Imagining the Penitentiary

Imagining the Penitentiary

*Fiction and the Architecture of Mind
in Eighteenth-Century England*

John Bender

THE UNIVERSITY OF CHICAGO PRESS

Chicago and London

JOHN BENDER,
professor of English and comparative literature
at Stanford University, is the author of
Spenser and Literary Pictorialism.

Published with the assistance of the
J. PAUL GETTY TRUST.

The University of Chicago Press, Chicago 60637
The University of Chicago Press, Ltd., London

© 1987 by The University of Chicago
All rights reserved. Published 1987
Printed in the United States of America

96 95 94 93 92 91 90 89   5 4 3 2

Library of Congress Cataloging-in-Publication Data

Bender, John B.
  Imagining the penitentiary.

  Bibliography: p.
  Includes index.
  1. English fiction—18th century—History and
criticism. 2. Prisons in literature. 3. Crime and
criminals in literature. 4. Law in literature.
5. Prisons—England—History—18th century. 6. Art,
English. 7. Art and literature—England—History—18th
century. I. Title.
PR858.P7.B4 1987   823'.5'09355   86-25074
ISBN 0-226-04228-6

TO

Ann Williams Bender

Contents

Illustrations and Acknowledgments

Preface

A preface is the most convenient place for an author to notice what his book has left unsaid. One such thing needs attention here. It concerns Michel Foucault.

The word "departure" has two senses, and this work sets out from Foucault in both of them. Without his precedent, my ideas could scarcely have been thought, but instead of pursuing his project, I have moved in directions he left unexplored or did not foresee. Readers familiar with Foucault's writings will continually notice points of difference or contradiction between his work and mine. I have let these pass because I did not want them to structure my argument. But one fundamental issue must be raised. Foucault's history of discourse treats literature as one of the many self-regarding disciplines among which reality was parceled out when, during the Enlightenment, language ceased to be a unified medium of world-making. Certainly, the specialized designation of literature as an autonomous, aesthetically privileged artistic domain has tended ever since to isolate it—or at least to foster the appearance of isolation. Yet while Foucault's tacit equation of all modern literary activity with the aesthetic discipline called "literature" served his heuristic requirements, it also obscured and left unanswered the question of how literary production is engaged in the ongoing process of cultural construction. This is my subject.

The obligations incurred during the research and composition of this book can never be sufficiently acknowledged. At least they may be recorded. The most profound of these are personal. Richard Chapman's tactful intelligence has borne witness to, and uniquely assisted, the life of this work. Ann Bender, while reaping few of the rewards of my authorship, has steadfastly endured most of its agonies. The dedication in her name scarcely begins to express my gratitude.

Some of my important obligations are to scholars I know only, or chiefly, through their works. But intellectual and professional indebtedness also has a collegial side that I am pleased to be able to acknowledge here. A few people have helped me in such various ways for so long that I wish to thank them first. They are Bliss Carnochan, Stephen Greenblatt, Herbert Lindenberger, Loy Martin, Stephen Orgel, John Richetti, James Thorpe, and David Wellbery. Many others have offered assistance or encouragement at significant junctures in the history of this work. They are Russell Berman, Morton Bloomfield, John Brewer, Max Byrd, Terry Castle, William Chace, George Dekker, Margaret Doody, Robin Evans, Robert Ferguson, Jay Fliegelman, Albert Gelpi, Thomas Grey, Shirley Kenny, Jerome McGann, Ron and Anne Mellor, Steven Mullaney, Ronald Paulson, Robert Polhemus, David Riggs, Renato Rosaldo, Helen Tartar, Robert Thorne, William Todd, and Hayden White. Frank Murray has been the ideal research assistant, often working beyond any reasonable requirement to complete the necessary checking, proofreading, and processing. The title of chapter 2 is intended as tribute to Ian Watt.

Several institutions have supported my efforts with grants of money, time, and expertise. The John Simon Guggenheim Foundation freed me from other obligations for a critically timed year. The Huntington Library and the National Endowment for the Humanities each supported a summer of research. The deans of Humanities and Sciences and of Graduate Studies at Stanford University have met most of the bills for computers, typing, photography, permissions, and research assistance. The *Stanford Literature Review* published an essay in which I worked out certain arguments that figure in the book. The Mellon Foundation sponsored the Stanford Faculty Seminar on Interpretation, during the first few years of which I reconceived a work in progress along the lines set forth here.

The list of illustrations credits numerous owners for granting me the right to reproduce photographs. Staff members at the following libraries and collections were especially helpful: the Stanford University Libraries, the Huntington Library and Art Gallery, the William Andrews Clark Memorial Library, the Lewis Walpole Library, the Metropolitan Museum of Art, the National Gallery (Washington, D.C.), the Yale Center for British Art, the British Library and Museum, the Warburg Institute, the Museum of London, the Guildhall Library, the Corporation of London Records Office, the National Monuments Record, the Archives Department of the Westminster City Libraries, Woburn Abbey, the Bibliothèque Nationale, the Musée Carnavalet, the Bibliothèque Historique de la Ville de Paris, and, in Milan, the Raccòlta

Bertarelli, the Archivio Storico Civico, the Bibliotèca Trivulziana, and the Bibliotèca Nazionale Braidense. Robin Evans loaned me original photographs that would have been difficult or impossible to obtain otherwise. John Harris guided me through the Royal Institute of British Architects, Drawings Collection. Peter Lovesey corresponded with me about the popular response to nineteenth-century executions. Evelyn Newby at the Paul Mellon Centre for Studies in British Art in London helped me seek out and gain permission to publish photographs of paintings in private collections. Undine Concannon, the archivist at Madame Tussaud's, searched their files to find a much needed illustration and other records.

*Psycho-analysts . . . are prepared to find several
motives for one and the same mental occurrence, whereas
what seems to be our innate craving for causality
declares itself satisfied with a single
psychical cause.*

SIGMUND FREUD
Clark University Lectures

*Subjectivity does not properly exist until
it is . . . organized, art forms generate and regenerate the very
subjectivity they pretend only to display. Quartets,
still lifes, and cockfights are not merely reflections
of a pre-existing sensibility analogically represented;
they are positive agents in the creation and
maintenance of such a sensibility.*

CLIFFORD GEERTZ
The Interpretation of Cultures

Introduction

This book investigates the subtle process of generation, representation, and regeneration that Geertz attributes to works of art in their cultural context. Above all I want to reach beyond the assumption that literature and art merely reflect institutions and attitudes: art, culture, and society are not separate or separable. I want to treat "motives" in Freud's sense of their multiplicity, and in Kenneth Burke's sense of categories or material conditions through which we can understand "language and thought primarily as modes of action."[1] I consider literature and the visual arts as advanced forms of knowledge, as cognitive instruments that anticipate and contribute to institutional formation. Novels as I describe them are primary historical and ideological documents; the vehicles, not the reflections, of social change.

I shall argue that attitudes toward prison which were formulated between 1719 and 1779 in narrative literature and art—especially in prose fiction—sustained and, on my reconstruction, enabled the conception and construction of actual penitentiary prisons later in the eighteenth century. Eighteenth-century prison reform found its form in the sphere of novelistic discourse, where, through the material of language, an emergent structure of feeling took shape and, like an image floating into focus, became subject to conscious experience. In other words, the earlier eighteenth-century novel bore the form within which the seeming randomness inside the old prison boundaries would later be restructured into a new penal order. Fabrications in narrative of the power of confinement to reshape personality contributed to a process of cultural representation whereby prisons were themselves reconceived and ultimately reinvented. The new penitentiaries, whose geometric disposition of individual cells and rigid daily routines we often take as inevitable, sprang suddenly into being about two hundred years ago, first in England and then across the whole of Europe and America. These penitentiaries assumed novelistic ideas of character and re-presented the sensible world (both to their inmates and to the public at large) in order to alter motivation and, ultimately, to reconstruct the fictions of personal identity that underlie consciousness.[2]

We must look outside of the strictly legal sphere to English narrative between Defoe and Goldsmith to trace the cultural formulations that endowed the penitentiary idea with its ultimately dominant force. As Durkheim observed in arguing that legal systems are themselves symbolically constituted,

> a representation is not simply a mere image of reality, an inert shadow projected by things upon us, but it is a force which raises around itself a turbulence of organic and psychical phenomena. . . . It arouses images, sometimes excites beginnings of illusions and may even affect vegetative functions. This foothold is as much more considerable as the representation is itself more intense, as the emotional element is more developed.[3]

Or as Fredric Jameson has suggested more recently, "fantasy or proto-narrative structure" is "the vehicle for our experience of the real."[4] The eighteenth century witnessed the emergence—in the novel, in philosophy, in reformist thought, in juridical practice, and in the transformation of prisons—of social and cultural systems framed within those structures of finely graded self-consciousness that, even today, serve to validate everyday life in metropolitan culture.

Broadly, then, this book concerns the role of novelistic representation in institutional formation. In the first chapter, while outlining my argument and introducing some necessary terminology, I contrast the old prisons with the new penitentiaries and discuss the relationship both of the novel and of reformist doctrine to eighteenth-century theories concerning the fictional construction of reality—especially of personal identity.

Next comes the heart of my case, which I argue by reference to specific writers and artists of the period. The two chapters on Daniel Defoe show how, beginning in 1719 with *Robinson Crusoe*, his narratives subtly introduced time, sequence, and developing consciousness of character into the happenstance experience of confinement in the old prisons. In chapter 4, I discuss how John Gay and William Hogarth regenerated this new structure of feeling in paradoxical, overtly contradictory forms that bridged customary generic types and proceeded, relative to the audience, in ways closer to the realist novel than to traditional drama or history painting. Under novelistic conditions, when literary discourse entered into what Mikhail Bakhtin calls a "dialogic" relationship with everyday life, the old practices of confinement began to split apart and became subject to a corrosive irony that set the stage for their rejection and reformulation even when reform of the social function of prisons was not explicitly at issue.[5] Gay and Hogarth brought contradictions that had been implicit in Defoe's depiction of the old prisons to the level of discourse in the public sphere. In chapters 5 and 6, I trace Henry Fielding's adaptation of Gay's paradoxes into a functional, intellectually accessible omniscience. Fielding's novels and his measures as Bow Street magistrate to improve the actual juridical practice of law enforcement through careful control of narrative procedures and resources inaugurated, during the 1750s, the phase of explicit action with which most accounts of prison reform commence. It is no accident that Fielding was the founder of the London police. According to my analysis, Defoe, Gay, Hogarth, and Fielding all predicate the new prisons in the very act of depicting the old.

Chapter 7 turns from the prehistory of reformative confinement in the work of specific novelists to the larger question of transparency—that is, to the technical convention whereby character and reflective conscience are isolated both in the realist novel and also in the social system epitomized by the penitentiary. Novelistic discourse becomes part of the culture's means of understanding. Jeremy Bentham's theory of knowledge and Adam Smith's account of the impartial spectator as the agent of conscience assist me, no less than Bentham's Panopticon, in linking the realist novel to the full-scale reformist movement that marked the 1760s and 1770s and to the emergence of prison architecture as an identifiable genre in England, beginning with the New Newgate of George Dance, Jr. This chapter delves broadly into the implications of the Penitentiary Act of 1779, which, in the first instance, defined narratively ordered penal institutions as we know them still. At last, in a postscript, I turn to some paintings by Wright of Derby and to certain dramatic alterations in the conduct of London executions in order to suggest ways in which public policy can be understood aesthetically.

This preliminary summary leaves aside collateral arguments and omits the analysis and evidence upon which my main thesis must stand or fall. It merely offers the reader a rough abstract of the story spelled out below. In order to address my particular concerns, I have had to consider some basic theoretical issues. For readers who are curious in such matters, I shall devote the rest of this introduction to laying them out in the briefest possible way. I group these issues under three headings: (1) historical causation; (2) the relation of form in art and literature to social and institutional structures; (3) the interrelated nature of discourse and ideology. What follows, then, are some declarations about the hypothetical framework that allows me to tell my story.

As Gregory Bateson argues in one of his "Metalogues," hypotheses are stories that enable us to create explanations (the characters are Father and Daughter):

> D: But then what does explain gravity?
> F: Nothing, my dear, because gravity is an explanatory principle.
> D: Oh. Do you mean that you cannot use one explanatory principle to explain another? Never?
> F: Hmm . . . hardly ever. That is what Newton meant when he said, *"Hypotheses non fingo."*
> D: And what does that mean? Please.
> F: Well, you know what "hypotheses" are. . . .
> D: Yes—and I know what *non* means. But what's *fingo*?
> F: Well—*fingo* is a late Latin word for "make." It forms a verbal noun *fictio* from which we get the word "fiction."
> D: Daddy, do you mean that Sir Isaac Newton thought that all hypotheses were just *made up* like stories?
> F: Yes—precisely that.
> D: But didn't he discover gravity? With the apple?
> F: No, dear. He invented it.[6]

The specific case presented in this book indicates that the complex relationships between art and social institutions have yet to be theoretically accounted for by an explanatory principle. Therefore, though analytic procedures exist on which I have drawn freely in order to construct viable hypotheses, loose ends and inconsistencies are inevitable in this kind of study so long as we lack an integrated theory. Even if we possessed such a theory, we might be like the structural chemist who, in order to gain a full description of the bonds between atoms in molecules, needs to invoke the principle of "resonance," which recognizes formally that the same structure must be viewed as existing simultaneously in different arrangements. This does not mean that an infinite number of accounts are valid, but that a certain number can coexist consonant with observable fact.[7]

· CAUSATION ·

In the matter of causation, two paradigms coexist in this book, and they correspond in turn to two perspectives on the material. The first model is descriptive. It views the novel and the penitentiary as autonomous but comparable social texts, both structured by a kind of narrative form that treats the material world, character, consciousness, personality, authority, and causation itself in a distinctive manner that I associate with realism in prose fiction. On this view, the simple fact that one of these two social texts demonstrably precedes the other—that the formulations of the novel come before those of the penitentiary—enjoys no privilege either as an explanation or as something to be explained. When the form of story-telling now called the "novel" emerged in the 1720s, it at once evinced an intimate self-consciousness concerning prison and confinement. The pervasiveness of the subject of confinement in the novel strongly indicates the presence of some cycle of generation and regeneration such as Geertz proposes. Where one enters the cycle and how one apprehends its shape or direction turns ultimately on the choice of analytic procedure. Whether or not a causal relationship might govern this cycle is inevitably open to question since, strictly, one can never prove causal sequences in history because it is impossible to discover what would have happened if a given set of conditions had not pertained (e.g., if there had been no novel). The chapters that follow can be read, with few allowances, entirely within the descriptive paradigm.

The second paradigm is generative and views the novel as a constructive force in the rise of the penitentiary. Literature and art are usually considered to be effects rather than causes of social institutions; this is precisely the theory of reflection I wish to avoid. But I hope the reader will come to see that I am not crudely adopting its mirror image. I consider that there is a certain particular sense in which the novel enabled the penitentiary by formulating, and thereby giving conscious access to, a real texture of attitudes, a structure of feeling, that I call the "penitentiary idea." I use the term "enabled" in a careful way. Belief in causes may well be no more than a conventional acceptance of argumentative categories that are embedded in narrative forms of inquiry. With regard to history, then, I may be able to persuade you that x caused y in the sense that y would not have existed without x, but I cannot demonstrate this as a fact because the very act of constructing a hypothesis imposes causal—that is, fictional—shape on the past. Althusser attacks just such beliefs and categories when he objects to "expressive causality" as a product of rhetoric rather than of science.[8]

Nonetheless, I accept the problem-laden baggage carried by the terms "constructive force" and "enabled." I do so because there is reason to believe that causation is a trope that has had a historical life of its own.[9] The attempt to trace its efflorescence in the eighteenth century seems worthwhile even though present methods of inquiry must themselves be governed in some measure by that century's epoch-making restructuring of culture within causal paradigms ordered by perceptual sequence.

Although I view a degree of uncertainty as inevitable, I contend that an age which ordered consciousness and its every representation along narrative lines may also have *behaved* causally.

Jürgen Habermas describes the social conditions under which causally ordered behavior could have come into being when he argues that with the emergence in eighteenth-century life of a public sphere (by which he means an arena of conversational and written exchange, epitomized by early English coffee houses and newspapers, in which participants relinquish their social and economic status by tacit agreement), discourse was reordered to allow easy flow of ideas from one field of interest to another and from one social stratum to another. He shows that the structures of discussion and the forms of writing in the prepolitical phase of this discourse governed political forms as power shifted during the period from the court sphere to that of public politics. The key idea here is that formal values are preserved in the shift from the arena of aesthetic discussion and writing to that of political argumentation and action. Habermas shows how the institutions of eighteenth-century culture were arranged to allow literary discourse to have causative force.[10] He shows that we are dealing with a period where expressive causality is itself the mode within which discourse is undertaken and by which it is organized.

Thus, within my second paradigm, I consider that the enablement I hypothesize may actually be a historical product—a mode of social action determined by the causal tropes in which the eighteenth century represented itself to itself. For techniques of representing sequence, perception, character, education, and material causation in terms of mental experience that emerged in eighteenth-century fiction characterized a wide range of cultural, social, and institutional phenomena in the period. Among them I would stress especially psychological representation in philosophy, critical and political discourse, and legal and philanthropic institutional practice.[11] The summation most relevant to my argument lies in Hume's constitution of personal identity as a "chain of causes and effects."[12]

· FORM ·

In considering the role of aesthetic works in cultural change, I view them—analytically and theoretically—as material productions that, because they are governed autonomously by their own specific requirements and conventions, provide finite arenas within which cultural formation becomes clear. Works of art attempt the unified representation of different social and cultural structures simultaneously in a single frame of reference. In literature and art the very attempt to contrive formal coherence out of disparate materials allows us to glimpse—through what have been called eloquent silences—the process of generation and re-generation that drives all cultural formation.[13]

Aesthetic works are peculiarly revealing as compared with the infinite sequences of historical process as a whole because of those breaks in tone, conflicts in representational method, and tensions among generic expectations that occur within their formal boundaries. Alterations in form, the emergence of new subject matter, and the adoption of techniques previously outside of an art can enact broader cultural change. But we can see more in works of art than mere reflections. They clarify structures of feeling characteristic of a given moment and thereby predicate those available in the future. This is the specific sense in which they may serve as a medium of cultural emergence through which new images of society, new cultural systems, move into focus and become tangible. I use the term "structure of feeling" to identify qualities that are contained within a culture at any given moment and that emerge *in process* as conventions play out their relationships within literary and visual forms. As Raymond Williams says, "What matters, finally, in understanding emergent culture, as distinct from both the dominant and the residual, is that it is never only a matter of immediate practice; indeed it depends crucially on finding new forms or adaptations of form. Again and again what we have to observe is in effect a *pre-emergence,* active and pressing but not yet fully articulated, rather than the evident emergence which could be more confidently named."[14] Such forms have constructive force as the bearers of a culture's organizing principles and master narratives.

Form in works of art has historical significance because it reveals relationships among the interwoven practices that make up reality, and it records traces of these practices that will bear interrogation and yield to decipherment. This is why the precariousness of the old prisons is so clear in the narratives wrought by Defoe, Hogarth, and Fielding between 1719 and the 1750s. At one with the magical vitality of the old prisons had been their unselfconscious, almost mythic, standing as elements of life lived in unexamined process. But these novelistic narratives, along with Gay's *Beggar's Opera,* both revealed and created the very self-consciousness about confinement that I am describing because their peculiar, paradoxical mode of story-telling shaped the stuff of day-to-day existence into decipherable form. This form, especially that of the novel, fused the minutiae of everyday life indissolubly with ideas about their meaning.

· IDEOLOGY ·

Ideas in ordinary life, in the specific sense that ideas are representations, rarely are subject to examination because they are continuously enacted culturally in detail after detail of living; then they cease to be simply ideas and become ideology. By "ideology" I intend not merely an articulate framework of belief, but the symbolic practices through which we manifest our social presence, or subjectivity. Such practices produce material institutions but also structures of domination, as well as the imagery through which emergent social and cultural formulations come into focus and gain conceptual status.[15] A primary medium of these symbolic practices is linguistic behavior, which produces kinds of discourse ranging from everyday speech, through argumentation and exposition, to literary representation in the technically discrete language of written narrative fiction. As Bakhtin says, "No cultural sign, once taken in and given meaning, remains in isolation: it becomes part of the unity of the verbally constituted consciousness. . . . Every ideological refraction of existence in process of generation, no matter what the nature of its significant material, is accompanied by ideological refraction in word."[16] Whether or not language is distinctively ideological, ideology is distinctively encoded in discourse. On the whole, therefore, I work within a communicational, or semiotic, definition of "behavioral ideology" as abiding in the continuous formation and reformation of systems of meaning through linguistic and social communication.[17] The novel, stretching in Bakhtin's description over vast reaches of history, catches in literary form the essentially "dialogic" character of social life, language, and therefore of ideology—the fact that "each person's inner world and thought has its stabilized *social audience* that comprises the environment in which reasons, motives, values, and so on are fashioned."[18]

From the eighteenth century onward, the realist novel has attempted the appearance of having removed all distance between itself and the processes of daily life: it pretends to be a transparent, unmediated form of knowledge about that life. As Bakhtin says, "When the novel becomes the dominant genre, epistemology becomes the dominant discipline."[19] The master fiction of the realist novel lies in the pretense that it shows the actual processes whereby material things and consciousness are all produced simultaneously through sensory experience. This book explores the historic institutional embodiment in the penitentiary prison of the underlying assumption that narrative processes can reproduce (re-present) human behavior so as to recreate personality. One way to view the task of this book is as the observation of this master fiction at work.[20]

Self *is that conscious thinking thing . . . which is sensible,
or conscious of Pleasure and Pain, capable of Happiness or Misery,
and so is concern'd for it* self, *as far as that consciousness extends. . . .
In this* personal Identity *is founded all the Right and Justice
of Reward and Punishment.*

Person, *as I take it, is the name for this* self. *Where-ever a Man
finds, what he calls* himself, *there I think another may say is the same*
Person. *It is a Forensick Term appropriating Actions and their Merit;
and so belongs only to intelligent Agents capable of a Law, and
Happiness and Misery. This personality extends it* self *beyond present
Existence to what is past, only by consciousness, whereby it becomes
concerned and accountable, owns and imputes to it* self *past Actions,
just upon the same ground, and for the same reason, that it does the
present. All which is founded in a concern for Happiness the
unavoidable concomitant of consciousness.*

JOHN LOCKE
An Essay Concerning Human Understanding

1

Prison and the Novel as Cultural Systems

When the form of story-telling now called the "novel" emerged in eighteenth-century England, it displayed an essential self-consciousness concerning prison and confinement. This fact should be unsurprising. The noun *novella,* which yields our term, meant an "addition to a legal code" in late Latin and, as Bakhtin observes, "legal-criminal categories in general have an enormous organizational significance" in the history of the novel.[1] More startling will be my argument that novelistic representation, which restructured the chaotic (though once culturally functional) experience inside the old prisons, implied a new kind of confinement—the penitentiary—conceived narratively on the lines of the realistic, consciousness-centered novel. Though distinctive in their means, the eighteenth-century novel, philosophy from Locke to Bentham, and the penitentiary as conceived in the 1770s all share an impetus toward realism, that is, toward a fine, observationally ordered, materially exhaustive grid of representation that accounts for behavior, in fact constructs it, in terms of sensory experience. The chapters that follow explore the ramifications of these ideas using Daniel Defoe, John Gay, William Hogarth, Henry Fielding, Adam Smith, George Dance, Jr., Jeremy Bentham, and others as specific instances. First, however, I must contrast the old prisons with the new penitentiaries and discuss the epistemological problematic that accompanied both the novel and the rise of the penitentiary.

· I ·

The old prisons were not intended, in themselves, as penal instruments but as places of detention prior to judgment or disposition (fig. 1).[2] Death was the common penalty, though often commuted to transpor-

Publish'd according to Act of Parliam? Price 6?

THE HUMOURS OF THE FLEET.

Welcome Welcome Brother Debtor
To this poor but merry place
Where no Bayliff, Dun, or Jettor,
Dare to shew his horred Face
But kind Sir as your a Stranger
Down your Garnish you must lay
Or your Coat will be in danger
You must either Strip or Pay

Neer repine at your Confinement
From your Children or your Wife
Wisdom lyes in true resignment
Through the various Scens of life
Scorn to shew the least resentment
Though beneath the frowns of fate
Knives & Beggars find Contentm?
Fears & Cares attend the Great

Though our Creditors are spightful
And restrain our Bodys here
We will make a Goal delightful
Since there's nothing else to fear
Every Islands but a Prison
Strongly guarded by the Sea
Kings & Princes for that Reason
Prisoners are as well as We.

What was it made great Alexander
Weep at his unfriendly Fate
Twas because he could not wander
Beyond the Worlds strong Prison gate
For the world is also bounded
By the Heavens & Stars above
Why should we then be confounded
Since there's nothing free but love.

Printed for B. Dickinson the Corner of Bell Savage Inn on Ludgate hill London 1749.

1. Frontispiece to W. Paget, *The Humours of the Fleet,* 1749. New prisoners had to pay "garnish" to buy drinks all around, or be stripped of their coats; games with rackets (background left) and many other less healthful diversions took place in the yard.

12

tation abroad. At mid-century in England, petty offenders could be hanged or transported for any simple larceny of more than twelve pence or for any robbery that put a person in fear. Even bankrupts who failed to surrender themselves or who concealed assets were subject to capital threat.[3] The typical residents of eighteenth-century prisons were debtors and people awaiting trial, often joined by their families like Hogarth's Rake (fig. 37), Goldsmith's Vicar, or the household that Francis Wheatley's painting shows receiving relief from the great prison visitor, John Howard (fig. 2). Their society might include convicts awaiting transportation or execution as well as innocent witnesses held by the court. All were serviced by a free traffic of tradesmen, lawyers, and simple curiosity seekers.

Like Old Newgate, most eighteenth-century prisons were not built purposely for confinement but were domestically organized, and the

2. Francis Wheatley, *John Howard Visiting and Relieving the Miseries of Prison,* 1787. An imagined family gathers about the miserable father while a jailer attends to Howard's remonstrances concerning their condition. The fanciful background, which is reminiscent of stage scenery, bears little relation to the actual architecture of any specific old-style prison.

very few specially constructed ones, York Prison for example, resembled grand houses (fig. 3). Prisons were temporary lodgings for all but a few, and the jailer collected fees from prisoners for room, board, and services like a lord of the manor collecting rents from tenants. Still, documentary inquiries indicate that life inside the old prisons spontaneously derived its own structure and its own rather exacting methods of governance.[4] As Smollett observed, these prisons microcosmically condensed the society that created them. They were mirrors of social and economic class, though like coffee houses they brought a cross-section of society together on special terms that suspended the ordinary rules. The heterogeneous interiors of these jails bore little relation to whatever network of walls and facades happened to enclose them. Their slight administrative structure derived from the keeper's contractual obligation to hold the prisoners fast, and from his pursuant right to impose fees on those compelled to lodge within his bounds.

An easy familiarity existed between prisons and the world they so pungently distilled. Crowds of visitors sustained familial communication and supplied tradesmen; and prisons, like Bedlam, were treated as holiday curiosities (fig. 4). Horace Walpole complained to Sir Horace Mann, for example, of a glamorous young Irish highwayman, James Maclaine, whose exploits ended at Tyburn in 1750:

> The first Sunday after his condemnation, 3000 people went to see him; he fainted away twice with the heat of his cell. You can't conceive the ridiculous rage there is of going to Newgate; and the prints that are published of the malefactors, and the memoirs of their lives and deaths set forth with as much parade as—as—Marshal Turenne's— we have no generals worth making a parallel![5]

Such routine traffic easily provided means of escape, as the condemned Jack Sheppard proved on the first of his brilliantly contrived flights from Newgate when he walked out in female disguise as the turnkeys were nodding. They ordered things similarly in France, where Diderot, translating Plato while a prisoner of state at Vincennes, simply bribed the keeper to sanction his nightly flight over the walls to visit Madame de Puisieux, his mistress in Paris.[6]

Debtors accounted for a large fraction of all prisoners. Debtors, whom the law assumed to be solvent and therefore liable to confinement until they paid up (or their creditors relented, or Parliament voted one of its sporadic "gaol delivery" bills), might be held indefinitely. Criminals remained in custody only until they had been tried and acquitted, discharged with slight corporal punishment, transported, or executed. Of course, anyone who failed upon acquittal to pay fees owing the jailer

3. York County Gaol, attributed to William Wakefield, c. 1705. The first specifically designed prison in England resembled a baroque palace and was laid out on a domestic plan.

The London rairey Shows or who'll step into Ketch's Theatre.

Amongst the Works which Nature doth produce	Newgate appears & how John Sheppard lay	But here's one thing to be admir'd the most
As well for Admiration as for Use	In heavy Irons till the fatal Day	Of which the earliest Ages cannot boast
A most surprizing Ostrich here we find	The crouding Populace flock in to see	Nor England ever had the same before
By Nature large & largest of its kind	This Man who did the Jayl and Law defy	Two Lions young brought forth in London Town
His Height Prodigious but above the rest	Who twice being taken twice did make escape	The like of this in such a Northern Clime
He hardest Steel or Iron can digest.	But now He's caught & Tyburn is his Fate	Has not been known since the first date of time.

4. *The London Rairey Shows or Who'll Step into Ketch's Theatre,* 1750. A fanciful view of Old Newgate as the centerpiece of a street carnival. Ketch, the executioner, appears at the upper left as master of a peep-show featuring Jack Sheppard and Jonathan Wild (whose house had been directly opposite the prison).

5. *Debtors and Condem'd Criminals Log'd Togeather*, from Moses Pitt, *The Cry of the Oppressed*, 1691. Civil and criminal offenders mixed at close quarters in the old prisons.

remained confined, now as a debtor. Like other prisoners, the debtors rented quarters that varied in quality according to the size fee they could muster for their keepers. While in theory they occupied special wards, often they were but haphazardly separated from felons (fig. 5).[7]

Commonality was central to the experience of the old prisons. Prisons, compters, and other places of detention intended primarily for civil offenders and debtors dotted the London streets; yet Newgate, the major strong house for accused felons and condemned criminals, contained numerous debtors too.[8] Equally indiscriminate were the bridewells and houses of correction. The Tudor legislation that had founded them in order to reform vagrants and minor offenders against the peace, as well as to provide work for the able-bodied poor, so little affected practice that, by the early eighteenth century, "it became, in fact, in most counties, difficult to discover any practical distinction between the House of Correction and the common gaol, whether in administration, discipline or the character of the inmates. In many cases the gaol and the House of

Correction were one and the same. In many others, though the two institutions were nominally distinct, they were kept in the same or adjacent buildings, under one and the same officer."[9] Theoretically, London drew perhaps the clearest demarcation among places of confinement; but there, as elsewhere, even the rudimentary classification of prisoners had little practical force.

In London, where the vast establishments of the Fleet and the King's Bench dealt chiefly with debtors (fig. 6), many of whom purchased the privilege of living in adjacent neighborhoods that lay outside the physical walls but within the legal boundaries or "the rules" of the prison, actual practice at the Fleet, as reported by the Oglethorpe Committee (1729), paralleled that at Newgate, as recorded in the *Memoirs of the Right Villainous John Hall* (1708).[10] Both offered lodging that ranged downward from the private apartments which technically formed part of the keeper's quarters. Next came decent if crowded chambers still on the master's

KINGS BENCH PRISON.

6. *Kings Bench Prison,* from Thomas Rowlandson and A. C. Pugin, *The Microcosm of London,* 1808. The prison as rebuilt on its old plan following the Gordon Riots of June 1780.

side, then common side wards where crowds of half-naked prisoners huddled in filthy straw, and finally the collective dungeons, where solitude could be considered a blessing by inmates who might expect to share quarters with the insane, the desperate, or even the deceased (fig. 7). The fees, the tap rooms, the prison yards, the "colleges" of prisoners that governed most internal affairs, the "garnish" or initiatory fee to purchase drinks for established inmates all reflected customary practice for felons and debtors alike.[11]

Even the use of irons on debtors in the Fleet, like the presence of dungeons there, paralleled the treatment of felons at Newgate and appears to have been common, though roundly condemned as a denial of ancient English rights by the parliamentary investigating committee of 1729. The "gaols committee" was chaired by James Oglethorpe, then a comparatively obscure M.P. of seven years' experience (see figs. 29 and 30 below). Several members of the 1729 committee would soon join in the project that won Oglethorpe still greater fame, his leadership of the movement to found a Georgia colony. The two ventures had related philanthropic aims: the first to mitigate the sway tyrannical jailers held over imprisoned debtors, the second to relieve the poor by resettling them abroad. Charges of brutality and extortion in the jails were hardly new, but the high level of Oglethorpe's investigations, his nearly comprehensive coverage of the major metropolitan prisons, and above all, the publicity and adulation that marked England's reception of his exposé all mark 1729 as a signal date in reformist thought. Abuses like those Oglethorpe exposed in fact were commonplace, but fifty years would elapse before Parliament began to replace the contract system of prison management. If the indignation of a celebrated parliamentary committee had such brief effect in the Fleet (as would appear from accounts of later visits by the Committee of 1754 and by the greatest of all prison visitors, John Howard himself), only the most barbarous extortions of its frightful warden, Bambridge, can have been unusual.[12] The prisoners' subjugation to the jailer as objects of profit transcended their individual offenses; the categories relevant to the jailer were economic, not legal.

The keeper ran a monopolistic utility, a business whose captive clients were forced, like the users of most eighteenth-century institutions, to subject themselves to bare survival on charity or to pay piecemeal charges for specific services or privileges: room, board, bedding, beverages, booking of admission, putting on of chains, delivery of legal papers, removal of chains, recording of dismissal, and so forth. Since containment and profit motivated the keepers, a prisoner, once having paid certain extortionate fees and having contracted for the best quarters he could

7. *Debtors in a Dungion 9 Foot under Ground,* from *The Cry of the Oppressed,* 1691. Debtors were often, though illegally, treated like felons.

afford, joined a largely unsupervised population within the guarded boundaries. Usually irons restrained the dangerous or obstreperous, but in some few jails the dilapidation of the physical structure had advanced so far that all felons of consequence had to be chained—a cheaper alternative than the reconstruction of walls.[13]

The Enlightenment reimagined the old, domestically ordered prisons, conceiving instead the penitentiaries later perfected by industrial society. This reconception occurred in stages. As impulses to reform became intellectually focused during the 1760s and critics attacked the old practices, prison exteriors were reimagined, although their interiors remained much as before. While the old contract system based on jailers' fees sturdily resisted change, prisons began during this decade to be envisioned with an outwardly fearful, awesome, intimidating aspect—sublime imagery set forth in the graphic arts by Piranesi's *Carceri* and in architecture by George Dance's 1768 design for London Newgate (figs. 8, 9).

In general, the reformers considered criminals different from the rest of humanity because malign rather than benign external effects had shaped their natures. Deterrence was therefore a chief objective of punishment. Deterrence had two aspects. The first was to forestall the repetition of crime by measuring out the displeasures and inconveniences of punishment to overbalance, ever so slightly, any pleasure or advantage to the criminal. The second was to represent this measured, expository system of punishment—primarily through orderly laws and rational adjudication—in institutions that would deter ordinary citizens whose more balanced, yet still precarious, natures might somehow be moved to crime. It followed from this reasoning that an excess of severity in the economy of deterrence would lead potential criminals to commit crimes equal to the punishment they expected to be imposed upon those who were apprehended. This Dr. Johnson argued in his *Rambler* paper on capital

8. Left: Giovanni Battista Piranesi, *Le Carceri*, VII, 1749–50; as heavily revised and augmented, 1761. George Dance, Jr., the architect of New Newgate, was living in Rome when the reworked version of these prison fantasies appeared.

9. Below: George Dance, Jr., New Newgate, London, designed 1768. An early twentieth-century photograph, taken before demolition in 1902, shows the prison as rebuilt following the Gordon Riots of June 1780.

punishment: if the penalty for robbery and murder are the same, the robber thinks little of adding murder to his crime.[14] The preoccupation with horrific prison facades that characterized the last half of the eighteenth century coincided with the wide dissemination of these ideas in Cesare Beccaria's *On Crimes and Punishments* (1764).[15] Prison interiors would shortly be reshaped into a powerful expository system, while horrific facades continued as mandatory exhibits in architectural portfolios and as frontispieces, entry lodges, or gatehouses to the new penitentiaries (fig. 10). Their *architecture parlante* reminded all who would enter, or even pass by, of the power of confinement to alter the spirit through material representation.[16]

The empiricist secularism that underlay reformist thought about punishment was apparent even in John Howard, the crusader around whom reform most visibly coalesced during the 1770s. He approvingly quoted

10. William Blackburn, Littledean Bridewell, entry lodge, 1785. Even reformed penitentiaries with technologically innovative interiors continued to address the public with massive portals that spoke architectural terror.

Henry Fielding's opinion "that it is religion alone which can effectually accomplish so great and so desirable a work" as to reform the morals of prisoners, but a guilty sense of shared mortal frailty brought him to adopt a humanist position. He was motivated to document abuses and squalor in the old prisons and to reshape the physical conditions, the governance, and the manners to which inmates were subjected because "debtors and felons . . . are men, and by men they ought to be treated as men." Even when he admired the "*constant* attention that is paid to *impress* the prisoners with a sense of RELIGION" in European houses of correction, Howard's phrasing indicated an approach that, despite his own intense spiritual conviction, was articulated within a utilitarian framework derived from Beccaria and other profane theorists: "We have too much adopted the gothic mode of correction, *viz.* by *rigorous severity,* which often *hardens* the heart; while many foreigners pursue the more *rational* plan of *softening* the mind in order to [encourage] its amendment."[17]

The reformers, beginning especially in England of the 1770s and prevailing throughout America and Europe during the 1840s, envisioned prison interiors as precisely refined instruments. Inspired to infinite elaboration within Beccaria's sketchy utilitarian analysis of human nature, they aimed to reshape the life story of each criminal by the measured application of pleasure and pain within a planned framework.

The Penitentiary Act of 1779 phrased their general ideal in a subjunctive, fictionalized language appropriate to that moment just prior to the penitentiary's assumption of architectural shape in the 1780s:

> If many offenders, convicted of crimes for which transportation hath been usually inflicted, were ordered to solitary imprisonment, accompanied by well-regulated labour, and religious instruction, it might be the means, under providence, not only of deterring others from the commission of the like crimes, but also of reforming the individuals, and inuring them to habits of industry.[18]

Each convict would be assigned upon entering one of the new penitentiaries to live out a program or scenario that took as its point of departure a generic classification based upon age, sex, type of offense, and social background.

Beginning in the 1780s, English prison buildings underwent huge changes in interior plan. Each structure was contrived as the physical setting implied by a narrative—or series of narratives—of criminal reformation. In Sir George Onesiphorus Paul's famous Gloucestershire system, for example, male and female felons were confined in penitentiaries under detailed rules setting forth regimes of work and diet appropriate to different stages of the sentence, which was analyzed into segments like the stages of a classic plot.[19] Following the Penitentiary Act, numerous counties and towns rebuilt their prisons to conform with the latest thinking about hygiene, reformatory punishment, and solitary confinement. Governmental authorities began to pay all expenses and to dictate every detail of penitentiary architecture along with every movement in the prisoner's carefully specified daily regime.

The new penitentiary structures, especially those planned by the remarkable young architect William Blackburn, bristled with innovations, ranging from geometric radial plans that allowed guards full view of all exterior yards and apertures, to ingenious details of construction that supported the architecturally contradictory aims of ventilation, cleanliness, and isolation (fig. 11). Inspiring and instructing the authors of the 1779 act, Blackburn was in steady demand as a consultant ready to condemn even recently built prisons as inadequate to the new ideals. For example, he had to inform the Dorset Grand Jury that the newly built Dorchester County Gaol did not allow that "solitude and separation from whence the hope of reformation springs."[20] Bentham's Panopticon designs of 1787–91 epitomized these innovations. He suspended inmates in a transparent medium dominated by a hidden omniscient authority. Bentham fused narratively structured reformative confinement with the principle of supervision: an imaginative projection in the subject's consciousness of the jailer's eye watching, as if eternally, from a centrally placed, curtained observation tower in full view of every cell (fig. 12). Increasingly, confinement itself became the punishment, and by the mid-nineteenth century, penitentiary sentences had virtually supplanted other criminal sanctions except execution for murder or treason.

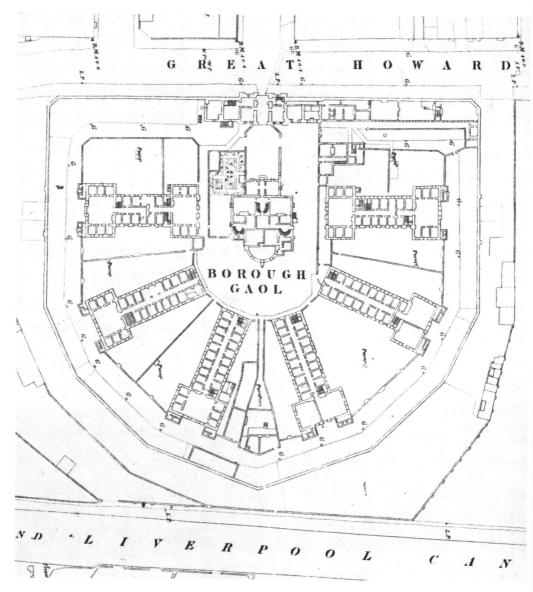

11. William Blackburn, Liverpool Borough Gaol, 1785–89. The new penitentiaries combined cellular confinement, optimal ventilation, and relative cleanliness. Security depended upon visual openness within and surrounding walls without.

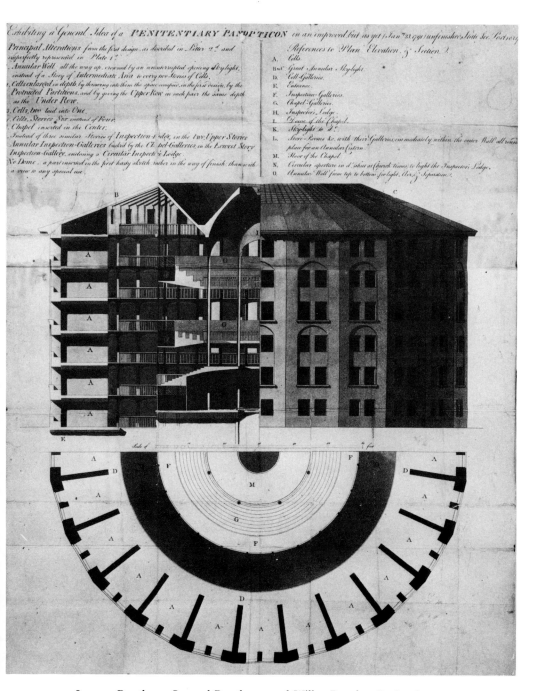

12. Jeremy Bentham, Samuel Bentham, and Willey Reveley, *Penitentiary Panopticon,* 1791. Section, elevation, half-plan, corresponding closely but not exactly to the description in Bentham's *Postscript.* The legend identifies the major elements.

· II ·

Victor Turner's anthropological terms provide a basis upon which to understand the old-style prisons that preceded penitentiaries as cultural systems. I shall introduce one of them now as the hinge on which many particulars of my analysis will turn.

One of the most explicit motifs in seventeenth- and eighteenth-century prison accounts is the identification of the experience of imprisonment with the point of view of the initiate or neophyte in a ritual.[21] The old-style prisoners were subjects who, to use Turner's word, underwent the "liminal" experience characteristic of rites of passage. The application of this term to prisons has a credence beyond that of suggestive metaphor since, as Turner says, "often the indigenous term for the liminal period is . . . the locative form of a noun meaning 'seclusion site.' " Indeed, the English word "jail" derives ultimately from the medieval Latin diminutive of *cavea* meaning "hollow," "cavity," "dungeon," "cell," or "cage" (*OED*).[22]

The "liminal" rite of passage enacts symbolic demise and takes for granted a randomness that, quite unpredictably, can bring about real death. "The essential feature of these symbolizations is that the neophytes are neither living nor dead from one aspect, and both living and dead from another. Their condition is one of ambiguity and paradox, a confusion of all the customary categories" (p. 340). Incessant complaints by eighteenth-century reformers that the old prisons were confused in tone—sites at once of misery and hilarity, punishment and immorality, death and generation—serve, in this context, to affirm their liminality. Captain Alexander Smith, for instance, wrote in his often reprinted history of highwaymen:

> Newgate, which dismal prison is enough to deter all men from acting an ill thing, if they would but consider that it is a place of calamity, a dwelling in more than Cimmerian darkness, an habitation of misery, a confused Chaos without any distinction, a bottomless pit of violence, and a tower of Babel, where all are speakers and no hearers. There is mingling the noble with the ignoble, the rich with the poor, the wise with the ignorant, and debtors with the worst of malefactors. . . . There, he that yesterday was great, to-day is mean; he that was well-fed abroad, there starves; he that was richly clad, is stark naked; he that commanded, obeys.[23]

The old prisons neither told stories nor assigned roles. Rather, the "coincidence of opposite processes and notions in a single representation characterizes the peculiar unity of the liminal: that which is neither this nor that, and yet is both" (p. 341). In the larger perspective taken by formal analysis and interpretation, liminal space has a double structure visible only in part to the passenger who acts within it and who experientially finds it out during initiation.

In the old prisons the real, if transient, danger to the liminal passenger depended, as in carnival, upon losing control within a demarcated arena where new patterns of life could be formulated. "Initiation," at the threshold (*limen, liminis*) separating one role in the larger social structure from another, "is to rouse initiative at least as much as to produce conformity to custom." Randomness was one of the rules in the old prisons: the squalor, the disease, the possibility of escape, the periodic jail deliveries voted by Parliament; the chance that your creditors might relent, the courts miscarry, the judges commute death to transportation, your patrons gain a reprieve, your friends revive your corpse after hanging. This rule of randomness of course adopts the point of view of the "passenger"—or that of the carnival spectator temporarily subject to misrule—one who engages in "liminal . . . forms of symbolic action, those genres of free-time activity, in which all previous standards and models are subjected to criticism, and fresh new ways of . . . interpreting . . . experience are formulated."[24] Finally, however, as Turner suggests, liminality does not posit change in personality but change in status; it fosters the outlook appropriate to a new social standing (p. 345).

Perhaps the best way to understand how the old prisons could embody all of the different aspects of liminality is to fragment the experience of entering them, first into temporal sequence and then into architectural space. The passenger in the old prison encountered first and last the jailer and his aides, who exacted fees at entry and exit and who applied or struck off irons according to the fees the prisoner could muster: the lighter the irons the higher the price. The jailer's chief responsibility was to secure the perimeters; his chief right, to gain fees for every service supplied the prisoner. Legal authority waited at the gate. Within the geographic and economic boundary defined by the jailer, most prisoners came and went through lodgings and yard, pub and coffee house, as fancy and their fellows guided them.

The liminal boundary was perhaps sharpest at the moment when the prisoner stepped clear of the keeper and his turnkeys into the yard or public rooms where he was subjected to the custom of "garnish." This was not a keeper's fee, but a charge levied by the associated prisoners. As the hackneyed poet put it in verse on the frontispiece to *The Humours of the Fleet:*

Welcome Welcome Brother Debtor
To this poor but merry place
Where no Bayliff, Dun, or Settor,
Dare to show his horred Face
But kind Sir as you'r a Stranger
Down your Garnish you must lay
Or your Coat will be in danger
You must either Strip or Pay.[25]

Though Paget's verse catches the jocular tone typical of hazing rites, reformers universally deplored this as the most degrading moment of the prisoner's initiation into his new life: if upon entry he could not pay a rather large set fee or "garnish" to purchase drinks all around, his clothes were stripped off to be sold for the purpose. This is one of Booth's first indignities in Fielding's *Amelia*.

For all its randomness, the rite of passage is governed and contained by the relation among neophytes on the one hand and between them and their instructors on the other. As Turner puts it, "There exists a set of relations that compose a 'social structure' . . . of a very simple kind: between instructors and neophytes there is often complete authority and complete submission; among neophytes there is often complete equality" (p. 341). Thus it is consistent with the character of the old prisons to view them, simultaneously, as arenas of randomness and as structured microcosms of society. They were at once the site of individual rites of passage and the collective embodiment of liminality in institutional and topological form. They physically expressed the liminal paradox through their enclosure of classless liberty. But since by the seventeenth and eighteenth centuries the rite of passage was becoming residual, the authority of the instructors or elders, which Turner describes as independent of legal sanctions, had been institutionalized in the keeper who served as an agent of the legal system though not as one of its officers. Still, the old prison keepers could function because they represented "the self-evident authority of tradition . . . the absolute, the axiomatic values of society in which are expressed the 'common good' and the common interest" (pp. 341–42).

Suggestive terms on which to understand the social situation of eighteenth-century prisons lie in E. P. Thompson's argument that the increasingly theatrical, yet isolated, grand gestures of "cultural hegemony" on which the eighteenth-century aristocracy and gentry founded their rule signified a decline in traditional paternalistic control over the lower social orders. This paternalism, in its turn, had depended implicitly upon mutual feeling and concern, and upon values held in common by patrician and plebeian alike. The erosion of this alliance of values, as labor became "decade by decade, more 'free' of traditional manorial, parochial, corporate and paternal controls," led to "the paradox of a customary culture . . . not subject in its daily operations to the ideological domination of the rulers":

> The gentry's hegemony may define the limits or the 'field-of-force' within which the plebeian culture is free to act and grow, but since this hegemony is secular rather than religious or magical it can do little to determine the character of this plebeian culture. The controlling instruments and images of hegemony are those of the Law. . . . Its subjects do not tell their rosaries nor go on pilgrimages of the faithful—instead they read broadsides in taverns and attend public executions, and at least some of the Law's victims are regarded, not with horror, but with an ambiguous admiration. The Law may punctuate the limits of behavior tolerated by the rulers; it does not, in the eighteenth century, enter into cottages . . . decorate the chimney-piece with icons, or inform a view of life.[26]

Nor did the agents of the law enter the classic eighteenth-century jail to inform the view of life within its precincts.

Life inside the old prisons, notwithstanding the emphasis on disease, drunkenness, and promiscuity through which reformers so effectively shaped later opinion, had its own spontaneous structure and its own methods of governance; the typical prisoner enjoyed a wide range of freedoms and pleasures that were to be eradicated in the new penitentiaries, where the reformed discipline sought to enforce solitude and penitence, cleanliness and work. The reformers subjected their institutions to discursive order by replacing with explicit regimes the customary forms of governance that had prevailed inside the old prison walls. The new penitentiary system of imprisonment, while religiously motivated and often narrated in evangelical terms, was based analytically in a materialistic utilitarianism and proceeded according to its behaviorist ordinances.

Three facts about the old prisons—all surprising from a modern point of view—demonstrate the force of traditional authority in their maintenance. First, the easy traffic of visitors—which sustained familial communication and enabled supply by franchised tradesmen—depended upon consensual boundaries. Second, the guard was strikingly light even at Newgate, where one official to each hundred prisoners sufficed during the 1760s to secure the walls and gateways.[27] Third, the old prisons literally penetrated life in surrounding neighborhoods by extending outside their own walls into legally drawn sectors known as the "rules," where prisoners might be detained in private buildings called sponging houses. Like the prison itself, these were businesses run for profitable fees by keepers, bailiffs, and landlords. Besides serving as way stations for those entering or leaving prison, sponging houses and "rules" were devices for managing crowded prisons; they provided quarters where those under detention could minimize their discomfort and danger while engaging tolerable, quasi-respectable lodging to share with their dependents. In 1776 the King's Bench had 395 prisoners, 279 wives, and 725 children, for a grand total of 1,399, about one-third of whom were in the rules.[28] In short, the boundaries were at once fixed and fluid, legally set and socially enacted: to the prisoner, opaque as a wall; to the visitor, transparent as a veil.

Perhaps the strongest sign of the reciprocal relation between the old prisons and the culture that produced them is that the structure "found" during the rite of passage was a version of surrounding social order. The requirement of garnish is a case in point. In general, a newcomer's compulsory purchase of drink for his entire company or shop enjoyed widespread acceptance as an initiation into trades and occupations—even at the higher levels of the magistracy—right through the eighteenth century and beyond.[29] This is not surprising since, according to Turner, rites of passage "are not restricted . . . to movements between ascribed statuses. They also concern entry into a newly achieved status, whether this be a political office or membership of an exclusive club or secret society" (p. 339). Similarly, the old prisons signified liminal equality to initiates by granting them the absolute social freedom of the coffee house (for that most egalitarian innovation among eighteenth-century institutions also existed within prison walls). In coffee houses, according to Habermas, lord and commoner could converse on equal terms in the "public sphere," outside the rules of status governing the period's usual social intercourse.[30] At the same time, the system of fees for lodging and services imposed by the jailer transparently demystified social standing by reducing it to the terms of a purely economic code. As Turner says, "Liminality may be partly described as a stage of reflection. In it those ideas, sentiments, and facts that had been hitherto for the neophytes bound up in configurations and accepted unthinkingly are, as it were, resolved into their constituents" (p. 345).

The campaign to change the regime, the governance, the finance, and the architecture of prisons appears to have coincided with a broad shift of economic power and social leadership away from the aristocracy and squirearchy, the actors in Thompson's cultural hegemony and the objects of Howard's quotation from Fénelon's *Télémaque:* "The prosperous turn away their eyes from the miserable, not through insensibility, but because the sight is an interruption of their gaity."[31] With a few exceptions, the impetus to reform was traceable to the merchants, the factory owners, the managers of resources and labor, whose sons tended to move into the professions or, like John Howard himself, into the new gentry. The rise of penitentiary prisons paralleled the emergence of interests alien to the old establishment as Thompson describes it.[32] A full understanding of the penitentiary idea must note not only that the chief reformers' economic welfare was linked directly, or through immediate relatives, to trade, to manufacture, to entrepreneurial agriculture, none of which could thrive without an orderly labor force largely free of old paternalistic ties, but that a dissenting religionism motivated the reformers' sincere belief that humanity could be improved and that a materialistic rationalism provided the institutional forms within which innovation could be carried out. The new penitentiaries, supplanting both the old prisons and houses of correction, explicitly reached toward all three goals: maintenance of order within a largely urban labor force, salvation of the soul, and rationalization of personality. Ultimately, reform in pursuit of these goals would work to the interest of "the middling sort," those small property holders, businessmen, merchants, and professionals who lived on the whole outside the realm of values, tacitly shared by patrician and plebeian alike, that sustained the cultural hegemony described by Thompson.[33]

In view of Thompson's argument that in England at least until the last part of the eighteenth century there was no industrial or professional middle class that could curb effectively the power of the old order, the prevalence of industrial and professional background among the major spokesmen for prison reform in the 1770s suggests that, consciously or not, further motives undergirded the reformers' philanthropy. Just as the Wesleys' deeply felt evangelical mission into spiritual terrain abandoned by the established church—often into the deepest recesses of London's or Bristol's Newgate—ultimately established a new religion by appealing to popular superstitions, so the humanitarian campaign to reform the prisons pointed to a new hegemony founded on control of cultural terrain the old regime had abdicated to the plebs.[34] This terrain included the arena bounded by old prison walls and their surrounding "rules."

The unofficial nature of governance within the old prisons illustrates in specific practice that "mutuality of relationship" between traditional authority and plebeian culture that Thompson notes in the middle decades of the century, "a *reciprocity* in gentry-plebs relations" that implied a degree of abdication of control to plebeian or "mob" interests. In the logic of this analysis, the liberty inside the legal boundaries of the old prisons emerges as a detailed, if powerfully symbolic, fraction of the "price which aristocracy and gentry paid for a limited monarchy and a weak State" in the form of "the licence of the crowd."[35] Lord Chesterfield recognized such an idea when, speaking to the House of Lords about the Licensing Act of 1737, he related the threat of theatrical sedition to larger questions of social order:

> There is such a Connection between licentiousness and Liberty, that it is not easy to correct the one, without dangerously wounding the other. It is extremely hard to distinguish the true limit between them like a changeable silk, we can easily see there are two different colours, but we cannot easily discover where the one ends, or where the other begins.[36]

When reformers objected to the old prisons, they used the words "licence," "riot," "mob," "disorder" in a tone wholly opposite Chesterfield's. Real riots often focused on prisons which were thrown open to aggrandize the "mob." A mob assault on prison walls symbolized a temporary breakdown of the precarious social accommodation between patrician and plebeian cultures. Well before the storming of the Bastille, prisons were emblems to the crowd both of ruling authority and of its limits (fig. 13). Thompson's general analysis helps us to decode specific traits of the furious sublimated energy these emblems contained.

An Exact Representation of the **Burning, Plundering** *and* **Destruction** *of* **NEWGATE** *by the Rioters on the memorable 7th of June 1780.*

13. *The Burning, Plundering, and Destruction of Newgate by the Rioters on the Memorable 7th of June 1780.* Many popular prints commemorated the Gordon Riots, during which several prisons were sacked and their inmates liberated.

The old prisons visibly situated the transient structures of liminality in the topography of the early modern city. They were representational no less than the new penitentiaries; the difference lay in the principles governing their form. The old prisons were loose structures bounded by authority yet out of its reach, even as their randomness sustained tradition by clarifying its elemental value. Structurally articulate, yet unpenetrated by systematic governance or precisely formulated rules, the old prisons maintained an account of reality that had informed earlier religious, governmental, and narrational practice and that continued to permeate much of eighteenth-century popular culture.[37]

At stake in the public debates and governmental struggles over reform were two different ways of apprehending social order, two different representational modes. Those who conceived no reason to change could be found in every walk of life from the lowest to highest. Among the lowest types, largely outside the sphere of patronage but aware of the license the old system tolerated, were the numerous vagrants and criminals who fled the counties where arrest might lead to reformatory punishment in one of the new penitentiaries, and who considered these districts "as Europeans would the Gold Coast or a Hindoo the Arctic regions."[38] Further up the social scale would have been Solomon Wisdom, the old jailer at Oxford who honored the hygienic regime instituted in the new penitentiary there by heaping manure in the courtyard. Having ornamented the front gate of the prison with a caricature of the official who reprimanded him, Wisdom was dismissed for "general conduct . . . repugnant to every plan of reform lately introduced by the Magistrates into the said gaol." The reformers were depriving Wisdom of his profits and the prisoners of their improvisational self-government.[39]

The famous clergyman Dr. William Paley spoke from a superior vantage point representative of Thompson's patrician hegemony in his *Principles of Moral and Political Philosophy* (1785), a work often invoked by the parliamentary majority that, until the 1830s, forestalled any broad reform of England's "Bloody Code" specifying death for hundreds of offenses against property and person. Paley voiced the skepticism of those who believed the old codes of punishment to be sound though subverted by erratic enforcement and excessive leniency:

> In . . . the *reformation* of criminals, little has ever been effected, and little I fear is practicable. From every species of punishment that has hitherto been, from imprisonment and exile, from pain and infamy, malefactors return more hardened in their crimes, and more instructed. If there be any thing that shakes the soul of a confirmed villain, it is the expectation of approaching death.[40]

Paley also observed that "of the *reforming* punishments which have not yet been tried, none promises so much success as that of *solitary* imprisonment." He speaks hypothetically of how solitude would "augment the terror of the punishment" much as he argues for enlarging the scale of punishment, "without offending or impairing the public sensibility by cruel or unseemly exhibitions of death," by destroying murderers "in a manner dreadful to the imagination, yet concealed from the view." He proposed death in hidden dens of wild animals as a form of execution most engaging to the imagination.

Dr. Paley envisioned a freshly concentrated version of the old order, but even he was touched by the currents of reform. Where once prisons had been unregarded except for the occasional charity call or curious visit, like elements of nature or features in the landscape (what Hume and Bentham called "fictions" in the technical language of philosophy), they now became puzzles to be solved—sites of speculation for projectors of schemes.

The new penitentiaries banished chance and fortune—the providential order of things—in favor of human planning and certitude imagined in material terms. Our very words make the case: "rebirth" through initiation or baptism implies mysterious re-creation, whereas "reform" assumes rationally ordered causal sequence and conceives human invention as capable of reconstructing reality. In the words of Sir William Blackstone, one of the several men who shaped the Penitentiary Act and guided it through Parliament during the 1770s:

> If the plan be properly executed, there is reason to hope that such a reformation may be effected in the lower classes of mankind, and such a gradual scale of punishment be affixed to all gradations of guilt, as may in time supersede the necessity of punishment, except for very atrocious crimes.[41]

Penitentiaries have regimes, schedules, disciplines; their inmates progress or regress; and they have stories, not to be told upon release or just prior to execution (like the liminal subjects of the old *Newgate Calendar*), but to be lived out in the penitentiary itself. Much of the history of penology subsequent to the establishment of penitentiaries in England during the last quarter of the eighteenth century is properly described as an attempt to order the prison story generically with divergent classifications of plot for each age, sex, and type of convict. This idea stands, then, at the heart of my argument: the form prisons took when they were remade in correspondence to and collaboration with the period's new systems of political and moral consciousness was narrative form of a distinctively novelistic kind that I associate with early realist fiction.

The very notion of a penitentiary sentence assumed ideas of time and determined sequence. Before the rise of penitentiaries, the "sentence" was a judicial decision on guilt versus innocence, or it was a determination of punishment—both absolute, instantaneous pronouncements that referred themselves and their objects of judgment to principles outside of time.[42] But linguistically a sentence unfolds in time like a plot and its elements have grammatical roles to play; narratives are made of such sentences. Indeed, as Roland Barthes has argued, narratives are properly viewed as expanded sentences with their own distinctive grammatical rules and syntactic structures.[43] The novel is a special kind of narrative that arose when sentences became accepted as surrogates of reality, that is, as I observe in the final part of this chapter, when reality itself came to be regarded as a fictional construct. The liminal prison became the penitentiary when, through a conflation of the legal and grammatical notions of a "sentence," randomness gave way to narrative order and "sentences" came to be served rather than executed. Punishment—previously the simple binary pronouncement "innocent/guilty," followed by its consequence "life/death"—was reformed into a programmatic course of events with the end of shaping personality according to controlled principles.[44]

· III ·

The comparison of the novel and the penitentiary advanced in the last few paragraphs and developed in the following chapters needs to be understood in the context of Locke's forensic conception of the self (see epigraph), which in turn has to be situated in the broad trend of philosophy in England from Locke, through Hume, to Bentham. These writers helped to articulate the predicament of a culture in which the lines between fiction and reality were becoming problematic. They located reality in the instantaneous present of impressions and stressed the constructed, "fictional," aspect of concepts such as self, character, justice, law, nature, final causation, any stable or self-evident notion of which they refused to accept.

For Hume, and later for Bentham, reality as ordinarily conceived was just a special form of fiction that, in daily life, we consider natural and concrete merely by way of convention or habit and, especially, of linguistic convenience. They examined the epistemological basis of "natural" fictions. Bentham, inspired by Hume but stopping short of his radical skepticism, instead accepted as irreducibly "real" the mechanisms of pleasure and pain founded in sensory experience and material circumstance.[45] This acceptance enabled Bentham to extend Hume's examination of fictions pragmatically into the realms of politics, legislation, education, and punishment. He sought laws and institutions that would be founded upon, and would foster, less convention-ridden, more realistic, more rational accounts of individual experience (epistemology) and of the social order (law) than had prevailed in the past. He wished to master reality by reshaping, and by rendering visible, the modes of its fictional construction. Bentham's theory of "fictions" is thus centrally important to a consideration both of novelistic representation and of the penitentiary's narrational structure as invented in the last quarter of the eighteenth century. His ideas can help us to understand the novel and the penitentiary as fundamentally similar social texts.

Bentham, retracing Hume's path, worked to distinguish the fictionality of poetic inventions from harmless natural fictions on the one hand and from the dangerous mystifications of priests and lawyers on the other:

> Of nothing that has place, or passes, in our minds can we give any account, any otherwise than by speaking of it as if it were a portion of space, with portions of matter, some of them at rest, others moving in it. Of nothing, therefore, that has place, or passes in our mind, can we speak, or so much as think, otherwise than in the way of *Fiction*. To this word Fiction we must not attach either those sentiments of pleasure, or those sentiments of displeasure, which, with so much propriety, attach themselves to it on the occasion in which it is most commonly in use. Very different in respect of purpose and necessity, very different is this logical species of Fiction from the poetical and political; very different the Fiction of the Logician from the Fictions of poets, priests, and lawyers.[46]

Bentham's "fabulous" entities, be they mythological gods or concepts like Natural Law, are merely the cast-off fables of past cultures:

> A *fabulous* Entity is one which has been believed in by others, but to the existence of which we attach no belief. Such are, with relation to us, the Heathen Gods, which were inferential entities with relation to those who believed in them. Between real or inferential and fabulous entities there is no distinct line of separation, even with relation to one individual mind, as belief admits of every degree from *positive* to *negative* certainty.[47]

But the very existence of this struggle to comprehend fictions by categorical type indicates a cultural situation in which their similarities have become problematic because they are assuming instrumental qualities. Bentham, for all his minute reasoning, has to admit that subjectivity blurs the boundaries he defines. The blurring of such boundaries between fact and fiction is, of course, one of the commonplace strategies

of the early realist novel.[48] Compelled by his own devastating forthright-
ness, Hume had been forced to admit that he could distinguish between
belief in logically fictional real entities, the object of which as Bentham
says is "neither more nor less than the carrying on of human converse,"
and belief in manifest fictions (including literature) only because they
feel different.[49] This feeling remained so indistinct that Hume found
himself incapable of naming it. Bentham enjoyed a cast of mind far
more practical than Hume's, so his faith that fictions might be identified,
mastered, and turned to socially useful ends was correspondingly greater.

Locke had linked his forensic concept of the self directly to pleasure
and pain, reward and punishment; in this sense the self is a continuing
legal and rhetorical fiction bounded by its own perceptions, which are
retained individually in memory and collectively in laws. The very act
of conscious being becomes fictive, and the self a legal entity. Hume's
idea of personal identity offered a more comprehensive account of the
same problem than Locke's:

> The true idea of the human mind, is to consider it as a system of
> different perceptions or different existences, which are link'd together
> by the relation of cause and effect, and mutually produce, destroy,
> influence, and modify each other. . . . Had we no memory, we never
> shou'd have any notion of causation, nor consequently of that chain
> of causes and effects, which constitute our self or person.[50]

Narrative makes precisely the substitution of succession for identity that
Hume says we make in attributing personal identity to ourselves. Narrative sequence and the fiction of personal identity are inseparable.

Once personal identity was viewed as a fiction, it also could be considered subject to artificial creation. Bentham's description of the laws
that govern the formation of identity in his *Introduction to the Principles
of Morals and Legislation* (written in the 1770s; printed in 1780; published
in 1789) fully rationalized an idea of the self, and therefore of punishment, derived from Hume's observation that vice and virtue do not exist
in external objects, in relations, or in facts:

> Vice and virtue, therefore, may be compar'd to sounds, colours, heat
> and cold, which, according to modern philosophy, are not qualities
> in objects, but perceptions in the mind. . . . Nothing can be more real,
> or concern us more, than our own sentiments of pleasure and uneas-
> iness; and if these be favourable to virtue, and unfavourable to vice,
> no more can be requisite to the regulation of our conduct and
> behaviour.[51]

It follows, then, that should one wish to shape the sense of identity
educationally or—as in the case of criminals undergoing reformative

punishment, to alter character—one must change the "succession of related objects" from which, according to Hume, the idea of identity is fictionally extrapolated in everyday life:

> The controversy concerning identity is not merely a dispute of words. For when we attribute identity, in an improper sense, to variable or interrupted objects, our mistake is not confin'd to the expression, but is commonly attended with a fiction, either of something invariable and uninterrupted, or of something mysterious and inexplicable, or at least with a propensity to such fictions. . . . And as the relation of parts, which leads us into this mistake, is really nothing but a quality, which produces an association of ideas, and an easy transition of the imagination from one to another, it can only be from the resemblance, which this act of the mind bears to that, by which we contemplate one continu'd object, that the error arises.[52]

The realist novel and the penitentiary are literary and social systems that re-present the fiction of self conceived as real, on these empiricist terms, through mistaken but imaginatively persuasive resemblance. To manipulate identity by recomposing the fictions on which it is founded is the exact aim of the penitentiary as an institution. Philosophy as exemplified by Locke and Hume, the realist novel, and the penitentiary as envisioned by Bentham all tell the story of the materially constructed self as it emerges in the practice of the period.

In his *Introduction to the Principles of Morals and Legislation*, Bentham describes the precise sensory basis of punishment in terms of a poetics or narratology of character as construed from circumstance. He discusses thirty-two categories of causes that will effect different circumstances, hence influence sensibility, and therefore call for specific gradations of punishment.[53] Then he shows how these categories can be taken into account in estimating the subjective force and impression of punishment on individual delinquents. Bentham offers a convenient summation while answering "specious objections":

> It is allowed that the greater part of these differences of sensibility are inappreciable: that it is impossible to prove their existence in individual cases, or to measure their force or degree; but fortunately these interior and hidden dispositions, if it may be so said, have external and manifest indications. These are the circumstances which have been called secondary: *sex, age, rank, race, climate, government, education, religious profession;* circumstances evident and palpable, which represent the interior dispositions. Here then the legislator is relieved from a part of his difficulty. He does not stop at metaphysical and moral qualities: he lays hold only of ostensible circumstances. He directs, for example, the modification of a certain punishment; not

on account of the greater sensibility of the individual, or on account of his steadiness, strength of mind, or knowledge, but on account of his sex or age.[54]

Bentham argues that the individual self, both initially and in its changed version after punishment, is the product of a detailed array of circumstance that can be described in exact narrative terms and altered by a renarration within a precisely controlled material grid that specifies exact new circumstances of "sensibility." The specimen penal code that he appends to the work specifies the legislative terms on which this can occur.[55] Bentham's theory of punishment, for all his zeal and contentiousness, enunciated a substantial consensus among the reformers on fundamental points. This consensus embraced the basic rules or laws governing punishment as part of the social mechanism, but not the specific methods that might follow from them.[56] The doctrine, for instance, that punishment should be "exemplary" and "characteristic" or "analogous to the crime," a principle that Bentham shares with virtually all of his compatriots in the 1770s, could support divergent practical schemes but, in general, sanctioned only realistic systems of penal representation.[57]

Bentham's ideas deserve emphasis here because they are specifically grounded in a theory of fictions and because of the unique explicitness with which, during the 1770s, he spelled out their implications for penology. He was able to join with Blackstone and the other authors of the Penitentiary Act even though he had attacked many of their ideas in *A View of the Hard Labour Bill* (1778). What separated Bentham from them, in his own view, was that the others were working from within a system of fictions that controlled them, whereas he was describing the laws that governed fictions and could thereby master their representations. Later, in his Panopticon project, Bentham summed up a broad attempt to account for human motives in terms of chains of cause and effect and to shape them fictionally, to reform them, by manipulating narrative sequences in a closely controlled grid of material circumstance—the penitentiary:

> If it were possible to find a method of becoming master of everything which might happen to a certain number of men, to dispose of everything around them so as to produce on them the desired impression, to make certain of their actions, of their connections, and of all the circumstances of their lives, so that nothing could escape, nor could oppose the desired effect, it cannot be doubted that a method of this kind would be a very powerful and a very useful instrument which governments might apply to various objects of the utmost importance.[58]

The world is Bentham's text and he himself the omniscient narrator with a story to tell.

Bentham aimed to correlate real and fictional entities by using the device he termed "paraphrasis" or "exposition" to represent fictitious entities. Paraphrasis consists in the definition of meaning through its restatement in alternate sentences employing both the simplest possible elements and reordered syntax. Bentham is thought to have been the first to see the sentence rather than the word as the primary integer of linguistic significance, and he worked to ground fictions in referentiality by harnessing the expository power of sentences. It is a short step from his theory of paraphrasis—from the rendering of complex significations and conditions of meaning through the minute restatement of material particulars in expository syntax—to a theory of realist narrative.[59]

A century before, in a capricious thought experiment, Leibnitz had dreamed of educating the senses in palaces of pleasurable representations under a kind of surveillance that anticipated the Panopticon: "These buildings will be constructed in such a way that the master of the house will be able to hear and see everything that is said and done without himself being perceived, by means of mirrors and pipes, which will be a most important thing for the State, and a kind of political confessional."[60] Working under the aegis of utilitarian behaviorism, Bentham, Blackburn, and other architects of the 1780s devised technologies that brought such a fantasy to the threshold of actuality. In a significant sense, both in the Panopticon and in his theory of knowledge, Bentham proposed the ultimate in realism—the ultimate representational system.

There are in London, *and the far*
extended Bounds, which I now call so,
notwithstanding we are a Nation of Liberty,
more publick and private Prisons,
and Houses of Confinement,
than any City in Europe, *perhaps as many*
as in all the Capital Cities of
Europe *put together.*

DANIEL DEFOE
A Tour Thro' the Whole Island of Great Britain

2

The Novel and the Rise of the Penitentiary

Moll Flanders and *Robinson Crusoe*

Defoe's fictional representation of the old prisons implied the conception of a new kind of imprisonment structured narratively along the lines of the realistic, consciousness-centered novel. Of course, any fabulist could tell stories about the old prisons too, but as institutions they were not internally ordered by narrational rules. The old prisons socially inscribed the principle that the true order of things had to be discovered through discord (*discordia concors*), and that final causes lay hidden beneath appearances. Romance narratives—by their magical strategies and implicit causes—bore this cultural fiction in literary form. The novel bears another fantasy entirely, that of a reality constituted from material causes. It articulates reality within a fine network of visible, observationally discoverable causes which are the motor factors of the narrative itself, for example, the internal forces of psychological motivation, the details of perceptual experience, the "natural" requirements of physical survival, the social demands of law and decorum. The reader experiences this complex matrix as "reality" by accepting the fiction of a governing consciousness in narrator and characters alike.

Defoe took two crucial steps toward the full novelistic schematization of confinement in the penitentiary: (1) he subjected experience to a detailed narrative articulation and thereby revealed the high degree of control latent in the novel as a representational form (even if he himself did not always attain it); (2) he showed how, in confinement, the internal forces of psychological motivation fuse dynamically with the physical details of perceptual experience. Here is the penitentiary imagined as the meeting point of the individual mind and material causes.

Contemporaries of Defoe considered him a specialist in prison narratives. One of them, grouping works of Newgate fiction, included *Rob-*

inson Crusoe, Moll Flanders, and *John Sheppard* in this category and indicated that these books represented crime and punishment to "the better Sort" whereas broadsheet biographies and last speeches did so to the mob: "How indulgent we are to the *Biographers* of *Newgate,* who have been as greedily read by People of the better Sort, as the Compilers of *Last Speeches* and *Dying Words* by the rabble." This critic took it that literary form implied societal differentiation, and he argued that writing had tangible consequence. So, for reasons entirely different from his, do I.[1]

This chapter and the next elaborate the significance I find in Defoe's fusion of an emergent narrative form with a subject matter previously limited to broadside accounts and penny pamphlets and the scribbles of popular court reporters. In *Moll Flanders* (1722), *Robinson Crusoe* (1719), and *A Journal of the Plague Year* (1722), I trace the novelistic reformation of liminal boundedness—the principle whereby the old prisons accommodated a reign of randomness and license within the precinct of confinement. Defoe's narratives array the old prisons on detailed representational grids of elapsed time, causal sequence, perceptual registration, and associative psychology. Under these conditions, the liminal prototype gives way to an ideal of confinement as the story of isolated self-consciousness shaped over time, within precise material circumstances, under the regime of narrative discipline: the key terms of what I call the "penitentiary idea."

The traditional figuration of authority in the early modern cities where the old prisons found their place (almost invariably in the walls or at the civic center) was external, hierarchic, and hegemonic; its emblematic formulations crystallized at boundaries (topographic, social, psychological), leaving discontinuous arenas subject to tacit or sporadic governance, as well as to chance and free play. These "liberties," in the double sense of physical places and of license, were covalent with established modes of order and, in a real sense, partook of their presence. Parodies of established governmental, legal, religious, or social structures at carnival time, in heretical movements, in the criminal underground—and inside the old prisons—revealed the systemic bonds that yoked demonstrative authority to its "other." By contrast, power is diffused everywhere within the sprawling grid of the modern industrial metropolis, to which the realist novel refers and with which it developed in tandem. The forces that order the metropolis become implicit, unbounded, undemonstrated—at once everywhere and nowhere—invisible except through partial but formally whole and apparently complete representations, like the novel and the penitentiary, that displace and re-project the boundaries in materially perceptible forms. Representation itself symbolically enacts the role of constituted authority; and, I argue, within the novelistic container as within the physical regime of the penitentiary, the self is perceived through and by its narrative construction. The point is not that Defoe proposes penitentiaries but that he delineates the subjective order—the structure of feeling—that they institutionalize and discloses to that order the power latent in the minutely sequential representations of realist narrative.

· I ·

Let me turn now to Defoe's narration of the liminal prison in the 1720s. In Moll Flanders's fictional world, "Newgate" as a word and as a place in general signifies liminality at its most concentrated. At the denouement of her story, Moll is cast into Newgate for stealing two pieces of brocaded silk:

> 'Tis impossible to describe the terror of my mind, when I was first brought in, and when I look'd round upon all the horrors of that dismal Place: I look'd on myself as lost, and that I had nothing to think of, but of going out of the World, and that with the utmost Infamy; the hellish Noise, the Roaring, Swearing and Clamour, the Stench and Nastiness, and all the dreadful croud of Afflicting things that I saw there; joyn'd together to make the Place seem an Emblem of Hell itself, and a kind of an Entrance into it.[2]

Moll conceives of her imprisonment emblematically, as if she were an allegorical figure, whereas Defoe's presentation requires us to situate her in a much more immanent, "naturally" motivated narrative structure. Moll describes life in prison as a death of her old self, again emblematically, in terms of the old psychological category of *acedia,* the sin of spiritual sloth:

> I degenerated into Stone; I turn'd first Stupid and Senseless, then Brutish and thoughtless, and at last raving Mad as any of them were; and in short, I became as naturally pleas'd and easie with the Place, as if indeed I had been Born there. (p. 278)

Moll has forgotten (in a famous lapse) that she has just decried Newgate as "that horrid Place! . . . where my Mother suffered so deeply, where I was brought into the World" (p. 273). The lapse, whether Moll's or Defoe's, characterizes her status as a liminal passenger. As Victor Turner says,

> In so far as a neophyte is structurally 'dead,' he or she may be treated, for a long or short period, as a corpse is customarily treated. . . . They

45

are allowed to go filthy and identified with the earth. . . . Often their very names are taken from them. . . . The other aspect, that they are not yet classified, is often expressed in symbols modeled on processes of gestation and parturition. The neophytes are likened to or treated as embryos, newborn infants, or sucklings by symbolic means which vary from culture to culture.[3]

So far, so good. Moll appears to be undergoing a symbolic rebirth that displaces her sense of first origins. Next should come either death or new social placement.

But suddenly the account splits. Defoe interposes Moll's retrospective judgment in her description of "the compleatest Misery on Earth," which is a mind weighed down with immense guilt, yet unrelieved by remorse or repentance. Now we hear two stories. The first is of collapse and failure in face of the liminal challenge presented by the rite of passage:

> I was become a meer *Newgate-Bird*, as Wicked and as Outragious as any of them; nay, I scarce retain'd the Habit and Custom of good Breeding, and Manners, which all along till now run thro' my Conversation; so thoro' a Degeneracy had possess'd me, that I was no more the same thing that I had been, than if I had never been otherwise than what I was now. (p. 279)

The second story begins at once with Moll's trauma of seeing her Lancashire husband brought into Newgate under arrest as a highwayman, combined with her own indictment by the grand jury. Repentance, reunion with a husband she always had loved, transportation to Virginia in lieu of execution, and ultimately a new life of prosperous gentility will ensue:

> My Temper was touch'd before, the harden'd wretch'd boldness of Spirit, which I had acquir'd in the Prison abated, and conscious Guilt began to flow in upon my Mind: In short, I began to think, and to think is one real Advance from Hell to Heaven; all that Hellish harden'd state and temper of Soul, which I have said so much of before, is but a deprivation of Thought; he that is restor'd to his Power of thinking, is restor'd to himself. (p. 281)

Thus Defoe both employs the model of spiritual autobiography and decisively breaks with it, for self-consciousness here replaces the ascent from hell to heaven, thought replaces salvation, and private awareness rather than emblematic public expression defines meaning.[4] Time, sequence, and causation—the predicates of novelistic narrative—have subtly altered the liminal place. The ironic counterpoint woven through Moll's story, far from obscuring this mutation, underscores the point. Moll's repentance, viewed from the religious perspective, remains doubtful, but her secular rehabilitation is complete. Defoe's irony verges so close to indecipherability because he uses the language of penitence and redemption to trace a salvation that is equally well comprehended in terms of mercantile economics.[5]

At the simplest level Moll's conversion leads to wealth, not to any spiritual sustenance. The "Newgate-Bird," a thief contributing no labor but syphoning value away from its natural repositories, reforms into a plantation owner generating wealth in the range of £300 per annum. This arbitrary denouement would follow easily from Moll's rite of passage in Old Newgate were there no attempt on Defoe's part to explicate it in spiritual terms. But Moll asserts that she has undergone a revolution of conscience, and Defoe's use of conventions drawn from Puritan spiritual autobiography leads us to expect one. Although Defoe depicts the old type of prison, when his imagination reforms it into narrative, it splits apart into different stories, whose contradictions register irony and paradox. Thus, while the social role of prisons is not explicitly at issue, we can see the unselfconsciousness of the liminal prison slipping away in the juxtapositions that occur in *Moll Flanders*.

No doubt what I have called Moll's second story (the spiritual one) could be told from a purely liminal perspective, for with that lucid simplicity possible only in fantasy or fiction, Moll's account outlines the cultural significance of the old prisons. Their filth, their dangerousness, their mysterious randomness, their carnival subculture, their absorption of the divine and otherworldly imagery of hell into a secular and social context all point to their provision of transformational experience on privileged ground where both festivity and profound danger are structurally central. This is precisely my argument: that Defoe takes the material surfaces of an institution that operates according to one set of principles and from those surfaces constructs a mentality that views the world quite differently. This may appear to be no more than the simple notion that his narrator holds a recognizable point of view. But this is not really the case since Moll is the sole narrator, and she undergoes both experiences. Finally, I want to emphasize that change itself is not the essence of the penitentiary as opposed to the liminal prison; change may occur in both, but the rite of passage is merely an occasion, while the penitentiary experience seeks out reasoned causes driven on the one hand by physical circumstance in all its detail, and on the other by the assumption that human behavior is—to use Moll's term—governed by thought acting in response to circumstance.

The point is that, at the very same instant Defoe's plots represent the old prison in all of its externally arbitrary, emblematic circumstance, he is reimagining punishment causally and sequentially as the reformation of inner thought. The peculiar quality of the novel as Defoe conceived it enabled ideas to be realized culturally through their enactment in a minutely particular mental world. The mere presence of ideas is not enough. The reception of early tracts such as Dr. Thomas Bray's *Essay Towards the Reformation of Newgate and Other Prisons in and about London* (1702), which remained unpublished until the nineteenth century, underscores this fact. Intellectual history is but one strand in the skein of cultural history. Thus, for all its richness, the modern scholarly picture of Defoe as an eclectic, intellectually informed writer who purposefully drew upon a wide range of literary traditions—those of spiritual autobiography, casuistry, pilgrim allegory, exempla in the "guide" literature aimed at youth, criminal narratives, and so forth—obscures the stroke of intuition with which he placed the general and the particular into a wholly new structural relation.[6]

Defoe's realism ensues from his master stroke. It comprises his unwavering focus on an individual character's mental world and his construction of each character's mentality out of the minute particulars, the very superficies, of physical objects. But the condition of possibility that enables Defoe's "realism" lies in a structural innovation at once peculiar to his moment and so fundamental to our own world view that ordinarily we pass it over.

Here is the briefest possible account of this innovation. Defoe's narratives employ a distinctive mechanism to foster the belief that everyday experience is meaningful. He constructs apparently true life stories whose plots purport to accord with established paradigms of moral significance even though these plots contain a discordant profusion of thought and incident. Because Defoe leads us to ascribe meaning to a tangible fictional world that includes attributes of the everyday, we come to think of human destiny as intentional or preconceived. But only the inconsistencies and contradictory materials that belong to our idea of realism, or even of reality itself, enable this meaning to emerge and validate the proposition that the flux of ordinary experience signifies. This situation is profoundly paradoxical, for the nature and function of novelistic realism lie in its ability to produce meaning by containing its own contradictions and thus to leave the impression that consciousness and subjectivity are stable across time.

One way to describe Defoe's contribution is to say that he took the traditional Puritan methods of reading the world allegorically and ran them backwards. Before, divinely validated stories had been sought in actual lives (as in spiritual autobiography), but he contrived fictional lives that could be construed as material validations of spiritual order. With Defoe, salvation becomes a matter of self-confirmation through psychological insight. This is not merely to propose a commonplace: that Defoe started with meanings and constructed a fictional world out of which they could be extracted in turn. Every classically oriented poetics I know of claims some such constructive essence for fiction. Herein lies much difficulty, for even during the Renaissance the theory of fictional meaning continued to be argued in a remarkably stable terminology while narrative procedures were shifting radically.[7] Indeed, my own description of Defoe's innovation appears to fail in this respect, for how can it distinguish between the sort of moral fable envisioned by Sidney's *Apology for Poetry* and typified by great exemplary fictions such as the *Aeneid, The Faerie Queene,* or Sidney's own *Arcadia* and works such as Defoe's? Obviously these earlier stories also construct worlds out of which meaning can be extracted; the vital difference is that they presume their entire contents to be homologous with the moral prototypes they represent. This may not always in fact be so (for a variety of reasons including failures of execution), but the presumption of both author and reader in these works is that all elements and details refer themselves ultimately to moral significance—even if only as devices to delight the reader and keep hold of his attention.[8]

Defoe describes his own enterprise in the same traditional terms I have been discussing when, in the preface to Robinson Crusoe's *Serious Reflections* (1720), the third and least often read volume of his most famous work, he says:

> I come now to acknowledge to my reader that the present work is not merely the product of the two first volumes, but the two first volumes may rather be called the product of this. The fable is always made for the moral, not the moral for the fable.[9]

This terminology is retrospective, and it forces Defoe's remarkable work into traditional categories that grant priority to invention over execution and deem fictional events valid when they can be seen to correspond to moral prototypes. Defoe says his *Idea* preceded its mere fictional exposition. At the same time, however, he asserts the temporal precedence of the fable—that is, he wrote it first. He seems at pains to deny his innovation, the essence of which had been in finding a new way to validate fictional meaning.

The way is so simple that we assume it: Defoe constructs fictions whose contents are not consistent with reference to any moral but only with reference to a central consciousness. His idea of "just history" and of "fact" is such that, in order to convey his moral, he has to recreate the predicament of finding meaning in the world at large. The truthfulness to fact that, in Defoe's view, grants credence to his moral can exist only under materially realistic conditions that erode or even contradict it.

Moll's repentance is but one of the more obvious examples. His archetypal plot represents a central consciousness constructing a moral world in face of this contradiction. His fiction purveys the myth—or ideology— that such representational constructions are real and material in themselves. Defoe formulates this myth most powerfully in *Crusoe*, where material phases in the fabrication of an island estate rehearse the course of self-discovery and change the castoff hero undergoes. The opposite occurs in *Roxana*, the tragic work that ended Defoe's brief novelistic career. Despite every material advantage, Roxana not only fails to assemble a morally coherent world, but her consciousness splits off into Amy, an ungovernable servant-double who, by contrast with Crusoe's Friday, cannot be restrained from murder.[10]

Defoe's reversal of the traditional method of reading the world allegorically becomes a radical innovation because he takes it so realistically, that is, with such material literalism. Defoe's very conception of personality derives from materialistic ideas of how the human mind and character are constructed from sense impressions. These ideas, on which Locke had founded his theories of personality, education, and government, have been cited by Maximillian Novak as formative to Defoe's intellectual world and by Ian Watt as instrumental to the rise of the novel.[11] They presage the utilitarian analysis of pleasure and pain as motive forces on which the penitentiary depends for its theoretical impetus. In these institutions, the sentence consisted of a reformation according to a narrative sequence of rewards and punishments over time. The sudden clarity of liminal conversion does not figure in these clean, well-ordered places.

We have now returned to the center of my argument. The penitentiary, which uses the material instruments of architecture and daily regime to recreate the convict, who has been sentenced for a crime that signifies failure to extract moral order from experience, parallels the novel in which a facsimile of the material world is shaped by a central consciousness discovering ordering principles among contradictions. It is worth recalling here that penitentiaries were constructed as narratives in the tracts of reformers long before the institutions were built. The idea of starting with categories of prisoners divided according to age, character, nature of crime, or the like, and ending with an "ordinary" person is fundamental to the reformist arguments. Since no one had ever seen these things done in prison, every account of what would ensue once the penitentiaries were built was a fiction.

At the simplest level, Defoe makes the link I have been discussing when, in the preface to the *Serious Reflections*, he says:

All these reflections are just history of a state of forced confinement, which in my real history is represented by a confined retreat in an island; and it is as reasonable to represent one kind of imprisonment by another, as it is to represent anything that really exists by that which exists not. (p. xii)

But representation alters as it preserves, creates as it maintains, and Defoe, for all his defensiveness here, cannot forestall the generative power of his narrative. Because Defoe writes in new forms that will accommodate contradictions and crosscurrents, he makes structures of feeling accessible that will not be institutionally constituted for decades and that are available to consciousness during the 1720s only in fictional modes.

A few years later Defoe's *Complete English Tradesman* (1725–26) shows the old punishments undergoing metaphorical redefinition as the idea of reformative confinement emerges:

> Now in order to have a man apply heartily, and persue earnestly, the business he is engag'd in, there is yet another thing necessary, namely, that he should delight in it: to follow a trade, and not to love and delight in it, is a slavery, a bondage, not a business. The shop is a bridewell and the warehouse a house of correction to the tradesman, if he does not delight in his trade; while he is bound, as we say, to keep his shop, he is like that galley-slave chain'd down to the oar; he tuggs and labours indeed, and exerts the utmost of his strength for fear of the strappado, and because he is obliged to do it, but when he is on shore, and is out from the bank, he abhors the labour, and hates to come to it again.[12]

The Tradesman's prisoner serves a fixed term under rigorous supervision, but the sentence is displaced onto an imaginary galley. This is a representation in fantasy, not the thing itself, and what tells here is not the corporal labor of correctional workhouses—themselves no more functionally institutionalized in the England of Defoe's day than were the galleys—but an idea of punishment as prospective and psychologically formative. The Tradesman's mental protopenitentiary measures time, out of public view, in controlled rations of inner pain. His stress in the paragraphs surrounding this quotation lies on the delights of diligence founded upon training and knowledge; punishment is a natural consequence of their absence. Although displaced metaphorically into emblematic lashes on the back of a galley slave, the force of punishment in the Tradesman's mental world is penitential and reformative.

· II ·

How does the narrative prison emerge elsewhere in Defoe's fiction? Experiences of transformation in marginal places of confinement figure centrally in both *Robinson Crusoe* (1719) and *A Journal of the Plague Year* (1722). At the same time, as in *Moll Flanders*, these works present materially realistic delineations of consciousness shaped through the narration of confinement.

Here is Crusoe's situation liminally considered. Prior to the wreck, Crusoe lays stress on the unceremonious break with his parents and on the immaturity of obeying "blindly the Dictates of my Fancy rather than my Reason."[13] After the wreck, invoking the metaphor of condemnation and reprieve, he hovers at the boundary between life and death:

> I believe it is impossible to express to the Life what the Extasies and Transports of the Soul are, when it is so sav'd, as I may say, out of the very Grave; and I do not wonder now at that Custom, *viz.* That when a Malefactor who has the Halter about his Neck, is tyed up, and just going to be turn'd off, and has a Reprieve brought to him: I say, I do not wonder that they bring a Surgeon with it, to let him Blood that very Moment they tell him of it, that the Surprise may not drive the Animal Spirits from the Heart, and overwhelm him. (p. 46)

Crusoe's thinking here catches the primitive doubleness of marginal symbolism in the notion of bloodletting at the moment of reprieve: the wound that heals. His overarching metaphor assumes the liminal prison because Newgate launched the condemned onto the infamous road terminating at Tyburn gallows and held the fortunate few who returned with reprieves until their transportation abroad. Indeed, we later discover that Crusoe has been simultaneously alive and dead throughout most of the book, for legally he has undergone *"Civil Death"* (pp. 283–84).

During the island confinement he subjects his entire previous standard of life to criticism; his initiative rises to the re-creation, often in parodic forms, of virtually every craft or social comfort known in England. Time becomes conjectural after he loses track during a delirious, nearly fatal, illness, and its value becomes immeasurably small during his ceaseless labors to shape the island into a microcosm of European life. Having undergone his own rite of passage, Crusoe undertakes Friday's instruction and eventually institutes a facsimile of civil society on the basis of truths he has discovered about human nature. Finally, Crusoe himself, as the Governor, reprieves certain mutineers and commutes their sentences to a form of transportation: the colonization of the island. He thus closes the liminal cycle with full acceptance of axiomatic social values, including the use of reprieves as tokens in the system of patrician patronage through which the gentry exercised authority.[14] Although Crusoe never settles down to realize them, the social prospects implied by his entry into the class of substantial landholders have been enacted prospectively on the island through his journeys from sea coast fort to inland country seat, as well as by his exercises in governance. In the end, however much greater his fortunes might have been had he remained in Brazil instead of undertaking the fateful voyage, Crusoe does achieve a new economic status well above his father's "middle state."

Yet the liminal account, like Crusoe's metaphor of reprieve, seems artificial—not false, but insufficient or old-fashioned—because Defoe centers the work on Crusoe's obsession with finding an account of his mental life that coheres sequentially, causally, and spiritually. Solitude is the occasion, narrative the medium, and prison the overarching figure:

> Now I began to construe the Words mentioned above, *Call on me, and I will deliver you,* in a different Sense from what I had ever done before; for then I had no Notion of any thing being call'd Deliverance, but my being deliver'd from the Captivity I was in; for tho' I was indeed at large in the Place, yet the Island was certainly a Prison to me, and that in the worst Sense in the World; but now I learn'd to take it in another Sense: Now I look'd back upon my past Life with such Horrour, and my Sins appear'd so dreadful, that my Soul sought nothing of God, but Deliverance from the Load of Guilt that bore down all my Comfort: As for my solitary Life it was nothing; I did not so much as pray to be deliver'd from it, or think of it. (pp. 96–97)

Here, as in the wreck, Crusoe's terms are more directly religious than in Moll's turn to thought. But in context the theological referents are wholly subordinate to the machinations of Defoe's narrative as it struggles—repeatedly retelling the early phases of the story—to trace the reformation of Crusoe's conscience. We move from "just history of fact," to straight journal, to journal interrupted and dissolved by reflection. Defoe uses the "real" words of Crusoe's chronicle to certify the truth of reflections that at first break into the texture of the vital pages surrounding the delirium and eventually overtake them entirely. Narrative in its relation to consciousness is the actual subject here: accounts of the self *are* the self, and fuller, more circumstantial accounts placed in a reflective context are more true than mere chronicles or journals. This section of *Robinson Crusoe* stands at a decisive juncture in the history of the novel because of its literal quest through generic types for some material equivalent to the formation of thought. This quest structures Defoe's "realism" as a mode of representation that incorporates and subordinates the others into what Bakhtin calls polyglossia.[15] Before our very eyes, the new, reflective, consciousness-centered form displaces the genres it has subsumed, a state of affairs traced in Defoe's text by Crusoe's progressive dilution of his ink until the journal fades into illegibility a few pages following the passage quoted above.

During Crusoe's "solemn" observance of the second anniversary of his shipwreck, the prison metaphor recurs, again yoked with solitude. Here the two terms fall into clear opposition, signifying states of mind before and after Crusoe's correct understanding of deliverance some two months earlier. To be imprisoned is to be subject to random misery:

> I was a Prisoner lock'd up with the Eternal Bars and Bolts of the Ocean, in an uninhabited Wilderness, without Redemption: In the midst of the greatest Composures of my Mind, this would break out upon me like a Storm, and make me wring my Hands, and weep like a Child: Sometimes it would take me in the middle of my Work, and I would immediately sit down and sigh, and look upon the Ground for an Hour or two together; and this was still worse to me; for if I could burst out into Tears, or vent my self by Words, it would go off, and the Grief having exhausted it self would abate. (p. 113)

But to comprehend solitude is to be spiritually and mentally whole, as well as to function materially:

> I spent the whole Day in humble and thankful Acknowledgments of the many wonderful Mercies which my Solitary Condition was attended with. . . . I gave humble and hearty Thanks that God had been pleas'd to discover to me, even that it was possible I might be more happy in this Solitary Condition, than I should have been in a Liberty of Society, and in all the Pleasures of the World. That he could fully make up to me, the Deficiencies of my Solitary State, and the want of Humane Society by his Presence . . . supporting, comforting, and encouraging me to depend upon his Providence here, and hope for his Eternal Presence hereafter. (p. 112)

Meanings outnumber terms here as the notion of prison slides from the liminal, arbitrary, openly public realm into the private realm of reflective thought.

Several things are happening. First, the liminal experience, while present, is losing its tangibility, and its habitual, external forms are assuming a negative tinge. Second, the outcome of punishment is now being represented as mental reformation. Third, errant personality is reconstituted as self-consciousness by solitary reflection. Finally, the ability to function materially is specifically attributed to the proper inner comprehension of life as a story, each circumstance of which is meaningful. We see the mythology of reform taking shape here. Prison, now equated with solitary reflection, is first viewed as negative, random, punitive, vengeful; but it slides into another thing entirely—something salubrious, beneficent, reformative, and productive of wealth and social integration. Crusoe's illness can be read, in this light, as a prospective allegory of the move from the old, fever-ridden jails to the clean, healthy, contemplative solitude of the penitentiaries.

Crusoe equates having a self with being able to account for his crime, and his story literally enacts a quest for some narrative equivalent to personality. Just as his construction of material surrogates of European civilization is indistinguishable from the narration of his story, so is novelization inseparable from the reformation of his consciousness. Friday's advent enables Crusoe to test the power of narrative to constitute the self. Crusoe must teach him the causes and raise him up into the crafts before Friday is recognizable as human and Crusoe's self-construction is socially validated.

When Crusoe ends his confinement by subjugating the mutineers with the purely fictional personage of the Governor, both the self and the authority it projects are shown as narrative constructs that effect material ends.

> When I shew'd my self to the two Hostages, it was with the Captain, who told them, I was the Person the Governour had order'd to look after them, and that it was the Governour's Pleasure they should not stir any where, but by my Direction; that if they did, they should be fetch'd into the Castle, and be lay'd in Irons; so that as we never suffered them to see me as Governour, so I now appear'd as another Person, and spoke of the Governour, the Garrison, the Castle, and the like, upon all Occasions. (p. 271)

The fiction of the Governor becomes real through its own enactment: the mutineers are divided, maneuvered into submission, and, where of sound character, reconverted to the service of established order. The five incorrigibles, imprisoned in the island's fortified cave during the recapture of the English captain's ship, benefit ultimately from clemency at Crusoe's hand in his role as the Governor; they are left to colonize the island under threat of execution should they return to England. Viewed one way, they, like Moll, are reprieved and transported; but from another perspective they have become convicts in Crusoe's penitentiary, condemned to reformation according to a narrative of his making. His story will be their regime:

> I then told them, I would let them into the Story of my living there, and put them into the Way of making it easy to them: Accordingly I

gave them the whole History of the Place, and of my coming to it; shew'd them my Fortifications, the Way I made my Bread, planted my Corn, cured my Grapes; and in a Word, all that was necessary to make them easy: I told them the Story also of the sixteen *Spaniards* that were to be expected; for whom I left a Letter, and made them promise to treat them in common with themselves. (p. 277)

Crusoe has altered from a lord of nature, alone with the savage Friday, to a lord of men who appears at last, ceremoniously clothed, in *propria persona* as the Governor. Having defined a consciousness located at the juncture of the mental and the material, having mapped it first on the terrain of his island and then on Friday's malleable mentality, Crusoe now rehearses his authority and renders it tangible through fiction. Once he has construed himself and discovered the enabling force of narrative, Crusoe uses the explanatory power of story-telling to exert control over the mutineers and to police the future civic order he envisions upon the arrival of the sixteen Spaniards. Upon Crusoe's departure, the island and its furniture exchange their metaphorical standing as prison for that of an actual penal colony with his fortress at its civic center and his story as its master narrative.[16]

· III ·

Although Defoe's hero is castaway on a deserted island, the formulation of imprisonment that lies at *Robinson Crusoe*'s figurative core assumes and incorporates the experience of the city as the seat of power. Defoe's tale is an archaeology of urban geographical, social, psychological, and legal forms. Crusoe maps the island according to the polarity between city and country even before he is able to populate it, and the architectural traces of his ingenuity, so minutely fabricated in the telling, become instruments of power once the mutineers arrive. This is especially clear in the case of Crusoe's fortified cave, the evolution of which is synonymous with the narration of his story, because it serves at once as a prison in which he holds the mutineers and the seat of authority personified in the Governor. Built first to shield its resident from harm and then elaborated to provide a base for his farming and hunting, the fortress becomes a walled city that can contain and subjugate as well as defend. Crusoe's building program retraces the ancient etymology of the English word "town" and the French word "ville," earlier forms of which referred first to enclosed places or camps, then to farms or manors, and finally to governed urban habitations.

Crusoe tests and revalidates forms of hegemony characteristic of urban culture, the ordering principles of the governed city. With the convergence of Friday, the Spanish captain, the mutineers, the English captain, and the prospective arrival of sixteen Spanish castaways from the mainland (signifying, like so many tribes, the varying modes of social order), Defoe retrieves that moment in human history described by Lewis Mumford as "the first time the city proper becomes visible": "The first beginning of urban life . . . was marked by a sudden increase in power in every department and by a magnification of the role of power itself in the affairs of men."[17] Of course Defoe's narrative cannot re-create the original city but instead must represent it from the vantage point of modern civilization—thus Crusoe's salvage operations, and his construction of what amounts to a deserted city waiting for its test of viability. The architectural fabric by which Crusoe laboriously masters the island, like the articles reclaimed from the shipwreck, store up power as surely as gunpowder stores propulsive force. They form a stockpile of the urban estate that, no less than Crusoe's hoard of gold, must wait to be expended.

It has become a commonplace of literary history to trace the emergence of the realist novel to the concentration of literate audiences in early modern cities.[18] Collaterally, from the broad perspective of social theory, the origin of written history within the purview of the city situates narrative in "a special form of 'container,' a crucible for the generation of power on a scale unthinkable in non-urban communities."[19] Critics of the novel risk more by making too little of these congruent analyses than by making too much.

Traditionally the two most distinctive spatial traits of the city were, at its center, the compound containing governmental and religious buildings and, at its periphery, the surrounding walls.[20] These also were the two habitual sites of prisons, which thus lay deep in the syntactic structure articulating the space of the city.[21] Viewed on the large canvas of world time, written narrative rests with prison at the generative axis of the city as the enclosed seat of authority and the site of surveillance. In ancient Sumer, for example, the origins first of written language and then of inscribed narrative have been traced to the requirements of civic administration:

The keeping of written "accounts"—regularised information about persons, objects and events—generates power that is unavailable in oral cultures. The list is . . . not just an aid to the memory, but a definite means of encoding information. Lists do not represent speech in any sort of direct way, and . . . the early development of writing thus signals a sharper break with speech than might be imagined if we suppose that writing originated as a visual depiction of the spoken word. In Sumer, listing led eventually to the further development of writing as a mode of chronicling events of a "historical" nature. . . . These "event lists" form the first known "written histories," and eventually built up to span a large number of generations.[22]

Considered on this scale, the claim that novels often lay to the narration of historical truth becomes an assertion of the authority latent in written representation.

As Mikhail Bakhtin says, all of the traditional literary genres, "or in any case their defining features, are considerably older than written language and the book, and to the present day they retain their ancient oral and auditory characteristics. Of all the major genres only the novel is younger than writing and the book: it alone is organically receptive to new forms of mute perception, that is, to reading."[23] The novel, the genre of writing par excellence, formally embodies the fabric of urban culture: the very self-consciousness concerning the narration of minute particulars that defines it implies not merely an awareness of being watched but the technical ability to keep track by writing and to retrieve by reading. Compilation, investigation, justification, adjudication, letters, lists, receipts, journals, records, evidentiary detail, testimony—the written traces of merchandise and manners—here is the stuff both of cities and of novels.

Defoe's pervasive listings—his accountings, inventories, census reports, bills of lading, logs, and diaries—fictionally reinscribe the origins of writing as the medium of power. Among the first products of Crusoe's confinement are the lists contained in his journal, at once prototypes of his ultimate published narrative and integral parts of it. But early in the story we see writing, the means of civic commerce, go faint as Crusoe dilutes and finally exhausts his ink in a trail of scarcely legible script. Defoe underscores the social structure implicit in records when, because of his delirium, Crusoe's marking of the calendar also becomes indefinite. On the island Crusoe's solitary, gestural use of writing calls attention to its usual function as a medium of exchange. For written language, which represents its objects abstractly and renders them transferable across time and space, is to talk and oral fable as money, which gains value only as a medium of exchange, is to labor and its tangible products. Defoe probes and reoriginates the link between money and writing, which, in recent times, has been traced archaeologically to exceedingly ancient trade tokens, impressions of which appear to have formed the earliest inscriptions, a primitive, protocuneiform script.[24] Crusoe is forced back into an existence based only on use value rather than exchange. He must put aside his hoards of money and stash his manuscripts.

In *Robinson Crusoe*, Defoe stages an explanatory myth showing how Crusoe's isolation and enclosure enable him to constitute power through the storage and allocation of resources.[25] Only gradually does Crusoe master the physical potential of the island and store up enough provisions to consider allocating some to another person. At first his sense of control seems childish or illusory, and he suffers horrible fears that his authoritative resources might not be sufficient to protect him from visiting savages. However, his power becomes instrumental when luck and skillful deployment enable him to subdue the two cannibals who separate from their clan to pursue Friday, the object of their feast. His rescue of Friday provides a subject on whom to exercise authority.

As Friday becomes Crusoe's loyal subject (a human resource), he participates in an elementary linguistic, educational, and social structure in which Crusoe accumulates enough power to mount a direct assault, destroying all but four of the twenty-one cannibals who visit the island intent upon making a banquet of Friday's father and the Spanish captain. Defoe's representation of the signal stages of civilization is lucid. Crusoe represses the primitive, devouring power latent, as Elias Canetti suggests, in the sharp, smooth, orderly array of teeth.[26] His island government sublimates cannibalistic dominance into a mimicry of toleration as state policy:

> My Island was now peopled, and I thought my self very rich in Subjects; and it was a merry Reflection which I frequently made, How like a King I look'd. First of all, the whole Country was my own meer Property; so that I had an undoubted Right of Dominion. *2dly*, My People were perfectly subjected: I was absolute Lord and Law-giver; they all owed their Lives to me, and were ready to lay down their Lives, *if there had been Occasion of it,* for me. It was remarkable too, we had but three Subjects, and they were of three different Religions. My Man *Friday* was a Protestant, his Father was a *Pagan* and a *Cannibal,* and the *Spaniard* was a Papist: However, I allow'd Liberty of Conscience throughout my Dominions: But this is by the Way. (p. 241)

When Defoe has the Spanish captain interpose an objection to immediate colonization of the island by shipmates abandoned among savages on the mainland, he goes out of his way to elucidate the relationship between physical resources and power in social formations:

> He told me, he thought it would be more advisable, to let him and the two other [*sic*], dig and cultivate some more Land, as much as I could spare Seed to sow; and that we should wait another Harvest, that we might have a Supply of Corn for his Country-men when they should come; for Want might be a Temptation to them to disagree, or not to think themselves delivered, otherwise than out of one Difficulty into another. You know, says he, the Children of *Israel,* though they rejoyc'd at first for their being deliver'd out of *Egypt,* yet rebell'd even against God himself that deliver'd them, when they came to want Bread in the Wilderness. (p. 246)

In this same context, though implements are lacking, writing becomes an issue for the first time since the ink was exhausted more than twenty years before. The authoritative language that Crusoe intends to have the force of a written charge assumes the marked stiffness of legislative prose:

> And now having a full Supply of Food for all the Guests I expected, I gave the *Spaniard* Leave to go over to the *Main,* to see what he could do with those he had left behind him there. I gave him a strict Charge in Writing, Not to bring any Man with him, who would not first swear in the Presence of himself and of the old *Savage,* That he would no way injure, fight with, or attack the Person he should find in the Island, who was so kind to send for them in order to their Deliverance; but that they would stand by and defend him against all such Attempts, and where-ever they went, would be entirely under and subjected to his Commands; and that this should be put in Writing, and signed with their Hands: How we were to have this done, when I knew they had neither Pen or Ink; that indeed was a Question which we never asked. (p. 248)

Only eight days later Crusoe sights the mutinous vessel, the mastery of which will prove his salvation.

Except for the one invocation of writing in Crusoe's charge to the Spanish captain, his ambassador to the mainland castaways, his demonstrations of power remain oral and physical until after he has staged the appearance of a settled government so as to overcome and imprison the mutineers. But at the moment of departure, when he tells the technical secrets of life on the island to the prison colony he leaves behind, Crusoe's letter to the expected Spaniards reintroduces writing in order to explain the constitution of his city-state and to govern its future behavior. His letter attempts to store up authority across time just as his treasure has stored up value. And indeed, as if to acknowledge the ancient covalence of writing and money, within a page of text Defoe refurbishes the disused currency:

> When I took leave of this Island, I carry'd on board for Reliques, the great Goat's-Skin-Cap I had made, my Umbrella, and my Parrot; also I forgot not to take the Money I formerly mention'd, which had lain by me so long useless, that it was grown rusty, or tarnish'd, and could hardly pass for Silver, till it had been a little rubb'd, and handled; as also the Money I found in the Wreck of the *Spanish* Ship. (p. 278)

Money, writing, listing, urban enclosure, social authority, forced confinement—all are obsessions of Defoe's, and these elements remain central to our sense of the novel in general.

Reference to large-scale social theory merely works to confirm motive forces embedded in the novel. The novel acts out, it represents iconically, the interplay between the unbounded heterogeneity of population in cities (their polyglot assembly of voices) and the bounded unity of their walls, fortified compounds, governmental structures, and systems of communication (their inscription of "facts," their insistence on point of view, and their assimilation of authority from approved genres through parody, burlesque, irony). "From the beginning," as Lewis Mumford says, "the city exhibited an ambivalent character it has never wholly lost: it combined the maximum amount of protection with the greatest incentives to aggression: it offered the widest possible freedom and diversity, yet imposed a drastic system of compulsion and regimentation."[27] My stance necessarily stresses the subordination of diversity to civic rule and, in the case of the novel, to narrative order. But the novel's generic instability persists because the diversity it encompasses and the authority it projects are reciprocal opposites, each defined by the representation of its antithesis, each always containing the other. Still, while it remains permissive in many respects, the novel oscillates between points of view that imply surveillance and enclosure. On the one hand stand novels in which readers enter the mental world of a single character and thereby fictionally view reality as a network of contingencies dependent upon observation; on the other lie novels in which readers ally themselves with the controlling power of an omniscient narrator. In this light, it is of more than incidental significance that Defoe served as a spy and a government agent—the very human medium of surveillance—and that he repeatedly suffered imprisonment.[28]

·

Good and Evil, as hath been shewn . . .
are nothing but Pleasure or Pain,
or that which occasions, or procures Pleasure or
Pain to us. Morally Good and Evil, *then,*
is only the Conformity or Disagreement of our voluntary
Actions to some Law, whereby Good or Evil is drawn
on us, from the Will and Power of the Law-maker;
which Good and Evil, Pleasure or Pain,
attending our observance, or breach of the Law,
by the Decree of the Law-maker, is that we call
Reward *and* Punishment.

·

JOHN LOCKE
An Essay Concerning Human Understanding

·

3

The City and the Rise of
the Penitentiary

A Journal of the Plague Year

Thus far, I have considered ways in which peculiar traits of the modern novel, as set forth early in the eighteenth century by Defoe, contradict the cultural predicates of the liminal prison and shape the penitentiary idea. The analysis of this process in *Robinson Crusoe* revealed how the narrative representation of instrumental self-consciousness validates the penitentiary idea as the logical outcome of Crusoe's rehearsal in miniature of the history of civic settlement. My argument has followed a course leading from discussion of the novel in a customarily delimited sense—the kind of realistic fictional prose narrative that defined itself in eighteenth-century Europe and prevailed through various permutations for about two hundred years thereafter—to a series of generalizations about the novel as the characteristic urban narrative genre. The novel in the latter, global, sense embraces the former and is an implicit subject of this chapter.

The large view traces both written narrative and prison, along with the authority they represent, deep into the original structure of the city. With such an understanding as an index, we can gauge the specific predicates of confinement in the novel of a given historical era (in Defoe's case, that of the emergent industrial metropolis) over and against the norms of a genre which, because of its tacit affinity to the subject of prison, recurrently implies observation and enclosure. In the case of the eighteenth-century novel, with its material particularity, its causal sequences, and its fine-grained rendering of personality as a summation of perceptual experience, the emerging formulations are those of the penitentiary. Of course cultural change never occurs uniformly or universally; not until the decade of William Godwin's *Caleb Williams* (1794) is penitentiary confinement institutionalized with equal explicitness in the spheres of social action (with local, county, and national governments moving under the stress of the American and French revolutions) and in novelistic prose. In the age of Defoe, since actual prisons were of the old type and since novelistic realism dictated many details of their depiction, we must read through gaps, breaks, and formal contradictions to discover the lineaments of reformative confinement. Even so, novelistic representation at once rendered the outline formally whole and ideologically accessible. Later, on the verge of the public movement toward reform, emergent predicates become arguments, and we find the fictional texture of a work like Oliver Goldsmith's *The Vicar of Wakefield* (written 1761–62; published 1766) fractured by polemics that are all but indistinguishable from reformist tracts.

· I ·

Defoe's narratives record the onset of an epoch-making revision in men's exercise of final authority over one another. This change occurred as London was assuming distinctive metropolitan features, including an unprecedented immensity of scale. Just as cities had originally implied walls and bounded, hierarchical social forms,[1] they also had dictated the transient use of prison—a threshold marking off ordinary life from death, banishment, or vindication. Thus both the decrees of imperial Rome and civil law, right through the seventeenth century, ruled against imprisonment as a punishment.[2] Liminal prisons had meaning only within a network of social boundaries, and frequently were built at the civic threshold or gateway directly within city walls. These walls by their nature could shield and govern, or enforce exile. But the London of Defoe's youth already had outgrown its walls. The original enclosure of the old City increasingly merged into sprawling suburbs at once congenial to real estate speculation and necessary to accommodate the commerce and the luxurious display that supported early urban industry.[3]

Defoe lived through the period when the prototypical pattern of blocks and squares characteristic of the modern metropolis unmistakably asserted itself in the speculative development of the West End (figs. 14, 15, and 16 [coordinates G/g, H/e, E/g, F/e, E/h, G/d, F/e, G/b]). The economic and social implications of this development were considerable. London moved swiftly from a distribution of real estate on the medieval pattern of irregular precincts, parishes, and plots to modern gridiron development whereby land is parceled out and standardized as a commodity subject to exchange. Roger North's autobiography indicates that speculative building on a large scale began with Dr. Barbone's ventures following the Great Fire: "He was the inventor of the new method of

building by casting of ground into streets and small houses, and selling
the ground to workmen by so much per front foot, and what he could
not sell, built himself. This had made ground rents high for the sake of
mortgaging, and others, following his steps, have refined and improved
upon it, and made a superfoetation of houses around London."[4] Immediately after the fire, Wren presented a new plan for London to
Charles II and a rebuilding committee was established by royal procla-
mation. Wren and Evelyn swiftly proposed schemes in which largely
regular gridirons of blocks were overlain by axial radiants linking major
monuments (fig. 17). These schemes adopted the outlines of authoritarian baroque order even though they were somewhat hobbled by the
absence of the court, traditionally resident upriver. Wren's city would
have focused on a gigantic circus centered by the Royal Exchange and
surrounded by the Mint, the Post Office, the Excise Office, and the
Insurance Office—a grand seat of commercial power to which even Saint
Paul's was subordinated. Under pressure of circumstance, London opted
instead for renovations superficially following the ancient street plan but
conducted in the manner of modern parceled development, with zoning
and codes of construction specified by the government. Thus Richard
Newcourt's rebuilding scheme (fig. 18), extending the ancient walls and
realigning parishes on a strict grid with a church at the center of each
block, graphs the reorientation of London's growth during Defoe's lifetime more meaningfully than Wren's or Evelyn's.[5]

The novel represented "this great and monstrous Thing, called *London*" to itself, rendering its sprawling scope accessible, comprehensible,
and controllable.[6] Coherence now lay not in the permanent shape of the
city as a whole (its acropolis, its close, its bounding walls, its social hierarchy), but in the formal order, the internal governance, of partial
representations of metropolitan life (its consumption of goods, its cultural and social foundations, its state institutions, its literature and art).
The realistic novel is above all a means of perception and disposition
that validates itself in the multifarious urban setting by means of an
apparent reflective completeness. The novelistic refiguration of the liminal prison into the narrative penitentiary is part of the web of generation, representation, and regeneration that creates and maintains the
identity of the modern city. As Mumford says, "The abstractions of
money, spatial perspective, and mechanical time provided the enclosing
frame of the new life. Experience was progressively reduced to just those
elements that were capable of being split off from the whole and measured separately." Or again, in a passage citing Defoe's eulogies to the
sheer size of London as a force in magnifying trade, "The expansion of
the market . . . is involved in the whole scheme of substituting vicarious

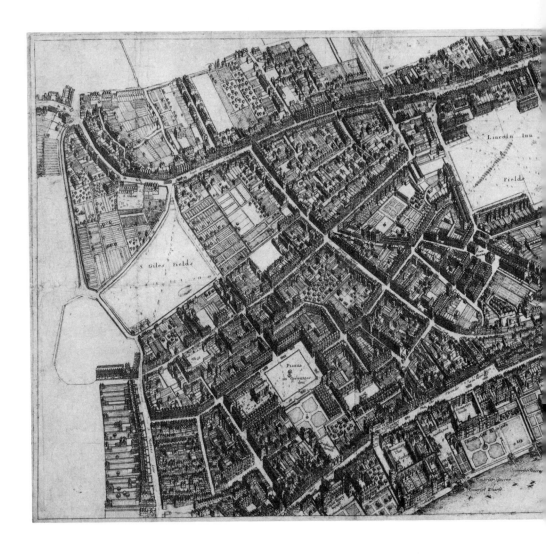

satisfactions for direct ones, and money goods for life experiences."[7]
More specifically, we may add, the substitution of private novel reading
for action in the public sphere.

One characteristic method of abstraction mentioned by Mumford is
casuistry, an analytic procedure for correlating general principles and
particular cases that provides the matrix within which Defoe weaves his
fictional universe. Casuistry is "that part of Ethics which resolves cases
of conscience, applying the general rules of religion and morality to
particular instances in which 'circumstances alter cases,' or in which there
appears to be a conflict of duties."[8] A recognition of the affinity of
casuistry to the novel allows us to grasp the paradox that realism is a
method of schematization that employs dense particularity of reference
as its means. The novel appears as the veritable opposite of abstraction

66

14. Wenceslaus Hollar, *Bird's Eye Plan of the West Central District of London*, c. 1658. Just prior to Defoe's birth, old developments abutted squares built on the new grid pattern, like Covent Garden and Lincoln's Inn Fields.

15. Sutton Nichols, *Covent Garden*, c. 1720. The first of the West End squares, planned during the 1630s by Inigo Jones for the duke of Bedford.

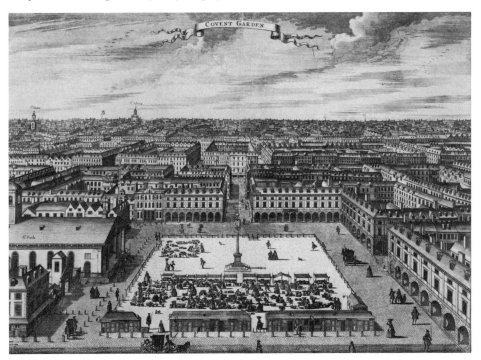

only if we look at its content rather than its methods. As Bakhtin says of the distinctively modern moment in the vast history of the novel as he embracingly defines it: "When the novel becomes the dominant genre, epistemology becomes the dominant discipline."[9]

In the particular kind of material realism that Defoe initiated (the novel of "Things" as Novak has called it, following Defoe's division of the "Subject of Trade" into "Things" and "Persons") what is abstracted is not the referents—the narrative content or subject matter per se—but the medium itself.[10] Modern novelistic realism in general is marked by its self-representation as a transparent medium, a mode of writing that one sees through rather than a form one looks at. The convention in Defoe's fiction that his novels are transparent or, as Ian Watt has suggested, "ethically neutral," requires prior acceptance of the abstract

16. George Foster, *A New and Exact Plan of the Cities of London and Westminster,* 1738. By mid-cent (left) contrasted sharply with the old City's tangled streets (right).

orderly patterns of West End development

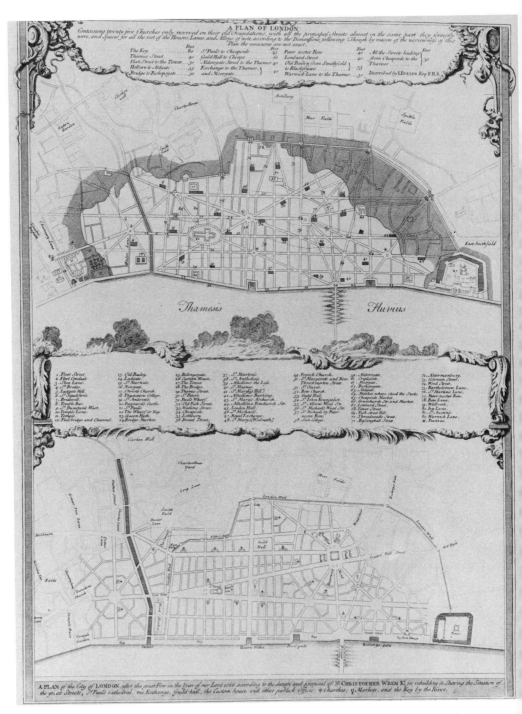

17. John Evelyn's and Christopher Wren's plans for rebuilding the City of London after the Great Fire of 1666. Visions of absolutist order were offered to the king after the conflagration (Wren's plan appears below and Evelyn's above).

70

premise that formal realism itself is intrinsically fair and evenhanded—requires in short the unacknowledged acceptance of a certain kind of authority diffused throughout the text. Watt assumes this point in his basic definition of the realist novel:

> The narrative method whereby the novel embodies this circumstantial view of life may be called its formal realism; formal, because the term realism does not here refer to any special literary doctrine or purpose, but only to a set of narrative procedures which are so commonly found together in the novel, and so rarely in other literary genres, that they may be regarded as typical of the form itself. Formal realism, in fact, is the narrative embodiment of a premise that Defoe and Richardson

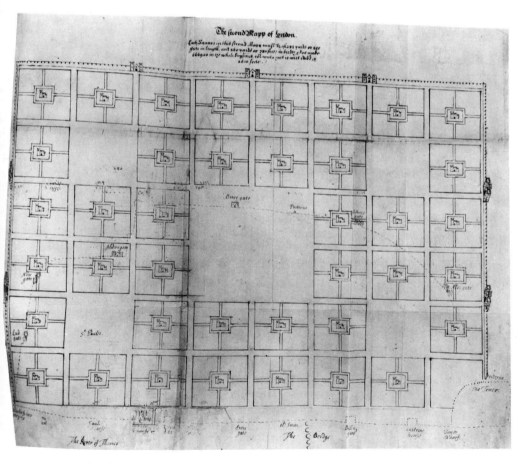

18. Richard Newcourt's scheme for rebuilding the City of London, 1666. The City reimagined on a perfect grid.

accepted very literally, but which is implicit in the novel form in general: the premise, or primary convention, that the novel is a full and authentic report of human experience. . . . Formal realism is, of course, like the rules of evidence, only a convention; and there is no reason why the report on human life which is presented by it should be in fact any truer than those presented through the very different conventions of other literary genres. The novel's air of total authenticity, indeed, does tend to authorise confusion on this point.[11]

The authority latent in the convention of representational neutrality is explicitly manipulated in novels such as Fielding's. While pretending all the while to hew to the values of formal realism, his narrator shapes our judgment, leading us along and supplying or withholding information so as to order our perceptions.

Even in *Moll Flanders* the author, speaking out in the preface, claims manipulative authority over both language and incident with a view to representing the heroine in words appropriate to "one grown Penitent and Humble":

> The Pen employ'd in finishing her Story . . . has had no little difficulty to put it into a Dress fit to be seen, and to make it speak Language fit to be read. . . . All possible Care however has been taken to give no leud Ideas, no immodest Turns in the new dressing up this Story, no not to the worst parts of her Expressions; to this Purpose some of the vicious part of her Life, which cou'd not be modestly told, is quite left out, and several other Parts, are very much shortn'd. . . . To give the History of a wicked Life repented of, necessarily requires that the wicked Part should be made as wicked, as the real History of it will bear; to illustrate and give a Beauty to the Penitent part, which is certainly the best and brightest, if related with equal Spirit and Life. (pp. 1–2)

I am arguing at the most general level, then, that novelistic conventions of transparency, completeness, and representational reliability (perhaps especially where the perceptions being represented are themselves unreliable) subsume an assent to regularized authority. This assent finds its cultural counterpart in the societal consent whereby, according to Weber, our reliance on the consistency, orderliness, and rationality of bureaucratic institutions—our acceptance of them as transparent and ethically neutral—validates the power of the state and indeed enables us to conceive its existence.[12] The penitentiary idea represents this acceptance at an extreme of ideological concentration in which it is rarely formulated except in what Erving Goffman has described as "total institutions."[13] Because of that doubleness and paradox specific to art and literature (what Althusser calls "internal distantiation"), there probably is no such thing as the "total" novel, but a profound affinity exists between the penal law and the traditional canons of consistent representation, which the novel brings to their most detailed realization. As Roland Barthes maintains, "That particular psychology, in the name of which you can very well today have your head cut off, comes straight from our traditional literature, that which one calls in bourgeois style literature of the Human Document."[14]

· II ·

Whereas Moll Flanders's Newgate had held a topographically and emblematically distinct place within London's delineating walls, sites of imprisonment in *A Journal of the Plague Year* (1722) are diffused into every street marked by the disease. Defoe's feigned historical memoir, published only two months after *Moll Flanders*, tacitly abandons the old prisons by granting them no delimited location in a text otherwise obsessed with places. H.F., the narrator of the *Journal*, never describes a single one of the twenty-seven public gaols listed in Defoe's *Tour* nor says anything about their condition during the plague.[15] Instead, H.F. considers the whole of London as a place of confinement bounded by hostile villages whose citizens allow no passage by road. In London and its environs, where sick people are guarded under quarantine in their own houses, there "were just so many Prisons in the Town, as there were Houses shut up" (p. 52).

When H.F. laments at the very end of his journal that most people who survived the scourge went back to their own routines without registering the transformational force of their experience, he chooses the overtly liminal metaphor of the Israelites' passage into the promised land:

> I must own, that for the Generality of the People it might too justly
> be said of them, as was said of the Children of *Israel*, after their being
> delivered from the Host of *Pharaoh*, when they passed the *Red-Sea*,
> and look'd back, and saw the *Egyptians* overwhelmed in the Water, *viz.*
> That *they sang his Praise, but they soon forgot his Works.* (p. 248)

This amounts to a denial of the liminal magic to Londoners who lived out the plague confined in the city at large.

The whole *Journal* depicts the uncertainty, danger, and sense of finality characteristic of rites of passage, but liminality is shorn of its transformative effects. H.F. allows lasting alteration only to those few sick people who recovered against odds. And, as to them, "confining the sick was no Confinement; those that cou'd not stir, wou'd not complain, while they were in their Senses, and while they had the Power of judging: Indeed, when they came to be Delirous and Light-headed, then they wou'd cry out of the Cruelty of being confin'd" (p. 170). Alone among others, he as narrator receives a perfect score. His final test is the remembrance over time of the sentence of plague under which the city had suffered, measured against his awareness of how self-conscious discipline and reflection validated his own sense of being an individual with a place in the order of things:

> I wish I cou'd say, that as the City had a new Face, so the Manners of the People had a new Appearance: I doubt not but there were many that retain'd a sincere Sense of their Deliverance . . . but except what of this was to be found in particular Families, and Faces, it must be acknowledg'd that the general Practice of the People was just as it was before. . . . Some indeed said Things were worse, that the Morals of the People declin'd from this very time; that the People harden'd by the Danger they had been in, like Sea-men after a Storm is over, were more wicked and more stupid, more bold and hardened in their Vices and Immoralities than they were before; but I will not carry it so far neither. (p. 229)

Although H.F. here seems to retreat from opinions closely similar to those of later reformers who attacked the old prisons, his doubts arise in a context of generalizations about the whole populace of London. But the alleged moral decline, even the terminology in which H.F. characterizes it, is precisely that of Moll and her cohorts in the Old Newgate. In the *Journal*'s archaeology of urban crisis, we find Defoe's account of the social and mental states requisite to the reformation of confinement that I have traced in *Robinson Crusoe* and *Moll Flanders*. H.F. prefigures the absolute contradiction of the liminal prison later found in Gay; and, through his real if tentative or casuistic embrace of authority, he assumes traits of the judgmental narrators in Fielding's novels.[16]

In the *Journal* Defoe looks back from the period when the novel was becoming a recognizable mode of writing to the time, following the Restoration and prior to the great depopulations of plague and fire, when London, already engulfed by suburban progeny, had assumed an early modern form and was on the verge of its endless sprawl into an industrial metropolis. Defoe formulates a multiplex account of urban values by adopting the fiction of a retrospective journal assembled at least thirty years afterwards from memoranda supposedly kept during the plague of 1665 by one H.F., a saddler now deceased and buried in Moorfields.[17] H.F. reflects as follows on the spread of the town after the Civil War:

> It must not be forgot here, that the City and Suburbs were pro-
> digiously full of People, at the time of this Visitation . . . for tho' I
> have liv'd to see a farther Encrease . . . the Numbers of People, which
> the Wars being over, the Armies disbanded, and the Royal Family and
> the Monarchy being restor'd . . . was such, that the Town was com-
> puted to have in it above a hundred thousand people more than ever
> it held before; nay, some took upon them to say, it had twice as many. . . .
>
> I often thought, that as *Jerusalem* was besieg'd by the *Romans*, when
> the *Jews* were assembled together, to celebrate the Passover . . . the
> Plague entred *London*, when an incredible Increase of People had
> happened occasionally, by the particular Circumstances above-nam'd:
> As this Conflux of the People, to a youthful and gay Court, made a
> great Trade in the City, especially in every thing that belong'd to
> Fashion and Finery; So it drew by Consequence, a great Number of
> Work-men, Manufacturers, and the like, being mostly poor People,
> who depended upon their Labour. (pp. 18–19)[18]

Defoe's history, staged in multiple repetitions within the psychology of
a single narrator, allows him to preserve the contradictory sense that
H.F. lives simultaneously in modern, metropolitan London and in an
old city that, following presentiments of future growth after the Civil
War, died away at the height of the plague into a kind of archaeological
site:

> The great Streets within the City, such as *Leaden-hall-Street, Bishopgate-
> Street, Cornhill*, and even the *Exchange* it self, had Grass growing in
> them, in several Places; neither Cart or Coach were seen in the Streets
> from Morning to Evening, except some Country Carts to bring Roots
> and Beans, or Pease, Hay and Straw, to the Market, and those but
> very few, compared to what was usual. (p. 101)

Defoe immerses the disease whereby "the Face of *London* was now indeed
strangely alter'd" in the reflective consciousness of a narrator whose
recollection, from a vantage point following the Glorious Revolution,
encompasses the decimation of the old "Mass of Buildings, City, Liberties,
Suburbs, *Westminster, Southwark* and altogether" by plague and fire, as
well as their resurgence with the "mighty Throngs of People settling in
London" during the rebuilding thereafter (pp. 16, 18).

The *Journal*, through its exacting literalism of reference, fuses the
metropolitan grid into realist narrative. H.F.'s story unites inseparably
with the history of a London that confines him under martial law. Such
is the *Journal*'s historical precision that, having for some while been taken
as a real document, it has since inspired a commentary obsessed with
grading the degree of its accuracy and with certifying its title to one
generic description or another. At the same time, the London of 1665

depicted in the *Journal* is really composed of landmarks that survived, however altered, in Defoe's city of the 1720s.[19] The lifeblood of the work seems to lie in an obsessively overdetermined double representationality: it behaves as if any depiction short of the literal is somehow insufficient. In reducing realism to an essence, the *Journal* risks becoming another substance—the zero degree of novelism. Paradoxically, by this same token, the work approaches a standing as the impossible "total" novel alluded to above.

The literalism of the *Journal* constitutes a narrational move to project authority by presenting the text as a real documentary account of London under sentence of plague. Since the factuality of the work therefore cannot be questioned within its own boundaries (indeed H.F. preempts doubt by incorporating continual disclaimers concerning what he can and cannot know precisely), questions about the authenticity of the text as regards London are displaced into issues of authority in the mind of H.F.[20] Given that Defoe wrote the *Journal* in part to justify the unpopular Quarantine Act, proposed by the government following the spread of plague from Marseilles in the early 1720s, the issue of the proper relationship between the force of the state and individual freedom presents itself directly in the work's history.[21] Thus I view the refiguration of the authority latent in cities, especially as its representation directs and inhabits mental life in the urban metropolis, as the *Journal*'s elemental concern.[22] And therefore I join with other critics who have treated the passages on the shutting up of houses as tropes for the claustrophobic, solipsistic, isolating aspects of the modern city—qualities that attain "total" representation in the penitentiary. As W. B. Carnochan suggests, H.F.'s watching from windows "prefigures Bentham's inspector":[23]

> I cannot speak positively of these Things; because these were only the dismal Objects which represented themselves to me as I look'd thro' my Chamber Windows (for I seldom opened the Casements) while I confin'd my self within Doors, during that most violent rageing of the Pestilence; when indeed, as I have said, many began to think, and even to say, that there would none escape; and indeed, I began to think so too; and therefore kept within Doors, for about a Fortnight, and never stirr'd out: But I cou'd not hold it. (p. 103)

H.F.'s self-confinement, though for want of enforcement he cannot "hold it" at this comparatively early stage of the narrative, anticipates his later acceptance of the role of examiner despite strong disagreement with official policy. The good citizen is both watched and watcher.

Defoe adopts the conceit that fully deployed legal authority in the city turns its houses into prisons and its citizens into criminals. From the specific case the *Journal* proposes, a generalized version of the reformist penitentiary follows by converse inference: "total" authority represented through physically enforced mental solitude—through a narratively ordered, sequential control of the particulars of daily life—will make citizens of criminals. Of course the bluntness of these propositions is a function of their exposition here. Defoe naturalizes their shading in a thousand ways by embedding them in the historically specific and highly unusual events of his journal, and by personifying them psychologically through his casuistic narrator's exposition of the debate over the shutting up of houses. The viability of the narrative depends upon a certain density of factual and emotional texture, upon the ebb and flow of multiple reports and competing interpretations.[24]

A number of strands lace through Defoe's network of claim and counterclaim, fact and counterfact, case and countercase. First, H.F. discredits liminal confinement by depicting the policy of shutting up houses as unfair and cruel in terms that precisely describe rites of passage. Second, permanent mental reformation, not mere change of status, is the standard against which H.F. judges the effect of confinement under siege of plague on the populace. Third, he traces the reach of authority into every aspect of urban life and illustrates the force of its psychic claims through his acceptance of the official role as examiner despite his deep reservations concerning the shutting up of houses. In the metropolis, as in prison, one is either watched or watcher, and those who refuse to be examiners are themselves "committed to Prison until they shall conform themselves accordingly" (p. 38). Finally, H.F.'s narrative certifies isolation, reflection, and solitude as means of survival and thus as final values. In H.F. we witness the private self being constituted narratively through isolated reflection on its relation to circumstance; individual personality appears as the internal restatement of external authority, as a principle of order in face of chaos, comprehension in face of the arbitrary, representation in face of endless disordered perception, a principle of life as opposed to death, reformation as opposed to execution.

H.F.'s all but obsessive recurrence to the issue of shutting up houses throws these ideological predicates into relief. The debate about the effectiveness of sequestering any household touched with plague symptoms dates back as far as the practice of shutting up houses itself, and Defoe's use of this controversy, along with his literal inscription of the entire legislation on which the decrees of 1665 were based, is part of his minute re-creation of social practices that accommodated rites of passage and used them expressively.[25] But the terms in which H.F. couches his rejection of this type of forced quarantine strongly condemn the liminality that he sees as characterizing the shut-up houses. Recall from our discussion in chapter 1 that liminal places are, etymologically, "seclusion sites"; that the inmates are at once neither living nor dead and both living and dead; that the randomness, the reign of chance, and confusion of categories so abhorrent to reformers prevails horrifyingly within the shut-up houses. It is precisely the chaotic, uncontrolled mixture of categories—well and sick, master and servant—that H.F. deplores most strongly. He attends much to the numerous methods of escape from shut-up houses—to the lack of system and regularity in enforcement—though from the liminal perspective the possibility of escape is itself part of the symbolism. The myth of the penitentiary is, conversely, that one cannot get out except by a regulated course of life.

Although H.F. views the measure of shutting up houses as inhumane, his objections focus at least as much on its ineffectiveness as on its cruelty: "I believed then, and do believe still, that the shutting up of Houses . . . was of little or no Service in the Whole; nay I am of the Opinion it was rather hurtful, having forc'd those desperate People to wander abroad with the Plague upon them who would otherwise have died quietly in their Beds" (p. 71). He advocates a more discriminating quarantine in pesthouses, where only those stigmatized with signs of the disease would be confined in solitary rooms, and therefore effectively monitored:

> I say, had there instead of that one been several Pest-houses, every one able to contain a thousand People without lying two in a Bed, or two Beds in a Room . . . I am perswaded, and was all the While of that Opinion, that not so many, by several Thousands, had died. (p. 74)

H.F. seems to envision a system of voluntary confinement in the pest-houses, for he denies the intention of "forcing all People into such Places" (p. 182). Yet his proposal is directed chiefly at servants, who spread the plague by coming and going to fetch necessaries for their households, and he vests the power to commit them in their masters, not in the servants themselves.[26] Similarly, for all that it contradicts his conviction that shutting up houses by force was ineffectual, H.F. never wavers in his belief that forcible confinement would prevent spread of the disease by crazed victims dashing frantically about the streets:

> Had not this particular of the Sick's been restrain'd . . . *London* wou'd ha' been the most dreadful Place that ever was in the World; there wou'd for ought I know have as many People dy'd in the Streets as dy'd in their Houses; for when the Distemper was at its height, it generally made them Raving and Delirious, and when they were so, they wou'd never be perswaded to keep in their Beds but by Force; and many who were not ty'd, threw themselves out of Windows, when they found they cou'd not get leave to go out of their Doors. (p. 164)

Thus, while opposing the method of shutting up houses, H.F. endorses its most practical aim, advancing a scheme in which solitary confinement would protect society and increase the survival rate of the infected.[27]

More important than the specific content of H.F.'s objections, however, is his rejection of symbolic boundedness as a method for organizing and allocating authority. The shutting up of houses was an old practice by which authority placed itself in a distinct relation to material circumstance, drawing putative boundaries around arenas within which the arbitrary and the bizarre not only were tolerated but expected. Liminal symbolism forms part of a cultural system alien to H.F.'s way of conceiving reality, and thus to his proposals. He advocates a much more individual and focused discrimination, a much finer symptomatic classification for separating the diseased from the not-diseased. In the old system, one could talk of infected houses; H.F. would deal in infected persons. By contrast with the demonstrative power that liminal boundaries symbolize, his representation of authority is more penetrating, diffused, and internalized. A person is no longer one with a status (bachelor, widow, citizen, councillor, magistrate, etc.) but one who has a self that continually rehearses, situates, and internalizes the force of authority. This is why casuistry takes such a central place in the formal structure of Defoe's fictions, and why it serves as an element of structure as well as style. H.F.'s representational mode is consonant with Defoe's Hobbesian ideas on government as a construct devised by men to protect themselves against the savagery of human nature, and consonant as well with the Lockean presumption that the self remains in total subjection to perceptual experience. Reality lies within, and therefore to the degree any external authority is realized, it must be as a mental phenomenon represented in words or images.[28]

H.F.'s position on shutting up houses unfolds during a course of extended personal deliberation in which he comes to identify with the established order in the city and, while rejecting liminality, to endorse solitude as a final, life- and self-preserving value. This occurs despite H.F.'s specific disapproval of and distaste for the formal policies of quarantine. To the degree the book tells his inner story, these events outline its plot. But he is caught up during the historical time of the plague itself in the contradiction of living between old world and new: H.F. the compulsive walker and watcher; H.F. the man who believes himself providentially sheltered yet tries to shut himself up to gain safety; H.F. the reluctant examiner; H.F. the social projector and reformer. His supposed plague journal is fused with retrospection and reflection, and his narrative, as opposed to its historical object (the plague in 1665), formulates the self in a private, internally isolated manner. His final values consist of solitude and respect for the balanced, moderate, bureaucratic order of modern society:

> Every thing was managed with so much Care . . . that *London* may be a Pattern to all the Cities in the World for the good Government and the excellent Order that was every where kept, even in the time of the most violent Infection. . . . One thing, it is to be observ'd, was owing principally to the Prudence of the Magistrates, and ought to be mention'd to their Honour, (*viz.*) The Moderation which they used in the great and difficult work of shutting up of Houses. . . . But after all that was or could be done in these Cases, the shutting up of Houses, so as to confine those that were well with those that were sick, had very great Inconveniences in it, and some that were very tragical . . . but it was authoriz'd by a Law, it had the publick Good in view, as the End chiefly aim'd at, and all the private Injuries that were done by the putting it in Execution, must be put to the account of the publick Benefit. (pp. 155, 158)

In context, the stress lies solidly on H.F.'s transaction with authority in itself, for a flat denial of the value of shutting up houses follows at once. Yet again, a few pages later:

> The Lord Mayor and the Sheriffs, the Court of Aldermen, and a certain Number of the Common Council-Men, or their Deputies came to a Resolution and published it, *viz.* 'That *they* would not quit the City themselves, but that they would be always at hand for the pre-serving good Order in every Place, and for the doing Justice on all Occasions. . . . These things re-establish'd the Minds of the People very much. . . . Nor were the Magistrates deficient in performing their Part as boldly as they promised it; for my Lord Mayor and the Sheriffs were continually in the Streets, and at places of the greatest Danger. (pp. 183–84)

Significantly, these passages enclose the episode in which H.F., "greatly afflicted" by the "Hardship" of being appointed an examiner for his parish, gains slight remission by pleading opposition to official policy.

But H.F. does serve, and the crisis of his personal history comes when, as an appointed bureaucrat, he must himself maintain order and respect for authority by enforcing the quarantine. The random fury of the plague opposes the systematic conduct of the urban magistrates who encounter it with written legislation, computation of casualties, printed plague bills, routine sweeping away of bodies, control of food supplies, and, above all, the shutting up of infected houses. To have a self is to take individual narrative account of the regulating, discriminating forces that control the chaos of human nature just as they display and order the abstract grid of the metropolis. Otherwise, like many people at the

height of the plague, he would begin to give up himself to "Fears, and
to think that all regulations and Methods were in vain, and that there
was nothing to be hoped for, but an universal Desolation" (p. 171). Authority both requires coherent personal identity and supplies the occasion for its production.

H.F. lives at a historical threshold, himself betwixt and between, a
personified contradiction. He simultaneously considers his "own Deliverance to be one next to miraculous," a special providence that saved
him personally, yet condemns "*Turkish* Predestinarianism" and insists that
the plague was "really propagated by natural Means, nor is it at all the
less a Judgment for its being under the Conduct of human Causes and
Effects" (pp. 193–94). Certainly his recommendations and his relation
to secular authority embrace human causes and effects—the regulated,
measured order of the metropolis, the private house, the individual
consciousness, and the penitentiary cell. When H.F. once approaches the
despair he has earlier described, schemes of social engineering allay his
doubt:

> Now let any Man judge . . . if it is possible for the Regulations of
> Magistrates . . . to stop an Infection, which spreads it self from Man
> to Man, even while they are perfectly well and insensible of its Ap-
> proach. . . . Tho' Providence seem'd to direct my Conduct to be oth-
> erwise; yet it is my opinion, and I must leave it as a Prescription, (*viz.*)
> *that the best Physick against the Plague is to run away from it.* I know People
> encourage themselves, by saying, God is able to keep us in the midst
> of Danger, and able to overtake us when we think our selves out of
> Danger; and this kept Thousands in the Town, whose Carcasses went
> into the great Pits by Cart Loads. [But] were this very Fundamental
> only duly consider'd . . . on any future occasion of this, or the like
> Nature, I am persuaded it would put them upon quite different Mea-
> sures for managing the People, from those that they took in 1665 . . .
> in a Word, they would consider of separating the People into smaller
> Bodies, and removing them in Time farther from one another.
> (pp. 197–98)

While noticing himself as a seeming exception, H.F. turns not to worship but to a rationalistic authoritarian project for thinning out the city
by systematic evacuation to a density below that critical to the spread of
plague. His cure dissolves the city into its solitary citizens, a cure appli-
cable to the fire and, by extension of H.F.'s language about the poor, to
crime:

> I could propose many Schemes, on the foot of which the Government
> of this City . . . might ease themselves of the greatest Part of the
> dangerous People that belong to them; I mean such as the begging,

starving, labouring Poor, and among them chiefly those who in Case
of a Siege, are call'd the useless Mouths; who being then prudently,
and to their own Advantage dispos'd of, and the wealthy Inhabitants
disposing of themselves, and of their Servants, and Children, the City
and its adjacent Parts would be so effectually evacuated, that there
would not be above a tenth Part of its People left together, for the
Disease to take hold upon. (pp. 198–99)[29]

For all this, as H.F. immediately points out, the fact remains that even
among those who fled, many had died, and even retreat implies confinement elsewhere. The only unimpeachable method of survival cited
in the entire *Journal* is in fact total self-imposed isolation based on fore-
sight, rational planning and storage of provision, and relentless vigilance:

Many Families foreseeing the Approach of the Distemper, laid up
Stores of Provisions, sufficient for their whole Families, and shut themselves up, and that so entirely, that they were neither seen or heard
of, till the Infection was quite ceased, and then came abroad Sound
and Well: I might recollect several such as these, and give you the
Particular of their Management; for doubtless, it was the most effectual secure Step that cou'd be taken for such, whose Circumstance
would not admit them to remove, or who had not Retreats abroad
proper for the Case. . . . Nor do I remember, that any one of those
Families miscary'd; among these, several *Dutch* Merchants were particularly remarkable, who kept their Houses like little Garrisons be-
sieged, suffering none to go in or out, or come near them. (p. 55)

While H.F. advocates self-imposed physical isolation as the only sure
method of survival, he cannot require it of himself both for want of
provision and patience. Yet psychologically he remains more alone on
the streets of plague-stricken London than the Dutch merchants barri-
caded in their houses. Their siege retreat invokes the proto-urban form
of the garrisoned tribe. H.F.'s project for guarding the city by stripping
it down to a molecular array of isolated citizens anticipates metropolitan
civil defense and could be implemented only by a disciplined population
in collaboration with bureaucratic authority.

The *Journal* hovers near an explicit denial of liminality as a principle
of justice. Counteractively, the mental life of Defoe's narrator illustrates
the sustaining power of reflective isolation, which is validated within the
fiction by the narrator's acceptance of authority, and maintained within
the larger novelistic construct as a principle of absolute representational
order diffused throughout the whole text. The interior affirmation of
consistently present authority registers psychologically as the persistence
of self. As in *Robinson Crusoe*, the narrative acts this out in terms of a
mental plot that hinges on a contract with God on the one hand and

with societal order on the other. The *Journal's* minute realism certifies the truth of its basic metaphor of London as prison and demonstrates total confinement as a mode of positive self-construction. The narrative is deeply contradictory, however, because the authority it validates enforces those old methods of confinement that it rejects. In this respect, Defoe has moved toward greater explicitness than in *Robinson Crusoe* and *Moll Flanders*, where the surface detail that refers to liminal practice is used to construct a mentality organized along quite different lines. Here the narrator questions liminal boundedness outright and proposes specific alternatives. But the casuistry of the narration tends to erode their concreteness in turn, and Defoe's narrative never breaks over into reformist discourse. Instead, what counts is the *Journal's* demonstration of the salubrious, life-giving, self-creating effect—the formulative power—of the contract between authority and isolated self. The work lays bare the central paradox of the urban metropolis (so vividly and totally crystallized in its corollary, the penitentiary) that the more tightly people pack together the more isolated they become, and concomitantly, the more dependent for their conception of self and their communication with others upon the authority latent in fine-grained representational forms: rationalized bureaucratic government, realistic narration, geographic placement in the metropolitan grid. As Crusoe says in "Of Solitude," the first chapter of *Serious Reflections*:

> I can affirm, that I enjoy much more solitude in the middle of the greatest collection of mankind in the world, I mean, at London, while I am writing this, than ever I could say I enjoyed in eight and twenty years' confinement to a desolate island. (p. 4)

Solitude is redefined not merely as a physical state, not merely as a state of mind, but as a condition of being.

My argument, then, is not that the *Journal* advocates the penitentiary but that Defoe articulates the conditions of its possibility by formulating the network of subjective circumstance—the structure of feeling—under which reformative confinement becomes part of the institutional texture of the city. Prison and the authority it assumes lie deep within the origins and structure of the city, but the city changes and so too do forms of confinement. The shift from the liminal to the penitentiary prison that I have been describing in terms of Defoe's rendering of consciousness can be viewed as a shift from the emblematic display of power within bounded walls, which also were literally prisons, to schematic forms of power that are increasingly removed, projected, and displaced into symbolically transparent, ideologically reified forms such as the novel and the penitentiary. This is not to assert that metropolitan life, the realist novel, and the penitentiary regime are identical. On the contrary, I view the penitentiary as the extreme case—the "total" instance, to use Goffman's term—of the narrative construction of self that the realistic novel portrays as normative. The novel bears these forms early and persuasively by virtue of its structural identity with urban life and its authoritative fusion of material specificity with detailed narrative causation. Finally, in attempting to anchor the rise of the penitentiary in novelistic form, one must observe the simple fact that the reformers of the modern penitentiary are not its occupants any more than the heroes and heroines of Newgate novels were readers. In other words, the penitentiary idea originally was a representation, a reformist construct, aimed at the literate public; only later, once having attained architectural form, could it claim an audience of criminals, and even then its literary life continued through interminable debates over its refinements, controversies that preoccupied the nineteenth century and continue even to the present day.

For Powers *are Relations,*
not Agents: and that which has
the power, or not the power to operate,
is that alone, which is, or
is not free, *and not the*
Power it self.

Jᴏʜɴ Lᴏᴄᴋᴇ
An Essay Concerning Human Understanding

4

Generic Conflict and Reformist Discourse in Gay and Hogarth

The Beggar's Opera (1728) changed the way in which the idea of Newgate signified and the level of awareness at which it did so. Gay, working in "a new species of composition," makes explicit the rejection of the liminal prison implied by the opposite structures of feeling delineated in Defoe's narratives.[1] Instead of the place of marginality, Newgate becomes the place of contradiction. Of course the liminal world symbolized by Newgate was always a world of paradox and contradiction, but with Gay, contradiction becomes an issue at the level of discourse. Habitual social forms, like the traditional genres that Gay set at odds, lose their explanatory power and, instead of subsuming paradox, are consumed by it. *The Beggar's Opera* exposes the capricious formulation of conventional authority by correlating it with arbitrary generic regulation. The old acceptances become untenable because in Gay's Newgate every meaning is contradicted by some other. All categories cancel one another out. Peachum is warm-hearted and predatory; Polly is innocent and rapacious; Macheath is hero and highwayman, husband and adulterer, hanged and reprieved, great man and scoundrel—a pure paradox. Gay's "total irony," as Ian Donaldson has called it, dissolves all boundaries, whether between criminals and prime ministers or between gentlemen and highwaymen, and fosters a "general sense of the interchangeability of men."[2] These total ironies sap Newgate's liminal structures by discrediting the very distinctions and delineations that its randomness worked ultimately to sanction.

There is no need here to rehearse the details of Gay's multiple discourse, which virtually every critic of *The Beggar's Opera* has described in one guise or another. Rather, partly by invoking Bakhtin's argument concerning the novelization of culture, I wish to show how this well-recognized strategy of Gay's sets reformist thought in motion by subjecting the old prisons and the social order they symbolized to a scrutiny that brings their character to consciousness. Gay does not control or direct interpretation. He was no activist. Instead, he transposes the spectator's awareness of generic contradiction—the dialogue among genres that Bakhtin finds at the heart of novelistic discourse—into cognitive form by affixing it, metonymically, to the contradictions being lived out in society. He set thought in motion, but the reformist outgrowth of his work was an unforeseen consequence of technique. This technique subjects social practice to consideration from multiple, unmediated points of view, which in turn imply choices.

One index of the radical nature of *The Beggar's Opera* is that its treatment of villainy as a profession horrified Defoe, who condemned its jocular pardon of Macheath the highwayman hero.[3] No doubt Gay's Newgate, compared with Defoe's, becomes a place of cynicism in terms of character, sarcasm in terms of tone (note the dance of prisoners in chains), and arbitrariness in terms of plot (note the rescue of Macheath). Yet *The Beggar's Opera* was considered subversive not because it exposed authority to temporary ridicule, as festive comedies had done for thousands of years, but because it depicted all existing public authority as permanently corrupted by self-interest. The virtues that survive are the strictly personal ones that adhere almost exclusively to Polly and Macheath. The closest approximation to stable truth lies in the ruling passions of individual personality as it comprehends experience. Although Polly and Macheath are far from ideal human beings, one tends to imagine human nature on their terms and to exaggerate their virtues as defenses against the sardonic urban province they inhabit.

The simultaneity of liminal and penitential views of prison found in Defoe's narratives no longer is possible after *The Beggar's Opera*. Gay's irony discredited the fabric of established order by using Newgate's mysteries as a central metaphor, and generic contradiction as a dominant formal strategy. Gay burst upon London at the same time that Hogarth and Fielding were becoming independently known. Both took up their public careers with performances closely affined to Gay's. Fielding opened his first London play two weeks after *The Beggar's Opera*, and his plays thereafter explored generically mixed forms such as Gay had introduced in *The What D'Ye Call It* (1715) and perfected in *The Beggar's Opera*. Later, Fielding turned to Peachum's original, Jonathan Wild, as the subject of one of his first novels. Hogarth, one of whose earliest commissions in oil yielded a series of paintings showing the climactic scene of *The Beggar's Opera* on stage (see figs. 20 and 21 below), soon adopted Gay's method of likening low life and high life in two sequences of unprecedentedly large visual satires, *A Harlot's Progress* (painted 1730–31, published 1732) and *A Rake's Progress* (painted 1734, published 1735) (see figs. 31–39 below). In these series, he attempted the visual equivalent of the narratives in which Defoe had shaped the penitentiary idea out of the material of the liminal prison. Hogarth took up Gay's challenge by making contradiction itself into a generic principle. He refabricated existing forms into a new mode of visual narration closely allied to the novel. Hogarth claimed credit for this invention when he attributed to his pictorial series "something of that kind of connection which the pages of a book have." Fielding soon dubbed the new form "comic history painting."[4]

This chapter shows, then, how the interplay of genres in Gay and Hogarth formally rehearses a new, overtly paradoxical structure of feeling that both erodes the liminal functions of the old prisons and brings their contradictions to consciousness. Although Gay and Hogarth show strong affinities to the novel, they also provide points of contrast because they show the effects of paradox cut loose from the exhaustive context of the novel, unregulated by its formal authority. Hogarth's reach toward narrative in his cycles is an attempt to draw back from the abyss of paradox by embracing novelistic means that locate contradiction in sequential chains of cause and effect. He ventures to impose narrative form on a society adrift between systems of authority and structures of feeling. As Fielding wrote of Hogarth in the *Champion,* "In his excellent works you see the delusive scene exposed with all the force of humour, and, on casting your eyes on another picture, you behold the dreadful and fatal consequence."[5] Fielding himself will later regenerate both Gay's paradoxical discourse and its containment in Hogarth's serial compositions. This chapter anticipates the authoritatively structured novels that accompanied Fielding's juridical and polemical contributions to the reformist movement that culminated in the Penitentiary Act of 1779.

· I ·

The Beggar's Opera enters this book about the novel and the penitentiary because Gay used essentially novelistic techniques of realism and generic contradiction to achieve a potent demystification of the reigning social structure, which he identified with the corruptions of a penal system infiltrated by Peachum, the prime minister of crime. Although other terms might apply to the sociorhetorical transaction that Gay brought to such a pitch of intensity in *The Beggar's Opera,* the one most relevant here is Bakhtin's "novelization." I have alluded previously to Bakhtin's delineation of the novel's power to absorb official genres through parody and burlesque. Here I want to stress his account of the novel's capacity to set these genres into "dialogic" commerce with one another and, in the process, to establish a "zone of contact" between the literary work and the social practices that inform daily life. Here are "the salient features of this novelization of other genres":

> They become more free and flexible, their language renews itself by incorporating extraliterary heteroglossia and the "novelistic" layers of literary language, they become dialogized, permeated with laughter, irony, humor, elements of self-parody and finally—this is the most important thing—the novel inserts into these other genres an indeterminacy, a certain semantic openendedness, a living contact with unfinished, still-evolving contemporary reality. . . . All these phenomena are explained by the transposition of other genres into this new and peculiar zone for structuring artistic models (a zone of contact with the present in all its openendedness), a zone that was first appropriated by the novel.[6]

Thus the novel, on Bakhtin's account, enters into continual dialogue with established social institutions through its byplay with established literary genres. The novel, properly speaking, is not a genre at all, but a mode of explication that establishes relationships among genres and thereby among the ideologies they crystallize. Bakhtin shows the formal, literary means whereby the novel brings social practice to consciousness.

Gay's realism has been associated from the beginning with the era's thriving production of criminal narratives, especially with the stories of Jonathan Wild, the notorious thief-taker, and Jack Sheppard, the celebrated robber and prison escape artist. As the standard compendium says, "The realism of *The Beggar's Opera* is apparent to one who has examined contemporary documents relating to the London of 1728, and especially Newgate and its inmates."[7] Despite the many differences between theatrical and novelistic realism, *The Beggar's Opera* shares important traits with prose narratives of the 1720s. It is seldom remarked, however, that the realism of *The Beggar's Opera* reached also to its initial stage production.

John Rich, the producer of Gay's work, had specialized in pantomimes that, in the vogue of the 1720s, contrasted with plays and operas by their elaborate scenery showing real places. Four years before *The Beggar's Opera*, in response to the competition with Rich, a pantomime of the famous escapades of Jack Sheppard had been devised by Cibber and Company at Drury Lane with scenery "painted from the real Place of Action," and the script included Gay's song, "Newgate's Garland."[8] Hogarth's popular print, *A Just View of the British Stage* (1724), though satiric and perhaps exaggeratedly theatrical, shows the character of Drury Lane's

19. William Hogarth, *A Just View of the British Stage*, 1724. A satiric version of the stage at Drury Lane set with realistic scenery of the kind used in pantomimes. The fireplace (left) suggests lodgings or a dining chamber in the better part (master's side) of Old Newgate.

Newgate scenery for the *Harlequin Sheppard* pantomime (fig. 19).[9] The earliest versions of Hogarth's canvases of *The Beggar's Opera* on stage at Lincoln's Inn Fields indicate that Rich probably used realistic pantomime scenery rather than the lofty Italianate backdrop substituted in the later paintings (figs. 20–22).[10]

Further instances of Gay's realism have to do with the way in which both the topographic situation of Newgate in the City of London and

ARCH.^e FERDINANDO BIBIENA INV DEL̃   PIETRO GIOANI ABATI FEC.^e

20. Opposite top: William Hogarth, *The Beggar's Opera*, 1728. Hogarth's
    first renditions of act 3, scene 11 appear to reflect John Rich's use of
    pantomime scenery in the production at Lincoln's Inn Fields.

21. Opposite bottom: William Hogarth, *The Beggar's Opera*, 1729.
    Hogarth's final version supplies a lofty, palatial setting that employs the
    double perspective often used in scenery for Italian operas.

22. Above: Ferdinando Galli Bibiena (1657–1743), *Interior of a Prison*.
    Etching by Pietro Giovanni Abbati. Prison settings that imitated designs
    by the Bibienas spread throughout Europe during the seventeenth
    and eighteenth centuries.

the specific details of the prison's physical structure and personnel are dramatically epitomized in his realization of Swift's idea that he write a "Newgate Pastoral." Gay literalizes Newgate's ancient marginal standing as a gateway or place of passage, reformulating it into a generic contradiction between terms drawn from pastoral romance and those drawn from heroic drama and opera. From this germ grew the inspired edifice of contradiction in genre, character, plot, and tone that make up the total irony of *The Beggar's Opera*. Both Swift and Gay had to have had the literal place in mind. Everyone was familiar with Newgate's location neither inside nor outside the City, but actually in and part of its walls. Everyone feared the rural terrain surrounding London, where one was much more likely to encounter highwaymen than swains. (In the 1720s, Jonathan Wild's luxurious house stood outside the wall, across the street called Old Bailey.)[11] And of course Tyburn, where most of the London executions took place, lay on a stream bank in the countryside beyond the City walls to the west of Newgate.

Gay enters the zone of the everyday in other fashions too. The deathly journey began at Newgate, where condemned prisoners were loaded onto carts along with their own coffins, under the pastoral care of the prison clergyman or Ordinary. From 1719 to November of 1727, a few months before *The Beggar's Opera* opened (and certainly during the time of its composition), the post of Ordinary at Newgate lay with the author of two volumes of pastoral poems after Theocritus and Spenser, the Reverend Thomas Purney, whose title to originality rests with his concept of the "Gloomy" as the "Soul and Essence of Tragedy."[12] Purney draws his examples of the gloomy from scenes in Shakespeare and, more especially, from scenes in Otway of the kind on which Macheath's soliloquy in Newgate's condemned hold is modeled (3.8). Finally, Swift and Gay had the classical education to have noticed that Old Newgate, as rebuilt after the Great Fire, was ornamented in the Tuscan order (fig. 23). In the Vitruvian and Palladian architectural vocabulary, this order signified the strength called for in prisons, arsenals, and treasuries; and also the rusticity and rural simplicity appropriate to farmhouses, stables, grottoes, and dog kennels. These qualities had signified opposite potentials of civic enclosure and rural freedom, both latent in the liminal perspective and both sculpturally personified at Old Newgate with statues that included not only Severity, Justice, Fortitude, and Prudence, but Peace, Plenty, and Liberty (fig. 24).[13] In *The Beggar's Opera*, the Newgate that personified the seven civic virtues becomes instead the seat of corruption.

Gay's realistic depiction of low life, his absorption of popular scenic realism, and his assimilation of the literal presence of Newgate ally his work with the novel. But the novelization of *The Beggar's Opera* also occurs at its structural core, where realism is used parodically to provoke continuous dialogue among genres. In his treatment of Macheath as hero and highwayman, for example, Gay fuses the "factuality" that inspired belief in and admiration for the daring exploits typical of criminal biographies of the 1720s (especially Defoe's *History of the Remarkable Life of John Sheppard,* where the hero's superhuman prison breaks culminate in his "most astonishing and never to be forgotten" escape from Newgate)[14] with the larger-than-life character and bold indifference to consequence that marked the protagonists of heroic tragedy. Generic permutation and interchange are the rule in this work, which imitates, burlesques, parodies, and engages in every imaginable kind of oblique discourse with an enormous range of genres, both established and emergent: epic, heroic tragedy, pastoral romance, Italian opera, sentimental comedy, popular pantomime, criminal narrative (both biographical and fictional), the amorous lyric, the epigram in the manner of La Rochefoucauld, and so forth. Thus Gay may be understood, in the perspective established by Bakhtin, as manipulating the dialogue between genres from which the novel takes life. His realism is actually part of a system of exchange in which heroic situation, dress, and language are in communication with their social opposites. A smattering of cant in the language of Gay's characters, for example, leaves the impression of a careful rendering of dialect even though the manner of speech, far from being modeled on low life, is that of gentlemanly discourse. This is the convention of realism, not reality itself.

Gay's talent lay in his capacity to carry the "interweaving" of genres and tones to its utmost extreme, so that the various kinds "cannot be distinguish'd or separated."[15] Similar, if less synoptic, generic mixtures mark a number of works written during Gay's career in the circle of Swift and Pope, including *The Rape of the Lock, Gulliver's Travels, The Dunciad,* and *The Memoirs of Martinus Scriblerus,* a collaboration in which Gay played some part. All illustrate, in one degree or another, the novelization of culture that Bakhtin describes. But as Gay and Pope suggest in a joint letter composed following the early success of *The What D'Ye Call It,* the novelty of Gay's work expressed itself above all in the remarkably unfocused, contradictory response it evoked from his audience:

> Some looked upon it as a mere jest upon the tragic poets, others as a satire upon the late war. Mr. Cromwell hearing none of the words and seeing the action to be tragical, was much astonished to find the audience laugh. . . . The common people of the pit and gallery received it at first with great gravity and sedateness, some few with tears; but after the third day they also took the hint, and have ever since been loud in their clapps. There are still some grave sober men who

NEWGATE:

Chamberlains Gate, a most miserable Dungeon, was rebuilt by Rich? Whitington, in the style here represented, and from its nearness call it Newgate, from which Newgate Street was named. Against the west front were four emblematical figures viz Liberty, Peace, Security, & Plenty, and on the east front were three figures, Justice, Fortitude, & Prudence, this Building was destroyed in the Conflagration 1666, & again rebuilt 1672, with great magnificence though nearly on the same plan, as appears by the print given in Maitlands London. At the entire demolition of this Gate, four of the figures were put up on the South wing of the present awfull structure.

see Elstracks, print of Whitingtor Stow p.48 Howell London, Camden part. Maitland p.42 Northouks London, p.615 London in Miniature p.216 Ralphs critical Review p.90, 91 Pennants London.

Pub? April 5 1791 by N? Smith N? 131 b? View Buildings.

23. *Newgate*, from the east side, as rebuilt after the Great Fire. On the old gateway prison, the Tuscan order framed statues of Justice, Fortitude, and Prudence (their attributes are vaguely generalized in this print).

cannot be of the general opinion, but the laughers are so much the majority, that Mr. Dennis and one or two more seem determined to undeceive the town at their proper cost, by writing some critical dissertations against it.[16]

As the gleeful reference to the sobriety of Dennis (the self-appointed legislator of literary boundaries) suggests, generic mixture by its nature subverted the established authority of the hierarchy of genres, forcing the rules of various socioliterary modes into competition with one another. But while the specifically formal dimension of Gay's strategy had been among his hallmarks, and while he already had realized some of its potential for social satire, the unique force of *The Beggar's Opera* arises because of the corrosive effect this formal construct assumes when Gay unleashes it on the fundamental institutions of society: not merely upon

24. *Liberty* from Old Newgate, as reinstalled on New Newgate of George Dance, Jr.

individuals or types, but upon the government, upon the idea of public morality, upon the very possibility of social order itself. This is Bakhtin's multivoiced discourse shorn of the assimilating narrational presence of the novel and set loose to raise the tacit rules of social practice to the level of consciousness.

The timing that made Gay's synthesis in *The Beggar's Opera* so powerful is worth examining more precisely since neither his mode of generic contradiction nor his satiric identification of Newgate society with the corruptions of the age was unprecedented. Gay's *Shepherd's Week* (1714), his *Trivia; or, the Art of Walking the Streets of London* (1716), and his *Fables* (1727) had employed literary incongruity as a satiric device. However, as in *The What D'Ye Call It*, which levels criticism at the squirearchy for abuse of their power over the poor tenants, these works focused chiefly on the interplay between literary conventions themselves. During this same period, whether in hack productions like *A Match in Newgate* (1715; restaged 1727) or sophisticated adaptations of popular forms like Gay's own "Newgate's Garland" (1724), the Newgate literature was likening thievery and thief-taking to official corruption. Newgate already had begun to assume the attributes of a theater (figs. 4 and 19). More pointedly, articles in *Mist's Weekly Journal* during June of 1725 had invited detailed comparison of Wild's methods with Walpole's. In fact *The Beggar's Opera* can be anatomized in this manner down to its very sinews, but not to the life of its design.[17]

The access of novelty that overtook Gay's audience may be traced to a difference—elusive from our vantage point but forcibly present in the astonished sense of newness that struck London in the wake of the *Opera*'s opening—a difference that consists in shock at the entry the piece required into what Bakhtin calls the "zone of contact with the present in all its openendedness." The sense of reality as a multifarious presence, the zone of contact, is preserved in the very form of the work and, to some extent, reenacted whenever it is played or revised. Thus the peculiar juncture of circumstance that originally compounded the effect of specific, previously exploited elements that Gay took up, accounts at once for the work's elusiveness and for its sustained impact. (It was played annually throughout the eighteenth century, often at two theaters, and it held the stage in numerous nineteenth-century revivals.)[18] *The Beggar's Opera*, through its exhaustive application of formal devices that Gay had perfected earlier (and through the latent tendency of the conflict of genres to neutralize authority), established a dialogue that, at the very least, engaged the following constituents: modes of expression and action that cross the full range of class boundaries from beggar to aristocrat and, in large measure, an actual theater audience that did so as well;

the sense of coopted justice and heroic criminality that the Wild and Sheppard cases had served to define during the mid-1720s; the opinion that the fashion for Italian opera was an expression of the moral and aesthetic absurdity of the court (especially after 1720 when operatic performances resumed, following an interval of three years, under the king's patronage at the Royal Academy of Music); the emergence of the realist novel in close association with criminal narrative as popular forms; a corresponding awareness of the particulars of Newgate as a real place; the spectacle of Walpole at the zenith of his power following his momentary decline and dramatic retrenchment during the first days of George II's reign; and finally, because of Gay's connections at court, and because of Walpole's responsive presence on the first night, an awareness in every audience of the awareness of the most powerful people in the land.[19] *The Beggar's Opera* at once revealed and fostered the transposition of boundaries. It demonstrates how, in London culture of the 1720s, realism was produced as a convention through the counterposition of genres not necessarily realistic in themselves.

Gay takes his place in my story about the novel and the penitentiary because *The Beggar's Opera* is a novelized work that discredits the old prisons and the forms of justice they implied. Gay depicts the contradictions and confusions that had been institutionalized in the old, liminal Newgate as tools of authorities who willfully corrupt the moral order rather than establishing and shaping it. Wild had deployed Newgate and the system of justice that hinged upon it as part of the apparatus governing the criminal underground. It was but a short step to Lockit, the keeper criminal. As we shall see, criminal manipulation of authority for personal gain was exactly the charge that Oglethorpe's parliamentary committee of 1729 leveled against the extortionate and cruel keepers of the Fleet. Prison could not serve as a valid symbol of the interplay between authority and the random happenstance of liminal conversion once Newgate, the chief exemplar, had become the seat of out-and-out corruption and malevolence.

It is worthwhile to contrast Gay's satiric transvaluation of Newgate with Fielding's and Pope's attacks on the laureateship of Colley Cibber in *The Author's Farce* (1730) and in *The Dunciad* (1743). To Fielding and Pope, the laureateship stands for the debasement of the court, of taste, of literature in general, and therefore of the wellsprings of social order. But in *The Beggar's Opera,* Newgate not only stands for the whole system of justice, and therefore the system of order and patronage that governs society, but also is the literal seat of that order: the thing itself, a foundational institution of authority, one of the most ancient symbols of governmental power in civic life. The laureateship is a metaphor for the degeneracy of society; Newgate tangibly represents the authority of the City to its citizens. Newgate was not merely like the government; it really was part of it. Wild was not merely like Walpole; they both, for profit, ran systems of patronage that governed the actual dispensation of criminal justice. The fusion of prime minister with thief-taker in Peachum's role has the rhetorical structure of an oxymoron: it adopts the form taken by the miniature fiction that governs that particular figure of speech. But Peachum also represents a literal statement: great men are criminals. Gay simplifies and literalizes rhetorical figures; unlike Pope, he moves not toward abstract generalization but, like the realist novel, toward inference from juxtaposed particulars.

When the impetus toward the dissolution of authority implied by Gay's specialized kind of generic dialogue came together with the Newgate scene of *The Beggar's Opera*, it formed a corrosive satiric mixture. Writing in the preface to his *Miscellanies* (1743), where *Jonathan Wild* first appeared, Fielding well understood Gay's Hobbesian equation of all human motives with the lowest common denominator.[20] Fielding narrows the target, leaving aside the opera's devastating parallel between Peachum's diction and the speech of honest mercantile London, and squirms to dissociate himself from the extremism of Gay's fiction:

> But without considering *Newgate* as no other than Human Nature with its Mask off, which some very shameless Writers have done, a Thought which no Price should purchase me to entertain, I think we may be excused for suspecting, that the splendid Palaces of the Great are often no other than *Newgate* with the Mask on. Nor do I know any thing which can raise an honest Man's Indignation higher than the same Morals should be in one Place attended with all imaginable Misery and Infamy, and in the other, with the highest Luxury and Honour. Let any impartial Man in his Senses be asked, for which of these two Places a Composition of Cruelty, Lust, Avarice, Rapine, Insolence, Hypocrisy, Fraud and Treachery, was best fitted, surely his Answer must be certain and immediate; and yet I am afraid all these Ingredients glossed over with Wealth and Title, have been treated with the highest Respect and Veneration in the one, while one or two of them have been condemned to the Gallows in the other.[21]

Fielding shies away from the pervasive indictment of human nature in the "shameless" metonymy upon which Gay founded *The Beggar's Opera*, for although Gay complicates matters by granting genuine aristocratic and heroic graces to Macheath and sincere sentimental affection to Polly, Fielding is right that he casts the net wide. Gay not only insists that an identity exists between the lowest and highest extremes of the social hierarchy but, when he associates the rapacious Peachum and Lockit with the genteel affectations and pretentious morality of bourgeois social climbers, also parallels the methods of thief-takers with those of England's self-appointed moral aristocracy.

Gay's equation of social, moral, and ethical antitheses exposed the postulates, motives, and methods underlying the exercise of power through social and economic patronage, the common currency of governance in English society. One measure of the radical consequence of Gay's irony—the shock of awareness it brought—is that Peachum's modus operandi can be described by direct quotation of Douglas Hay's remarks about the ways in which the British ruling classes of the period used the sanguinary laws of the nation as a framework within which to exercise power and maintain position by intervening as patrons seeking pardons or commuted sentences for their clients:

> The Pardon is important because it often put the principal instrument of legal terror—the gallows—directly in the hands of those who held power. In this it was simply the clearest example of the prevailing custom at all levels of criminal justice. Here was the peculiar genius of the law. It allowed the rulers of England to make the courts a selective instrument of class justice, yet simultaneously to proclaim the law's incorruptible impartiality, and absolute determinacy. Their political and social power was reinforced daily by bonds of obligation on one side and condescension on the other, as prosecutors, gentlemen and peers decided to invoke the law or agreed to show mercy. Discretion allowed a prosecutor to terrorize the petty thief and then command his gratitude, or at least the approval of his neighbourhood as a man of compassion. It allowed the class that passed one of the bloodiest penal codes in Europe to congratulate itself on its humanity.[22]

While Gay's medium is theatrical, not that of post-Marxian historical analysis, his point is comparable to Hay's. Nor was it missed in his own day.

The outcry against *The Beggar's Opera* that began with its premiere and continued throughout the eighteenth century was led by some of the highest notables in the land, among them the Reverend Thomas Herring, who was to become archbishop of York and of Canterbury; Sir John Fielding, magistrate in Bow Street, where his brother Henry had presided; and Sir John Hawkins, chairman of the Bench of Justices of Middlesex. Hawkins, writing in his *History of Music* (1776) is perhaps most interesting because he specifically addresses the question of authority as well as raising the more common complaints against the morality of the piece and its alleged tendency to encourage thieves by glorifying them:

By inculcating that persons in authority are uniformly actuated by the same motives as thieves and robbers [it tends] to destroy all confidence in ministers, and respect for magistrates, and to lessen that reverence, which, even in the worst state of government, is due to laws and to public authority, a character is exhibited to view, of a libertine endowed with bravery, generosity, of the qualities of a gentleman, subsisting by the profession of highway robbery, which he defends by example drawn from the practice of men of all professions. In this view Macheath is as much a hero as the principal agent in an epic poem. . . . The effects of this Beggar's Opera on the minds of the people, have fulfilled the prognostications of many that it would prove injurious to society. Rapine and violence have been gradually increasing ever since its first representation: The rights of property, and the obligation of the laws that guard it, are disputed upon principle. . . . Young men, apprentices, clerks in public offices, and others, disdaining the arts of industry, and captivated with the charms of idleness and criminal pleasure, now betake themselves to the road, affect politeness in the very act of robbery; and in the end become victims to the justice of their country.[23]

Hawkins was no crank; his complaint was characteristic and his views echoed those of many a thoughtful citizen. But Swift, who had ridiculed such attacks as shallow at best and politically motivated at worst, credited Gay with a "happy performance" in which "all the Characters are just, and none of them carried beyond Nature, or hardly beyond Practice." Swift stressed the *Opera*'s revelation of poverty as the basis of crime and patronage as its means: "It discovers the whole System of that Common-Wealth, or that Imperium in Imperio of Iniquity established among us. . . . It shews the miserable lives, and the constant fate of those abandoned Wretches; for how little they sell their Lives and Souls; betrayed by their Whores; their Comrades; and the Receivers and Purchasers of these Thefts and Robberies."[24]

Sir John Fielding, who succeeded his half-brother Henry as magistrate in the Bow Street Court, thought *The Beggar's Opera* threatening enough to write in 1772 to the managers of Covent Garden and Drury Lane asking that it be suppressed, and although the magistrate suffered some derision for having intervened, the ending finally was altered and given specific moral point for competing performances at the two theaters during the autumn of 1777. At Covent Garden, Macheath's sentence was commuted to three years of hard labor on the prison hulks: "Here he is visited by Polly and Lucy; acknowledges the lenity of his sentence, and resolves to become a virtuous member of the community."[25] More than forty years after its premiere, Gay's work was still in dialogue with contemporary society—a changed society in which a reformative sentence could replace the old choices of execution or reprieve.[26] Garrick at Drury Lane substituted a specific royal pardon for the poetic reprieve of the original. Both productions managed to bring the ending within the ken of formal law and order, yet *The Beggar's Opera* remained so multivalent a social critique that its irony could subsume even the alterations of its moralizers: Garrick's change might well have been taken, in the spirit of Gay, as an allusion to the king's refusal to pardon the celebrated clergyman forger, Dr. Dodd, who had been executed during the summer of 1777 despite petitions for mercy signed by twenty-three thousand loyal subjects.[27]

Gay brought contraries that had been present in the old prisons to conscious scrutiny by drawing them into the novelized "zone of contact" between fictional discourse and social practice that, for Bakhtin, distinctively marks the emergence of the realist novel in eighteenth-century life. As we have seen, liminal Newgate had been tacitly rejected in *Moll Flanders* (as well as in other works of the 1720s). Defoe had imposed novelistic shape on the randomness of liminal confinement, ordering it into causal sequences and situating the multiple voices of society in the authoritative container of narrational form. But where Defoe's novels tended to personify contradiction, treating it as moral conflict within the characters of his narrators, Gay yoked contraries into an oxymoron that implicated the whole of society and disclosed the contradictions of liminal Newgate to awareness as a social issue. Hogarth's conversation piece, *A Scene from 'The Indian Emperor'* (1732) (fig. 25), reveals the extent to which the old imagery of prison had been discredited by the early 1730s. Using the mode of painting he devised to encapsulate *The Beggar's Opera* on canvas, Hogarth places the climactic prison scene from one of the previous era's most esteemed tragedies in a contemporary drawing room and shows its enactment by children before a select domestic audience.[28]

· II ·

The novelistic dialogue with everyday linguistic and social practices described by Bakhtin embraces both of the polarities of the city as I have discussed it in previous chapters: the extreme of the multiple, heterodox babble of dialects, and the extreme of authority projected through standard language and official architecture. But since Gay's work is novelized, yet not a novel, only half of this equation is present, and generic contradiction in itself cuts loose from authoritative control. *The Beggar's Opera* mixes so many genres and sets them in such conflicting relations that these genres are disabled and virtually cease to function in their

25. William Hogarth, *A Scene from 'The Indian Emperor, or The Conquest of Mexico,'* 1732. Children in a noble drawing room enact a heroic prison scene of the kind recalled at the climax of *The Beggar's Opera.*

own right. As Ian Donaldson argues, for instance, the climactic scene of the work (3.11), which Hogarth painted six times, employs the device from heroic tragedy of suspending the imprisoned hero between the irreconcilable demands of two leading ladies.[29] But parody of Thomas Otway's *Venice Preserved,* the chief play alluded to in this scene, is not the aim or consequence even though it is one of the means. Nor is parody of Gay's own heroic tragedy, *The Captives* (1724), at issue (fig. 26). Rather, Otway's play becomes part of a novelized fabric in which it is one of many objects of representation, not itself the medium. The standing of Dryden's *Conquest of Mexico* in Hogarth's painting is exactly comparable. The novelization of traditional genres, then, does not ensure free dialogue with social fact or, as Bakhtin puts it, full entry into the zone of contact; rather, the process of novelization tends to disable the established genres, to reformulate them in self-conscious, artificial ways.

During the 1720s the novelization of London culture also coincided with the emerging narrative schematization of confinement that I have traced in Defoe's fictions. The general character of this emplotment is nowhere more apparent than in the many narrative, dramatic, and pictorial accounts of Jack Sheppard that appeared during the decade. In one broadsheet, for example, minutiae of the kind supplied by Defoe in *A Narrative of All of the Robberies &c. of John Sheppard* and scenic realism like that associated with pantomimes and with *The Beggar's Opera* already coexist with the idea of a "progress" (fig. 27). The eleven narratively captioned frames in this minutely specific sequence show every mechanical and temporal detail of Sheppard's great escape from Newgate

26. William Kent, frontispiece to John Gay's *The Captives*, 1724. The setting is Persia yet the veiled captive appears in heroic Italianate scenery combining attributes of palace and prison.

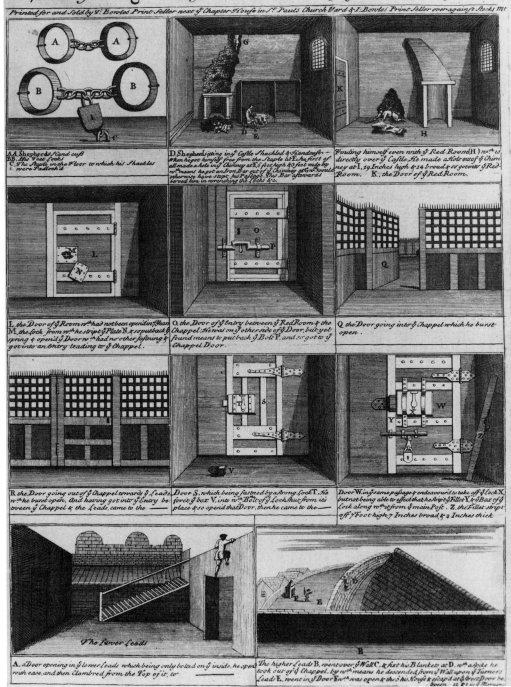

27. *An Exact Representation of . . . Shepherd . . . His Wonderfull Escape out of Newgate*, c. 1724–25. A chapter of eleven episodes in Shepherd's progress toward Tyburn.

28. Nathanial Parr, *A Criminal's Progress,* frontispiece to *Select Trials at the Old Bailey,* 1742. The story of a criminal life in seven chapters.

between four in the afternoon and one in the morning of 15 October 1724. The print writes a chapter in his progress toward Tyburn. Later, imitating Hogarth in small, Nathaniel Parr realized the progressive character implicit in the Sheppard material. His frontispiece to *Select Trials* (1742) (fig. 28) divides an archetypal criminal career modeled on Sheppard's into seven framed scenes ranging from the debut as a boy pickpocket through exploits as a housebreaker and highwayman to the judicial ceremonies of commitment, trial, and execution (this climactic episode occupies a double frame).[30] During the 1730s the narrative reformulation of the liminal scene, which we have found implicit in *Moll Flanders* and other works by Defoe, will recur openly in Hogarth's cycles.

What I am tracing, then, is the concurrent disablement of traditional genres through novelization (the process whereby they become subjects in social discourse and objects in novels) and the emerging imposition of narrative order on the old prisons. This disablement shows most clearly when established genres are used to criticize social abuses or to advocate reform—when they attempt to enter the zone of contact. Analogously, the old prisons (considered as a societal genre), with their rule of randomness, are progressively cut loose, especially in the urban metropolis of London, from the cultural hegemony that had made their procedures functional. A new, rationalized, sequential order was materializing, and the first step in its validation was to confront the old prisons, to reformulate their story narratively.

Before turning to Hogarth's cycles, it is worthwhile to illustrate the disablement of established genres by considering, at some length, James Thomson's use of high poetic diction and Hogarth's adaptation of the conventional group portrait to address abuses in the old prisons that were uncovered by James Oglethorpe, chairman of the famous Committee to Enquire into the State of the Gaols, appointed in 1729 by the House of Commons.[31] The marmoreal poetic drapery in the manner of the Miltonic baroque that Thomson sought to hang about Oglethorpe suggests the dimensions of the task encountered by an accomplished poet who wished to treat a contemporary social evil as among the "great and serious subjects" of poetry, that is, to treat it with a gravity appropriate to epic. Comparison of his tirade with the devastating, matter-of-fact particularity of Oglethorpe's reports renders suspect the strained elevation of these lines from *Winter:*

And here can I forget the generous few,
Who, touch'd with human woe, redressive sought
Into the horrors of the gloomy jail?
Unpitied, and unheard, where Misery moans;
Where Sickness pines; where Thirst and Hunger burn,

And poor Misfortune feels the lash of Vice.
While in the land of liberty, the land
Whose every street, and public meeting glows
With open freedom, little tyrants rag'd:
Snatch'd the lean morsel from the starving mouth;
Tore from cold, wintry limbs the tatter'd robe;
Even robb'd them of the last of comforts, sleep;
The free-born BRITON to the dungeon chain'd;
Or, as the lust of cruelty prevail'd,
At pleasure mark'd him with inglorious stripes;
And crush'd out lives, by various nameless ways,
That for their country would have toil'd, or bled.
Hail patriot-band! who, scorning secret scorn,
When Justice, and when Mercy led the way,
Drag'd the detected monsters into light,
Wrench'd from their hand Oppression's iron rod,
And bad the cruel feel the pains they gave.
Yet stop not here, let all the land rejoice,
And make the blessing unconfin'd, as great.
Much still untouch'd remains; in this rank age,
Much is the patriot's weeding hand requir'd.
The toils of law, (what dark insidious men
Have cumbrous added to perplex the truth,
And lengthen simple justice into trade)
How glorious were the day! that saw these broke,
And every man within the reach of right.[32]

Thomson's advocacy of reform goes well beyond Oglethorpe's philanthropic wish to expose the "little," though deadly, "tyrants" who ran
the Fleet Prison. Neither a radical nor an innovator, at least in 1729,
Oglethorpe remained content to see that existing rules were enforced
and, refusing to intervene in the prosecution of justice once charges had
been brought, stood by while the government manipulated the trials of
the villains in order to obtain dismissals or acquittals. The socially well-
placed warden of the Fleet, John Huggins, though deprived of further
office and prosecuted by the Commons for benefiting from the business
of extortion he had farmed out to Bambridge (an underling jailer to
whom he had sold the wardenship in 1728), was legally absolved, with
Bambridge, of any crime. Although Oglethorpe's prosecution of these
offenders in some measure "bad the cruel feel the pains they gave," there
he stopped. But Thomson goes on to attack the prevailing legal system
for subverting the noble spirit of the British law by running it for individual profit derived from "trade." Four decades later, the wish to
prove this telling point moved John Howard, newly appointed sheriff

of Bedfordshire, to begin his quest to locate a single English prison that was supported by the government rather than by fees levied against prisoners by their jailers.

Nonetheless, Thomson's ceremonial poetic diffuses the impact of his progressive thought just as it works to generalize Oglethorpe's findings. For instance, the Portuguese prisoner Jacob Mendez Solas had been confined for almost two months in a dungeon "wherein the Bodies of Persons dying in the said Prison are usually deposited, till the Coroner's Inquest"; the "Strong Room," as they called it, was "built over the Common-Shore, and adjoining to the Sink and Dunghil where all the Nastiness of the Prison is cast." After a friend liberated Solas,

> tho' his Chains were taken off, his Terror still remained, and the unhappy Man was prevailed upon by that Terror, not only to labour *gratis* for the said *Bambridge*, but to swear also at random all that he hath required of him: And the Committee themselves saw an Instance of the deep Impression his Sufferings had made upon him; for on his surmising, from something said, that *Bambridge* was to return again, as Warden of the *Fleet*, he fainted, and the Blood started out of his Mouth and Nose.[33]

Thomson, of course, could not attempt the literal, documentary tone of a report to the House of Commons. But in *Winter* the moving specificity of the committee's report—a catalog of abuses so prolific that it overflows into generous appendixes filled with affidavits—evaporates into such vague Shakespearean mist as "Tore from cold, wintry limbs the tatter'd robe."[34] The forced sublimity of these lines obscures the horror of Oglethorpe's documentation behind an ennobling scrim. The paraphernalia of poetic grandeur—for instance that ostentatious Miltonism "redressive"—obtrude themselves on the subject matter like coronation robes worn on a charity call.

Although Thomson glances at the possibility of larger causes, he fosters the idea that injustice in Britain arises from the petty tyranny of a few individuals acting outside the law on impulses essentially foreign to the British spirit. Thomson encourages self-congratulation in the "land of liberty" by associating the oppressed prisoners whom Oglethorpe discovered in illegally constructed "strong rooms" at the Fleet with state captives marked by "inglorious stripes" in the Bastille-like dungeons and torture chambers of Europe.[35] Gay fosters a much more penetrating analysis in which crime and injustice are seen to arise from the corrupt and corrupting system of patronage and payoffs on which the whole of society is structured. The precious terms that Thomson had chosen in his preface of 1726 to defend poetry from those who would "declare against that DIVINE ART" suggest that his attempts at sublimity are actually evasions: "It is declaring against the most charming Power of Imagination, the most exalting Force of Thought, the most affecting Touch of Sentiment; in a Word, against the very Soul of all Learning, and Politeness."[36] Thomson, yoking charm to imagination, learning to politeness, and all of these attributes to the "divine art" of poetry, recalls the teasing manner of Gay's rhetoric but omits its satiric thrust, its profound engagement with present reality. The affecting touch of sentiment in Gay had substantiated the paradox that the charming, the learned, and the polite could also be criminals, prisoners, and jailers.

Hogarth's two depictions of Oglethorpe's committee at work in the Fleet Prison (1729–30) reveal that a disabled genre could entrap the painter no less than the poet; that is, both could be driven by generic and stylistic imperatives—presumably self-imposed by Thomson and to some degree imposed by patrons upon Hogarth—to produce work that attempts dialogue with the multiplicity of the present but remains awkwardly poised on its margins.[37] Yet Ronald Paulson's discovery that the adolescent Hogarth very likely lived for five years within the Rules of the Fleet while his father was imprisoned for debt must remove any doubt that Oglethorpe's inquiry into gross abuses of authority at the Fleet touched some of his deepest concerns. As Paulson says,

> Hogarth produced for his contemporaries the definitive image of that dark room of the mind by which Locke figured the process of perception. The individual's world is a closed room which has little access to the outside and is stocked with the impressions, the objects and collections, that make up the owner's character, or (in Lockean terms) his ideas. The imprisonment is self-imposed in that he has chosen these ideas himself, but they determine his every action, and they are themselves imposed on him because they are what he has seen when looking out through those narrow chinks upon the world.[38]

Hogarth's disclosure of human folly and corruption, the minute engagement of his art with contemporary life, cannot be traced to single causes, but his experience as a youth beside an imprisoned father surely figures in his ultimately successful construction of a new mode of painting within which the particulars of liminal confinement could be exposed, analyzed, and sequentially ordered.

The Fitzwilliam sketch for the Oglethorpe picture (fig. 29) indicates that the young Hogarth could show how indignation must have flared on 8 March 1728/29 as the committee and a prisoner confronted Bambridge—warden of the Fleet, extortionist, and author of the cruelties documented in the Oglethorpe report. The sketch renders a drama that

29. William Hogarth, *The Committee of the House of Commons*, 1729–30. Hogarth's oil sketch for the painting, possibly drawn during actual hearings at the Fleet.

seems intrinsic to the situation.[39] Here committee members all but leap from their places around a table set in plunging diagonal, toward this Bambridge who had originally sparked the inquiry by his barbaric treatment of Oglethorpe's friend Robert Castell, an architect, the author of *The Villas of the Ancients Illustrated* (1728), and a translator of Vitruvius. Castell, committed to the Fleet for debt and, after a time, unwilling to meet Bambridge's extortionate fees for airy lodging in the Liberty of the Rules, was placed by the warden in a smallpox-ridden "spunging house," where he died of the disease. In this sketch the committee, which upon its first visit to the Fleet found Sir William Rich, Bart., loaded with irons and in a foul dungeon, confronts and seems almost to evict from the picture the craggy Bambridge (who, in an act of defiance and foolish overconfidence, returned Sir William to his hole immediately upon their departure). Bambridge's ferocity registers in his piercing, forward-set eye, while the expression of terror on the face of the uniformed figure standing to the rear signals us with the correct response.[40]

In the National Portrait Gallery's painted version (fig. 30), a few hints survive to indicate that outraged social conscience is here confronting hardened inhumanity, but the conventional demands of face painting have shoved the drama aside. Now the solitary and authoritative Bambridge might well be investigating the committee. The prisoner is reduced to an anonymous suppliant in emblematic irons, the forceful diagonal of the table is obscured, and the members' solemn, studio-posed faces hover under their full-bottomed wigs in even marches across the picture surface. The scenographic background Hogarth has done up for the occasion all but mocks the static actors it now accommodates, while a plunging vista of prison vaults reminiscent of baroque stage settings (fig. 22) and grand portraiture of the previous century has to carry a disproportionate burden of meaning.

30. William Hogarth, *The Committee of the House of Commons* 1729–30. Oglethorpe and his colleagues interrogate the Warden and a prisoner in irons about conditions in the Fleet. The setting is imaginary.

The stagelike prison background, with no less than four heavily barred openings, is one of Hogarth's significant iconographic additions between sketch and finished version. Another is his heavy rhetorical emphasis on irons, which appear in the painting at Bambridge's feet, around the prisoner's neck, and emphatically brandished by Chairman Oglethorpe. Possibly they are not merely atmospheric but topical additions since Bambridge's offenses included not only extortion (perhaps recalled by what appears to be a torn table of fees above his head) but the far greater crimes of putting debtors in irons, using tight irons as torture instruments, and constructing dungeons—"Strong Rooms" or "prisons within a prison"—contrary to English custom and law.[41] The Oglethorpe report documents the committee's search into the very depths of the Fleet's illegal dungeons. Hogarth may be struggling to suggest this quest on a single flat surface by surrounding the committee with a profusion of threateningly foreclosed apertures. Samuel Wesley's poem in praise of the committee, *The Prisons Open'd,* also visualizes Oglethorpe's achievement in concrete terms as the removal of bars and irons.[42]

Hogarth's curious picture, like Thomson's panegyric of the Oglethorpe Committee in *Winter,* is produced from an alliance of stylistic elements originally derived to serve other subject matters. These works pay awkward duty to their modern cause. They reveal the incapacity of traditional forms to engage social issues. The choices remaining to artists in the early 1730s included continuation of Gay's dramatic mode, as Fielding did in his plays; Pope's alliance with classical authority through close imitation, so as to certify contemporary diction, satiric posture, and formal values by a nearly literal retracing of Horatian masterpieces; the turn to philosophically driven generalization such as Pope attempted in *An Essay on Man;* and, of course, Hogarth's ventures into the largely uncharted terrain of realist narrative. Gay had decentered both literary diction and the conventionally oriented systems of metaphoric reference (like oxymoron in *The Dunciad*) that had given satire its social force. Hogarth's reach toward the novel draws him away from the abyss of total irony by lending narrative shape to a social discourse momentarily adrift between structures of feeling.

· III ·

My emphasis in the balance of this chapter lies on Hogarth's construction of a novelized genre in the visual arts, his use of realist narrative in *A Harlot's Progress* and *A Rake's Progress* to analyze the social contradictions that Gay set forth by ordering them into causal sequences and situating them in webs of particulars centered in each case on a distinctive, if typical, personality. Hogarth's narrative method enabled him to detail the personal, practical, material consequences of power exercised socially through forms of cultural hegemony that were traditional in external appearance but corrupt within. At the turning points of his two series of the 1730s we find institutions of liminal confinement whose former symbolic multivalence has been supplanted by their instrumental role in narratives of tragic inevitability. I am saying, then, that Gay found the formal means to identify the disfunctional old prisons and the judicial system they served with the contradictory forms of cultural hegemony that enforced both. This identification, objectified by Oglethorpe's inquiries, and bolstered by the popular cynicism about prisons promoted by the boom in criminal narrative of the 1720s, created a shock of recognition that then took time to absorb. Gay's generic innovations in the ballad opera provided means of acting out contradictions in the old social forms and institutions with a transparency sufficient to expose them, but Gay's method did not enable sustained inquiry. Hogarth's novelized cycles allowed a more structured analysis in which irony and dialogue were subordinated to narrative coherence. Hogarth thus provided a means of sustained awareness and inquiry that cut across social boundaries and economic classes. As Hogarth's competitor George Vertue observed in 1732: "The most remarkable Subject of painting that captivated the Minds of most persons of all ranks and conditions from the greatest Quality to the meanest was the Story painted and designed by Mr. Hogarth of the Harlots Progress and the prints engravd by him and publishd."[43] It is worth emphasizing, and important to understand, that the 1730s and 1740s did not witness the publication of explicit tracts on prison reform.[44] To the degree the values later expressed in such tracts were born to consciousness during these decades it was in the novel, in Hogarth's prints, in the theater, and in popular literature.

When Hogarth examines the social behavior of the isolated self in *A Harlot's Progress* (figs. 31–36) and *A Rake's Progress* (figs. 37 and 38), he depicts protagonists who are the willing if naive victims of corrupt or hostile institutions. There are no positive external structures. As the Harlot begins her career in London, a clergyman turns away in quest of the bishop who looks after Walpole's ecclesiastical preferments, while the twice-pardoned gentlemanly rapist, Colonel Charteris, leers at her from an open doorway (fig. 31). Thus the spiritual guide and the feudal protector both abandon their traditional roles in favor of self-satisfaction. Both histories implicitly question whether there are any social institutions worth associating with: the high life that occupies the ruling establishment corrupts with diseases of lust and profligacy (figs. 32 and 33), while

31. William Hogarth, *A Harlot's Progress*, plate 1, 1732. Mother Needham, the procuress, inspects newly arrived country goods while a potential client, Colonel Charteris, looks on approvingly and a clergyman seeking preferment turns away.

32. William Hogarth, *A Harlot's Progress*, plate 2, 1732. Soon established as a mistress, Moll Hackabout creates an accident to prevent the rich Jew who keeps her in luxury from noticing the flight of a young lover.

33. William Hogarth, *A Harlot's Progress*, plate 3, 1732. On the verge of arrest as a common whore, the infected Moll keeps to hand a masquerade costume, the spoils of thievery, and a portrait of Macheath.

34. William Hogarth, *A Harlot's Progress*, plate 4, 1732. Wearing one last luxurious gown, Moll works off her sentence in a rendition of a decaying London Bridewell that reduces the idea of reform to an economic transaction.

35. William Hogarth, *A Harlot's Progress*, plate 5, 1732. Confined to impersonal, cell-like lodgings and mocked by useless cures, Moll succumbs to disease.

36. William Hogarth, *A Harlot's Progress*, plate 6, 1732. The behavior of a Fleet parson who attends more to his companion's petticoats than to the license that reigns at Moll's wake symbolizes the failure of institutions to endow exemplary stories with reformative force.

labor is merely an alternative to the pillory, the whipping post, or the gallows—the three choices presented to the Harlot in Bridewell (fig. 34). In fact both the Harlot and the Rake die of inner corruption—syphilis and madness—not at the hand of the law (figs. 35 and 38).[45]

The pillory, the whipping post, and the gallows, like the prisons, bridewells, and houses of correction, symbolized power. The actual use of them represented the failure rate, the last resort, of a social order based on patronage for service, which had been progressively transformed into a system of preferment for pay.[46] Moll Hackabout's true alternative, as revealed by a fellow prisoner in *The Jew Decoy'd; or, the Progress of a Harlot,* a ballad opera that joined hosts of competitors for a share in Hogarth's success, is not shown in the plate depicting her beating hemp in London Bridewell:

> I can assure you the folks here are very reasonable; you need not beat hemp, if you can afford but a trifle to pay them for your time.[47]

Moll is expected to pay the keeper for preferring her while one and all keep up the appearance that the system of patronage retains old significances based on work and service. The scene just prior to Moll's entrance shows the motives of the keeper, whose livelihood is supposed to come from the produce of the same forced labor that redeems his prisoners:

> Most of the poor devils that comes here have scarce rags to their backs, and though I think I know the art of squeezing as well as most of my brethren, yet I have much ado to keep my chaise and pair out of the profits. . . . I believe most of my customers will grow honest by force, for want of having something to lay their hands on.[48]

The old instruments of punishment, as Oglethorpe's committee discovered at the Fleet and other prisons, had become weapons of extortion for grasping, social-climbing keepers, just as the collective bonds that validated government by patronage had been replaced under Walpole by the individualistic drive for personal wealth and power, leaving no more than the shell of titles and honors intact. In the words of the song just prior to Moll's entrance in *The Jew Decoy'd,*

> Since the laws come from power, then grant it you must
> What ever power does is lawful and just:
> For justice to it must owe its free course,
> And statutes are trifles, if not back'd by force.[49]

Walpole's government was itself a parody—a representation under patrician guise—of the urban, commerce-based, Whig ascendancy.

In *A Harlot's Progress*, Hogarth's crisp realistic focus on low life necessarily limits his range of direct commentary (though in figure 34, at the simplest emblematic level, he shows the decay of liminal punishment by the decrepit state of the building in which we find Moll beating hemp under a roof ventilated by gaping holes). But his narrative works to condemn the whole social order along with its laws, justices, keepers, and prisons. Far from delivering Moll Hackabout from prostitution and placing her in the way of honest work, Bridewell is merely a stage in her destruction. Still, I want to stress that for all the negative, satiric thrust of Hogarth's series, its very nature as a narrative account structures the idea of imprisonment sequentially. And though Moll's story is tragic, the implication is always that it might be otherwise—that the institutions we see might intervene to retell it. This is especially so as Hogarth chooses to put his harlot in a "house of correction," a species of institution that long since had strayed from its original disciplinary purpose (in that the bridewells had become just another kind of liminal prison) but one which, at least in theory, might have turned Moll Hackabout onto another path. The bridewell we see in *A Harlot's Progress* mocks the liminal prison by exposing the pretense to the improvement of prisoners evident in actual houses of correction. It raises the issue of altering behavior while showing the system as corrupted and worse than fruitless. The story's devolution into one of decay and antireformation—a story of death by rot—at once mocks established order and proposes the possibility that the narrative and the institutions it encompasses might be different. Only much later, in *Industry and Idleness*, does Hogarth separately articulate good and bad, prosperity and adversity, comedy and tragedy, in a double progress. Even then they remain recognizable as versions of one another.

In *A Harlot's Progress*, each stage of the tragedy presses the observer to reflect on some positive comic alternative, and the devices of comedy are present even in Hogarth's most scarifying plates. We are encouraged, especially in the first plate of the series, to imagine what might have been had the clergyman been a watchful shepherd, or the noble lord in quest of an honest servant rather than a victim to serve his turn. The Bridewell plate (fig. 34) gives us to notice correctional punishment as a substitute for the modes of corporal abuse illustrated on the walls behind the prisoners and, though Hogarth's realism limits his capacity to propose explicit alternatives, his omission of any reference to Moll's option of buying out her time at least implies the possibility of a system in which fixed correctional sentences and common currency are not interchangeable—one of the fundamental principles of the reformative penitentiary. Unlike the comparable scenes in *A Rake's Progress* (figs. 37 and 38), the last two plates of Moll's story do not show forcible institutions, but, as Paulson observes, the walls close in on her, ultimately forming the sides of her coffin.[50] The reformational antidote to the fifth plate in her story (fig. 35), in which she hovers at the verge of death while false doctors quarrel over their useless cures, would substitute the medicine of spiritual education—a reversal, a revelation of "thought" or insight like Moll Flanders's experiences in prison. In the final scene, rather than finding herself restored to productive life through insight and reformation, Moll Hackabout regains a social place only in death (fig. 36). The sort of clergyman who might, in a better world, have guided her path (in fact he is a chaplain of the Fleet, notorious for conducting nefarious weddings) instead assists at her wake by groping under the skirts of one of the more respectable-looking mourners. Not even Moll's ultimate confinement bears any instructional or exemplary burden, and I think, in the context of a story whose crisis takes the form of a scene in Bridewell, we are required to consider that it might have. Thus, when I say that *A Harlot's Progress* represents the narrative penitentiary, I mean it does so by way of its antitype. Although Hogarth glances at a correctional institution in the series, he does not pose explicit alternatives to existing punishments; but he establishes the narrative form of reform in the very act of showing the old prisons. Henceforth social criticism takes the form of a story.

Thus Hogarth resolved Gay's total irony—its quality of being fixed, frozen in time, and in that sense unreformative—into causally comprehensible narrative. Gay's work is novelized, but Hogarth's approaches the standing of the novel per se, though frustrated because the cycles want extensiveness of plot and, above all, because Hogarth's medium, like Defoe's choice of first-person narration, limits his power to regulate the implications of his stories in any container of narrational authority. In *The Analysis of Beauty,* Hogarth shows a full awareness of the link between stories and discourse, that is, of narrative's power to advance conclusions and, above all, of the viewer's insistent delight in drawing them out:

> It is a pleasing labour of the mind to solve the most difficult problems; allegories and riddles, trifling as they are, afford the mind amusement: and with what delight does it follow the well-connected thread of a play, or novel, which ever increases as the plot thickens, and ends most pleas'd, when it is most distinctly unravell'd?[51]

Hogarth takes narrative understanding as a cultural presumption, as the mode of comprehension within which his audience can be assumed to operate. His cycles record traces of an emergent cultural system in which realistic narrative governed by detailed sequences of cause and effect is both a means of presentation and a mode of perception.

The reception of *A Harlot's Progress* documents Hogarth's thorough-going appropriation of life in Bakhtin's novelized "zone of contact with the present in all its openendedness." A cheap unauthorized pamphlet, based on garbled descriptions of the paintings, all but preceded the artist's distribution of engravings to the subscribers and began the lively eighteenth-century tradition of narrative accounts of Hogarth's prints.[52] The story was retold in variants ranging from the pornographic to the moralistic, and the prints were copied onto articles of daily use such as fan-mounts or cups and saucers. The genesis of the series, the origins of its major characters, and much of its almost inexhaustible density of meaning are embedded in a web of topical reference traceable in news-paper accounts of contemporaneous events.[53] There can be little doubt either of Hogarth's intention to introduce realistic narrative into painting or of the entry of his work into the novelized zone of contact where, according to Bakhtin, thought about contemporary experience takes linguistic, generic, and conceptual form.

Bakhtin says that the zone of "unfinished, still-evolving contemporary reality . . . was first appropriated by the novel," but one can witness Hogarth's quest, following close upon Defoe, to imitate novelistic realism in narrative as a means of annexing contemporaneity to the visual arts as well.[54] We can see a push toward seriality in Hogarth's painting even before *A Harlot's Progress,* which, by Vertue's account, exfoliated at the urging of visitors to Hogarth's studio from one picture, to a pendant pair, to the ultimate half-dozen.[55] Between 1728 and 1730, Hogarth painted no fewer than six canvases showing act 3, scene 11 of *The Beggar's Opera.* In them, as Paulson argues, Hogarth perfected the delicate coun-terpoint, within a single mode of realistic representation, between fic-tional characters and notable contemporary personages.[56] This was the mode, distinct from that of caricature, that he would use so effectively in *A Harlot's Progress.*

Although the paintings of *The Beggar's Opera* do not form a narrative series, they show Hogarth thinking sequentially in the sense of recording shifting points of view. They map the path by which he discovered how to assemble images in a novelized form. The first paintings focus close in on characters acting their parts before a comparatively realistic setting; the surrounding audience of notables appears in caricature, drawn flat in a manner that removes them from the scene by draining away their tangibility (fig. 20). For all the freshness of Hogarth's painting in certain passages, the genres that coexist in this picture remain unenlivened by dialogue with one another and interact no more than the posed figures they render. The last two paintings, larger in size and more distant in perspective, present actors and audience in a unified transparent style that allows Hogarth's painterly irony and humor to glance among any number of genres in a manner precisely analogous to Gay's verbal and dramatic irony (fig. 21). As if to call attention to the realism of his figural presentation, Hogarth surrounds his personnel with elaborate baroque theatrical paraphernalia, including a sculptural proscenium and a spacious Italianate setting of the kind used for prison scenes in opera and heroic tragedy.[57] The depiction within this frame views figures in a manner akin to the situational group portrait or conversation piece, establishing relationships between the on-stage audience and the actors through precisely calibrated details of gesture, dress, and color; but the poses are adopted from history paintings in the grand manner, while the whole is imbued with the odd mixture of analytic detachment and high seriousness that characterizes theater pieces by Rembrandt or Watteau.

Considered with the idea of a stretch toward seriality, Hogarth's own studio accounting notes from this period allow the interpretation that the last of *The Beggar's Opera* group (Tate Gallery) was sold as one of a pair with the version of the Oglethorpe Committee visiting the Fleet Prison now in the National Portrait Gallery. The pictures are linked by complementary themes and settings, as well as by a shared theatricality of approach and a comparable disposition of actors and audience in the manner of conversation pieces. Eighteenth-century accounts strongly suggest that they were similarly framed for hanging as a pendant pair.[58] The evidence is perhaps too slight to support extended speculation, but if one considers the two works as a sequential pair, the notion of a move toward reform becomes part of their meaning.[59]

In fact, the idea that Gay's opera could be recast into a progress setting forth the affinity between the powerful and the criminal yet moving finally to the prospect of reform inspired by the Oglethorpe Committee is more than a product of strenuous modern interpretation. Exactly this sequence occurred in *The Prisoners Opera*, a work combining scenes of popular pantomime with episodes in Gay's manner, which played at Sadler's Wells during the summer season of 1730. The Head-Turnkey sings, for instance:

Why should Mortals think us base,
   For extorting double Fees?
Since each Jaylor buys his Place,
   At what Price his Betters please:
Were the Purchase-Money low,
   Wonders might perhaps be seen,

And we Rogues as honest grow
  As those Saints that put us in.

Since, like Monsters in the Sea,
  Mighty Knaves the less devour,
Why should not such Wolves as we,
  Prey on those within our Pow'r?
But what we from others drain,
  Greater Bites new Ways have found
To extort from us again,
  So the sharping World goes round.[60]

Yet following a variety of scenes centering in turn on garnish, drunkenness in prison, family misery, begging, and the decline of charity for debtors, *The Prisoners Opera* ends with a general chorus that, however modified by contextual irony, has to be taken as a hymn praising Oglethorpe's exposure of corrupt jailers:

Our Keepers, who of late, like Leeches, suck'd the Poor
  And made us still more wretched by unlawful means,
By Justice have been fleec'd of their illgotten Store,
  And punish'd for their Avarice and other Sins.
  We now shall know our Fees,
    And live in greater ease;
The Law has giv'n 'em Bounds, to our content;
  And since we Wretches find
    The Government so kind,
God save our noble King, and bless the Parliament.[61]

Representations such as this of course transpired at the margins of articulate discourse in the public sphere, as Habermas terms the arena of reasoned public communication; but to the degree that Gay and Hogarth were the subjects of imitation and explanation in both popular and polite discourse, their work occasioned a sustained rehearsal of attitudes toward the failings of the old prisons that would dominate reformist arguments later on.

Hogarth's series of "comic history paintings" repeated in the visual arts Defoe's innovation in written narrative of more than a decade earlier. Defoe had posed an alternative to liminal confinement by representing it causally and sequentially as an individual quest for meaning. Gay enacted the contradiction of the liminal prison that had been implicit in the structure of feeling Defoe revealed, and dissolved all meaning derived from social institutions. Hogarth's narrative plates accept Gay's rejection of liminal transformation and the patriarchal social forms it implied. The skepticism concerning the traditional bases of morality implicit in the two earlier series becomes cynicism in *Marriage à la Mode* (1745), where the first plate shows the merchant (the line of work) and the earl (the line of fixed aristocratic hegemony) forming a contractual alliance by the marriage of their children. Hogarth commences with a scene illustrating the fabled English method of renewing the patrician social order by joining the egalitarian virtues of industry and self-improvement to stable aristocratic institutions. But the story is one of vanity, corruption, and dissolution ending in murder and suicide. The issue of this classic marriage is a diseased and crippled girl-child in whom both lines are doomed to fail, and the story finishes as the merchant removes the wedding ring from his dying daughter's finger—suggesting that hard assets are the only stable reality. The Harlot and the Rake both die pursuing passion in the predatory social world Gay set forth. Hogarth's endings are of the kind found in bourgeois tragedy, specifically George Lillo's *London Merchant* (1731), not the arbitrary heroic sort Gay ridiculed in his comic conclusion to *The Beggar's Opera*.

Hogarth's visual narratives reject the old prison and in so doing they reintroduce, to more systematic purpose, the kind of sequence and moral causation I have found in Defoe. In *A Rake's Progress*, the liminal prison splits into the Fleet and Bedlam, which appear sequentially in the series as stages of development in the plot. In the Fleet scene (fig. 37) Hogarth represents the farcical aspect of the old prison, but rejects its comic potential by ending the series tragically in Bedlam (fig. 38). The Fleet in its carnival dimension has become a step on the way to insanity and death, not an arena of free play from which any outcome can issue. The rite of passage, outside of ordinary time and full of potential either for rebirth or sudden death, now splits into the opposites of caprice and terror seen in sequence. The life of caprice leads to a death of terror.

In the Fleet, we see Rakewell at the moment of no return—evidently just after arrival since the turnkey is demanding garnish. The means are those of farcical stage comedy in the manner of Jonson's *Alchemist* but the humor drains away into a sense of threat, entrapment, and potential tragedy. The figure of the turnkey sums up this strangely hollow tone of comedy without laughter since garnish, which was supposed to be a charge of pleasure for the other prisoners, here becomes a threat. If the walls and the very air seemed agents of Moll Hackabout's incarceration, contorted inhumanity persecutes the catatonic Rakewell in the Fleet. Rakewell's surroundings in prison and in the madhouse show him trapped within a defective self whose formation by the society that fostered it, and in some measure shares it, is symbolized by institutional walls and bars. Although the crowd of people and objects around Rakewell are part of his story, in the last two plates at least they exist for us rather than for him to interpret. *A Rake's Progress* takes a more emblematic approach than *A Harlot's Progress;* its moralized narrative is more explicit, and its assignment of blame more specifically personal.

Should we balk in pursuit of Hogarth's visual clues linking crime to madness and prisons to madhouses, the caption written for the prison plate by Dr. John Hoadly sanctions us to proceed:

> Not so the Guilty Wretch confin'd:
> No Pleasures meet his roving Mind,
> No Blessings fetch'd from early Youth,
> But broken Faith, & wrested Truth,

37. William Hogarth, *A Rake's Progress,* plate 7, 1735. The Rake's comedy becomes tragic farce in the Fleet Prison.

Talents idle, & unus'd,
And every Gift of Heaven abus'd,—
In Seas of sad Reflection lost,
From Horrors still to Horrors tost,
Reason the Vessel leaves to Steer,
And Gives the Helm to mad Despair.[62]

In the Fleet, Rakewell's skull has become the prison and his body, as compared with the earlier plates, has begun to assume the stiff, statuesque pose that emerges fully at the end when he resembles C. G. Cibber's statue of melancholy madness on the gates of Bedlam.[63] Lunatic self-absorption immures Rakewell's companions in the Fleet and in Bed-

38. William Hogarth, *A Rake's Progress*, plate 8, 1735. When the Fleet turns despair to madness, barred confinement at Bedlam replaces the prison cell. The spectacle amuses ladies of fashion.

lam more surely than the bars hovering in the background. In prison the others are scientific or literary "projectors" whose struggles to get free by alchemy, Icarus-like flight, schemes to pay the national debt, or, in Rakewell's case, authorship, imply some recognition that a world exists outside. However, in Bedlam the only attempt at human interchange, beyond the trio gathered about Rakewell as if posed for a pietà, is whispered commentary from one of the two elegant visitors, who are conspicuous to us partly because of their irrelevance to the madmen. Beyond the helpers who isolate the Rake in Bedlam roam lunatics so much more threatening than the bars enclosing the place that one puzzles over how these well-dressed ladies got in unaccompanied. True, they had paid admission, but ultimately the answer is revealed at the end of Hogarth's life, and it parallels Gay's: with the revision of the plate in 1763, Hogarth added a medallion of Britannia as lunatic to the other graffiti on the wall above Rakewell's head (fig. 39). Inside and outside it's all the same!

Finally, Hogarth's cycles, not to mention the explicit captions on his *Rake's Progress* plates, imply alternative stories, other social constructs, in which the victims might prosper, and the plates spur consideration of social institutions that might foster rather than destroy. Hogarth's later double progress, *Industry and Idleness* (1747), actually tells both stories at once and, while recognizing the difficulty of restraining passionate natures, veers toward the supervised workshop as a social model (figs. 40–45). Although Hogarth departs from his earlier practice in showing a positive alternative and employs dozens of parallels between the two apprentices to reveal, I think quite radically, that the ideally good and the quintessentially bad are inseparable versions of one another, Idle's fate on the Road from Newgate to Tyburn seems irreversible. Hogarth does not explicitly push through to the conclusion that Tyburn Fair might be avoided, that Idle might be sentenced to relive the positive half of the narrative. This remains a possibility latent in Goodchild's part of the story (figs. 40, 41, 43, and 45). Instead, he spells out parallels between Idle's procession from Newgate at the margin of the City to his death amid the tumultuous carnival at Tyburn and Goodchild's progress through the heart of town to assume the office of lord mayor (figs. 44 and 45).[64] Hogarth has novelized, and thereby exposed sequentially to view, the covalence between authority and its abdication in the liminal arena—the definition of each by an alien or "other." He anatomizes a kind of governance typical of the closed city.

By contrast, the sprawling metropolis must absorb, regulate, and rectify its aliens for want of any power to exclude them physically; and the sense of injustice one feels at Idle's fate arises at least in part from the metropolitan scene in which Hogarth has situated him, a narrative con-

Madness, Thou Chaos of y Brain, | With Rule disjointed Shapeless Measure | Shapes of Pleasure, that but Seen | The headstrong Course of youth thus run, | See Him by Thee to Ruin Sold.
What art: That Pleasure giv'st, and Pain : | Fill'd with Horror, fill'd with Pleasure : | Would split the Shaking Sides of Spleen | What Comfort from this darling Son : | And curse thy self, & curse thy Gold.
Tyranny of Fancy's Reign : | Shapes of Horror, that wou'd even | O Vanity of Age : here See | His rattling Chains with Terror hear.
Mechanic Fancy, that can build | Cast Doubt of Mercy upon Heaven. | The Stamp of Heaven effac'd by Thee | Behold Death grappling with Despair, | Retouch'd by the Author 17
Vast Labyrinths, & Mazes wild. | | Invented & Etch'd by W. Hogarth & Publish'd according to Act of Parliament June y.e 25. 1735.

39. William Hogarth, *A Rake's Progress*, plate 8, 1735. Third State revised, 1763. An added halfpenny showing Britannia as lunatic (upper left) suggests that madness has become the coin of the realm.

text governed by causal and sequential rules that implies his story might be retold or relived if authority were redisposed along metropolitan rather than civic principles. One thinks ahead to Fielding's Bow Street constables and to his proposals for a metropolitan police.[65] The association of Hogarth's cycles with the idea of reform remains powerful at least through mid-century when, in *Amelia* (1751), Fielding lines the study of his beneficent authoritarian moralist, Dr. Harrison, with them— at once a sign and a source of the good man's philanthropic zeal. With Fielding's juridical innovations during the late 1740s and early 1750s, and with his later social tracts, the structures of feeling I have been tracing in narrative forms emerge with full force in reformist discourse.

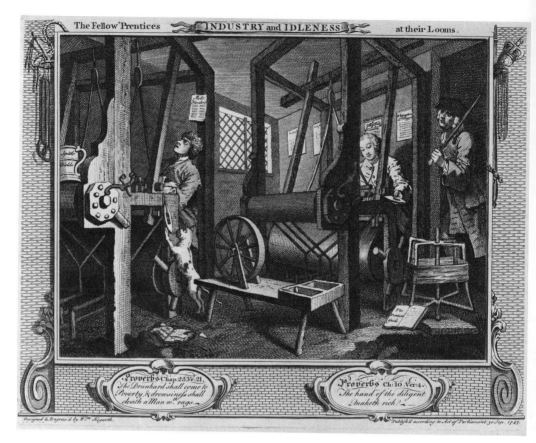

40. William Hogarth, *Industry and Idleness*, plate 1, 1747. Idle and Goodchild begin opposite courses of life in a supervised workshop.

41. William Hogarth, *Industry and Idleness*, plate 2, 1747. Goodchild dedicates his leisure to worship as he embarks on a successful career in trade.

42. William Hogarth, *Industry and Idleness,* plate 3, 1747. Idle, cheating some fellow laggards in a churchyard furnished with emblems of mortality, reveals thievery as his true calling.

43. William Hogarth, *Industry and Idleness*, plate 10, 1747. Much later,
the divergent paths of business and crime cross a second time when
Alderman Goodchild, acting as magistrate, must commit Idle
to Newgate.

133

Plate 11

44. William Hogarth, *Industry and Idleness*, plate 11, 1747. Idle's progress ends outside London at Tyburn Fair, where a rowdy carnival engulfs the theater of execution and a Methodist preaches reformation while an official clergyman, the Ordinary of Newgate, rides at a distance.

During the 1760s, the fictional materiality of the novel will give way to the physical materiality of the architectural facade and, at last, to the penitentiary itself.

Hogarth's cycles signal the end of a system in which the civic humanism of palatial public buildings like the new Bedlam Hospital (fig. 46) and the prison at York (fig. 3), or for that matter Old Newgate with its emblematic statues (fig. 23), could function in harmony with the ungoverned arenas behind their columns and pilasters. These buildings were monuments to demonstrative forms of authority exercised through personal patronage—to what E. P. Thompson has called the theatricalism of patrician hegemony—and vestiges of an architectural ideal of the city formulated in the Renaissance under the inspiration of Vitruvius and epitomized by Palladio. The residential character of palatial architecture in itself implies the personal agency of king, duke, or baron.[66] Bars to segregate violent inmates were added to Bedlam in 1729, and Hogarth's

Proverbs CHAP: III.Ver:16.
Length of days is in her right hand and
in her left hand Riches and Honour.

45. William Hogarth, *Industry and Idleness*, plate 12, 1747.
Goodchild, honored by a procession through the heart of the
City during his installation as lord mayor of London,
reaches the pinnacle of success.

representation of the Rake's lunatic death leads one to question how
many subscribers to the series could any longer accept the bland assertion, made only a few years before by John Styrpe in his revision of
Stow's *Survey of the Cities of London and Westminster* (1720), that the idyllic
conditions at Bedlam Hospital inspired many a cured lunatic to beg to
remain instead of returning home to his relations.[67] Hogarth, following
Defoe, had anatomized the contradictions of liminal confinement by
subjecting them to the logic of realistic narrative—by insisting that they
make discursive, evidentiary sense rather than play a ceremonial or ritual
role. This re-enactment of ceremony and ritual in novelized literary and
visual forms has profound consequences, for it promulgates a discourse
situated in the public sphere, a discourse in which the multiple voices
of the present can take concrete form, relating to one another analytically
rather than magically. A struggle to control the means of observation
and to dispose the resources of narrative must ensue as the realistically

The Hospital of Bethlehem? L'Hospital de Fou?

London, Printed for Bowles & Carver, 69 St. Pauls Church Yard, and Rob Wilkinson, 58 Cornhill.

46. *The Hospital of Bethlehem—L'Hospital de Fou*, 1751. An engraving that emphasizes Bedlam's palatial elegance.

illustrated minutiae of present life become subject to the discourse of debate—a discourse in which evidence based on observation is central and in which narrative coherence forged from multiple voices delineates authority, government, and reality itself.

*There appear to me to be four sorts of political power;
that of bodily strength, that of the mind, the power of the purse, and
the power of the sword. Under the second of these divisions may be
ranged all the art of the legislator and politician, all the power
of laws and government. These do constitute the civil power; and a
state may then be said to be in good order, when all the other
powers are subservient to this. . . .*

*In plain truth, the principal design of this whole work is to
rouse the civil power from its present lethargic state. A design, which
alike opposes those wild notions of liberty that are inconsistent with all
government, and those pernicious schemes of government
which are destructive of true liberty.*

HENRY FIELDING
Preface to *An Enquiry Into the Causes of the
Late Increase of Robbers*

5

Narration and "Civil Power"
Jonathan Wild in Fielding's Career

Fielding brings us to the moment when, because of the novelization of eighteenth-century culture that I have illustrated above with reference to Gay and Hogarth, formal innovation in the novel becomes a mode of action.[1] Fielding at once articulated a cultural system in his fiction and took a vital formative role in shaping a paradigmatic social system.[2] The peculiar engagement between his legal and novelistic careers, which always has been cited as thematically central to *Amelia* and to certain incidents in the earlier novels, now must itself be considered as characteristic of a distinct phase in the penitentiary's emergent representation to public awareness. On the whole, then, my chief attention in this chapter and the next rests neither on the fine points of Fielding's fictional technique nor on the details of his reformist proposals. In this chapter I notice, rather, Fielding's overriding concern—in his novels, his judicial practice, and his reformist writings—with the deployment of narrative as an authoritative resource. In the next chapter, while investigating Fielding's systematic revision of law enforcement during his magistracy, I stress his repetition, in the seemingly divergent spheres of discourse and juridical action, of patterns of narrative construction that are integral to the penitentiary idea. The realization of this idea would have been impossible without the development of interrelated social systems. Fielding was directly responsible for some of them: specifically, for the establishment of a centralized agency dedicated to the collection, cross-referencing, and dissemination of information on metropolitan crime and for the organization of a professional police force engaged in crime detection. These innovations accompanied larger trends toward evidentiary precision in the construction of legal narratives in the criminal courts. The penitentiary idea as unfolded in these chapters increasingly comprehends alterations in the system of law enforcement itself.

The idea of narrative as an authoritative resource was partially explored in my chapters on Defoe, where written records and civic power were viewed as correlative.[3] Narrative resources include the capacity to store up information in the tables, lists, registers, and chronicles associated with the origins of written language in cities. These resources also encompass the facility both to shape data into instrumental knowledge through sorting, indexing, and other devices of access characteristic of early modern bureaucracy and, beyond keeping track, to create controlled sequences ordered by cause and effect—sequences with explanatory power. This potential is implicit in the syntax of writing itself but is fully realized only in the densely stored, cross-referenced informational networks that characterize written accounting in the modern metropolis, where many of the systems of classification and integration necessary to command masses of written information were first fully actualized. I count the realist novel as one of these systems.

Cities long had numbered governmental archives, church registers, institutional libraries, and, more recently, municipal banks and exchanges among their authoritative repositories, but the rapidly evolving London metropolis presented conditions under which the capacity to hold and employ information was dispersed and struggles for the control of narrative resources ensued.[4] Written data became merely preconditions of the authority they once encoded; the question was who could most actively, coherently, and inclusively dispose them into effectual sequences. Who could create and maintain the master narratives that would shape the social order? It is possible, for example, to consider the theatricalism E. P. Thompson has attributed to the patrician hegemony that dominated eighteenth-century England as a strategy of self-preservation whereby the residual hierarchy achieved a visibility that could be apprehended without reference to the allegiances it originally represented.[5] This theatricalism, though effective during the early stages of metropolitan development, met with increasingly formidable competition. For it emerged that the extended power made possible by cross-referencing aggressively compiled, up-to-date information within the interlocking coordinates of metropolitan time and space could be wielded either by civil authority or by enterprising individuals or associations. In the 1720s, for instance, Jonathan Wild devised a system of indexed registers to keep track of London robberies. By gaining detailed information about the circumstances of crimes from the victims and correlating it with knowledge about the goods involved, Wild made a fortune fencing stolen property back to its original owners in exchange for handsome, supposedly voluntary, rewards. Simultaneously, by using the facts he had obtained about the thieves' methods of operation and their specific movements as evidence against any who held back goods or otherwise betrayed him, the "thief-taker" both collected a handsome bounty for scores of successful indictments and posed as a public benefactor—a kind of private police detective. Wild exercised a new kind of power under the guise of public service, while Walpole employed similar methods in a parody of traditional hierarchy and patronage. The two were perfect analogues of one another, and by the 1740s, the pursuit of private interest by their kind had, according to commentators like Fielding, reduced the resources of "civil power" in London to a level that scarcely exceeded that of private individuals and entities. Fielding set about to rectify the situation, in part by copying Wild's methods.

· I ·

Henry Fielding lived and worked all of his London life within an area roughly marked out by Temple Bar, Charing Cross, Saint Martin in the Fields, and Covent Garden, where he presided as magistrate of the Bow Street court beginning in October of 1748.[6] Covent Garden had been the first of the squares developed in the seventeenth century on land to the west of the City. Begun in 1631, at the initiative of the fourth earl of Bedford, on a noble Italianate plan by Inigo Jones, it set the pattern of building on speculation that was to burgeon after the Great Fire (figs. 15 and 16 [coordinates G/g]). Although it remained a fashionable place of residence for at least a generation, the Covent Garden Piazza (so called because its plan was inspired by the Piazza d'Arme at Leghorn) increasingly lost out to competition from newer developments farther west. This westward exodus of fashion accelerated after 1670 when the Bedfords gained a royal charter licensing them to operate a casual market that had sprung up in the square during the Civil War (fig. 47). By the time of Fielding's magistracy, the market contained more than a hundred shop stalls and the area had declined into a marginal suburb teeming with ventures that traditionally had flourished in the "liberties" that lay under the shadow of London's walls: theaters, coffee houses, brothels, gambling places, and rough taverns (fig. 48). As Fielding wrote in *The Covent-Garden Journal* for 9 May 1752:

> Within the memory of many now living, the circle of the People of Fascination included the whole parish of Covent Garden, and great part of St. Giles's in the Fields; but here the enemy broke in, and the

47. Balthasar Nebot, *A View of the Covent Garden Piazza,* 1735. The market and square as it appeared during Fielding's years as a London dramatist.

circle was presently contracted to Leicester Fields, and Golden Square. Hence the People of Fashion again retreated before the foe to Hanover Square; whence they were once more driven to Grosvenor Square, and even beyond it, and that with such precipitation, that, had they not been stopped by the walls of Hyde Park, it is more than probable they would by this time have arrived at Kensington.[7]

The streets of London and Westminster were secured chiefly by ill-paid watchmen and citizen constables, for the idea of a police force had yet to gain currency except in terms of vague negative associations with French absolutism. The very word "police" did not attain its modern meaning until the mid-eighteenth century.[8] Most defendants were privately detained at the scene of a crime, apprehended by a hue and cry, or impeached by accomplices. In the vast majority of cases before justice

HE AND HIS DRUNKEN COMPANIONS RAISE A RIOT IN COVENT GARDEN.

48. *A Riot in Covent Garden,* 1735. Fielding's precinct abounded in drunken revels like these, depicted here in a popular series that imitated *A Rake's Progress.*

of the peace courts like Fielding's, where misdemeanors were punished and indictments for felony were "made over," as well as in the somewhat more formal proceedings at the Old Bailey's criminal courts, the injured party conducted the prosecution and the accused mounted his own defense under the inquiring guidance of active judges unrestrained by any of the modern rules of evidence. No detectives assisted the citizen prosecutor in formulating or documenting the case against defendants and the rare appearance of counsel was chiefly for purposes of cross-examination.[9]

In the judicial sphere, Fielding devised idiosyncratic methods that became models of future law enforcement. Most striking, he introduced new strategies for identifying evidence through systematic advertisements and for assembling it through the use of a quasi-official police force called the Bow Street Runners. Fielding employed the information gained by his "runners" to draft indictments that increased convictions in the Old Bailey because they presented judges and juries in that court with coherent, authoritatively structured narratives of criminal action. He and his half-brother John, who continued the work in Bow Street after Fielding's health failed in 1754, are usually considered the founders of London's Metropolitan Police, an institution that was to wait until 1829 for parliamentary sanction. Fielding's inventive magistracy in Bow Street, no less than his novelistic innovation, signals a major stage in the emergence of structures of feeling that enable the narrative penitentiary because he takes the step from consciousness contrived as a narrative of the material world to the inclusion of omniscient, inquiring authority in that world. Viewed in this light, his major reformist works of the 1750s— *An Enquiry Into the Causes of the Late Increase of Robbers* and *A Proposal for Making an Effectual Provision for the Poor*—become more significant as symptoms of changes in practice than as causes.[10]

Fielding already had introduced authoritative moral control into the novel rather than leaving it implicit as in earlier fictions like Defoe's. Such realist narratives had shaped consciousness through novelistic specification of phenomenal detail and, implicitly, through direct first-person discourse by the main character. But consciousness needed governance in Fielding's view, and so did narrative. The misunderstandings to which Richardson laid himself open in his immensely popular *Pamela* (1740) proved the case. As Ronald Paulson says, "By reality Fielding means moral or factual truth apprehended by the reader, whereas he sees in Richardson a reality that means the true workings of a character's mind, without any concern for the truth or falseness of apprehension in relation to the external world."[11] From Fielding's belief arose both his attack in *Shamela* (1741) on the moral ambiguity of Richardson's first novel and his derivation in *Joseph Andrews* (1742) of the "comic epic-poem in prose," a narrative form best understood, in the present context, as a corrective to the lack of authorial presence in epistolary fiction.

At the time Fielding gained admission to the bar on 20 June 1740, after a comparatively short stay of just under three years at the Middle Temple, he was an experienced playwright and satirist approaching his mid-thirties. *Jonathan Wild* may already have existed in draft.[12] Legal and fictional discourse continually intersect during this same period in his contributions to *The Champion* where, as Paulson observes, he developed "a persona that began to move in the direction of the detached, fair-minded judge who would later be equated with the artist-creator or historian in the characteristic figure of the Fielding narrator."[13] Certainly by the winter of 1740/41, in the wake of *Pamela*'s enormous vogue and just prior to the publication of *Shamela* in early April, his attention had turned to the interrelated issues of moral significance, authoritative control, and formal order in the novel. Within a year, *Joseph Andrews* had appeared. To quote Pat Rogers's summation, "It is not true that Fielding *invented* the novel. . . . What *Joseph Andrews* did was to give the novel a more clearcut function, a more expressive literary form, and a wider range of resources."[14] The resource upon which Fielding most distinctively drew was the classical epic—especially its formal structure, its treatment of time as an objective continuum, and its intrusive narrator. He assimilated the epic, the official genre par excellence, into the novel by parodic means that Bakhtin identifies with ancient seriocomic literary species including the Socratic dialogue, Roman satire, Menippean satire, and dialogues of the type associated with Lucian (Fielding's favorite author).[15] Because of his transformation of the mock heroic into "the comic epic-poem in prose," Fielding's novels preserved at least some measure of the epic's authoritative ethos so as to contain the amorphous growth of narrative invention and to govern the interpretive fantasy of readers.[16]

In 1743, just two years after *Shamela*, came the *Miscellanies* containing *Jonathan Wild* as the third volume. All the while Fielding was riding the western circuit as a barrister and, in 1745, was advertised in the press as the author of a two-volume treatise on crown (i.e., criminal) law.[17] Right along there had been literary mock trials—of Colly Cibber at the court of Hercules Vinegar in *The Champion* (17 May 1740), of Julian the Apostate by Judge Minos at the gate of Elysium in *Journey from This World to the Next*. In the *True Patriot* for 19 November 1745, Fielding pictured himself in a dream where, wrenched from his hearth and children to go before Jacobite judges on the charge of treason for the crime of having defended King George in print, he is tormented by a priest in the guise of a Newgate Ordinary, thrown into a dungeon, and, once brought to the place of execution, awakened just as the hangman slides the noose about his neck.[18] As early as the autumn of 1747 he was named a justice of the peace for Middlesex, although he did not hold enough property to take the oaths until January of 1749. Already, during October of 1748, Fielding had been installed as justice for Westminster, an office he continued to hold in parallel. In February of 1749, he could anticipate the publication of *Tom Jones*.

In *Amelia* (1751), Fielding's last novel, reformist structures of feeling are at their most available. Good evidence exists that the work was begun during the late autumn of 1749, about twelve months after the novelist first assumed office and more than a year before the publication of *An Enquiry Into the Causes of the Late Increase of Robbers*.[19] The penitentiary idea serves as an organizing principle in the plot of *Amelia* and figures continually in echoes overheard from contemporaneous juridical discourse. The hero's every move takes place in prisons or in the sanctuary of "rules" and "verges" pertaining to them. The novel opens with an overt rejection of the old-style prison, a source of every possible corruption from fraud to adultery. In this extended Newgate sequence, Booth, the hero, is seduced during a protracted narrative told by the remarkable Miss Mathews in the consciousness-centered mode of Defoe. After matching her tale with his own story, also unmediated by alternative versions and ungoverned by an objective narrator, Booth commits the adultery upon which the central plot hinges. Thereafter, Booth and Amelia are kept under watch by the beneficent, all-knowing authority, Dr. Harrison. Much later, when Dr. Harrison has Booth committed for debt, this good man controls every detail. He enacts an exemplary story with Booth as the main character and creates a fictional surrogate of the narrative penitentiary. Harrison's procedure as omniscient warden stands in the sharpest possible contrast with that of the jailer who joins the prisoners in stripping Booth for garnish upon his entry to Newgate. Fielding staged this plot with a realism of detail in the depiction of metropolitan social conditions that would remain unmatched in the English novel until Dickens, and with a precise coordination of fictional chronology and urban topography that was entirely unprecedented.[20]

Early in the year 1751, during which *Amelia* first appeared, Fielding published *An Enquiry Into the Causes of the Late Increase of Robbers*, and exactly twelve months later he produced *A Proposal for Making an Effectual Provision for the Poor* (1753). One gradation of punishment he proposed in the second of these was solitary confinement, which was to become one of the leading notions of the reformers. In the sphere of reformist discourse, as Robin Evans has shown, Fielding's scheme for a huge Middlesex County House, "combining prison, house of correction and work-house," marked a step toward the penitentiary because the differing regimes of its variously classified detainees and prisoners were arrayed precisely within the material framework of a building designed, in collaboration with Thomas Gibson, to control and shape them (fig. 49):

> The Fielding/Gibson project would rely less on creating reflex obedience by chastisement, more on aligning institutional structure with the specification and distribution of space. The early houses of correction had made a place into a punishment but the place itself had no special properties. Like other early prisons they were, more often than not, colonizations of existing sites and structures, and were never conceived as works of architecture in any conventional sense; they were simply fixed abodes. The architecture of the Fielding/Gibson project was by contrast described in detail. At Bridewell chastisement ha[d] been inescapable: in the County House the space allotted to labour, supervision and recuperation would have been inescapable.[21]

Fielding presented a plan in which reformation would depend upon the manner in which activities were disposed within an architectural grid that would classify and order behavior under supervision. The Middlesex County House is an ideal metropolis governed by special rules of its author's creation; indeed, he considers it as "the idea of a body of men united under one government in a large city."[22]

In general, Fielding sought intermediate punishments that combined "correction of the body" with "correction of the mind." The recollection of Moll Flanders's statement that she "began to think, and to think is one real Advance from Hell to Heaven" hovers behind Fielding's words:

> Nothing can, I think, appear more strange than the policy of appointing a chaplain to Newgate, and none to Bridewell. On a religious account it is surely very fit to have a proper person for preparing men for death; but in a political view it must seem most extremely absurd to provide for the regulation of those morals in which the society are no longer concerned, and entirely to neglect the correction and amendment of persons who are shortly to be let loose again among the public, and who are even confined for the purpose of correction. The correction of the body only was doubtless not the whole end of the institution of such houses; and yet it must be allowed a great defect in that institution to leave the correction of the mind to the same hands. In real truth religion is alone capable of effectually executing this work. . . . The excellent Archbishop Tillotson . . . hath very nobly expatiated on the subject:—
>
> "Religion," says he, "hath a good influence upon the people; to make them obedient to government, and conformable to laws: and that not only for wrath, and out of fear of the magistrate's power—

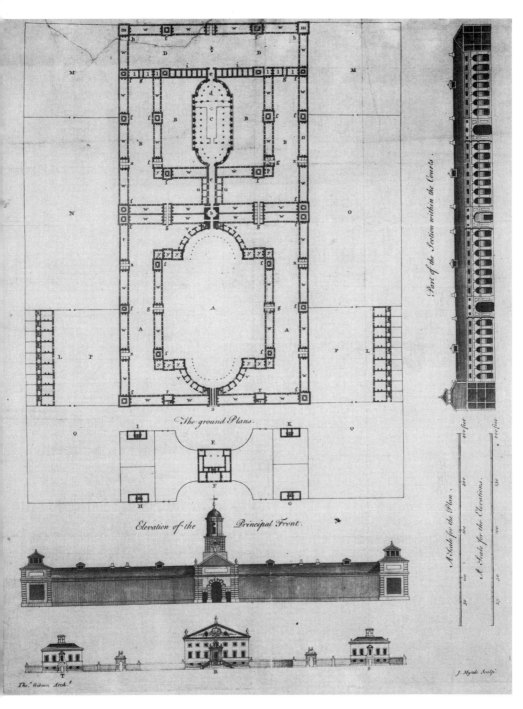

The ground Plans.

Part of the Section within the Courts.

Elevation of the Principal Front.

A Scale for the Plan.

A Scale for the Elevations.

Tho.ᵉ Gibson Arch.ᵗ

J. Mynde Sculp.

49. Thomas Gibson and Henry Fielding's project for a Middlesex
County House, plan and elevations. These plans for a protopenitentiary
accompanied Henry Fielding's *A Proposal for Making an Effectual Provision
for the Poor*, 1753.

which is but a weak and loose principle of obedience, and will cease whenever men can rebel with safety and to advantage—but out of conscience, which is a firm, and constant, and lasting principle, and will hold a man fast when all other obligations will break. . . ."

Nay the very deist and atheist himself, if such a monster there be, must acknowledge the truth of this doctrine; since those who will not allow religion to be a divine, must at least confess that it is a political institution, and designed by the magistrate for the purpose of guarding his authority and of reducing the people to obedience.[23]

While Fielding advocates the instruction of capital offenders "on a religious account," the immortal soul is not a social issue for him. Through the medium of religion, civil power gains access to conscience, and to a progress-ive model upon which to structure reformatory punishment. The wish to correct mind and body together suggests the intermediate state of purgatory, which, because of theological innovations during the course of the eighteenth century, the redemptive hell of the Protestants came increasingly to resemble. In Defoe's version of Old Newgate, Moll subjectively experiences both the unredemptive, early Protestant hell of eternal damnation and a purgatorial replacement as yet without its architectural representation in the penitentiary. A redemptive hell for the wayward soul, a reformative regime for the felonious mind, and a penitentiary architecture to contain and direct the resources of the criminal body are correlative inventions.[24]

· II ·

Like Hogarth's earlier progresses, Fielding's *Jonathan Wild* takes Gay's "total irony" as its point of departure. But while Fielding directly imitates *The Beggar's Opera* in his use of Jonathan Wild, the thief-taker, as a surrogate for Walpole, the "great man," he decisively abandons Gay's treacherous aplomb. Where Hogarth implied an alternative story shaped by reasoned human institutions, Fielding's plot supplies it: balancing Wild's grim progress (his *"Gradus ad Patibulum"* or *"step towards the gallows"*) against the comic outcome of Heartfree's all-but-tragic victimization, and seemingly vindicating Mrs. Heartfree's assertion that "Providence will sooner or later procure the felicity of the virtuous and innocent."[25] Fielding's approach resembles Hogarth's somewhat later in *Industry and Idleness* (1747), even though the careers of Wild and Heartfree are not paralleled as methodically as those of Idle and Goodchild. Fielding's introduction of Heartfree, the good man who first is imprisoned and then nearly hanged because of Wild's perverse manipulations of justice, underscores this novel's rejection both of liminal prisons and of a society in which their sanctioned license formed a structural part.

Fielding's story never slips from the control of his heavily ironic narrator who, at the denouement, declares that his plot will not be marred by an arbitrary reprieve like that in *The Beggar's Opera*. Instead, he rationalizes Heartfree's rescue by bringing forward a conscientious "good magistrate," whose inquiries unravel the willful perjury upon which Wild has founded his denunciation of the innocent Heartfree for capital fraud. As Ian Donaldson says, Fielding's "inversions of high and low in *Jonathan Wild* carry quite different implications from Gay's superficially similar inversions in *The Beggar's Opera*."[26] Total irony and sarcasm, though closely related, are not rhetorically the same: the former presents meanings that cancel one another out because no character or idea is exempt and no index or point of reference guides our judgment, while the latter steadily requires us to understand the opposite of apparent denotation. Irony, in its extreme specialized form as sarcasm, controls and confines meaning as Fielding does in *Wild*.

Fielding separates himself from Gay in the preface to the *Miscellanies* (1743) where, upon introducing *Jonathan Wild*, he draws a distinction between "considering *Newgate* as no other than Human Nature with its Mask off, which some very shameless Writers have done" and "suspecting, that the splendid Palaces of the Great are often no other than *Newgate* with the Mask on."[27] He is qualifying the passage near the end of *The Beggar's Opera* where, following the reprieve, the Beggar declares:

> Through the whole Piece you may observe such a similitude of Manners in high and low Life, that it is difficult to determine whether (in the fashionable Vices) the fine Gentlemen imitate the Gentlemen of the Road, or the Gentlemen of the Road the fine Gentlemen.[28]

Gay's Beggar, for all that he serves as author/presenter of the piece, abdicates control of the denouement to suit the town's operatic taste. He surrenders interpretive privilege along with his intended moral, becoming just another of those for whom the meaning of *The Beggar's Opera* is elusive.

Fielding's preface at first seems to consider playfully that the truth may be "difficult to determine," but the irony draws up short as he turns to a juridical metaphor:

> However the Glare of Riches, and Awe of Title, may dazzle and terrify the Vulgar; nay, however Hypocrisy may deceive the more Discerning, there is still a Judge in every Man's Breast, which none can cheat nor corrupt, tho' perhaps it is the only uncorrupt Thing about him. And yet, inflexible and honest as this Judge is, (however polluted the Bench

be on which he sits) no Man can, in my Opinion, enjoy any Applause which is not thus adjudged to be his Due. (p. 10)

When Fielding's Count does specifically echo the Beggar early in Wild's adventures, the sardonic narrator subdues Gay's ironic equation, framing and controlling it to suit the morally directive tone of fable:

> Can any man doubt whether it is better to be a great statesman or a common thief? . . . Doth it not ask as good a memory, as nimble an invention, as steady a countenance, to forswear yourself in Westminster-hall as would furnish out a complete fool of state, or perhaps a statesman himself? It is needless to particularize every instance; in all we shall find that there is a nearer connection between high and low life than is generally imagined, and that a highwayman is entitled to more favor with the great than he usually meets with. (pp. 16–17)

The Count, viewed as a person, speaks without irony like a character in *The Beggar's Opera*. But whereas Gay's total irony rose from the interplay of statements not in themselves ironic, the sarcasm of Fielding's narrator focuses meaning and guides interpretation. The difference is no longer "difficult to determine"; it is obvious to every reader, though not of course to Wild/Walpole, the Count's only audience at this point in Fielding's fable.

A crucial step has occurred. Both Fielding's discursive control and his polarizations of character reform Gay's total irony. Located thus within the confines of Fielding's narrational authority, the Count's speech, though built up from fragments of Gay's discourse, is invaded by the narrator's tone and subordinated to Fielding's satiric intention. The novelistic requirement that the Count, considered as a personage, speak with direct, uncolored persuasiveness, yields to a manner scarcely removed from the narrator's own. Thus he continues:

> If, therefore, as I think I have proved, the same parts which qualify a man for eminence in a low sphere, qualify him likewise for eminence in a higher, sure it can be no doubt in which he would choose to exert them. Ambition, without which no one can be a great man, will immediately instruct him . . . nay, even fear, a passion the most repugnant to greatness, will show him how much more safely he may indulge himself in the free and full exertion of his mighty abilities in the higher than in the lower rank; since experience teaches him that there is a crowd oftener in one year at Tyburn than on Tower-hill in a century. (p. 18)

Elsewhere, the narrator is at pains to illustrate the similar but much more manipulative exchange of voices between himself and Wild. He demonstrates the full extent of his intervention by printing a transcript of Wild's love letter to the "MOST DEIVINE AND ADWHORABLE CREETURE," Miss Laetitia Snap, from her "most passionate amirer, adwhorer, and slave." He notices that "spelling, or indeed any kind of human literature, hath never been thought a necessary ingredient" to "sublime greatness," and argues that, "if it should be observed that the style of this letter doth not exactly correspond with that of our hero's speeches which we have here recorded, we answer, it is sufficient if in these the historian adheres faithfully to the matter, though he embellishes the diction with some flourishes of his own eloquence" (pp. 115–16). Fielding brought the multiple, ungrammatical, variously colloquial, and jargon-laden voices of *The Beggar's Opera* into conformity with the rules of his own discourse. Gay's precarious assimilation of novelistic heteroglossia to drama had yielded a realm of ungoverned paradox that Fielding contained and reformed by mastering the authoritative resources implicit in narration.

Gay wielded total irony as an x-ray device to throw hidden motives and social affinities into descriptive relief. Fielding depicted total irony as a social condition, as an attitude personified in characters like the Count and, to a degree approaching the absurd, in Wild. Fielding considered personality as a compound of inborn traits and circumstance (including education). In the main, though with significant and increasing reservations, he thought love of the species—a benevolent instinct expressed through social bonds in general and romantic love in particular—indigenous to humankind as a whole if not to every single individual.[29] Wild is the extreme case, the exception that proves the rule. The odd seizures that overtake Wild's mother during her pregnancy indicate, ludicrously, that his will be a monstrous, unnatural birth:

> So did the mother of our great man, while she was of child with him, dream that she was enjoyed in the night by the gods Mercury and Priapus. . . . Another remarkable incident was, that during her whole pregnancy she constantly longed for everything she saw; nor could be satisfied with her wish unless she enjoyed it clandestinely [and] so had she at this time a most marvelous glutinous quality attending her fingers, to which, as to birdlime, everything closely adhered that she handled. (pp. 7–8)

By subjecting Wild to extreme ridicule, Fielding seeks to contain and correct the view, advanced by Hobbes and perpetuated by Mandeville, that the passion of self-love governs human nature. Human beings do not, on the whole, act like Wild. Intrinsically evil as "greatness" may be— that is, action on a pure principle of self-love—it is rare. In the words that close *Jonathan Wild*: "While it is in the power of every man to be perfectly honest, not one in a thousand is capable of being a complete rogue" (p. 207). The social bond governs even Wild's gang of criminals, a fact he ruthlessly exploits (e.g., pp. 138–43). The real harm lies, not in the aberrant emergence of a few truly great men, but in their glorification as ideals of human action. This idealization creates a pattern of emulation, a set of circumstances under which those of better nature, aspiring to greatness, believe they may be rewarded with wealth and high office by acting as if they were governed entirely by self-love. This is the sense in which I mean that Fielding depicted total irony as a social condition that required containment.

Because Fielding wanted to "rouse the civil power" over "mind," he had to distance himself from Gay's total irony by transforming it from a method into a subject matter. Since he believed that human beings in general, even if not every single individual, could be shaped by the collective rational faculty as set forth in legislation, his posture was fundamentally reformist even when certain of his views were not. Thus the idea in the preface to the *Miscellanies* of "a Judge in every Man's Breast" is not ironic with reference to humanity as a whole, although it is so with reference to Wild and with reference to the universalizing tendency of the "benevolists." For all his stress on good nature as a basic human trait, Fielding always gives prominence to the exceptions. On the other hand, while he assigns to individual rational judgment an ethical role that Hume's psychology denies, he joins the philosopher in accentuating the subjective bases of individual action. A passage from Hume's *Treatise of Human Nature* (1739–40), which Fielding's metaphor may glancingly parody, offers a sophisticated version of the benevolist position:

> Take any action allow'd to be vicious: Wilful murder, for instance. Examine it in all lights, and see if you can find that matter of fact, or real existence, which you call *vice*. In which-ever way you take it, you find only certain passions, motives, volitions, and thoughts. There is no other matter of fact in the case. The vice entirely escapes you as long as you consider the object. You never can find it, till you turn your reflexion into your own breast, and find a sentiment of disapprobation, which arises in you, towards this action. Here is a matter of fact; but 'tis the object of feeling, not of reason. It lies in yourself, not in the object. So that when you pronounce any action or character to be vicious, you mean nothing, but that from the constitution of your nature you have a feeling or sentiment of blame from the contemplation of it.[30]

Hume takes a much more extreme position than Fielding, but both consider that, whatever the exact place of reason in human affairs, it works primarily through conventional embodiments: collectively and externally through the legal, judicial, and moral institutions of society; personally and internally through conscience. In practice, then, Fielding ends up very close to Hume on the critical issue of the representational character of the interaction between judicial institutions and consciousness: "Those impressions, which give rise to [the] sense of justice, are not natural to the mind of man, but arise from artifice and human convention."[31] It remained for Adam Smith, in *The Theory of Moral Sentiments* (1759), to show precisely how those emotions of sympathy and disapprobation that Hume had described worked to create and maintain civilized behavior through the mechanism of the "impartial spectator"— the individual apparition of justice that represents public reason in every man's breast.[32]

Fielding everywhere declares himself the traditional Christian moralist. But while such a description accurately, if schematically, accounts for his articulate ideology, his practice greatly alters its meaning. The executive agent in his consideration of the struggle is no longer religion, which has become an instrument, but the state—"civil power" in its rational dimension—and the chief object of contention is no longer the soul, which has been left to religion in its mystical aspect, but the material "mind," the consciousness of Locke, Berkeley, and Hume. In terms of narrative representation, Christianity concerns itself with the choice between two archetypal romance stories: the life of Christ and the life of Satan. The liberal state, on the other hand, aspires to record as many stories as it has citizens or subjects; its mode is realism of the most extremely particularized kind.[33] The extended "time-space distanciation" that, for Anthony Giddens, characterizes large-scale social structures is sustained by and, in part, arises from the dense narrative categorizations required to protract authority through the "retention and control of information."[34] The state works to organize these stories categorically so that they will be comprehensible, that is, so that their subjects can be identified as controllable, storable resources. Significantly in this regard, Fielding recurs again and again to the waste of the labor value reposed in the common people and considers increased control by civil authorities as a way to recover wealth.[35]

· III ·

Fielding's novels record a struggle for control of narrative resources that is characteristic of early metropolitan society in London, and his juridical practice illustrates his practical intuition that power resides in the mastery and disposition of densely particularized narrative. As the following chapter will show in more detail, schemes to exercise authority through written instruments lie at the heart of Fielding's program as a justice of the peace, as founder of a police force, as inventor of newspaper advertising schemes that appropriated and extended the methods of thief-takers like the historical Wild, as projector of legislation, and as proponent of reformative correction contained within the legally exacting regime and the materially circumstantial architecture of his own ideal city—the Middlesex County House.

It is worth digressing here to recall that control of narrative resources is also of extreme concern in Richardson's novels of the 1740s. They depict the tools of writing as weapons. In them the composition, conveyance, concealment, and collection of letters, as well as every other imaginable manipulation of written documents (including forgery, itself a capital crime), become primary means of exercising power in the fictional present and of storing up future authority. Journals and collections of letters are envisioned as the ultimate, authoritative transcriptions of temporarily incommunicable experience; and in the extreme case of Clarissa's will, the actions of others are rigidly determined through a legal document requiring execution beyond the lifetime of its author. As Margaret Doody indicates, the mode of discourse in *Pamela* is revolutionary by its very nature: "It is not just the occasional phrase which gives the reader . . . contact with revolt, with the questioning of hierarchy. The novel itself lacks (ostensibly) the controlling, authoritative and soothing presence of the monarchical author."[36] *Clarissa* may, again, illustrate the point that in novels, as often in politics, the content of the narrative is not so much at issue as the exercise of control itself.

Usually in novels the struggle over the power to tell the story—to shape consciousness—unfolds thematically in terms of the narrational metaphor of *Bildung*, that is, as a contention over who will determine the growth, education, inheritance, or marriage of the central character. Richardson restages primal social conflicts within the scene of writing by initially granting all characters the implements of written narration. Paradoxically, however, Richardson's most authoritative figures (like the author himself and like Clarissa's "father" in the double sense she so insists upon of her biological father and God the Father) mainly hover outside the arena of direct conflict—vestiges of the divine authority that speaks what others write down but that, because of its aloofness, is subject now to misprision. Within Richardson's epistolary fictions, the ability to reform the characters of others and thus to resolve the plot—comically in Pamela's case, tragically in Clarissa's—lies with the one who possesses the fullest range of narrative powers. The tragic outcome of *Clarissa* is determined in part because Lovelace's strengths are nearly equal to the heroine's. In Fielding's mature novels, the resources to conduct this struggle are allocated by and contained within the authority of a narrator with exceptional powers of inquiry, adjudication, and sympathy.

Jonathan Wild recasts the romance of traditional Christian psychomachia between good and evil into a contention among abeyant narrators personified as characters. Fielding arranges the mortal struggle at the core of *Jonathan Wild*, the moral warfare between Wild and Heartfree, as a combat between variant novelistic accounts of material circumstance. The quest for the most natural, historically truthful narrative becomes a test of moral consciousness, and the narrator holds himself accountable by this standard:

> Here the reader must excuse us, who profess to draw natural, not perfect characters, and to record the truths of history, not the extravagances of romance, while we relate a weakness in Wild of which we are ourselves ashamed, and which we would willingly have concealed, could we have preserved at the same time that strict attachment to truth and impartiality which we have professed in recording the annals of this great man. (p. 157)

Willful distortions, the extravagances of romance, the machinations of unbridled self-interest—all corrupt and destroy the social bond.

Wild begins his assault on his old school friend, the merchant Heartfree, with an elaborate imposture in which the Count gives a false instrument in exchange for a suite of jewels Heartfree has obtained on credit. Wild, having set his gang to rob the jeweler of the cash down payment as well, assures Heartfree's arrest for debt and, while the ruined man languishes in the Fleet, uses another story to trick his wife into eloping to Holland with the family's remaining assets. Upon his return from the voyage, Wild founds an inveterate hatred of Heartfree upon fear that the good merchant will seek revenge, illustrating a principle basic to the understanding of true "greatness": "Never trust the man who hath reason to suspect that you know he hath injured you" (p. 108; originally all in capitals).

Wild's venture at luring Heartfree to destruction by proposing a prison break that might involve "a murder or two" marks the turning point. The moment is couched in terms specific to forensic narrative such as "evidence," "circumstance," and "fiction":

> Heartfree was unwilling to condemn his friend without certain evidence . . . but the proposal made at his last visit had so totally blackened his character in this poor man's opinion, that it entirely fixed the wavering scale, and he no longer doubted but that our hero was one of the greatest villains in the world.

Circumstances of great improbability often escape men who devour a story with greedy ears; the reader, therefore, cannot wonder that Heartfree, whose passions were so variously concerned . . . should at this relation pass unobserved the incident of [Wild's] being committed to the boat by the captain of the privateer, which he had at the time of his telling so lamely accounted for; but now, when Heartfree came to reflect on the whole . . . the absurdity of this fact glared in his eyes and struck him in the most sensible manner. At length a thought of great horror suggested itself to his imagination, and this was, whether the whole was not a fiction. (p. 125)

A war of warrants ensues during which Wild enforces his (false) narration of reality by using the official instruments of law as weapons. Heartfree actually makes the first move, but he lacks Wild's finesse in the language of writs and the proceedings of justice. Doubts are "raised by Mr. Wild's lawyer on his examination, he insisting that the proceeding was improper, for that a *writ de homine replegiando* should issue, and on the return of that a *capias in withernam*" (p. 129). When the justice inclines to committal anyway, Wild improvisationally supplements his original narrative by recalling (i.e., inventing) a companion on the voyage. This turns out to be Fireblood, a member of the gang whose perjured testimony prevails for all that "he was forced to collect his evidence from the hints given him by Wild in the presence of the justice and the accusers" (p. 129).

In due course, Wild retaliates with "a scheme so deeply laid, that it shames all the politics of this our age." Wild founds his counterfiction on the fact of Mrs. Heartfree's disappearance:

A scheme arose in his imagination which not only promised to effect [Heartfree's ruin] securely, but (which pleased him most) by means of the mischief he had already done him; and which would at once load him with the imputation of having committed what he himself had done to him, and would bring on him the severest punishment for a fact of which he was not only innocent, but had already so greatly suffered by. And this was no other than to charge him with having conveyed away his wife, with his most valuable effects, in order to defraud his creditors. (pp. 130–31)

Indictment follows and the court, convinced by Fireblood's perjury and on confirmation by Wild, "who counterfeited the most artful reluctance at appearing against his old friend," condemns Heartfree to death for capital fraud (p. 146). Fortune meanwhile plots independently to cause Wild and Heartfree to converge upon the ultimate scene of greatness, Newgate. Wild's definitive arrest caps a chain of events begun when the great hero, upon leaving Heartfree's trial, is stabbed by Blueskin, a former gang member impeached by Wild for insubordination:

> The knife, missing those noble parts (the noblest of many), the guts, perforated only the hollow of his belly, and caused no other harm than an immoderate effusion of blood. . . . This accident, however, was in the end attended with worse consequences: for as very few people . . . attempt to cut the thread of human life . . . merely out of wantonness and for their diversion, but rather by so doing propose to themselves the acquisition of some future good, or the avenging some past evil; and as the former of these motives did not appear probable, it put inquisitive persons on examining into the latter. Now, as the vast schemes of Wild, when they were discovered . . . seemed to some persons . . . rather to be calculated for the glory of the great man himself than to redound to the general good of society, designs began to be laid by several of those who thought it principally their duty to put a stop to the future progress of our hero; and a learned judge particularly, a great enemy to this kind of greatness, procured a clause in an act of parliament as a trap for Wild, which he soon after fell into. By this law it was made capital in a prig to steal with the hands of other people. (pp. 147–48)

Narrative cause and effect are clearly at issue here. The only plausible stories all work against Wild; every one that accounts for Blueskin's action also points to Wild's criminality. Fielding strengthens the causal force by greatly condensing the long interval between the passage of legislation against the historical Wild (4 Geo. 1, c. 11 [1717]) and his ultimate arrest on the statute in 1725. The act made it a capital felony to take a "Reward, directly or indirectly, under Pretence or upon Account of helping any Person or Persons to any stolen Goods."[37] Fielding also simplifies and clarifies the contention that existed historically among competing accounts of Wild's thief-taking. The actual reason for the delay between the enactment of the bill and Wild's fall was probably that for some while many people considered him a servant of the public interest because he arranged smoothly for the return of stolen goods and brought so many highwaymen and robbers to justice.[38]

Viewed as a force for good, the historical Wild was high commissioner of the police force London officially lacked. When Fielding the magistrate sought to meet this need, his methods, as we shall see, bore striking resemblances to Wild's. Wild crystallized for Fielding the insight that the authoritative resources of the metropolis might be "roused" selfishly for the private gain of criminals and great statesmen or magnanimously for the public benefit through abstracted "mind"—that is, through "all the power of laws and government." In the one he saw a tyranny of self-interest, in the other a liberty of reasoned benevolence. The activities of Wild and his kind showed that the resources would not go unclaimed.

Wild's scheme against Heartfree unravels when the "good magistrate" (named only in this way), who heard the successful prosecution for fraud but who "examined always with the utmost diligence and caution into every minute circumstance" (p. 163), notes that persuasive evidence for the allegation no longer exists because the only two witnesses, Wild and Fireblood, have since found their way to Newgate. This magistrate dedicates himself to constructing the true story of which Wild's "warrants," "writs," "evidences," and "informations" are false representations. Mrs. Heartfree's chronicle of her voyage completes the true account begun by the magistrate, fully cancels the indictment for fraud that might potentially be brought against her, and, because "the good magistrate was sensibly touched at her narrative," gains the promise of an "absolute pardon" for her husband (p. 188). This is why her protracted story needs to be heard by the magistrate, whose presence seems awkward when considered in other lights.

The narrator presents these stories by the good magistrate and Mrs. Heartfree as true "natural" discoveries, persuasive "historical" accounts that validate Heartfree's reprieve, which they follow sequentially in the novel, and that are supposed to distinguish the ending of this work from the implausible turn at the finish of *The Beggar's Opera*. For Fielding, the powerfully conjoined "rules of writing and probability" govern equally the novel and society itself:

> Lest our reprieve should seem to resemble that in the Beggars' Opera, I shall endeavor to show [the good-natured reader] that this incident, which is undoubtedly true, is at least as natural as delightful; for we assure him we would rather have suffered half mankind to be hanged than have saved one contrary to the strictest rules of writing and probability. (p. 163)

But the reprieve and the pardon also validate these narratives by giving them forensic standing; perhaps for this same reason Fielding specifically provides material evidence by arranging for Mrs. Heartfree to recover the original jewels of which Wild and the Count had robbed her husband, and by having an African chief bestow upon her a diamond of "immense value." The ability to give a satisfactory forensic account of oneself is to be recognized as a citizen at liberty; not to possess a story, to be without narrative resources, is to lack a comprehensible character within the metropolitan order and to be subject to a reformation of consciousness.

Why is Fielding so determined to separate himself from Gay in this respect? *The Beggar's Opera* displays the contradictions of liminal justice as a series of unresolvable paradoxes that suspend the conventional operations of plot. An arbitrary ending becomes bizarrely correct. But from Fielding's perspective in the 1740s, the cost at which *The Beggar's Opera* maintains its equipoise is a cynicism that seems as unacceptably capricious as liminality itself. Therefore, although Fielding repeats Gay's strategy of turning Wild's operation (headquartered first at Mr. Snap's sponging house and then at Newgate itself) into a representation of English government and society, he anchors the metaphor, as Gay does not, within a range of expository statements concerning political theory.

The role of government in society is debated on several occasions in Wild's gang and at Newgate. Wild consistently adopts Hobbesian positions. Dividing booty with Bagshot, he argues in contrast to Locke that labor does not confer proprietary rights: "The ploughman, the shepherd, the weaver, the builder, and the soldier work not for themselves but others; they are contented with a poor pittance (the laborer's hire), and permit us, the GREAT, to enjoy the fruit of their labors. Aristotle . . . hath plainly proved . . . that the low, mean, useful part of mankind, are born slaves to the will of their superiors" (p. 26). Later, in the climactic dispute with Blueskin, Wild demands a stolen watch: "I will undertake . . . to show I have an absolute right to it, and that by the laws of our gang, of which I am providentially at the head." But Blueskin objects that the gang put Wild in power to "contribute to their benefit and safety; and not to convert all their labor and hazard to [his] benefit and advantage" (p. 139). In Wild's reply the Hobbesian/Lockean debate hovers under a tissue-thin fiction:

> You are talking of a legal society, where the chief magistrate is always chosen for the public good, which, as we see in all the legal societies of the world, he constantly consults, daily contributing, by his superior skill, to their prosperity, and not sacrificing their good to his own wealth, or pleasure, or humor: but in an illegal society or gang, as this of ours, it is otherwise; for who would be at the head of a gang, unless for his own interest? And without a head, you know, you cannot subsist. Nothing but a head, and obedience to that head, can preserve a gang a moment from destruction. (pp. 139–40)

Fielding drives hard toward the conclusion that an alternative exists to the "illegal society" represented by Wild's gang and by Walpole's government. The term "illegal society," like Fielding's later account of English social history in the preface to *An Enquiry Into the Causes of the Late Increase of Robbers*, suggests that the London of his day had actually regressed to the siege mentality (whether of Hobbes's warfare or Locke's precarious peace) that immediately preceded the social contract. Defoe elucidated this historic moment in *Jure Divino*:

But *as* to wider Regions Nations spread,
And weaker Numbers made the Great their Head,
Eternal Feuds the Petty Lords invade,
To *Lust and Crime*, by *Lust and Crime* betray'd;
Necessity Confederate Heads Directs,
And Power United, Power Expos'd Protects;
The Nature of the Thing directs the *Mode*,
And Government was born in *Publick Good*:
Safety with *Right* and *Property* combines,
And thus *Necessity* and Nature *joins*.[39]

Fielding wants government to retrace within the boundless sprawl of contemporary life epitomized by modern London that original institution of state authority described by Defoe.

Once Wild arrives in Newgate, Fielding's political allegory makes it clear that party preference is not the issue. Wild, who suddenly stands for Walpole's successor (the earl of Wilmington), and Johnson (temporarily the Walpole figure) struggle for the position of "head of all the *prigs* in Newgate."[40] Johnson's office, like Wild's leadership of his gang, specifically involves governance through the manipulation of narrative resources: "He examined into the nature of [the prigs'] defense, procured and instructed their evidence, and made himself, at least in their opinion, so necessary to them, that the whole fate of Newgate seemed entirely to depend upon him" (p. 152). Wild extravagantly proclaims that Johnson is undermining "THE LIBERTIES OF NEWGATE" (p. 152). But high language merely disguises a clash over which prigs will control the debtors (citizens), "who were the destined plunder of both parties," since "*liberties* . . . in the cant language, signifies *plunder*" (p. 154). Once Wild prevails and his self-interested purposes become clear to all, "a very grave man, and one of much authority" among the debtors couches an appeal in terms closely akin to those in which Locke defines the liberal state:

> Every *prig* is a slave. His own *priggish* desires, which enslave him, themselves betray him to the tyranny of others. To preserve, therefore, the liberty of Newgate, is to change the manners of Newgate. . . . Instead of being ready, on every opportunity, to pillage each other, let us be content with our honest share of the common bounty, and with the acquisition of our own industry. . . . Let us consider ourselves all as members of one community, to the public good of which we are to sacrifice our private views. . . . While one man pursues his ambition, another his interest, another his safety; while one hath a roguery . . . to commit, and another a roguery to defend; they must naturally fly to the favor and protection of those who have power to give them what they desire, and to defend them from what they fear; nay, in

this view it becomes their interest to promote this power in their patrons. . . . What remains therefore for us but to resolve bravely to lay aside our *priggism*, our roguery in plainer words, and preserve our liberty, or to give up the latter in the preservation and preference of the former? (pp. 155–56)

The narrator immediately shrugs off this utopian alternative as lip service. Yet Fielding broaches the possibility of social change and, though blunted by irony, the edge of his fiction cuts toward reform. He considers that the status quo of Walpole's "illegal society" prevails not, as *The Beggar's Opera* implies, because of ungovernable paradoxes in human nature but because of social choice.

In 1754, when Fielding revised *Jonathan Wild* at the close of his judicial career, a brief "Advertisement from the Publisher to the Reader" retained the allusion to Gay that had set the tone of the *Wild* section in his 1743 preface to the *Miscellanies*. Now rejecting the attempts of some readers to make "personal application" by deciphering the work allegorically, he declares:

The truth is, as a very corrupt state of morals is here represented, the scene seems very properly to have been laid in Newgate; nor do I see any reason for introducing any allegory at all; unless we will agree that there are without those walls, some other bodies of men of worse morals than those within; and who have, consequently, a right to change places with its present inhabitants. (p. xv)

This strongly affirms the realism of the work—the appropriateness of its Newgate setting—while urging the necessity of reading it as a general satire, not against individuals, but against "bodies of men." The thought is much less involuted than in the 1743 preface and, more important, the end of Fielding's 1754 advertisement points to the speech about "priggism" just quoted above. He singles out the most specifically reformist passage in the novel: "To such persons, if any such there be, I would particularly recommend the perusal of the third chapter of the fourth book of the following history, and more particularly still the speech of the grave man" (p. xv). Fielding removes, or at least sharply qualifies, the possibility of treating the passage ironically, and guides us to read it instead as presenting an alternative to the present "illegal society" of England. By pushing the expository dimension of *Jonathan Wild* into the foreground and attributing extraordinary authority to one segment, he relocates the novel within the reformist enterprise that dominates *Amelia* and intertwines his every activity from 1749 to the last year of his life.

*Then as the only Purposes of Punishments less than capital,
are to reform the Offenders themselves and warn the Innocent by their
Example, everything which should contribute to make this Kind of
Punishment answer these Purposes better than it does, would be a great
Improvement. And whether it be not a thing practicable, and what
would contribute somewhat towards it, to exclude utterly all sorts
of Revel-mirth from Places where Offenders are confined, to separate
the Young from the Old, and force them Both, in Solitude, with Labour
and low Diet, to make the Experiment, how far their natural Strength
of Mind can support them under Guilt and Shame and Poverty;
this may deserve Consideration. Then again, some Religious Instruction
particularly adapted to their Condition, would as properly accompany
those Punishments which are intended to Reform, as it
does capital ones.
[Therefore] it cannot but be even more incumbent on us, to endeavour
in all Ways, to reclaim those Offenders, who are to return again
into the World, than those who are to be removed out of it: and the only
effectual Means of Reclaiming them, is to instil
into them a Principle of Religion.*

BISHOP JOSEPH BUTLER

*A Sermon Preached Before the Right Hon. the
Lord Mayor, the Court of Aldermen, the Sheriffs,
and the Governors of the Several Hospitals
of the City of London . . . Monday in
Easter-Week, 1740*

6

Fielding and the Juridical Novel

The first publication of *Jonathan Wild* predates the formal inauguration of Fielding's magistracy by more than five years. Yet his fictionalized history of Wild's life as a struggle to master narrative resources entirely complements his actual experimentation, as a justice of the peace, with methods to increase the number of viable indictments by improving the interception of evidence and suspects. In a certain particular sense, these usages are one and the same, for over and over again in his novels, as in his activities in Bow Street, the issue is who will have final control over narrative construction; the difference is that fiction can realize the fantasy of omniscient authority. The very potential for this congruent representation of Fielding's concerns in such divergent spheres attests to the remarkable convergence between novelistic discourse and reformist practice at mid-century. This convergence is traceable during Fielding's later career in the ideologically profound relationship between technical moves toward increased transparency of narration in his novels and juridical innovations in his Bow Street practice. These changes participate, by correspondence, in larger, slower patterns of alteration in legal procedure that were affecting the daily labor of magistrates.

The old civic order had been lodged in personal operators—the actors in Thompson's theater of cultural hegemony—who directly controlled the available narrative resources and improvised freely within the social framework they embodied. These actors were physically demonstrative, vocally present, and in the main ungoverned by the law they enforced (see chapter 1). By contrast, the constitutive impersonality of written rules, regulations, and procedures—printed coordinates, advertising, and systematic reporting and dispatch—shaped the emergent order that took representational form during Fielding's later career. The active, inquiring judge traditional on the English bench was increasingly transmuted during the last half of the eighteenth century into the rule-bound, traffic-conducting authority familiar in modern courtrooms. "Hue and cry" in pursuit of criminals gave way—along with its tendencies to forgetfulness and error—to the dissemination of stable, written information in the *Police Gazette* and to penetration of the metropolis by investigators like the Bow Street Runners. Fielding amplified control over the metropolis by finding ways to coordinate the movements of witnesses with individual criminals; ways to centralize the storage and cross-referencing of information; ways to exploit newspapers to extract and disseminate particulars of circumstance and physical description; ways to found written indictments, which were indispensable to criminal prosecution, upon probable sequences of cause and effect that had been closely correlated with material particulars. Concurrently, he took steps in *Amelia* toward the placement of individual subjectivity within the impersonal, all-embracing medium of transparent narration ordinarily associated with later realist fiction. *Amelia,* in contrast with Fielding's previous novels, employs a comparatively unobtrusive narrator who maintains pervasive control while delegating the appearance of omniscience to a character within the story—the benevolent Dr. Harrison. Fielding discovered a way to represent impersonal authority as subjectively immanent in personality.

Jonathan Wild, viewed as a struggle between civil and criminal power, helps us to grasp why Fielding's actual magistracy so strikingly reinscribed Wild's reign as "Thief-Taker General." Through his adoption of many of the "great man's" methods, Fielding the magistrate became a veritable reincarnation of the historical Wild as mediated through his own fiction. His response to competition with the metropolitan underground worked to reshape the traditional judicial postures he cherished and idealized. Contemporaneously, his narrative technique underwent changes that anticipate the later absorption of obtrusive omniscience into the realist convention of transparency, a convention that I associate with impersonal supervision in the penitentiary. Once discovered in the criminal underworld and in the heteroglossic realm of popular fiction, the organizational power of realist narrative—its dense particularity, its rules of cause and effect, its mastery of consciousness—had to be harnessed by authority. Realism can be fruitfully regarded as a network of technical innovations that, by increasing the representational power of narrative, brought about the necessity to command its means.

· I ·

Some facts about law enforcement and court proceedings in mid-eighteenth-century London are necessary to illuminate the nature of Fielding's work as justice of the peace and to disclose its significance in the present context. The basic framework within which the administration of order took place had been regularized in statutes dating from the reign of Queen Mary. The pivotal officials in this system were territorial justices of the peace appointed from among the local gentry by royal commission. Their duties included the examination of suspects and witnesses upon arrest, the transcription of resulting testimony, and the certification of these evidentiary records to the trial court in the form of written indictments (fig. 50). The lord mayor traditionally discharged these responsibilities in the City of London, but in 1737 a scheme was instituted to rotate the case load among "sitting aldermen." Alderman Goodchild in plate 10 of Hogarth's *Industry and Idleness* acts in precisely such a capacity (fig. 43). Both aldermen and justices of the peace, in sharp contrast to their present-day counterparts, were investigative officers with citizen constables at their command. In cases of serious crime, they served the criminal courts in a fashion that combined the roles of modern pretrial hearing-officers with those of detectives and police.[1]

During most of the eighteenth century, the idea of a professional police force continued to be as foreign as the French word itself, which retained the old meanings of "policy" and "civil government" right through the period. Fielding's half-brother John, who took up as justice in Bow Street in 1754, appears to have been the first writer regularly to use the word "police" in its modern sense, without self-conscious reference to its association with the enforcement of absolutism. Before there were police, a night watch guarded the streets while citizen constables kept the peace, sought out accused criminals, made arrests, and carried the malefactors before justices. Those who had been tapped for constabulary duty (in a manner akin to H.F.'s appointment as an examiner for his parish in *A Journal of the Plague Year*) might serve, pay a fine, or hire a substitute. What semblance of professionalism in law enforcement that existed in eighteenth-century London arose because a continuing core of substitutes was engaged by different appointees in successive terms. But the constables, no less than the beadles, watchmen, messengers, marshals, and sheriffs who discharged the duties of enforcement for various civil entities in different quarters, were seriously hampered by

Dodd delin   Taylor sculp

View of the **PUBLIC OFFICE** Bow Street, with Sir John Fielding presiding, & a Prisoner under examination

50. *A View of the Public Office Bow Street with Sir John Fielding Presiding & a Prisoner under Examination.* The Fieldings' court became famous enough to attract fashionable visitors and to evoke a plate in the *Newgate Calendar.*

the multiplicity of boundaries and jurisdictions in London. The watch as Fielding described it in *Amelia* epitomized the ineffectiveness of the whole higgledy-piggledy contrivance:

> I have often considered some of the lower officers in our civil government to be disposed [ridiculously]. To begin, I think, as low as I well can, with the watchmen in our metropolis, who, being to guard our streets by night from thieves and robbers, an office which at least requires strength of body, are chosen out of those poor old decrepit people who are, from their want of bodily strength, rendered incapable of getting a livelihood by work. These men, armed only with a pole, which some of them are scarce able to lift, are to secure the persons and houses of his majesty's subjects from the attacks of gangs of young, bold, stout, desperate, and well-armed villains.[2]

This picture of the watch exaggerates unfairly. Nonetheless, conditions were such that neighborhoods often organized private watch associations, some of which gained authority through local acts of Parliament. Fielding significantly altered the situation in his own district, and his moves toward centralization strengthened law enforcement in the metropolis as a whole. In part because his half-brother dedicatedly pursued the implications of his ideas for more than twenty-five years, Fielding is usually considered the father of the English police.[3]

The Sessions, which the central criminal courts held to try felonies and other serious crimes eight times yearly in the Old Bailey (immediately down the street from Newgate), differed greatly from modern proceedings on the same site. Neither methodical standards of proof nor rules designed to protect the jury from questionable evidence governed ordinary criminal procedure. For this and a variety of other reasons, trials were swift, verdicts swifter. Justices of the peace shaped cases for the courts during pretrial hearings, where frivolous charges were screened out and testimony was reduced to writing while it was fresh. Juries acted with dispatch because they gained experience by hearing numerous cases at a single Sessions and because many of the same jurors were impaneled repeatedly. Prior to the 1730s, defense lawyers could not appear in ordinary courts and, even then, could not address the jury. Counsel for the prosecution, though admitted, in practice did not appear in regular trials. For decades after lawyers entered the scene, most prosecutions were brought by injured parties, while most defendants spoke for themselves, examining and cross-examining witnesses, addressing the court, and offering summations. The principals did not go unassisted, however, for judges, untrammeled by rules, freely inquired, cajoled, and instructed. Besides taking many of the parts now assigned to lawyers, judges directed juries with a heavy hand—guiding them, returning them for further deliberation, refusing to accept verdicts, even threatening them with contempt.[4]

· II ·

The language that John Fielding used in 1761 to explain the system devised by Henry for reporting and investigating crime tersely recalls the practices of the historical Jonathan Wild and anticipates the fantasy of omniscience in Bentham's *Panopticon.* Bentham would reconceive prison as an artificially compartmentalized metropolis in total view of a single centralized watchtower from which each inhabitant was to imagine himself under perpetual inspection. John Fielding similarly described London itself as subject to official omniscience: "By bringing all Informations of Fraud and Felony into one Point, keeping a Register of Offenders, making quick Pursuits, [and] opening a general Correspondence with all the active Magistrates in the Country, Escapes are rendered difficult, and Discoveries easy."[5] This vision eliminates every trace of that oblivion always implicit in "hue and cry": the fleeting moments during which virtually all convicted felons once had been apprehended, immediately following their crimes, were extended into hours, days, and weeks when the police began to retain and circulate information. As early as 17 October 1754, not even two weeks after his brother's death, John Fielding was running a notice that fully outlined the scheme for readers of the *Public Advertiser:*

> *Whereas* many Thieves and Robbers daily escape Justice for want of immediate Pursuit; it is therefore recommended to all Persons, who shall henceforth be robbed on the Highway or in the Streets, or whose Shops or Houses shall be broke open, that they give immediate Notice thereof, together with as accurate a Description of the Offenders as possible, to *John Fielding,* Esq.; at his house in Bow Street, Covent Garden: By which means, joined to an Advertisement, containing an account of the Things lost (which is also taken in there) Thieves and Robbers will seldom escape; as most of the pawnbrokers take in this Paper, and by the intelligence they get from it assist daily in discovering and apprehending Rogues. And if they would send a Special Messenger on these Occasions, Mr. Fielding would not only pay that Messenger for his Trouble, but would immediately despatch a Set of brave Fellows in Pursuit, who have been long engaged for such Purposes, and are always ready to set out to any Part of this town or kingdom, on a Quarter of an Hour's Notice. It is to be hoped, that the late Success of this Plan will make all Persons for the future industrious to give the earliest Notice possible of all Robberies and Robbers whatever.[6]

As Langbein points out, this advertisement shows how Henry Fielding's specific measures formed a coherent network when centralized under the supervision of an examining magistrate charged with shaping indictments that would sustain the prosecution's case in trial at the Old Bailey. The Bow Street office served as a control point for reporting crime and maintaining an inventory of stolen goods. Newspapers that Fielding operated—first the *Covent Garden Journal*, later the *Public Advertiser*—rapidly spread this information through the metropolis and, most particularly, allowed cooperating pawnbrokers to identify stolen goods and collect legitimate rewards in lieu of profits they might have gained through dubious traffic. Finally, a standing police force (the "Set of brave Fellows" who came to be known as Bow Street Runners) stood ready to serve as the forcible arm of the magistrate's authority.

The brief notice used in the *Covent Garden Journal* specified quite precisely its demand for that exact detail expected both in legal documents like affidavits and depositions and in the realist novel: "To the Public—All Persons who shall for the Future suffer by Robbers, Burglars, etc. are desired immediately to bring, or send, the best Description they can of such Robbers, etc. with the Time and Place, and Circumstances of the Fact, to Henry Fielding, Esq., at his House in Bow Street."[7] The emphasis on time and place recurs in every description and advertisement: these are the crucial coordinates within which details of circumstance and material fact must be located in order to be centrally stored, sorted, and cross-referenced for use on real London streets, and also to yield convincing accounts at the Old Bailey. The aim was to match casual arrests against details on crimes and stolen goods and to coordinate both with information gained from confessions by crown witnesses who, like Fireblood at the end of *Jonathan Wild*, turned state's evidence against accomplices in order to protect themselves from prosecution and to collect rewards.[8] The same purpose guided Fielding when he advertised for the public to witness the questioning of suspects in Bow Street so that "if they should know them to give evidence against them," and when he kept an orderly and clerk on duty at all times "to keep an exact Register of all Robberies committed; Descriptions of all Goods lost; the Names and Descriptions of all Persons brought before the said Magistrate who stand accused either of Fraud or Felony, or suspected of either; of the Houses that harbour them and receive their stolen Goods."[9] Fielding systematized and stored up in writing records of the fragile kind that, in *Jonathan Wild*, exist uniquely in the memory of the good magistrate, who alone possesses all of the means necessary to unravel Wild's plot against Heartfree. He extended and reinforced the possibility of judicial inference, projected in the narrative form of indictment. Concurrently, he devised a remarkably exacting fictional chronology for *Amelia* and disposed the novel's action in a London that represented metropolitan geography with unprecedented specificity.[10]

Wild invented neither organized crime nor its syndication under the guise of law enforcement, but he probably was the first to establish open premises from which to conduct these activities as businesses and was the first private (i.e., non-officeholding) thief-taker to erect a public persona as servant of the state.[11] Certainly for these reasons he became the most notorious criminal of his age. While posing as a disinterested benefactor, he set himself up as a wholesale broker arranging the return of property that had been stolen with a specific view to collecting ransoms from owners who would answer his advertisements in newspapers or themselves publish notices for restitution.[12] Wild's closely interlocking and even more famous business as "Thief-Taker General" at once enforced discipline in the gangs that performed his robberies and burglaries, provided him with a handsome income from government rewards, and, again, allowed him to appear as a servant of the public interest. We see Wild the thief-taker at work in Fielding's novel when he impeaches Blueskin for refusing to surrender a stolen watch. Historically, Wild certainly would have gained the government's standard head money of forty pounds for turning over a robber, and probably would have received a reward from the watch's owner for its recovery. The capture of notorious criminals could bring further official rewards.[13] In the process, of course, he eliminated the competition and strengthened his sway over the surviving thieves. Wild cleared the metropolis of four large underworld gangs between 1721 and 1723, virtually preventing activity by highwaymen from then until his execution.[14] At Wild's trial in 1725, he distributed a printed listing of some seventy-five criminals he had "discovered, apprehended and convicted," of whom sixty-seven had been hanged and the balance transported.[15]

As Gerald Howson observes, Fielding's "Bow Street Runners were modelled to some extent on [Wild's] posse of thief-takers."[16] Highwaymen referred to the "runners" as "Fielding's gang," who never fully escaped the taint that hung about thief-taking.[17] The similarity of Fielding's "gang" to Wild's, though striking, in fact merely begins the story, for a survey of Wild's methods also reveals that the notion of a clearing house lay at the heart of his system. His network for the retrieval of stolen goods depended heavily upon written records and upon the dissemination of information through newspapers. Wild's "Lost Property Office," like the Fieldings' Bow Street premises, had the marks of a bureaucratic repository. He kept a register noting the exact details on every robbery reported. When these did not tally against the accounts of his thieves, Wild knew them to be holding out on him or employing other receivers; when they did tally, he placed a cross by the thief's name showing that ready testimony was available when the time came to purge him from the gang by impeaching him for the forty-pound reward. It is said that our expression "double-cross" originated in cant language because Wild added a second cross to the register when his victim had swung at Tyburn.[18] Howson declares that the warrant of detainer issued against Wild by the city recorder constituted London's "first official recognition of a system of crime, and for that matter crime-prevention, that had been progressively refined for a century and a half."[19] The warrant's eleven sections summarized the devices by which Wild played his role as mock governor of the metropolis. Two sections find special relevance here:

> III. That he divided the Town and Country into so many Districts, and appointed distinct Gangs for each, who regularly accounted with him for their Robberies. . . .

> VII. That, in order to carry on these vile Practices, to gain some Credit with the ignorant Multitude, he usually carried a short Silver Staff, as a Badge of Authority from the Government, which he used to produce, when he himself was concern'd in robbing.[20]

To one whose aspirations would turn like Fielding's to rouse the civil power, the warrant could epitomize both the strength of the enemy and the means to its defeat.

This warrant can hardly have been unknown to Fielding given its widespread distribution in accounts of Wild's life and his ownership of *Select Trials at the Sessions House in the Old Bailey,* which reprinted it.[21] But whatever specific sources lay in the background, Wild's history formed the vehicle around which Fielding's imagination crystallized his juridical practice—first as a struggle for narrative control in the novel *Jonathan Wild,* then as a reinscription of the historical Wild's system in Bow Street. On this basis he apprehended the contention between organized crime and civil power as a trial of jurisdiction over evidentiary and narrative resources. He depicted himself, with apparent justification, as locked in struggle against a criminal order that magnified its threat to the public by means of central organization. Without doubt, Fielding's pleas for governmental funds to support his activities were most successful in face of gang threats—the aspect of law enforcement on which he spent the most effort. The issue for Fielding was who would control the means of order that, both in his novels and in the exercise of judicial office, he represented as the means of narration. The outcome of this contention would be the deployment of narrative as an authoritative resource in law enforcement. The penitentiary regime, in particular, continually rehearses civil power as narrative structure.

· III ·

Alterations in criminal trial procedure that occurred during Fielding's career led to epoch-making developments in the law of evidence and the law of proof. This transformation was part of a turn toward increasingly systematic narrative representation of civil power throughout the legal sphere. Several things were happening together, with substantial interpenetration of emergent and residual forms, but as Langbein says, hindsight allows us to ponder outcomes that were unforeseen in the mid-eighteenth century.[22] Further consideration of changes in the eighteenth-century criminal trial can shed light on the situation of judgmental authority in the novel and on narrative representation in the penitentiary. The forms eventually taken by juridical authority in the realist novel, the courtroom, and the penitentiary have marked affinities.

In his pseudo-official role as impeaching officer, Wild represented the underworld analogue to the indicting justice of the peace. Both constructed narratives, based upon "circumstances of the fact," for use as evidence in trials at the Old Bailey. Fielding's novelistic Wild goes one better when he mounts the assault to dislodge Johnson, the chief prig of Newgate, who, in discharging his office as shadow counsel to the prisoners, heretofore has "examined into the nature of their defense, procured and instructed their evidence, and made himself, at least in their opinion, so necessary . . . that the whole fate of Newgate seemed entirely to depend upon him" (p. 152). Wild successfully dislodges Johnson by attacking him for dealing merely in unassimilated fact, that is, for failing to fabricate the kind of densely specified realistic fiction—the alibi—that may be effectively substituted for factual evidence.

> One man . . . hath engrossed to himself the whole conduct of your trials, under color of which he exacts what contributions on you he pleases: but are those sums appropriated to the uses for which they are raised? Your frequent convictions at the Old Bailey, those depredations of justice, must too sensibly and sorely demonstrate the contrary. What evidence doth he ever produce for the prisoners which the prisoner himself could not have provided, and often better instructed? How many noble youths have there been lost when a single *alibi* would have saved them! (pp. 152–53)

A fully elaborated alibi is the inverse image of an indictment, a story brought to court at the Old Bailey in order to counter or cancel a justice of the peace's narrative reduction of evidence to writing. Wild will replace reality with realistic fiction.

Johnson's duties mimic those of counsel for the defense, a figure who, by the time of Fielding's legal career, was beginning to reshape the struggle to control narration in the specialized context of the criminal trial. By the 1730s, as Langbein has shown, counsel for the defense were admitted at the Old Bailey.[23] Prior to this "the prosecuting victim, the accused, and the witnesses would be 'examined' and 'cross-examined' by the presiding judge, as well as by one another, in a relatively conversational way."[24] The introduction of counsel marked the beginning of a process in which casual modes of narrative construction that long had marked the English criminal trial—which Sir Thomas Smith once called an "altercation"—were gradually supplanted by the elaborated rules of evidence and consistently specified burdens of proof that distinguish modern criminal procedure. The introduction of defense counsel had enormous long-term consequences. The exact stages of development remain uncertain because articulated change occurred through countless minute shifts in practice, but Langbein's overall account rings true.[25]

Although defense counsel could not address the jury and thus could not speak entirely for the accused, they protected defendants from self-incrimination by relieving them of the need to cross-examine witnesses. They showed skill at gaining directed verdicts following cross-examination and at correctly estimating the risk of allowing their clients to speak when the prosecution's evidence had been weak. Since they could manage an effective defense without calling upon the accused, the old practice of active testimony by defendants began to slip away. Counsel, unable to address the jury and limited to cross-examination, needed to know the evidence against the defendant in order to proceed. By the 1750s, even in trials with no counsel, testimony was being articulated into cases *pro* and *contra*. This clarification pointed up the issue of burden of proof, and soon trials with or without defense counsel could end with a directed verdict following the prosecution case. The more clearly the burden of proof emerged as prosecutorial, the more defendants had to gain by falling silent. Finally, the presentation of inculpatory evidence as a sustained account allowed defense counsel to focus judicial attention on questions about the admissibility of evidence.

Despite these changes, counsel for the prosecution continued for decades to appear only in special circumstances because magistrates already had fixed the chief evidence in written depositions and indictments, while judges served as examiners at trial. But the Fieldings were responding at least in part to the need for a fuller gathering of evidence and a more systematic sifting of claim and counterclaim at the pretrial level. Detailed, fully specified cases were needed at trial, and far more than counsel for the prosecution, the justice of the peace structured this narration. Surviving documents suggest that systematic construction of cases by well-organized justices of the peace like the Fieldings bulked large in court. John Fielding served as examiner and committal officer in nine of the eighteen substantial Middlesex cases tried at the October 1754 sessions before Sir Dudley Ryder, a judge of the mid-1750s who left unusually full and informative shorthand notes.[26] By the same token, defense counsel could substantially affect the outcome of trials. The eight Ryder cases with defense counsel yielded three acquittals, four partial verdicts, and only one full conviction (in a case of grievous misdemeanor).[27]

The appearance of defense counsel moved the struggle for control of narrative resources to the center of judicial consciousness by subjecting the prosecution's evidentiary constructs to articulated standards of reliability (realism) and by introducing expert voices competitive with the judge's legal authority. In light of Bakhtin's discussion of "polyglossia" as the defining trait of novelistic discourse, which he considers as having increasingly penetrated the whole of culture during modern times, the "lawyerization" of the eighteenth-century criminal trial could be called a form of "novelization."[28] Langbein argues that the need to curb the lawyers explains the progressive introduction of rules of evidence and standards of proof:

> If the judges had continued to dominate jury trial, we doubt that they would have needed to develop the law of proof as an instrument of jury control. But various factors, in particular the rise of the lawyers, were about to cost the judges their commanding role in the procedure, and thereby to make the jury much more dangerous. The formation of the law of evidence from the middle of the eighteenth century is more or less contemporaneous with the onset of lawyerization of the criminal trial. My suggestion, therefore, is that the true historical function of the law of evidence may not have been so much jury control as lawyer control.[29]

The transformation of the free-ranging judge who dominated the old-fashioned "altercation" into "the passive traffic controller who presides over modern . . . adversary procedure" is the cost of lawyerization.[30] But what happened to the virtually unfettered powers, the free-ranging authority, of the inquiring judge?

The emergent rules of evidence and proof relocate juridical administration within narrative categories—ways of proceeding—rather than personifying authority in a visible actor. Rules are supposed to be passive, disinterested, objective, and transparent: their ideology is that they embody no ideology. The active, inquiring, demonstrative judge—effaced by rules—persists chiefly in the realms of sentencing and punishment and, even there, is displaced into other official roles such as the inspecting warden in the new penitentiaries and the parole officer in modern society. Control is lodged in rules and categories themselves through the very act of subscription to them. Formal realism, transparency, judicial objectivity, bureaucratic neutrality and consistency—the very instruments that allow the separation of relevant from irrelevant fact, of perjury from honest testimony, of the evidential from the incidental, of distortion from reality—are all representational systems of assent that at once constitute and validate authority as densely particularized, closely reasoned differentiation. As Weber said of jurisprudence in modern society:

> Juridical thought holds when certain legal rules and certain methods of interpretation are recognized as binding. Whether there should be law and whether one should establish just these rules—such questions jurisprudence does not answer. It can only state: If one wishes this result, according to the norms of our legal thought, this legal rule is the appropriate means of attaining it.[31]

The genius of modern forms of bureaucratic control is that they appropriate the heteroglossic diversity of the metropolis by keeping track of it and absorbing it into a container of authority projected as systematic rules, a controlled framework within which polyglossic discourse can be allowed liberal freedoms.[32]

The reformulation of authority in terms of ostensibly autonomous rules finds its counterpart in the convention of transparency that distinguishes the realist novel. Flaubert condensed the basic principle into a vivid formulation later echoed by Joyce: "The illusion (if there is one) comes . . . from the *impersonality* of the work. . . . The artist in his work must be like God in his creation—invisible and all-powerful: he must be everywhere felt, but never seen."[33] The convention awaited full incarnation with the flowering of "free indirect discourse" in novelists from Jane Austen onward. This specialized form of third-person narration, also known as *style indirect libre* and *erlebte Rede*, absorbs the narrator within an impersonal, apparently unmediated representation that creates the illusion of entry into the consciousness of fictional characters. Not that free indirect discourse was Fielding's basic technique. On the contrary, in *Tom Jones* above all, he brought to perfection the active narrator whose presence, transcending mere detachment, joins the objectivity that accompanies a certain distance from the scene of action to the vigorous mental engagement of an investigator probing for meaningful detail. But Fielding figures in the early history of free indirect discourse because of instances in which he adopts this "technique for rendering a character's thought in his own idiom while maintaining the third-person reference and the basic tense of narration."[34] In *Tom Jones*, for example, following the decisive break with Lady Bellaston:

> Though Jones was well satisfied with his deliverance from a thraldom which those who have ever experienced it will, I apprehend, allow to be none of the lightest, he was not, however, perfectly easy in his mind. There was in this scheme too much of fallacy to satisfy one who utterly detested every species of falsehood or dishonesty: nor would he, indeed, have submitted to put it in practice, had he not been involved in a distressful situation, where he was obliged to be guilty of some dishonour, either to the one lady or the other.[35]

Although *Tom Jones* personifies the active, inquiring judge as an obtrusive narrator, Fielding's novel partakes technically of a larger process whereby this manipulative presence is absorbed within the realist convention of transparent narration.

In many respects the narrator of *Tom Jones* is an idealized version of the kind of trial judge whose days already were numbered by the time Fielding became a magistrate. As Leo Braudy says of the novelist's frequent use of juridical analogies to characterize his narrator, "Fielding's judge works in the courts of equity, upholding the importance of specific situation and the individual nature of the case before him."[36] Actually, to put a finer historical point on the analogy, the narrator in *Tom Jones* amalgamates traits of the untrammeled judge at the traditional Old Bailey trial with those of the investigative justice of the peace. But while Fielding's novelistic idealization realizes a fantasy-ideal in which pervasive magistral insight entirely shapes and governs a struggle for control of the narrative (a contention that, from the perspective of characters like Blifil, Lady Bellaston, or Mrs. Fitzgerald, lies at the heart of the action), it also abstracts the judge and limits his capacity to intervene. Both the idealization of the active inquiring judge and his removal to a sphere of absolute control establish a mode of omniscience congenial to assimilation within the convention of transparency.

The "natural" resolution of Tom's predicament is left to the circumstantial intervention by Mrs. Miller and Square, in other words, to the conventionally invisible contrivance of the narrator.[37] Significantly, no judicial character within the plot acts effectually like the "good magistrate" in *Jonathan Wild*. Far from piecing out the truth from scattered fragments, Squire Allworthy has to be confronted with the declaration of a dying man before he arrives at an accurate judgment. In their function as justices of the peace, both Allworthy and Squire Western are caught helplessly in the struggle for authoritative control. Even the good-hearted Allworthy lacks the habits of mind and tools of inquiry necessary to unfold the complexities of concerted deception. Fielding rejects this kind of justice whether at its best, as with Allworthy, or at its worst, as with Western. In its place he proposes the justice of his narrator—a man of benevolent nature, intelligence, and tenacity who, like the "good magistrate" in *Jonathan Wild*, inquires into "every minute circumstance." This kind of justice is prospectively realized within the action itself by Tom Jones, an honest man who understands human nature through experience. Tom inherits Allworthy's goodness of soul and, in the end, gains not only Sophia but presumably assumes the position as local magistrate that would accompany Squire Western's reassignment of the family seat and estate to him.

Fielding subordinates the liminal randomness of patrician justice (see chapter 1) to consistently structured narrative procedure. He arrays fact and detail under the surveyorship of a new kind of authority who commands wide-ranging observational resources and enforces articulated standards of evidence and procedure. The discussion of some of these resources in Fielding's reformist tracts, and the practical employment of others in his judicial practice, directly succeeds his idealized personification of the inquiring, judgmental narrator in *Tom Jones*. The juridical and literary phenomena are recognizably comparable social texts. In assimilating the old tradition of the inquiring judge to metropolitan forms of investigation and adjudication, Fielding partakes of developments that transformed the trial court from a place of judgment in the traditional sense of direct determination into a scene of regulated narrative construction.

The plenipotentiary dimension of Fielding's narrator brings Bentham's inspector to mind. Fielding's narrator always has at heart the best interests of those whose lives he observes, shapes, controls, and judges. He understands contingencies and rules only on the basis of systematic inquiry and specific evidence. He personifies the conventions of transparency and objectivity implicit in formal realism and, through the juridical analogy, links them with the rational but invisible order of the metropolitan bureaucracy. Categorical differentiation, as Weber observed, represents the state and its official mechanisms as defending the interests of individuals. The very methods of judicial inquiry (systematic questioning, consideration of claim and counterclaim, standardization of procedure) validate the objectivity of the authority that conserves these qualities through laws, rules, and regulations. Even if individual judges err, the judiciary as an institution strives always to be fair and to ensure the best interest of citizens. The "Judge in every Man's Breast"—his senses and intellect protracted bureaucratically through organizations like the police and architecturally through institutions like the penitentiary—comes to be apprehended invisibly as authority in the liberal state, as the governance of law, as the rule of rules.

· IV ·

Fielding's approach to fictional narration changed significantly over the decade that passed between *Shamela* (1741) and *Amelia* (1751). Ironic distance, often reinforced by the ridicule that had figured in *Shamela*, accompanies a heavy schematization of characters in *Joseph Andrews* (1742), the first of Fielding's novels to attempt a narrative stance ʳombining detachment, the appearance of disinterested inquiry into factual detail, and a conversational alliance with the reader. The rather different, sardonic narrator of *Jonathan Wild* (1743) entirely dominates the novel with a demonstrative rhetoric resembling that of Swift's personifications in "An Argument Against Abolishing Christianity" or "A Modest Proposal." The narrator's all-seeing and all-knowing posture emphasizes contrivance and control. Even the major characters lack particularity, and lesser ones like the "good magistrate" live specialized, insubstantial lives as creatures of plot. In *Tom Jones* (1749), Fielding combines qualities of detached, often ironic, judgment with omniscient presence and authoritative governance of the narration. Although *Amelia* still employs what must be classified generally as a type of intrusive omniscience, its narration reveals major departures from the manner of *Tom Jones*. Braudy, remarking that "the world of *Amelia* is more shaky and uncertain than that of *Tom Jones*," describes how Fielding's narrative voice changed:

> The narrator of *Amelia* does not give us much help. . . . *Amelia* proceeds outward from the limited narrations of Miss Matthews and Booth that form the first half. The narrator gradually reveals his omniscience and begins to pull the reader up short more often. . . . In the later books the narrator is more concerned than he was earlier to justify and explain actions and bring the story up to date with flashbacks. . . . Fielding makes the world of *Amelia* seem less created than the world of *Tom Jones* because he is now more concerned with the relation of private perceptions to the world of external society— the world of public figures, public events, and public institutions.[38]

Fielding seems to have realized, in the wake of *Clarissa*, what Friedrich von Blanckenburg remarked in his *Essay on the Novel* of 1774: "A writer, lest he wish to dishonor himself, can not hold to the pretense that he is unacquainted with the inner world of his characters."[39] In *Amelia*, both as regards the comparatively elusive presence of the narrator and the characterization of omniscient authority in the benevolent Dr. Harrison, we find significant movement toward the transparency of the later realist novel. Neither the indifferent aesthetic success of Fielding's technical experimentation nor any supposed failure of imagination on his part is at issue here. In fact, the uncertainty and hostility that marked the novel's early reception underline my point in the analysis which follows because I take the splits and contradictions that have preoccupied critics of *Amelia* since its original publication to be symptoms of the novel's situation on the threshold of reformist discourse.[40]

Amelia begins with scenes that flatly reject the apparatus of liminal justice. The first named character, the blatant "trading justice" called Thrasher, is a living catalog of offenses to the historical Fielding's proud professionalism. As magistrate of "a certain parish . . . within the liberty of Westminster," he operates, next door to Bow Street, with a cynicism and venality that recur in varying registers in a wide range of public figures throughout the novel.[41] Absolute ignorance of English law is Thrasher's least dangerous attribute, for "he perfectly well understood that fundamental principle so strongly laid down in the institutes of the learned Rochefoucault, by which the duty of self-love is so strongly enforced. . . . To speak the truth plainly, the justice was never indifferent in a cause but when he could get nothing on either side" (6: 17). By the end of the second chapter, Thrasher has committed Booth, the hero, to a Newgate of substantial factuality, populated by a vividly particularized crowd of jailers, turnkeys, mythopoeic street figures like Blear-eyed Moll, habituated residents like Robinson (the freethinking cardsharper who serves as Booth's guide) and pathetic offenders caught between their poverty and the absurdity of the laws:

> Booth['s] . . . attention was suddenly diverted by the most miserable object that he had yet seen. This was a wretch almost naked, and who bore in his countenance, joined to an appearance of honesty, the marks of poverty, hunger, and disease. He had, moreover, a wooden leg, and two or three scars on his forehead. "The case of this poor man is, indeed, unhappy enough," said Robinson. "He hath served his country, lost his limb, and received several wounds at the siege of Gibraltar. When he was discharged from the hospital abroad he came over to get into that of Chelsea, but could not immediately, as none of his officers were then in England. In the mean time, he was one day apprehended and committed hither on suspicion of stealing three herrings from a fishmonger. He was tried several months ago for this offence, and acquitted; indeed his innocence manifestly appeared at the trial; but he was brought back again for his fees, and here he hath lain ever since." (6: 28–29)

This could be straight out of the affidavits that set the tone of the Ogle-thorpe Committee reports just four years before the time during which Fielding's novel is set. The third and fourth chapters, "Containing the Inside of a Prison" and "Disclosing Further Secrets of the Prison-house," survey human misery in a protosociological manner much closer to such affidavits than to the facsimiles of consciousness found in Defoe. The narration continually breaks over into explanation of the law and con-tention over its merit:

> Mr. Booth took notice of a young woman in rags sitting on the ground, and supporting the head of an old man in her lap, who appeared to be giving up the ghost. These, Mr. Robinson informed him, were father and daughter; that the latter was committed for stealing a loaf, in order to support the former, and the former for receiving it, know-ing it to be stolen.
>
> A well-drest man then walked surlily by them, whom Mr. Robinson reported to have been committed on an indictment found against him for a most horrid perjury; "but," says he, "we expect him to be bailed to-day." "Good Heaven!" cries Booth, "can such villains find bail, and is no person charitable enough to bail that poor father and daughter?" "Oh! sir," answered Robinson, "the offence of the daughter, being felony, is held not to be bailable in law, whereas perjury is a misde-meanour only; and therefore persons who are even indicted for it are, nevertheless, capable of being bailed. Nay, of all perjuries, that of which this man is indicted is the worst; for it was with an intention of taking away the life of an innocent person by form of law. As to perjuries in civil matters, they are not so very criminal." "They are not," said Booth; "and yet even these are a most flagitious offence, and worthy the highest punishment." "Surely they ought to be dis-tinguished," answered Robinson, "from the others: for what is taking away a little property from a man compared to taking away his life and his reputation, and ruining his family into the bargain? I hope there can be no comparison in the crimes, and I think there ought to be none in the punishment. However, at present, the punishment of all perjury is only pillory and transportation for seven years; and as it is a traversable and bailable offence, methods are found to escape any punishment at all." (6: 27–28)

Fielding etches life in the old prisons with an exactness unprecedented by any fictional work I know. He projects the feeling "pervasive in *Amelia*," as Claude Rawson observes, "of a cruel divorce between social institutions and the human purposes which they theoretically serve."[42]

At the entry to prison, where "a number of persons . . . all demanding garnish" beset Booth (6: 21), Fielding's narrator recedes from the prom-inent position he occupies at the foreground of the first two chapters into the roles of orderly and traffic controller. The intellectual posture of Booth's guide, Robinson, superficially justifies the framing of critical vignettes in an objective discourse resembling that of official reports or affidavits, but Fielding's retreat places the convention of transparency under severe stress in aggressively reformist passages like those quoted above. Once Miss Mathews gets under way with her story, the narrator effectively assumes the neutral role that he sustains through most of the prison sequence. Nonetheless, Fielding situates the first-person narratives of Mathews and Booth solidly within the framework of the liminal prison. He manages them as artifacts or objects of representation—as the kind of self-centered, morally unfocused story-telling attributable to dubious informants in a marginal place. Also guilty by association with this setting are Booth's deterministic ideas on the fixity of individual character (the "ruling passion") and on the "necessity of human actions." Densely factual first-person narration ceases to serve as the neutral medium we find in Defoe. Containment reveals the limitations of such narration and indicts it by consequences, which extend in this case to adultery stimulated in some measure by the stories themselves. Fielding's apparent withdrawal during these Newgate stories discloses an alliance between seemingly didactic first-person narration and self-serving immorality.

The moral indeterminacy of the liminal prison and the didactic indeterminacy of consciousness-centered narrative in the manner of Defoe discredit one another. This meaningful juxtaposition is shaped and manipulated by a reformist narrator who sets forth consequences like a scientist. This is Fielding's own metaphor in chapter 1:

> By examining carefully the several gradations which conduce to bring every model to perfection, we learn truly to know that science in which the model is formed: as histories of this kind, therefore, may properly be called models of HUMAN LIFE, so, by observing minutely the several incidents which tend to the catastrophe or completion of the whole, and the minute causes whence those incidents are produced, we shall best be instructed in this most useful of all arts, which I call the ART of LIFE. (6: 14)

The stress on observation goes hand in hand with an increased transparency in the narration of *Amelia*. For Fielding here equates knowledge with the apprehension of minute particulars under the disciplined circumstances that surround the behavioral study of a model, and life is viewed as an art (in the sense of "technique") that can be mastered through reasoned investigation. The implicit utopianism; the sense that facts, if fully known, require no mediation; the idea of the laboratory for controlled observation; the assertions, earlier in this chapter (on the novel's very first page), that "natural means account for the success of knaves, the calamities of fools, with all the miseries in which men of sense sometimes involve themselves" and that "to retrieve the ill consequences of a foolish conduct, and by struggling manfully with distress to subdue it, is one of the noblest efforts of wisdom and virtue" (6:13–14) together signal the changes of method and purpose that distinguish Fielding's stance. "The meditative and reformist narrator of *Amelia* defines himself . . . as an expert in law," and the novel, to continue in Braudy's words, "gives the closest scrutiny to the perversions and distortions of law. . . . But, like Hume, Fielding has a great hope for the ability of law to translate private virtue into public good."[43]

In *Jonathan Wild* and *Tom Jones,* the personal merit of a good magistrate or a good man can locally rehabilitate liminal justice. But Mrs. Heartfree's travelogue account of an African tribe, where once elected on grounds of "superior bravery and wisdom" the chief magistrate is a virtual prisoner of public duties and is privately kicked once a day to keep him humble, exoticizes the possibility of genuine alternatives to the existing judiciary in a fanciful vein reminiscent of *Gulliver's Travels.* Similarly alien is Tom's encounter with monarchic justice in a band of gypsies who "differ from all other people" in "that they have no false honors among them, and that they look on shame as the most grievous punishment in the world."[44] *Amelia* rules out the exotic. Until the appearance, ultimately, of a nameless justice who knows the law, the novel reveals a government corrupt beyond redemption by the piecemeal efforts of any good individuals it might employ. Nonetheless, Fielding draws back from the determinist metaphors of biological growth and decay with which the politically interested nobleman to whom Dr. Harrison appeals for Booth's promotion characterizes society. To this spokesman for contemporary politics, the meritocracy that Harrison seeks "is all mere Utopia . . . the chimerical system of Plato's commonwealth, with which we amused ourselves at the university; politics which are inconsistent with the state of human affairs" (7: 248). Yet, as with the idealistic invocation of the common interest to which Fielding called such marked attention in the advertisement to the 1754 *Jonathan Wild,* there is something in it. Fielding wore himself out as justice of the peace, pamphleteer, and proponent of legislation, acting on the belief that he could "rouse the civil power." Considered in the context of his practice as a magistrate, the familiar old terms used to justify satiric writing in the first number of his *Covent Garden Journal* (1752) assume fresh significance: "I cannot be supposed, by an intelligent person, to have any other view, than to correct and reform the public." When, in his summation of Fielding's purpose as the author of tracts and manifestos, the legal historian Leon Radzinowicz ignores the context that links the last six words to a long satiric tradition, he modernizes their meaning without distorting it. For Fielding, correction and reform had become modes of action.[45]

· V ·

Fielding's emergence as a reformist writer is fraught with complexities and contradictions, many of which cluster around Dr. Harrison, a figure who comes as close as a fictional character can to speaking for his creator—or, perhaps more precisely, a figure who personifies Fielding's fantasy-ideal of himself as juridical moralist. The ambiguities and paradoxes in Fielding's account of Harrison are characteristic, more generally, of discourse at moments of radical change: reform finds its initial representation within the existing boundaries of those formal, conceptual, terminological, or institutional species it eventually will alter. Again and again Fielding's writing of the 1750s sets forth projects and proposals for reform articulated in a language fabricated from the classical moralists and the latitudinarian clergy. On specifically modern social and economic questions, Fielding also is apt to rely, as Zirker has shown, on terminologies of the previous generation.[46] Significantly, the innovations in sheer scale and in the use of sequential regimes that Fielding proposes for his Middlesex County House—factors that point toward the use of architecture to shape reformation in the penitentiary—enter a superficially backward-looking project in large part through the medium of the architectural groundplan. The writer has to search for a new language through the old, and the novel is perhaps his ideal instrument since, as Bakhtin argues, it distinguishes itself as the genre that most hospitably records alien voices.

Having set the first quarter of *Amelia* in Newgate, from within which the story's earlier phases unfold in retrospective first-person accounts, Fielding works to establish liminal confinement as the archetypal experience of contemporary life. Amelia's little family lives throughout the present of the novel in the Verge of the Court, a sanctuary or "liberty" traditionally under royal protection, where unfortunate debtors like Booth could take refuge from the law. Pivotal episodes that open respectively onto the plot's crisis and its denouement occur in Bailiff Bondum's private jail (books 7 and 8; 11 and 12), and the shadow of Newgate looms repeatedly.[47] Endlessly replicated in the novel as the site of those "accidents" and "distresses" that the narrator makes it his business to account for, the liminal prison encodes the arbitrary, disorderly, narrowly self-regarding institutions of society as Fielding considered them. Both the omnipresence of prison as a container within which the novel unfolds and the fact that confinement itself occasions so many of Booth's errors (above all his adultery with Miss Mathews) and Amelia's misfortunes (especially her nearly fatal association with Mrs. Ellison and the "noble peer") confirm J. Paul Hunter's conclusion that in *Amelia* "Fielding's earlier Augustan faith in institutions as a check on human depravity seems very much shaken; these 'solutions' to immoral behavior now seem to him a major and continuing source of the problem."[48] The narrator and Dr. Harrison work to set things straight through narrative construction, that is, through inquiry into the "several small and almost imperceptible links in every chain of events by which all the great actions of the world are produced" (7: 292–93), and through the silent manipulation of those events into meaningful, causally coherent sequences.[49] In the end, Dr. Harrison cries to Booth, "Providence hath done you the justice at last which it will, one day or other, render to all men" (7: 327). But "Providence," as Terry Castle observes of this passage, "can be demystified . . . as a trope for plot itself—a figure concealing authorial, rather than supernatural, design."[50] I am arguing, further, that both providence and plot in *Amelia* are representations of reason in human affairs, explications that formulate social and mental life into causally saturated patterns that render them intelligible.

Yet Fielding will not embrace the despair that threatens Amelia when, following the revelation of Colonel James's duplicitous intrigue against her virtue, she cries out to Dr. Harrison, "For sure all mankind almost are villains in their hearts" (7: 145). Unwilling to yield to fatalism even when cruelly tricked by the appearances of human nature, Dr. Harrison replies:

> The nature of man is far from being in itself evil; it abounds with benevolence, charity, and pity, coveting praise and honor, and shunning shame and disgrace. Bad education, bad habits, and bad customs, debauch our nature, and drive it headlong as it were into vice. The governors of the world, and I am afraid the priesthood, are answerable for the badness of it. Instead of discouraging wickedness to the utmost of their power, both are too apt to connive at it. . . . I am convinced there are good stamina in the nature of this very man [James]; for he hath done acts of friendship and generosity to your husband before he could have any evil design on your chastity; and in a Christian society, which I no more esteem this nation to be than I do any part of Turkey, I doubt not but this very colonel would have made a worthy and valuable member. (7: 145)

Fielding utterly condemns the institutions of his day while clinging to the doctrines of an admittedly ineffectual Christian humanism. *Amelia,* as Battestin says, "is the expression—in some respects, the embodiment—of a theory of human nature virtually indistinguishable from the psychology it ostensibly repudiates."[51] Fielding is caught, intellectually and emotionally, between religious principles that seem to offer the only hope for moral responsibility in society and a skeptical, materialistic psychology that more persuasively accounts for reality.

The antiphonal that sounds throughout Fielding's work, between a deterministic view that human nature is helplessly driven by the passions and the latitudinarian position that steady education, good habits, and God's grace can effectively intervene, continues in *Amelia*.[52] At the same time, however, we begin to overhear alternative discourses. For instance, French Enlightenment thought figures but slightly in the earlier Fielding, yet ideas conspicuously associated with Montesquieu appear in *Amelia's* early chapters, as when the narrator observes that "good laws should execute themselves in a well-regulated state" (6: 15), or when, in the passage quoted above, Robinson alludes to the argument that punishments ought to be proportional to crimes (6: 28).[53] Perhaps most notable in the present context is the moment of Booth's final conversion after reading the sermons of Barrow (a latitudinarian divine) in prison. Dr. Harrison celebrates it in terms that, for all the religious aura of their context, could easily be found in Bentham:

> If men act, as I believe they do, from their passions, it would be fair to conclude that religion to be true which applied immediately to the strongest of these passions, hope and fear; choosing rather to rely on its rewards and punishments than on that native beauty of virtue which some of the ancient philosophers thought proper to recommend to their disciples. (7: 313)

Fielding's religious sincerity is not at issue. Rather, a way of proceeding that transcends but may include religious belief overtakes his thought and comprehends its other aspects. He stands at the threshold of a reformist discourse, conducted in the broadly shared vocabulary of sensationalist empiricism, that will unite in common purpose figures as diverse as dissenting Christian religionists like Jonas Hanway or John Howard and secular pagans like Jeremy Bentham.

The extent to which traditional ideas could remain superficially intact while undergoing sharp revision through restatement in the dominant discourse of empiricism may be illustrated by comparing the opening and closing of a famous passage from the beginning of Hume's *Enquiry Concerning Human Understanding* (1748) that Miller discusses in his summation of Fielding's writings as a moralist. Hume is contrasting moral philosophers who "consider man in the light of a reasonable rather than an active being, and endeavour to form his understanding more than cultivate his manners," with those who consider man "chiefly as born for action; and as influenced in his measures by taste and sentiment":

> As virtue, of all objects, is allowed to be the most valuable, this species of philosophers paint her in the most amiable colours; borrowing all helps from poetry and eloquence, and treating their subject in an easy and obvious manner, and such as is best fitted to please the imagination, and engage the affections. They select the most striking observations and instances from common life; place opposite characters in a proper contrast; and alluring us into the paths of virtue by the views of glory and happiness, direct our steps in these paths by the soundest precepts and most illustrious examples. They make us *feel* the difference between vice and virtue; they excite and regulate our sentiments; and so they can but bend our hearts to the love of probity and true honour, they think, that they have fully attained the end of all their labours.[54]

The idea that fictions can move to virtuous action could hardly be older. Certainly Hume's first two sentences could fit comfortably into many a Renaissance defense of poetry, but assimilated in the final sentence to his quite literal empiricist notions of feeling, excitation, regulation, and sentiment, this ancient doctrine assumes material force. It is no accident that Miller turns to *Amelia* and *An Enquiry Into the Causes of the Late Increase of Robbers* for illustrations of Fielding's commitment to the materialist explanations of perception and education. These theories supply the underpinning of the reformist exposition of the penitentiary idea and, I think, take considerably increased prominence in Fielding's later writings. Hume's *Enquiry,* of which Fielding owned a copy, and David Hartley's *Observations of Man, His Frame, His Duty, and His Expectations* (1749), containing the first complete exposition of the doctrines of associationalist psychology, have been taken to mark "the beginning of the Utilitarian century."[55] Given that within a month of *Amelia's* publication Fielding stated his intention "to correct and reform the public," and that he, like Dr. Harrison, could "no more esteem" the England of his day as a Christian society than "any part of Turkey," I think both his religious position and the doctor's have to be viewed at once as sincere and as subsumed by the terms of a secular reformism. The coloration of the doctor's words, "hope and fear" and "rewards and punishments," has to be substantially revised in light of their situation in the prehistory of utilitarian discourse.

Finally, however, the emergence of reformist discourse in *Amelia* is not limited to explicit statements and shifts in terminology. On the contrary, the formal steps toward transparent narration described above mark fundamental ideological transformations. The comparatively recessive narrator, while of course continuing to shape his story, transfers apparent omniscience to an actor within the fiction and thereby depicts impersonal authority as a function of individual character. (This way of accounting for character, so critical to the penitentiary idea, is the subject of my next chapter.) Dr. Harrison actively exercises judgment and manipulates narrative resources in order to yield reformative punishment for Booth. The plot substitutes supervised confinement with reformative purpose for the corrupt institutions of liminal justice that are obsessively reduplicated in the manifest content of the novel's realistic surface.

Fielding's judicial interventions as justice of the peace were analogous to his posture as narrator in *Amelia*. Fielding the personal agent, the literal judge, projected his authority through representational schemes of quasi-institutional character, as in his use of the *Public Advertiser* to organize pawnbrokers into a network serving law enforcement (a plan put into effect the year after the novel).[56] Fielding was creating the omniscience he wished to serve, the "civil power" he wished to "rouse." One measure of his success is that the system he devised for registering information on crime and disseminating it through publication expanded, under the guidance of Sir John Fielding, into a widespread network united by receipt of listings called the *Quarterly Pursuit of Criminals* and the *Weekly or Extraordinary Pursuit*. These publications developed ultimately into the modern *Police Gazette*.[57] In the course of his successful campaign to win government financing for the scheme, John Fielding declared that "the vigorous Circulation of the Civil Power, which on this Occasion has flowed in such a rapid Stream throughout every Jurisdiction, will keep it in constant and effective Action, to the great Benefit of the Community."[58] This circulation takes place through exchange of written information, and permits centralized matching of data obtained from disparate sources. Centralization, in turn, enables particulars about person, place, and time to be assembled into probable—forensically viable—accounts of identity on the basis of which arrests, indictments, and convictions can be obtained.

Nonetheless, the audience of *Amelia*'s first edition recoiled at the anachronistic literalism with which Fielding incorporated references to his brother's Universal Register Office (an exchange with listings of everything from lodgings to clerical livings to honest pawnbrokers) into an action ostensibly set between about 1727 and the middle of 1733. He had gone too far in signaling the remarkable entry of this work into "a zone of contact with the incomplete events of a particular present."[59] He later eradicated every vestige of these anachronisms; the revised version that we now read may leave Amelia's honest pawnbroker unmotivated, but it maintains a historically more consistent, if still less than perfect, chronology.[60] Anachronism became an issue because *Amelia* confronted the reader with contradictory appearances. The judging narrator, visibly alive and in personal communication with the reader, was giving way to the demands of realistic semblance as founded on the convention of transparency. The narrator was disappearing from view but, like Bentham's surveying inspector, not from phenomenological presence. Fielding so skillfully managed the contradictions implicit in the technique of *Amelia* that they assumed a workable conventionality of their own, but when he forced unmistakable references to the period of the novel's composition into a history of the Booth family set some twenty years previous, he violated an emergent convention of transparency that lacked articulate rules but had tangible force as a way of proceeding.

· VI ·

Fielding repeatedly presents Dr. Harrison as an ideal who, "unique among Fielding's characters . . . can both criticize his age and live within it." He realizes, to continue in Braudy's words, "a conflation of Fielding's good men with the kind of epistemological good sense possessed previously only by the narrators."[61] Amelia seems to speak for Fielding when she exclaims:

> Of all mankind the doctor is the best of comforters. As his excessive good-nature makes him take vast delight in the office, so his great penetration into the human mind, joined to his great experience, renders him the most wonderful proficient in it; and he so well knows when to soothe, when to reason, and when to ridicule, that he never applies any of those arts improperly, which is almost universally the case with the physicians of the mind, and which it requires very great judgment and dexterity to avoid. (6: 115)

One needs good reason to part company with Amelia when she declares late in the novel: "You know, doctor . . . I have never presumed to argue with you; your opinion is to me always instruction, and your word a law" (7: 303). He possesses that finely honed power of observation which Booth is said to lack when he fails to notice the visible marks of Amelia's confusion at Colonel James's unwanted dinner invitation: "they could not have escaped Booth's observation had suspicion given him the least hint to remark; but this, indeed, is the great optic-glass helping us to discern plainly almost all that passes in the minds of others, without some use of which nothing is more purblind than human nature" (7: 128–29).

Dr. Harrison plays a startling number of authoritative roles in *Amelia*. He contrives the turns of plot that bring Booth's courtship of Amelia to a successful conclusion, intervening as Booth's "friend and zealous advocate" to gain the consent of her mother, Mrs. Harris, and conniving "to get possession of Amelia by strategem" when the old lady threatens a forcible alliance with Mr. Winckworth's coach and six (6: 81, 85). Harrison finally gains their just union through sheer intimidation: "The doctor's voice, his look, and his behaviour, all [of] which are sufficiently calculated to inspire awe, and even terror, when he pleases, frightened poor Mrs. Harris, and wrought a more sensible effect than it was in his power to produce by all his arguments and entreaties" (6: 97). The idea of the calculated manipulation of sensibility as an authoritative resource is central here. In the flurry of action that concludes the novel, Harrison literally leads the hue and cry after lawyer Murphy at full sprint, crying " 'Stop the villain! stop the thief!' . . . Being in foot the nimbler of the two, he soon overtook him" (7: 323). He takes the role of arresting constable over the protests of the mob, which demands an official with a warrant. Meanwhile, because of Murphy's behavior during the inquiry by an honest justice of the peace who knows the law, Harrison realizes that "if his house was searched some lights and evidence relating to this affair would certainly be found" (7: 327). After successfully demanding a search warrant, he himself conducts the investigation like a Bow Street Runner at work for Justice Fielding: " 'And I will go and see it executed,' cries the doctor; for it was a maxim of his that no man could descend below himself in doing any act which may contribute to protect an innocent person or to bring a rogue to the gallows" (7: 328).

Yet Harrison has significant flaws and makes some critical errors. Among the doctor's failings and mistakes are his contentious dislike of Mrs. Bennet for her classical learning and his erroneous good opinion of Colonel James (not to mention his mixup over the roles of James and Major Bath at the masquerade). But these comparatively trivial lapses easily leave him qualified as one of Sheldon Sacks's "fallible paragons." Such characters "do not sin; they err." Harrison, like Parson Adams in *Joseph Andrews* and Squire Allworthy in *Tom Jones*, "becomes a standard of virtue in the novel in which he appears."[62]

Harrison's arrest of Booth (placed strategically by Fielding very near the centerpoint of the novel) is another matter entirely. As Amelia cries upon hearing the news, "Well, then, there is an end of all goodness in the world. I will never have a good opinion of any human being more" (7: 64). The masquerade provides the novel's moral turning point, but here lies its intellectual crisis. What is the explanation? One sign of crisis is that Fielding offers entirely too many explanations in the opening chapter to book 9 (7: 122–25). This overdetermination occurs, I think, because he confronts not merely a crisis in the plot but irreconcilable contradictions in the means of representation. His move toward more transparent narration—which in its fully developed form diffuses the narrator's authority throughout the text as a tacit, impersonal manner of proceeding that allows not only full access to subjective consciousness but also the power to structure that consciousness as if it existed in the third person (a power I correlate with that of the narrative penitentiary)—increases realism of presentation by muting that richly characterized narrator who figures so largely in *Tom Jones*. Unwilling or unable to surrender this presence (in my argument, because of the novel's situation on the verge of reformist discourse), Fielding fuses it with a character in the story. The contradictions arise because Harrison so fully realizes authorial design, precisely in the sense that he works constantly to lay the plot and complicate its movement. But authors, and even obtrusive, characterized narrators, do not live in the world of the plots they create and their plotting does not even have to be revealed, much less explicated. Dr. Harrison's does. Fielding must conserve his character at all costs; thus the overdetermined explanations.

With Dr. Harrison, the phenomenon of the "disappearing exemplar" or the "fallible paragon" is a symptom of intrinsically contradictory conditions of representation."[63] When the representational aspect of the state (its nature as an "artificial person") is itself personified, we get a jarring character like Harrison. His mistakes glare out as those of Fielding's other disappearing exemplars like Adams and Allworthy do not because he impersonates a means of governance—more an abstract principle than a person, yet not like the allegorical personifications of literary tradition.

The contradictions posed by Dr. Harrison go far beyond the often-cited novelistic requirement that idealized characters have humanizing flaws. Fielding attempts to present Harrison, not as an abstraction, but as the instantiation of abstracted authority. The early theory of the state defines terms on which to understand the difficulty he faced. Hobbes argues in the *Leviathan* that "a commonwealth or state . . . is but an artificial man, though of greater stature and strength than the natural."[64] He later defines a "person" thus:

> He whose words or actions are considered either as his own or as representing the words or actions of another man or of any other thing to whom they are attributed, whether truly or by fiction. When they are considered as his own, then is he called a *natural person*; and when they are considered as representing the words and actions of another, then is he a *feigned* or *artificial person.* . . . Of persons artificial,

some have their words and actions *owned* by those whom they represent. And then the person is the *actor,* and he that owns his words and actions is the AUTHOR; in which case the actor acts by authority.[65]

Hobbes's absolutist theory of sovereignty considered the natural person or individual character of the ruler and magistrate as indissoluble from his artificial or representational character, just as an actor is inseparable from his impersonation. The personification of abstracted authority (itself a likeness or impersonation) as a natural person is imponderable—a representation of the means of representation. As Hobbes indicated, only through the fiction of government itself can abstract entities rise even to the status of artificial persons: "Things inanimate cannot be authors, nor therefore give authority to their actors; yet the actors may have authority to procure their maintenance, given them by those that are owners or governors of those things. And therefore such things cannot be personated before there be some state of civil government."[66] The authority of the state is at once a representation itself—an "artificial person"—and the medium that renders entities, inanimate things, and incapable human beings like children, fools, and madmen capable of being "represented by fiction" as if they were persons. Its power works through human agents but cannot be fully personified.

The contradictions surrounding Dr. Harrison are products of Fielding's reach toward a new, abstracted kind of authoritative representation in which the realist novel and the impersonal, narratively structured regime of penitentiaries partake. With Harrison, Fielding personified his aspiration to the extent that, in the largest sense, the doctor indeed supervises, guides, and controls the novel. We must understand his arrest of Booth in this light even though, to the degree he acts as a character in the plot, he makes a serious mistake that must be explained. It is possible to interpret this disconcerting doubleness in *Amelia* as arising from Fielding's attempts to bind realistic vignettes of corrupt contemporary society into a plot that treats problematically his aspiration to structure juridical systems in terms of the novel's own conditions of representation. Dr. Harrison must, in other words, plot within a system of liminal justice that entraps him along with the other characters. He seeks reformation but must proceed within a social system whose institutions scarcely distinguish punishment from the "spirit of revenge" he rejects in conversation with the young clergyman (7: 165).[67]

Viewed in this light, the narrator's detailed explanation of Harrison's conduct makes good sense. The arrest is justified by the need to correct and reform Booth, and though the effects on Amelia and her children are potentially drastic, it appears to the doctor that she has been playing a contributory role in the distress and imprudence of the family. Harrison can be swayed by the malice of the Booths' former neighbors. He can mistake the significance of "ocular demonstration" in the form of rich trinkets he finds during his mysterious search of their lodgings because the "account tallied so well with the ideas he had imbibed of Booth's extravagance in the country" (7: 123). His conduct, as the narrator assures us, "however inconsistent it may have hitherto appeared, when examined to the bottom will be found, I apprehend, to be truly congruous with all the rules of the most perfect prudence as well as with the most consummate goodness" (7: 122). The stress here on rules, on proof, on evidence, is important. Fielding insists that judgment from evidence takes primacy over the possibility of error; that the corrupt character of the law does not absolve one of the responsibility to act within the framework of its institutions. Authority can be reasoned even if it is wrong and, indeed, authority resides in acting on reasoned, evidentiary bases even at the risk of reaching mistaken conclusions.

Here, as with the scramble at the end of *Amelia* to assign the largest possible number of juridical roles to Harrison, Fielding provokes consideration of the doctor as a representation of "civil power." The acts of which Booth stands accused are not literally but morally and figuratively criminal. Harrison, acting unofficially as a constable conducting a pretrial investigation, finds enough testimony and physical evidence to call for the equivalent of indictment and preventive detention—enough to submit Booth to the forms of trial and to expose him to punishment. In fact this is precisely the stage in the judicial process at which a majority of the prisoners in Fielding's Middlesex County House of Correction would have been. This is only a committal, not a conviction, though clearly at another level it works as an episode of reformative character along the lines of Moll Flanders's stay in Newgate. The difference is that Harrison's rationally structured authority supervises the process and integrates it into a larger pattern of correctional narrative, whereas in Moll's Newgate chaos reigns. Reformation in the old prisons operated entirely by chance. In Fielding's view, their occupants were far more likely to be entrapped and corrupted—the kind of moral devolution that Booth undergoes in the early prison episodes of *Amelia*—than to undergo reform.

Harrison acts out the wish for a regulated order of proportional punishments that Fielding would soon articulate in his reformist pamphlet *A Proposal for Making An Effectual Provision for the Poor* (1753):

> Nothing conduces more to the good order of any society than the moderate punishment of small offences; this is properly called correction, since by it the manners of the party are often corrected and he is prevented from the commission of greater crimes. Such pun-

ishments should be always attended with reproof, and an endeavour to persuade the offender that he is corrected only for his own good. It must be remembered, however, that they are the better and milder dispositions which are to be much amended this way; and therefore shame should as little as possible be mixed with such correction.[68]

Fielding himself did not propose to extend corrective punishment beyond the realms of pretrial detention and of committal for minor criminal offenses of the kind tried by justices of the peace. In fact, Robinson's relapse into crime, after the seeming reformation in which he gives evidence that restores Amelia's fortune to the Booths, signals Fielding's own doubts about the redemption of hardened offenders (7: 340).

The point is that Fielding first broached the prospect of reformative correction in *Amelia,* the composition of which began during the autumn of 1749 and was interrupted about halfway through by preparation of the *Enquiry.* These ideas emerge far more explicitly in *An Effectual Provision,* just over a year after the novel's publication in December of 1751.[69] Both the interconnections between these works in his own thinking and the extent to which *Amelia* was poised on the verge of full-scale reformist discourse become clear if we attend to the last words of Dr. Harrison's speech on the manipulation of the passions through reward and punishment quoted above (7: 313). The doctor's wish to "defer this discourse till another opportunity" seems natural enough as part of the breathless denouement of a lengthy novel. In fact, however, Fielding did continue exactly this argument in *An Effectual Provision:*

> Heaven and hell when well rung in the ears of those who have not yet learnt that there are no such places . . . are by no means words of little or no signification. Hope and fear, two very strong and active passions, will hardly find a fuller or more adequate object to amuse and employ them; this more especially in a place where there will be so little of temptation to rouse or to gratify the evil inclinations of human nature. . . . In such a place, and among such a people, religion will, I am satisfied, have a very strong influence in correcting the morals of men.[70]

I think Fielding became aware in *Amelia* of the tendency of reformist ideas to breach the texture of the novel, that is, of the extent to which the commitment of the realist novel to rendering the particularity of the present limits its reformist thrust by forcing the alternatives it poses always to some significant degree into the realm of metaphor. In such a context, concretely articulated alternatives are apt to incur charges of utopianism or anachronism because they threaten the representations that the novel defines as real. Unlike Goldsmith in *The Vicar of Wakefield* (written 1761–62; published 1766), Fielding was willing neither to adopt

the manner of a fable nor to rupture the fiction with a treatise on reformative punishment. In *Amelia* he elected a historical realism that limited
the scope of his reformism by confining it in the main to representation
within the institutions and customs of the social system he rejected. From
this choice follow both the obsessive reduplication of prisons and scenes
of confinement in the novel and its overdetermined explanations of Dr.
Harrison's contradictory behavior.

Fielding could not turn loose of humanized representations of authority any more than he could fully abandon obtrusive omniscience in
favor of complete transparency. He substantiated the emergent penitentiary idea in *Amelia* and *An Effectual Provision,* but he could not give it
full conceptual or formal articulation. That would be the work of the
full-blown reformist discourse onto which his later career opens. Like
the judges of the 1750s described by Langbein, he was at once the last
of the old and the first of the new, and his position led to representational
contradictions, the full implications of which are accessible only through
hindsight. His practice bears on the penitentiary idea much as that of
Langbein's Dudley Ryder on the law of evidence. The critical difference
is that Fielding both shaped his practice and set it forth through published writings of the widest accessibility. For him writing was a mode of
action.

· VII ·

As judged by the index of parliamentary attention, prison reform appears "to have fallen asleep" between 1729 and 1773, but vivid, half-
wakening dreams marked the intervening decades, and their subject was
the penitentiary idea.[71] In fact I have argued that, substantially because
of the rich interplay of Fielding's practice in varied spheres of discourse
and juridical action, authoritative mastery of narrative resources and of
structured reformative confinement were linked in practice during this
period and became institutionally articulate.

The partial awakening becomes evident upon comparison of Fielding's scheme for a Middlesex County House (fig. 49) with Bishop Butler's proposal in a sermon preached at Easter of 1740 before the "Lord
Mayor, the Court of Aldermen, the Sheriffs, and the Governors of the
Several Hospitals of the City of London." Butler's tentatively phrased
proposal for reformative solitude forms the epigraph to this chapter.
Fielding's argument that it makes as much sense, under civil principles,
to provide religious instruction to prisoners who will reenter society as
it does, under divine principles, to insist upon it for those who face
execution so exactly parallels Butler's that he must have had the sermon

in mind or have been indebted to a common source.[72] Fielding, too, endorses the reformative powers of solitude and fasting, but as part of a system governed by a theory of graduated punishments suitable to the character and condition of the offender:

> Indeed there can be no more effectual means of bringing most aban-
> doned profligates to reason and order, than those of solitude and
> fasting; which latter especially is often as useful to a diseased mind
> as to a distempered body. To say the truth this is a very wholesome
> punishment, and is not liable to those ill consequences which are
> produced by punishments attended with shame: for by once inflicting
> shame on a criminal we forever remove that fear of it, which is one
> very strong preservative against doing evil.[73]

Moreover, Fielding's emphasis on combining "correction of the body" with "correction of the mind," his closely detailed scheme with its fifty-nine articles of legislation for governance, the unprecedented metropolitan vastness of his projections, his system of classification, and his inclusion of Gibson's architectural plans spelling out the material structure within which progressive reformation is to be ordered—all set him worlds apart from Butler.

Fielding's plans for a "County House" containing a prison and a house of correction must be understood as part of a larger program of representational construction. Only as such can they be fully comprehended. His contribution to the rise of the penitentiary lies as much or more in his having established the need for authoritative mastery of narrational resources, and in his having roused the civil power to comprehend the value of instituting schemes to do so, as in his contribution to reformist discourse proper.

Fielding confronted a crisis in the possibility of personified, humanized representations of authority that ran in tandem with the emergence of reformist discourse. The new element present by the mid-eighteenth century, the factor unaccounted for by Hobbes, was the progressive emergence of authority from its traditional embodiment in personified representations (epitomized by the sovereign) and its projection through a grid of cultural and social systems. The authority of the modern bureaucratic state—lodged in detectives, bureaus of records, and circulars like the *Police Gazette;* in newspapers, court reporters, and traffic-controller judges; in the reign of rules and regulations, including the rules of evidence; in the metropolitan order, the conventions of transparent, "factual" narration; and, perhaps most accessibly, in the penitentiary idea with its principle of omniscient inspection—can be fully humanized only through illusionism. The whole nature and quality of abstracted authority—the very essence of its superior effectiveness—lies in the unrepresentability of its means of representation. As Bentham noticed, the operational fact in his Panopticon is the principle of inspection itself, not the person of the inspector. The inspector-keeper is not really omniscient, or even really a person; rather, Panopticon architecture forces the prisoner to imagine him as such. To quote Bentham's words, "In the condition of *our* prisoners . . . you may see the student's paradox, *nunquam minus solus quam cum solus,* realized in a new way: to the keeper, a *multitude,* though not a *crowd;* to themselves, they are *solitary* and *sequestered* individuals."[74]

*To say that, in discourse, fictitious language ought never, on any
occasion, to be employed, would be as much as to say that no discourse
in the subject of which the operations, or affections, or other phenomena
of the mind are included, ought ever to be held: for no ideas being ever
to be found in it which have not their origin in sense, matter is the
only direct subject of any portion of verbal discourse; on the occasion and for
the purpose of the discourse, the mind is all along considered and
spoken of as if it were a mass of matter: and it is only in the way of
fiction that when applied to any operation, or affection of the mind,
anything that is said is either true or false.*

JEREMY BENTHAM
Chrestomathia

*The violator of the more sacred laws of justice can never reflect on
the sentiments which mankind must entertain with regard to him, without
feeling all the agonies of shame, and horror, and consternation. When
his passion is gratified, and he begins coolly to reflect on his
past conduct, he can enter into none of the motives which influenced it. They
appear now as detestable to him as they did always to other people. By
sympathizing with the hatred and abhorrence which other men must
entertain for him, he becomes in some measure the object of his own
hatred and abhorrence. . . . The sentiments which they entertain with
regard to him, are the very thing which he is most afraid of. Every
thing seems hostile, and he would be glad to fly to some inhospitable
desert, where he might never more behold the face of a human creature,
nor read in the countenance of mankind the condemnation of his
crimes. But solitude is still more dreadful than society. His own
thoughts can present him with nothing but what is black, unfortunate,
and disastrous, the melancholy forebodings of incomprehensible misery
and ruin. The horror of solitude drives him back into society, and
he comes again into the presence of mankind, astonished to appear before
them, loaded with shame and distracted with fear, in order to supplicate
some little protection from the countenance of those very judges, who he
knows have already all unanimously condemned him. Such is the
nature of that sentiment, which is properly called remorse; of all the
sentiments which can enter the human breast the most dreadful.*

ADAM SMITH
The Theory of Moral Sentiments

7

The Aesthetic of Isolation as Social System

Τhe representation of reflective consciousness in fiction, the juridical definition of character and conscience, and the conception of reformative confinement under the penitentiary regime are interlocking developments whose collateral nature is best appreciated by examining the ideas of two very different figures—Jeremy Bentham and Adam Smith. Bentham's theory of knowledge and Smith's exegesis of the moral sentiments, taken together, go far toward accounting for the master narratives through which the aesthetic of isolation came to function as a social system during the later eighteenth century and continues, however decrepitly, in the present. In this chapter these two writers will stand, instead of a substantial number of novelists and reformers, as delegates who give voice to the large change in cultural formation—a change in the conception of humanity itself—that attended the penitentiary's foundation.

My account of Bentham and Smith reveals how novelistic discourse as defined in this book not only saturated reformist thought concerning new penal institutions but pervaded the means of comprehension—the cognitive instruments—employed by moral and social philosophers as they began to articulate the paradoxical modern conception of a self at once isolated and transparent to view. Transparency is the convention that both author and beholder are absent from a representation, the objects of which are rendered as if their externals were entirely visible and their internality fully accessible. As the final section of this chapter will show, Adam Smith's exposition of consciousness in *The Theory of Moral Sentiments* works to found a moral order upon the illusory experience of entry into the thoughts and sensations of others. Sympathetic projection and identification become, equally, aesthetic processes and modes of social formation.

The aesthetic of isolation, the penitentiary, and the transparency that attends them are productions of a culture in which experience is structured by a constitutive impersonality that locates the beholding subject in a private world of response and that penetrates the very essence of consciousness. These productions function through an absorptive engagement of the subject in semblances that present themselves as neutral and naturally or mechanically inevitable. The aesthetic of isolation takes shape when the spectator, the theorist, the artist, imagines and narratively structures consciousness in reciprocation with social power. It is an aesthetic of the sublime in which anxiety at the fantasy of subjection to unlimited force is displaced into a resolute embrace of finite social structure, an aesthetic that affirms the transcendent value of self by transmuting fear of external power into identification with its strength and thereby stabilizing both self and the social other.[1] In this light Dance's horrific New Newgate facade (fig. 9), though it screens a quite old-fashioned interior design, is psychologically as much part of the penitentiary movement as Bentham's Panopticon (figs. 12 and 52), or as that epitome and culmination of the solitary system, Pentonville Model Prison, completed in 1842.[2]

The old prisons were arenas physically accessible to the public, theaters in which paradigmatic social relations were tangibly enacted. Residues of prison as theater remained even in Bentham's *Panopticon*, the postscript to which describes visitors assisting in the act of inspection by witnessing a charade of masked prisoners staged in a theatrically disposed chapel. He likens the "emblematic" effect of this "masquerade" to the "serious, affecting, and instructive one" of the Spanish Inquisition's *auto-da-fé*. In this chapel, the prisoners become histrionic objects arranged to create a moral impact on a public audience. But fundamentally the penitentiary is a means of representation that removes prisoners into the mental realm of conscience. Even while advancing the scheme for a public chapel in the Panopticon, Bentham could attest that the "seeds of virtue [were being] buried in obscurity . . . in other improved prisons."[3] These others proved characteristic, for, as realized during the past two hundred years, the penitentiary has isolated prisoners from the public gaze, transforming them into subjects, characters, objects of imaginative projection.

Isolation in the penitentiary achieves distinct yet interrelated effects vis-à-vis the prisoner on the one hand and society at large on the other. Isolation divests the criminal of narrative resources and designates a "character" to be formulated. The old prisons had allowed prisoners full access to narrative instruments: writing and publication, visits by auditors, normal reading matter, even hedged participation in society at large within the surrounding neighborhoods denominated as "rules." The penitentiary deprives prisoners of direct communication with any audience—though usually not of reading one official narrative, the Bible. A secular and impersonal, yet god-like, supervision that holds the individual conscience materially subject replaces liminal randomness—the experience of survival or demise (comedy or tragedy on the literary account) in the transition between phases of life. Isolation is conceptually requisite in the penitentiary, not so that prisoners can reflect on the past—that would be old-style ritual penance aimed at forgiveness of sin rather than at alteration of being—but so that omniscience can restructure the inmate's identity through control of narrative resources.[4]

In the realist novel, fictional consciousness is experienced as actuality through the convention of transparency, epitomized by the device of free indirect discourse, which presents thought as if it were directly accessible. This technique is not a linguistic universal, nor even endemic to narrative; it is historical and occurs almost simultaneously in written fictional narration throughout Europe.[5] Correlatively, the penitentiary stages impersonal, third-person presence (above all, the principle of inspection as set forth in the new architecture, in regulations, and in sequential regimes) so as to represent actual character and conscience as fictions capable of alteration. The penitentiary habilitates, in its own technical practices, devices parallel to those of free indirect discourse. The mode of literary production and the social institution present collateral images of one another. They are stylized within analogous expository structures. The correlation holds even—perhaps especially— for the Panopticon, where Bentham sought to bypass the fictional operations of language and to provide a direct, sensory rehearsal of reality. He wanted to alter motives in his subjects by restructuring their perceptual apprehension or affect, ultimately to alter the physical basis of their calculations and thereby to improve their capacity for rational action. He thought of "real" entities as truly transparent, and of direct sensory experience as having an absolute structure capable of reference without the mediation of language. But his position was contradictory since he both opposed fictitious entities and devised a method of exposition (paraphrasis) for giving them real meaning; he both rejected and embraced them, revealing in the process that his own irreducible realities, the "two sovereign masters *pain* and *pleasure*," gained their significance from exposition no less than did the fictions of his opponents. In the end, Bentham, too, was caught in the convention of transparency and therefore was a realist in a sense quite opposite the one he cherished.

Bentham's attempt to eliminate manifest fictions and fabulous entities from discourse merely parallels the truth claims of "fact," "probability," and "causation" in the realist novel.[6]

· I ·

Instead of tracing the currents of reformist discourse in the novel after Fielding, I reflect here upon selected developments in thought about reformative punishment, about the representation of reality, and about the constitution of character during the half-century that pivots about the Penitentiary Act of 1779 (19 Geo. c. 74)—the act of Parliament that wrote narrational regimes of imprisonment into British law. Inevitably I also describe legal and physical practices that retain a place in our own penal institutions and, far more significantly, in the public imagination of them. For, although the penitentiary regime has proved operationally ineffectual and each of its successive redactions has been scrutinized in an ongoing process of reform, it has remained hypothetically compelling for some two hundred years.

Penitentiary architecture substantiated the dynamic field of thought within which Western society methodized and coordinated practices associated with the modern social order. While the penitentiary idea has been manifest in infinite permutations, both theoretical and practical, during the two centuries since its first legislative enactment, remarkably stable factors persist at its core. These factors include (1) a stress on the fearful but recuperative potential—psychological, moral, and social—of solitude (or isolation achieved through devices such as enforced silence); (2) the presumption that material circumstance will interact with consciousness to alter behavior and to reform character; (3) the premise, expressed in the principle of inspection, that the socialization of individuals depends upon the mental representation of impersonal juridical process; and (4) the inference that the structuring of these processes within the closely interlocked, finely articulated grids of time and space characteristic of metropolitan culture requires systematic control of information and deployment of narrative resources. However imperfectly this identity may have been realized in any single building or system, it has persevered ideologically and therefore forms my constellation of reference here.[7]

A conventional account of prison reform and the penitentiary movement would begin where my chapters on Fielding have concluded. In *The State of the Prisons* (1777), John Howard set the pattern followed by every historian to the present day when he found in the 1750s the origins of the consciousness that, variously dilated through the efforts of Beccaria, Blackstone, Eden, Hanway, Bentham, and Howard himself, legislated reformative punishment, authorized its regime, and predicated its architecture.[8] Howard quotes not only Fielding but Dr. Johnson's *Idler* paper objecting to incarceration for debt because of the morally corrosive society of the old prisons:

> The misery of the gaols is not half their evil; they are filled with every corruption which poverty and wickedness can generate between them; with all the shameless and profligate enormities that can be produced by the impudence of ignominy, the rage of want, and the malignity of despair. In a prison the awe of the publick eye is lost, and the power of the law is spent; there are few fears, there are no blushes. The lewd inflame the lewd, the audacious harden the audacious. Every one fortifies himself as he can against his own sensibility, endeavours to practise on others the arts which are practised on himself; and gains the kindness of his associates by similitude of manners. Thus some sink amidst their misery, and others survive only to propagate villainy.[9]

The old jails, which continued at mid-century on their traditional multivalent pattern, appear wholly discreditable to Johnson because they mark the failure of what Fielding called "civil power." Johnson, writing in the same year Smith's *Theory of Moral Sentiments* appeared, also imagines spectatorship—"the publick eye"—as the vehicle of authority. He confirms the liminality of prison, but the threshold gives onto the abyss of misery or the high road to crime. The "similitude of manners" in this topsy-turvy society yields, not constructive "fears" and "blushes," but vice and destruction.

As reformist ideas began to take hold in the 1760s, and especially following the publication of Beccaria's *On Crimes and Punishments* in 1764, prison buildings like Dance's New Newgate were projected as exemplary symbols facing the outside world and serving to regulate crime by illustration. Dance festooned his entrances with real fetters (fig. 61 below). The old prisons would continue side by side with the new, but never again could they be looked upon as carnivalesque or as sites of liminal passage. This transformation may be readily grasped in the juxtaposition of the younger Dance's horrific New Newgate facade to his father's 1755 project for the renovation of Newgate (fig. 51). George Dance, Sr.'s, building, unlike his son's, would still have functioned as a civic gateway, and would have alluded to its use as a prison only by employing the Tuscan order. With his son's horrific facade of 1768, an enormous change has occurred. Clearly something more than a decade had brought the material presence of prison to public attention in unprecedented fashion. Such buildings not only shut criminals in, they transfixed the citizen,

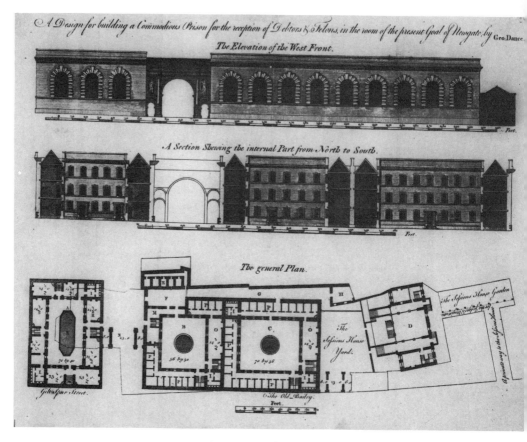

51. George Dance, Sr., *A Design for Building a Commodious Prison for the Reception of Debtors & Felons, in the Room of the Present Gaol of Newgate,* 1755. An unconstructed project by the elder Dance emphasized Newgate's function as a gateway to the City.

whom they stopped, gripped, and frighteningly engaged almost as if he had become a criminal. They inspired narrative creation on the part of the viewer—possibly the kind of story Defoe's *Tradesman* told about the shopkeeper who imagined delight in his work as preferable to a sentence under hard labor (see chapter 2). The definitive stage of reform takes the narrative of criminal punishment inside the new penitentiaries and leaves the citizen to introspection.

Thus the story of the novel and the rise of the penitentiary (at least as it concerns specific fictional writings) has been sufficiently told once the struggle for control of narrational resources begins to produce new authoritative practices during the 1750s, and once the penitentiary idea becomes established through reformist discussion in the public sphere. Yet an understanding of the novel's place in the prehistory of reform puts the rise of the penitentiary in such an unfamiliar light as to require selective reconsideration of the movement's first activist phase. During the 1760s and 1770s, emergent and residual modes of representation compete so vigorously within the distinct spheres of novelistic structure and prison design that they rupture existing forms, at once displaying the new mode of consciousness and fostering the establishment of a distinctively modern institution. Already, for example, when Oliver Goldsmith was composing *The Vicar of Wakefield* in the early 1760s, reformist ideas were splitting off into a separate discourse lodged within but not integral to the structure of the novel itself. Substantial passages that appear in the episode of the vicar's imprisonment are virtually indistinguishable from the reformist argumentation found in Fielding's treatises, Johnson's essays, Goldsmith's own *Citizen of the World* (1762), or periodical pieces of the 1760s. In fact, Goldsmith's novel was often excerpted in magazines and newspapers during the year of its publication in 1766. Chapter 27 on prison reform was by far the most frequent selection, and it was warmly discussed in these journals on the same footing with essays.[10] Once reformist ideas have entered the sphere of public discussion, the novel presents them in the forms of address they ordinarily assume there, no longer confined to acting them out in the tacit forms of plot, narrative technique, material reference, and psychological formulation. Conversely, the fundamentally narrative structure of the penitentiary idea permeates reformist discourse and, ultimately, the fabric and daily regime of functioning institutions.

The legislation of 1779 has itself to be considered an enabling fiction: the Penitentiary Act authorized two national institutions that never became operative because of executive conflict. Instead of providing physical structures, it set the conceptual pattern for any number of local acts and, in part because of a national architectural competition sponsored under its aegis in 1781–82, spawned the penitentiaries established in various counties during the next decade. The fictive power of the penitentiary idea extended well beyond the construction of the actual buildings that put it into daily practice. In fact its ideology was perpetuated in a reformist discourse that extends to the present moment—an endless counterpoint of variations aimed, first, at reshaping any surviving old prisons and, later, at modifying the penitentiaries themselves. This obsessive rehearsal had to become a permanent feature of the penitentiary as a social system because the representational means of the fully developed penitentiary are indirect and procedural rather than theatrical and emblematic: the penitentiary could not be conceived, nor can it function, outside of a specific, impersonally structured public discourse. Prior to the 1780s in England, the penitentiary existed only in the telling.

Thereafter, because ordinary visitors were rigidly excluded under the new penal regulations, the penitentiary had to live in the public mind through mediated accounts rather than through concrete experience. Criminals physically rehearsed their various narratively structured regimes within the framework of actual buildings. Society at large could conceive this discipline only through its representation in public discussion, in published schemes, and in the external fabric of prison architecture. No wonder the rise of the penitentiary in England required a neologism: the word "penitentiary" itself is a coinage that originated within Eden's and Blackstone's parliamentary coalition of the 1770s—a product, like the emergent institution it named, of the structure of feeling described in this book.[11]

· II ·

The evident transfiguration of prison design between Dance and Bentham is far less a matter of penal psychology than of the relative self-evidence of the means of representation. In the New Newgate facade, Dance's means are the visible, speaking surfaces of public architecture apprehended as a tableau. By contrast, Bentham sought in theory (by specifying the use of radically innovative materials such as cast iron) to press beyond what Blackburn did in practice. By exploiting conventional materials to their limit, he attempted to render the architectural means of penitentiary reformation transparent or even invisible (fig. 52; see also fig. 11 above).[12] Bentham and Blackburn marshaled the technical resources necessary to recreate criminals as subjects, to hold the prisoners, the jailers, the public, and legal authority itself in a predisposed array. Bentham called this set of relations the "Inspection Principle." At the heart of his social project lay institutions designed to create socially coherent motivation through the manipulation of physical and mental experience—in other words, to create a sensationalist mode of conscience.[13]

Men as seemingly opposite as the profane Bentham and the pious Jonas Hanway could agree that motivation might be altered by conscience operating in solitude under supervision. Bentham routinely likened the "apparent omniscience" and "omnipresence" of the governor, upon which his inspection principle depended, with that of God in heaven.[14] Even Hanway, the profoundly Christian philanthropist, placed more faith in secular than in religious institutions and for the same reason—their power to mold conscience:

Whether we build *prisons* to restore the morality and religion of the people; or *churches,* in which they are to worship God; the object is the same: but, to all appearance, the *repentance* and *amendment,* the *sorrow* for the past, and the *resolution* with regard to the future part of life, will be more sincere in the *prison,* than it usually is in the *church.* For Heaven's sake, let us try the experiment of *solitary imprisonment!*

Nor would the influence extend to the minds of convicts alone:

A malefactor put to death in the ordinary way of execution, is no object of terror, not even to him who attends the execution. . . . But even a distant view of such a prison-house, whilst it gave confidence in the security of life and property to peaceful citizens, it would strike the evil-minded with such terror as might *happily* keep it empty; which would be the *glory of the plan!* . . . The prison will soon appear as intended to render life useful and beneficial to society.[15]

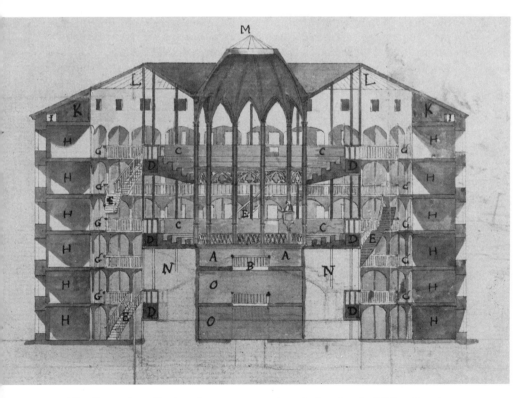

52. The Panopticon Penitentiary, 1791, section. A drawing by Willey Reveley, preparatory to Bentham's *Postscript,* reveals the lightness and transparency of Bentham's innovative structure. Four appearances of the letter "C" mark the chapel area.

The idea of character is central here, for as in the development of the realist novel, omniscient authority retreats behind the convention of transparency into the pretense that characters alter spontaneously, adapting to physical circumstance through the reflective operation of consciousness.

The claim that the massive systems of the penitentiary are only neutral, mechanical means to this end parallels the convention that characters in the realist novel have a being independent of their all-creating author when in fact, as Bakhtin argues, "authorial intonations freely stream into the reported speech."[16] Just as the realist novel presents "character" to an audience of readers as an autonomous phenomenon consisting in the development of consciousness, reformist discourse represents the penitentiary as shaping character without the direct interposition of personal authority. Jonas Hanway, for instance, declares in *Solitude in Imprisonment*:

> This proposal stands upon a principle, that man is a *reasoning, as well as a passionate creature. . . .* Reflection cannot lose all its power; nor can the heart of man be so petrified, but the consideration of his *immortal* part, under the terrors of solitude, will *open his mind.* He will feel his situation as an intermediate state between both worlds, and as a preparative for either. When released, the remembrance of such imprisonment will never be effaced. He will hardly fall into the same temptations, from the danger of being exposed to the same punishment, with more terrible circumstances with respect to duration of time, or a *horrible dungeon.* (pp. 102–3)

Penitentiary architecture and its attendant regimes are described merely as occasions, creations of appropriate circumstances, that foster the definitive process of self-reflection. The criminal who knows solitary by direct experience here personifies—in a sense exchanges characters with—a public that imagines the horror of isolation. A sympathetic introjection of terror is modulated through reflection into social order. Spectatorship is the vehicle of control here, the story of a prisoner's rehabilitation in solitude its tenor. Hanway, the reformer, leads one to enter the mind of a criminal through an act of identification that assumes both the transparency and interchangeability of consciousness.

In their account of Roland Barthes' *S/Z*, Rosalind Coward and John Ellis offer a cogent summation of contemporary thought on transparency as a convention:

> Realism stresses the product and not the production. . . . All that matters is the illusion, the story, the content. . . . "Not only do signifier and signified seem to unite, but in this confusion, the signifier seems

to be erased or to become transparent so as to let the concept present itself just as if it were referring to nothing but its own presence." Language is treated as though it stands in for, is identical with, the real world. . . . The identity between signifier and signified which is established in realist writing is the precondition of its ability to represent a *vraisemblable*, an accepted natural view of the world. It does not mean that all writing is absolutely transparent, but rather that the narration, the dominant discourse, is able to establish itself as Truth. The narration does not appear to be the voice of an author; its source appears to be a true reality which speaks. . . . So fragments of writing are confidently attributable to one character or another. And . . . the narration also establishes the basic positionality for these characters, by setting up antithetical oppositions between them, creating a system of mutually defining, separated spaces.[17]

I am not aware that Bakhtin used the term "transparency," but he early reflected along this same general line while considering the ideological significance of the phenomenon's chief technical manifestation in realist narrative, free indirect discourse, "a form for the direct depiction of the experiencing of another's speech."[18]

The device of free indirect discourse creates the illusion that the unvoiced mental life of fictional personages exists as unmediated presence. The representation of consciousness that it enables distinguishes the novel from nonfictional narrative on the one hand and from nonnarrative mimesis in drama and film on the other. It is the technical basis upon which the fundamentally novelistic *vraisemblable* of modern life rests, the dominant discourse that pervades modern cultural and social systems.[19] Such devices of communication, as Bakhtin argues, are not merely symptoms but rather the operative conditions that create and maintain the forms of mental life:

> Some displacement, some shift had to have occurred within socio-verbal intercourse . . . for that essentially new manner of perceiving another person's words, which found expression in the form of quasi-direct discourse, to have been established. . . . The inner subjective personality with its own self-awareness does not exist as a material fact, usable as a basis for causal explanation, but it exists as an ideologeme. . . . Personality, from the standpoint of its inner, subjective content, is a theme of language, and this theme undergoes development and variation within the channel of the more stable constructions of language. Consequently, *a word is not an expression of inner personality; rather, inner personality is an expressed or inwardly impelled word.* And the word is an expression of social intercourse, of the social interaction of material . . . producers. The conditions of that thoroughly material intercourse are what determine and condition the kind of thematic

and structural shape that the inner personality will receive at any given time and in any given environment.[20]

Both the realist novel and the penitentiary pretend that character is autonomous, but in both cases invisible authority is organizing a mode of representation whose way of proceeding includes the premise, and fosters the illusion, that the consciousness they present is as free to shape circumstance as to be shaped by it. In first-person narratives like Defoe's, or in epistolary fictions like Richardson's, we may question what a character says or does but not the concept of character itself. In the narrator-centered novel epitomized by *Tom Jones,* the concept of character is reinforced by doubling: we view the world of character through a character. Eighteenth-century novelists after Fielding in part maintain these approaches to the narrative presentation of character, but, increasingly, Fanny Burney and other female writers explore and consolidate the use of free indirect discourse. They in fact make it available to Austen, who often has been called its originator in English.[21] In the later realist novel, the device disperses authoritative presence into the third-person grammar and syntax through which the illusion of consciousness is projected; the material world is commuted into a function of character viewed, thanks to the convention of transparency, as if it defined materiality. Realism becomes a substitute for reality itself, the mode of practice within which life functions. Authoritative narrational presence exists invisibly—by force of convention—in every projection of consciousness.[22]

On Bakhtin's terms, the novel is the genre that defies genre because it freely and fully represents the dialogic nature of utterance, that freight of alien voices and implicit audiences born in every act of speech. The realist novel, more specifically, represents discourse as it participates in the formation of consciousness under the conditions prevailing in the early modern era. When dialogue becomes not just a matter of recording the otherness that, for Bakhtin, is intrinsic to all utterance, but of the creation of self-consciousness through the use of reported speech that represents discourse to the public sphere *in writing,* European culture confronts a new version of itself. Ann Banfield, in a parallel argument, writes that "the spontaneous appearance of narrative style and, in particular, of represented speech and thought in western literature, is the result . . . of the transformation of western culture into a literate culture." She maintains that "the dominance of the communicative function in speech . . . accounts for the absence of the features of narrative style in speech . . . and written composition . . . frees linguistic performance from the tyranny of the communicative function."[23] This technically autonomous fictional construction of spoken language—and of thought itself—

is the momentous but unspecified "displacement" to which Bakhtin refers in his discussion of free indirect discourse.

Bakhtin's global, panhistoric "novel" does indeed freely register alien voices, but in the realist novel the means of representation do more than record multiple voices: the convention of transparency treats the one presence within which all other presences are staged as if its embrace were invisible. Transparency absorbs the heterodox within tacit authority. Free indirect discourse represents the fullest possible control of narrative resources. Because Bakhtin romanticizes the novel by setting it against the "official" genre of epic, he largely neglects the containment of heterodoxy effected within the realist mode, where narration itself invisibly controls, contains, and becomes authoritative. Bakhtin does assert that the novel "alone is organically receptive to new forms of mute perception, that is, to reading" and, in an important passage, describes the "realistic and critical individualism" of the end of the eighteenth and early nineteenth century as defined by "its pictorial style and its tendency to permeate reported speech with authorial retort and commentary."[24] Finally, however, he believes the novel to be most fully realized when it is most "heteroglossic." For him, the novel evades the hegemony of official culture. Conversely, I have shown the place of the realist novel in the dense array of modern culture: its narrative devices, like those of the penitentiary, place the individual on an entirely revised footing vis-à-vis authority. They redefine the way of being in the world.[25]

· III ·

Bentham was the theorist who, given the historical limits of an eighteenth-century frame of reference, exposed most fully the fictional basis of character as accounted within jurisprudence (as well as its ideological dependence upon seemingly transparent concepts such as "nature" and the "social contract," which he also treated as fictional). Perhaps the best way to understand his long life's work is as an explication of the semio-technological production of social and mental life. His endeavor, which in the end had significant influence on the reform legislation of the 1830s, aimed consistently at the institution of laws founded on the truth of this production as he understood it. He considered sensory experience and physical circumstance to be "real"—the mechanisms of pleasure and pain—and he described the constructs of language, law, and ordinary thought as variously mystified representational "fictions." Bentham explained the concepts of "right" and "duty," according to Ross Harrison, "in terms of what someone is, in law, liable to be punished for not doing;

213

and punishment is explained in terms of the pain to which someone is liable for non-performance. Hence, since pain is a simple idea, a really existing entity, an analysis is possible which explains the central, fundamental, terms of jurisprudence, rights and duties, in terms of simple ideas or real entities."[26] Through such analysis, Bentham designed to lay the groundwork for reform by supplanting superstition with rational thought and calculation.

Fictions are at once obfuscations of reality and operational necessities (see epigraph to this chapter). The purpose of philosophy, for Bentham, is to show the fictional standing of ordinary, nonanalytic modes of discourse and to provide the logical instruments necessary to master (that is, to gain practical dominance over) fields such as jurisprudence and punishment through the critical inquiry into their real basis. He stepped out of the spiritualist frame of explanation that enabled reformers like Hanway and Howard to endow the penitentiary with attributes of the monastery and the confessional, but also outside the preoccupation of secular Enlightenment thought with issues like human nature, the social contract, and natural rights—all of which Bentham considered irretrievably fictional constructs, "non-entities." Bentham's attacks on Blackstone, in his early discussions of legal fictions, show that while he shared many of the legislative and institutional goals of the other reformers, he considered himself theoretically superior. He was able to look approvingly upon their goals but had to view their unselfconscious employment of fictions with a certain condescension.

Interestingly for my purposes here, the tool Bentham invented to dispel "the pestilential breath of fiction" and to advance his inquiry into the "springs of action"—the "real" bases of social systems—was the expository device of "paraphrasis." This seems to me a signal contribution to narrative theory. Bentham insists that substantives used in apparently significant sentences gain their meaning, even when they have no real reference, by the context of the whole sentence in which they appear and, critically, that the translation of such sentences into other sentences determines their significance (this is the process he called paraphrasis or exposition). He argues that the illusion of significance that attaches to fictional entities inheres in human language and that significance itself is intrinsically expository. He takes the "constitution of human language as the source from whence the illusion flows."[27] Harrison credits Bentham with the "highly important insight" that sentences, not individual words, are primary integers in the analysis of meaning, and Quine identifies Bentham as making "the crucial step forward" in this aspect of epistemology. Expository communication in sentences is central both to Bentham's fundamental analytic device of paraphrasis and to his theory of meaning.[28]

Although Bentham's views were held originally within his treatment of quite technical issues, I believe they bear upon the description undertaken in this book of the realist novel as a cultural system. The conventions of the realist novel—above all its creation of a dense array of terms that ordinarily refer to or specify material objects and real entities as the framework that validates, as substantive, certain wholly imaginary frames of reference and states of mind—are within the sense of Bentham's word "paraphrastic." This is to say that these conventions form the limiting case of the power of sentences to explicate one another in such a fashion that they create meaning through what Russell called "incomplete symbols," "things that have absolutely no meaning whatsoever in isolation but merely acquire meaning in context."[29] Bentham's inferential use of propositional exposition to test the referential content of fictions can be described as an advance in epistemological inquiry, but it can equally well be viewed as a technical practice within the cultural system that produced the penitentiary and the realist novel, genres in which the illusion of significance is projected contextually through facsimiles of referential sentences.[30]

Bentham takes on enormous importance here because he at once theorized and lived within the cultural system I am describing. Thus, despite its later epistemological subtlety, a doubleness remains in Bentham's thought because he continues to accept the premise that entities such as pain and pleasure exist physically as absolute facts, not merely as referents or "qualities." Since he gauges the significance of other, inferential, entities against these absolutes through the intrinsically expository medium of language—judging such entities as instrumental or fabulous according to their representational content as measured by his device of paraphrasis—he must be described as a realist for whom transparent reference remains the final index. "Realities," he says in a discussion of rights, "on this occasion as on all others, realities I prefer to fictions." He argues that apart from non-entities or fabulous entities like natural law and the devil, "every fictitious entity bears some relation to some real entity."[31] Paradoxically, while utterly opposed to the mystifications of fictitious entities, he invented the device of paraphrasis for giving sense to sentences that name them. He provides an exhaustive treatment of the realist aesthetic's epistemological structure, while "supposing," as Harrison succinctly declares, "that there is, in principle, a way in which things can be made ideally clear and so described really as they are without any trace of fiction."[32]

Inevitably, however, my comparison between the realist novel and the penitentiary must raise the objection, in point of the convention of transparency, that actual penitentiaries have to be massive and therefore opaque. True and not true. Bentham's Panopticon of glass was the extreme case, an invention that went beyond the most advanced technology of its day to envision the largest possible area of glass stretched over the slenderest of structural members (figs. 52–54).[33] Bentham condensed the ideal Panopticon into a single fantasy image, a French fairy tale in which "one of the occurrences is the imprisonment of the heroine in a palace, the boundaries of which were composed throughout of one solid mass of glass. Of this archetype, the Panopticon was as near a similitude as the limited power of human art could admit of."[34] Blackburn's radial designs pursued similar objectives within the practical limits of actual construction (fig. 11). Bentham turned the traditional prison inside out, placing the prisoners at its periphery and, at its center, the jailer (now depersonalized into the principle of inspection). Inside and outside became a single conceptual entity in Bentham's ideally transparent prison. Public and prisoner occupied different relative positions but both were subject to an inexorable system. One is either watched or watcher, and the two reflexively become one (see fig. 57 below). The lord lieutenant of Ireland who said of the Panopticon, "They will all get out," was both entirely right and entirely wrong. He might as well have said, "They will all get in." For Bentham, the solid peripheral wall to secure the Panopticon was an afterthought in response to critics who could not understand his metaphor.[35]

But the lord lieutenant was pointing to an obvious fact. The ideal penitentiary is transparent while, as Bentham certainly understood, real ones must be impenetrably fortified. The solution, historically, was to build transparent structures within peripheral walls breached only by massive portals intended to communicate horror to the passerby. Within such walls, penitentiary structures from the 1780s onward follow a pattern in which a maximum of light and visibility is sought inside through the use of galleries on slender supports, and a maximum of inside-outside penetration is provided through the use of glass on a scale unheard of in the old prisons. The ideal of transparency is, in other words, fully embodied up to the technical limits posed by the need to confine. Structures of feeling, as they take material form in different spheres of production, are subject to the technical requirements of each sphere. Vis-à-vis the public—the larger audience of the penitentiary narrative, as opposed to the subjects inside—transparency resides in the myth, originally underwritten by religious ideology, that the characters of the prisoners are growing, altering, and reforming through their own self-reflection. This aspect of the penitentiary must be understood as a mystified projection, an imaginative representation of authority in the form of conscience apprehended as a principle of inspection.

"Sublime" prisons like Dance's New Newgate had aimed at direct intimidation. Their *architecture parlante* communicated intrusively like a

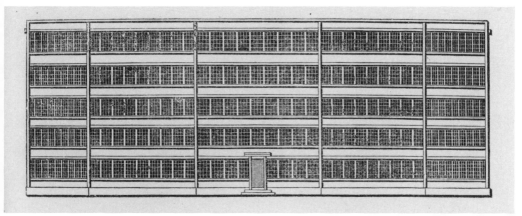

53. Samuel Bentham and Samuel Bunce, Panopticon House of Industry, 1797. The walls in this design become a curtain of glass, a conception actually realized in later factories.

54. Panopticon rotunda, Isle of Pines, Cuba, 1932. A naturally lighted modern photograph demonstrates the comprehensively detailed field of vision revealed from the central vantage point in a structure based on Bentham's transparent design.

moralizing narrator. A physical idea of deterrence motivated the horrific facades that mark the early phase of reform, especially on the Continent (figs. 55 and 56). These urban prisons were designed to shape public response through direct emotional communication. Although this approach survives residually in the entrance lodges to many penitentiaries, it becomes functionally as well as literally peripheral (figs. 10 and 11). The penitentiary in its fully realized form proceeds obliquely—not by intimidation but by inspection, not by force condensed into awe but by the manipulation of consciousness through time. Its discourse, like that of the realist novel, rehearses a cultural system in which character and conscience are produced as interrelated, transient forms of being without which one needs reformation and, in that sense, is criminal.

In a passage near the beginning of *The State of the Prisons,* John Howard urges upon advocates of the old prisons a state of mind appropriate to the new:

> Those gentlemen who, when they are told of the misery which our prisoners suffer, content themselves with saying, *Let them take care to keep out,* prefaced perhaps, with an angry prayer; seem not duly sensible of the favour of Providence which distinguishes them from the sufferers. . . . They also forget the vicissitudes of human affairs; the unexpected changes to which all men are liable; and that those whose circumstances are affluent, may in time be reduced to indigence, and become debtors and prisoners. And as to criminality, it is possible, that a man who has often shuddered at hearing the account of a murder, may on a sudden temptation commit that very crime. *Let him that thinks he standeth take heed lest he fall,* and commiserate those that are fallen.[36]

This fusion of empathy and objectivity, this recognition of the fragility of the conditions that enable personal identity, and this sense of consciousness watching and judging itself subsist as narrational inferences within the network of juridical exposition that the penitentiary epitomizes.

· IV ·

The interior personification of juridical presence as character—perhaps the element most central to the penitentiary idea—is best understood historically with reference to Adam Smith's explanation of the reciprocal nature of conscience in *The Theory of Moral Sentiments* (1759). In this work, Smith clarified the standing of moral sentiments as mental representations, an issue that had presented problems to materialist empiricism from the beginning. Bentham's obsession with the public sphere—

ORDRE TOSCAN RUSTIQUE.

PROJÊT DE LA FAÇADE D'UNE PRISON CRIMINEL.

Jl. Cuvilliés fils in.

55. Jean François de Cuvilliés, *Projêt de la façade d'une Prison Criminelle*, 1770–76. This project unmistakably declares the prison's function with rusticated Tuscan columns, spikes, draped chains, and statues of captives.

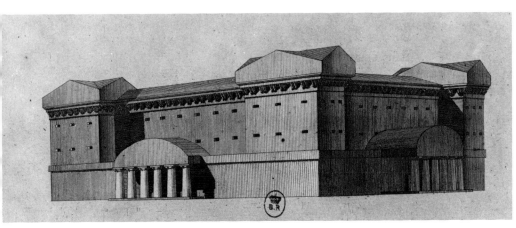

56. Claude-Nicolas Ledoux's project for a prison at Aix-en-Provence, designed 1784. The architectural symbolism of entombment bespoke the power to impose a living death through imprisonment.

with the underlying principles of legislation and jurisprudence—and his entirely behaviorist approach to social action limited his capacity to probe the psychology of reformative punishment. But Smith, though he employed numerous concepts that Bentham condemned as fictions (above all the idea of "Nature"), described the psychological mechanisms through which the project Bentham inherited from Helvétius and Beccaria was to be realized. This project aimed, as Harrison says, "to create an artificial identity of interests between the individual actor and the people as a whole by the creation of a system of rewards and punishments. Artifice would result in the self-interested actor acting in the general interest."[37] The analysis of conscience in *The Theory of Moral Sentiments* documents with considerable insight the structure of feeling that the penitentiary institutionalized. Smith's psychological theory provides a schematic account of the expository mechanism underlying an emergent social system that eventually all but supplanted the emblematic, rhetorical, and ceremonial presence which for centuries had ritualized authority as public theater (see, e.g., fig. 50). In the new, narratively structured system, the site of enactment becomes private, mental, and individual; the medium of representation particular, factual, evidentiary; the mode of processing experience inferential, procedural, systematic. The means of representation, indeed the very fact of representation itself, become transparent, abstracted, inaccessible to direct apprehension.[38]

Smith maintained that since, even in their physical presence, we have no "immediate experience of what other men feel," we must rely in forming moral judgments upon the imagination's "representing to us what would be our own [sensations]" if we were to take their place:

> Though our brother is upon the rack, as long as we ourselves are at our ease, our senses will never inform us of what he suffers. . . . It is the impressions of our own senses only, not those of his, which our imaginations copy. By the imagination we place ourselves in his situation, we conceive ourselves enduring all the same torments, we enter as it were into his body, and become in some measure the same person with him.[39]

Sensory isolation forms the elemental condition of existence for everyone. Imaginative sympathy is the medium through which any social formation must occur.

For Smith, there exist two levels or types of sympathy. An instance of the first kind, immediate sympathy, occurs when we draw back upon seeing a blow descend upon another person. The second, imaginative sympathy, involves a much more extended representational network centered on the mechanism Smith calls, variously, the "impartial spectator," the "indifferent person," the "man within," the "tribunal within the breast," "society," and so forth:

> We can never survey our own sentiments and motives, we can never form any judgment concerning them; unless we remove ourselves, as it were, from our own natural station, and endeavour to view them as at a certain distance from us. . . . Whatever judgment we can form concerning them, accordingly, must always bear some secret reference, either to what are, or to what, upon a certain condition, would be, or to what, we imagine, ought to be the judgment of others. We endeavour to examine our own conduct as we imagine any other fair and impartial spectator would examine it. If, upon placing ourselves in his situation, we thoroughly enter into all the passions and motives which influenced it, we approve of it, by sympathy with the approbation of this supposed equitable judge. If otherwise, we enter into his disapprobation, and condemn it. (p. 110)

Smith contends, centrally, that sympathy is situational. The operative forms of sympathy do not arise from any direct response to having witnessed expressions of pleasure or pain in another but rather from imaginatively occupying the situation of another—from experiencing another's emotions within the medium of one's own senses.

In the old European social order, shame and public disgrace had been major forces governing behavior, and fear that a lord's or patron's favor would be lost had been a genuine sanction. As we saw in chapter 1, even though the ties that bound this patriarchal order together had greatly loosened by the eighteenth century (especially in cities), its law was perpetuated for a time through the concentrated, demonstrative pageantry which marked the public theater of cultural hegemony that Thompson describes as governing earlier Georgian England. Smith accounts psychologically for an emergent order based on guilt rather than shame, and marked by the introjection of impersonal norms as character. In this new order, guilt is a permanent condition. It refers to the values of others, certainly, but rapidly takes on an independent life by generalizing and depersonalizing them. Guilt enforces its standard of behavior without reference to actual opinions of particular spectators. The agent of reproach, like sympathy itself, is private and individual.[40] Thus, for Smith, the true response of the object of sympathy remains incidental; the feelings of the other need have no real or specific existence:

> We sometimes feel for another, a passion of which he himself seems to be altogether incapable; because, when we put ourselves in his case, that passion arises in our breast from the imagination, though it does not in his from the reality. . . . The anguish which humanity feels, therefore, at the sight of [a lunatic, for example,] cannot be the

reflection of any sentiment of the sufferer. The compassion of the spectator must arise altogether from the consideration of what he himself would feel if he was reduced to the same unhappy situation, and, what perhaps is impossible, was at the same time able to regard it with his present reason and judgment. (p. 12)

The impartial spectator personifies a way of viewing the world, a special kind of attention. Smith anatomized this fictional construction of identity as if it were universally, intrinsically human. It appears now to exist only in certain places at specific historical times.

Smith's impartial spectator is the mechanism that underlies such fundamental, ordinarily transparent concepts as character and personal identity:

Were it possible that a human creature could grow up to manhood in some solitary place, without any communication with his own species, he could no more think of his own character, of the propriety or demerit of his own sentiments and conduct, of the beauty or deformity of his own mind, than of the beauty or deformity of his own face. . . . Bring him into society, and he is immediately provided with the mirror which he wanted before. It is placed in the countenance and behaviour of those he lives with, which always mark when they enter into, and when they disapprove of his sentiments. (p. 110)

Although Smith stops just short of declaring the self a social structure (the solitary human creature is said to possess a character even if it cannot be an object of his thought), he established the terms within which later social theorists could do so. George Herbert Mead, for example, argues that self-identity comes to being only when the sensations of a particular individual pass through the medium of social norms and expectations as personified in the "generalized other" or, in Dr. Johnson's terminology, "the publick eye." Only thus can the individual define a self in correspondence to, or in conflict with, these norms. This is not a matter of mere habit but of the construction of a humanized subject through an ongoing fusion of contingent, individual sensation with the impersonal norms of a generalized other.[41] The sympathetic feelings of Smith's impartial and well-informed spectator are functions of the impersonality that, so very paradoxically, structures individual subjectivity in modern life.

Governmental punishment follows spontaneously, for Smith, from public resentment generated by sympathy for individual victims and moderated through the psychological and social mechanisms of justice:

Resentment cannot be fully gratified, unless the offender is not only made to grieve in his turn, but to grieve for that particular wrong which we have suffered from him. He must be made to repent and be sorry for this very action, that others, through fear of the like punishment, may be terrified from being guilty of the like offence. The natural gratification of this passion tends, of its own accord, to produce all the political ends of punishment; the correction of the criminal, and the example to the public. (p. 69)

The sympathetic process of representation that Smith narrates is narrowly specific—existing only in the exact particulars of individual experience—but also central to social formation. Smith makes this clear though the institutions in question remain sketchy.[42]

The conception of an impartial spectator is first established in part 2 of *The Theory of Moral Sentiments*, which concerns reward and punishment. The epigraph to the present chapter—Smith's portrayal of the murderer's state of mind—forms the illustrative set-piece around which the section turns. He maintains that society cannot exist unless justice works in two ways: internally, through the presence of the impartial spectator, to moderate the kind of individual behavior that naturally leads to "resentment" (and therefore to revenge) on the part of others; and externally, through institutions, to confer validity upon the exercise of natural resentment through punishment. Conscience, personified as the impartial spectator, is fundamentally judicial, and justice is the linchpin of the social fabric: "Nature has implanted in the human breast that consciousness of ill-desert, those terrors of merited punishment which attend upon its violation, as the great safe-guards of the association of mankind, to protect the weak, to curb the violent, and to chastise the guilty" (p. 86). The breath of sympathy animates the whole system, which always remains, fundamentally, a matter of self-judgment and self-inflicted punishment:

> When I endeavour to examine my own conduct, when I endeavour to pass sentence upon it. . . . I divide myself, as it were, into two persons. . . . The first is the spectator, whose sentiments with regard to my own conduct I endeavour to enter into, by placing myself in his situation. . . . The second is the agent, the person whom I properly call myself, and of whose conduct, under the character of a spectator, I was endeavouring to form some opinion. The first is the judge; the second the person judged of. (p. 113)

Formal institutions merely enforce and regulate the juridical construction of self as the focal point of inspection by a potentially infinite number of imagined spectators—all collected into Smith's personification of the impartial spectator. For him, as for Bentham, punishment is the foundation of social order.

Smith's argument in *The Theory of Moral Sentiments* is persistently, stren-
uously normative. Certainly, the murderer depicted in the section on
reward and punishment, where Smith first presents the idea of the impartial spectator, is a rationalized ideal against whom all other criminals
are indexed: the socially assimilated man who, temporarily overcome by
passion, fully realizes the meaning of his crime and judges himself on
behalf of civilization. Smith's moral psychology—always and everywhere
a psychology centered on the issue of justice—allows us to understand
the penitentiary idea as centrally concerned with stimulating in criminals
the experience of "remorse" depicted in this paradigmatic narrative.
The mechanism is discursive and, of course, sympathetic: "By sympathizing with the hatred and abhorrence which other men must entertain
for him, [the murderer] becomes in some measure the object of his own
hatred and abhorrence" (p. 84). At first he thinks of flight to the utter
solitude of banishment, but its horror forces him to embrace judicial
punishment instead. He predicts that the judgment of his crime by society will be less severe than his self-condemnation unmoderated by
institutions. For as Smith declares at the start of his next section, official
consideration must look to his motives and to "the intention or affection
of the heart" from which an action proceeds. Worst of all would be to
remain undetected, living among others but subject to the depredations
of unmediated conscience:

> Men of the most detestable characters, who, in the execution of the
> most dreadful crimes, had taken their measures so coolly as to avoid
> even the suspicion of guilt, have sometimes been driven, by the horror
> of their situation, to discover . . . what no human sagacity could ever
> have investigated. By acknowledging their guilt, by submitting them-
> selves to the resentment of their offended fellow-citizens . . . they
> hoped, by their death to reconcile themselves, at least in their own
> imagination, to the natural sentiments of mankind; to be able to con-
> sider themselves as less worthy of hatred and resentment . . . and by
> thus becoming objects, rather of compassion than of horror, if possible
> to die in peace. . . . Compared with what they felt before the discovery,
> even the thought of this, it seems, was happiness. (pp. 118–19)

At least the judicial sentence is finite. Even while exacting death, justice
returns the criminal from the wasteland of inhumanity to the sphere of
social order and erases whatever monstrosity the crime revealed. Indeed,
Smith argues that "the rules of justice," unique among the virtues, "may
be compared to the rules of grammar" because they are "precise, accurate, and indispensable" (p. 175). Thus institutionally regulated, punishment becomes merciful because it draws the criminal back from the
abyss of irrevocable solitude into a demarcated isolation that punishes

while protecting consciousness from the horror of its own dissolution. As John Brewster wrote in *On the Prevention of Crimes* (1792), "There are cords of love as well as fetters of iron."[43] Smith's work delineates the psychological network within which the penitentiary idea will come to full growth; and, to the extent that he establishes a gulf between his idealistic account of human conscience and contemporary practice, he engages in a mode of reformist discourse.

Smith invokes the up-to-date notions of "correction" and "proportionable punishment," and certainly, in the context of his description of "the different shades and gradations of weakness and self-command," his assertion that the "control of our passive feelings must be acquired" is powerfully behaviorist (p. 145). More significant, however, is his consideration of justice as a system of interlocking psychological representations of punishment as experienced by the victim, by the criminal, and by the public at large. He provokes thought about how systems of punishment might alter states of mind. Conceptually, the step from his juridical theory of moral consciousness to penitentiary punishment is short indeed. The analysis of human motives that led Bentham to embrace the Panopticon differs greatly from that in *The Theory of Moral Sentiments*, but, within Smith's frame of reference, the effect of placing the convict under inspection in solitude would be to substitute institutional authority for the impartial spectator: to constitute artificially the character-defining structure that restrains criminal behavior. Bentham calls criminals "froward children" who cannot subject their passions to reasoned self-discipline.[44] Smith, in a passage that brings to mind Bentham's thirty-two "circumstances influencing sensibility,"[45] establishes a scale of character ranging from the very young child who has "not yet gone to school," through the weak man and the "man of a little more firmness," to "the man of real constancy . . . who has been thoroughly bred in the great school of self-command . . . and whether in solitude or in society, wears nearly the same countenance. . . . He does not merely affect the sentiments of the impartial spectator. He really adopts them . . . and scarce even feels but as that great arbiter of his conduct directs him to feel" (pp. 145–47). Smith's sympathetic self-consciousness rewrites the aesthetic of isolation as a social system. The penitentiary codifies and enforces this way of being in the world. The solitude it propounds cannot be that of the old-fashioned dungeon—at its worst a black hole in which vision ceases. Rather it must be isolation under inspection—solitude displayed in the glaring backlight of a Panopticon cell (fig. 54). But even in the Panopticon, actual beholders must view each person within the limits of physically constructed space, and therefore any real Panopticon will fail to make its population perfectly observable because it must run up against the technical limits of materials. The penitentiary acts out and strives artificially to reconstitute the structure of observation crystallized in the idea of the impartial spectator, but the institution can never fully reformulate in criminals the subjectivity that attends the ideal citizen in the society Smith delineates. The very nature of the penitentiary as a representation of a representation works to explain both its practical failure and its ideological persistence.

The children and weak men on Smith's scale of character require real spectators to maintain their rudimentary self-command.[46] But Smith's normative psychological process—embodied in the ideal man of constancy and, to a lesser extent, in the more typical man of firmness—involves an ever-unfolding, inevitably expository interior *dédoublement*. As David Marshall writes, each person "looks to his spectators for sympathy and in so doing imagines himself as a spectator to his own spectacle."[47] Character, conscience, consciousness, and society itself all partake in a cybernetic interchange where individuals continually adjust their responses into a register apperceptible within the distant, isolated subjectivity of others, and where others, living within their own cycles of self-consideration, continually reimagine external responses and adjust their own behavior accordingly. Subjectively, as Marshall argues, this involves an actual division of the self into alternative personifications or characters. One of these characters must always be the accused, the other an omniscient examiner.[48]

Sympathetic representation as Smith describes it shares significant attributes with transparent fictional construction in the realist novel. In fact, because emotions represented in the sympathetic imagination must compete with the intrinsically vivid affects of direct experience, the mechanisms of sympathy correspond to those of realism:

> That there may be some correspondence of sentiments between the spectator and the person principally concerned, the spectator must, first of all, endeavour, as much as he can, to put himself in the situation of the other, and to bring home to himself every little circumstance of distress which can possibly occur to the sufferer. He must adopt the whole case of his companion with all its minutest incidents; and strive to render as perfect as possible, that imaginary change of situation upon which his sympathy is founded. (p. 21)

Over and over again, Smith depicts the processes of sympathy as lodged within networks of precise material, situational, psychological, and causal reference of the kind that define realist narrative. Full sympathy involves unqualified entry into the mind of another—experienced transparently as if it were one's own. In the case of the death of a person wronged in a quarrel, for example, "we not only sympathize with the real resentment of his friends and relations, but with the imaginary resentment which in fancy we lend to the dead, who is no longer capable of feeling that or any other human sentiment. But as we put ourselves in his situation, as we enter, as it were, into his body, and in our imaginations, in some measure, [we] animate anew the deformed and mangled carcass of the slain" (p. 71). Or again, at the death of another's son, the sympathy that arises from "an imaginary change of situations" with the father "is not supposed to happen to me in my own person and character, but in that of the person with whom I sympathize . . . I not only change circumstances with you, but I change persons and characters" (p. 317).[49] Smith apprehends the processes of cultural and psychological formation as narratives in which members of society perpetually imagine the minutest circumstances of others as if they were their own and, in turn, imagine their own minute circumstances from the perspective of an imagined other. Therefore, I would shift the emphasis laid on Smith's theatrical metaphor by Barish, who says that it "puts the condition of spectatordom at the heart of the moral experience," or Marshall, who writes that it "represents a society where everyone and everything seem motivated by the gaze of spectators."[50] I have in mind a very simple point: namely, that while Smith's metaphor for consciousness is theatrical, its mode of representation is entirely mental. He considers spectatordom as the fundamental condition ordering social life, but the state of being he characterizes as theatrical must always be staged in a nontheatrical mental field that much more closely resembles the transparency of the realist novel than the non-narrative fictions of theater.

The act of imaginative construction in Smith's version of consciousness is not that of theater but of third-person narration—an unenactable kind of drama that has shed every trace of the histrionic and has become novelistic. He founds moral life in society upon the illusion of achieving what he takes to be impossible—absolute entrance into the sentiments of others. He personifies and, at times, theatricalizes the "tribunal within the breast" through which consciousness must, on his account, come into being. But its spectatorship actually is an impersonal fabrication analogous to the specialized use of the third-person position in transparent narration. Sympathy, operating through the medium of impersonal spectatorship, fuses the subjectivity of the beholder with other equally isolated but seemingly accessible consciousnesses. This staging of speech and thought in the third person, as if it were immediately present, is accomplished technically in the novel through free indirect discourse, the convention that permits fictional representation of consciousness as if it were unmediated experience. Ann Banfield, who argues that the technique appears only in written narrative, calls it "that style for representing consciousness which has almost become synonymous with novelistic style and which allows us to locate precisely the course of subjectivity."[51] Free indirect discourse transports the perspectives of beholder and first-person protagonist alike into an impersonal purview that can be achieved in writing alone. In fact, Smith's own style sometimes takes on the quality of narration and, with his instance of the murderer's remorse, verges on free indirect discourse as it was emerging in fiction of the period: "Every thing seems hostile, and he would be glad to fly to some inhospitable desert, where he might never more behold the face of a human creature, nor read in the countenance of mankind the condemnation of his crimes" (p. 84). Smith's theatricality is always manifest in a nontheatrical medium, like a play staged fictionally within a novel and presented, through the technique of free indirect discourse, as apparent direct experience within consciousness.

The penitentiary suspends the offender within a tightly specified topography of spectatorship which reproduces, as physical practice, an invisible masterplot that structures mental life in metropolitan society. This plot is capable of full enactment only through sympathetic construction, in the imagination, of those material particulars that govern the sensibility and behavior of others. Thus the penitentiary does not need to be accessible to visitors, or even physically present to view (in fact, by contrast with the old prisons, they came increasingly to be located outside of cities) because its rules are one and the same as those that govern consciousness itself. Citizens at large function, in imagination, as the beholders of penitentiary punishment, picturing themselves at once as the objects of supervision and as impartial spectators enforcing reformation of character on the isolated other. The essence of the Panopticon lies, as with Smith's impartial spectator, in its construction of an impersonal beholder. The principle of inspection functions, not because a single individual surveys the whole, but because anyone who occupies the surveyor's place—whether in fact or imagination—commands the whole (fig. 57). The impartial spectator is a personification, not a personality: its character exists, like the grammatical procedures of free indirect discourse, only as a general code. Although Bentham and other architects were able to specify every detail of structures in which the principle of inspection could be played out bodily—and in the mature Panopticon scheme every guard and turnkey, not just offenders, would have been subject to the gaze of others—inspection is not so much a physical condition as a way of living in a transparent world.

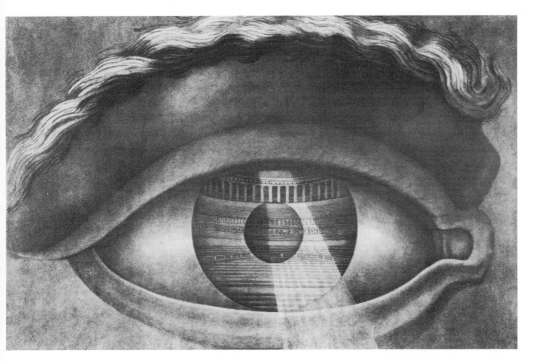

57. Claude-Nicolas Ledoux, *Coup d'Oeil du Théâtre de Besançon,* designed and built 1775–84. Spectator and spectacle fuse in Ledoux's image of an amphitheater reflected in the pupil of an eye placed on stage.

To feel is to judge.

HELVÉTIUS
De l'Esprit

For as all love is connected with a willingness to put ourselves in the place of the beloved object, so we must share all kinds of suffering with them, which is very expressively termed compassion. Why then should not fright, terror, rage, jealousy, revenge, in fact all forms of unpleasant emotions, even envy not excepted, spring from compassion?

G. E. LESSING
Hamburg Dramaturgy

I began these memoirs with the idea of vindicating my character. I have now no character that I wish to vindicate: but I will finish them that thy story may be fully understood; and that, if those errors of thy life be known which thou so ardently desiredst to conceal, the world may at least not hear and repeat a half-told and mangled tale.

WILLIAM GODWIN
Caleb Williams

8

The Absorptive Tableau and the Public Execution

A Postscript on Transparency as Practice

In this postscript, a brief consideration of two intimate pictures by Wright of Derby of prisoners in isolation opens onto the great world of public executions and, glancingly, onto the nineteenth century. This is not the place for anything approaching a full account of these subjects. Rather, a sketch may suggest ways in which historical developments ordinarily thought of as events in the sphere of policy can be understood to have an aesthetic dimension. I am less concerned to track a specific kind of painting in eighteenth-century England than to suggest that Adam Smith's psychology of conscience sheds light on the relationship between a particular manner of constructing (and beholding) pictorial images, which following Michael Fried I describe as "absorptive," and the exercise of spectatorship in contemporary English public life. Of course I refer to the rise of the penitentiary, where the panoptic array isolates both spectator and captive within an impersonal, narratively ordered field of moral sentiment and conscience. But here I have chiefly in mind the age-old practice of ceremonial execution, revisions in the conduct of which reproduced absorptive spectatorship in later eighteenth-century London civic life and led, ultimately, to the withdrawal of these spectacles from the public eye following the last hanging in front of Newgate in 1868. This change in social practice partakes of the inward impulsion of spectatordom that accompanies the removal of penal confinement from the realm of direct experience— the projection of punishment into imagination—that went forward with the establishment of the penitentiary as a national and international institution.

The mechanism of Smith's moral psychology explicates the phenomenon of "absorption," a term that Fried has employed in describing the response of certain French painters and critics of the 1750s and 1760s to a perceived crisis in the status of the spectator. Fried analyzes the preoccupation, especially that of Diderot and Greuze, with scenes which depict figures so utterly absorbed in action that the tableaux in which they appear seem to deny the beholder's existence and thus, paradoxically, to intensify his fascination with the characters to such a point that he may wish to address them, comfort them, or, in some paintings, even to enter their pictorial world. The absorptive tableau refuses theatricality of address (which came under intense theoretical scrutiny during the latter half of the eighteenth century) in pursuit of internal coherence and causal consistency of dramatic enactment. These paintings, like Smith's psychology, define a spectator who is at once isolated and irrevocably fascinated with the sensations and thoughts of the beings he confronts—a spectator simultaneously at one with an imagined consciousness yet incapable of direct entrance into its realm. The absorptive aesthetic is founded, in my view, on the paradox that the more isolated human beings become, the more minutely they become engaged in imaginatively re-creating the existence of others. Absorption portends intervention; re-creation implies regulation.[1]

Fried traces the course of absorption as a distinct problematic in eighteenth-century French painting and aesthetics, but he also connects significant formal attributes of these pictures with an "absorptive tradition" that thrived in Europe at least from Caravaggio and Rembrandt in the seventeenth century to Courbet in the nineteenth:

> The tradition to which I refer is essentially a realist one, and there is every likelihood that the connection between absorption and realism that it evinces is functional rather than merely accidental: thus, for example, an absorptive thematics calls for effects of temporal dilation that in turn serve the ends of pictorial realism by encouraging the viewer to explore the represented scene in an unhurried manner; the same painterly chiaroscuro handling that lends itself to strong absorptive effects . . . also yields effects of modeling and atmosphere— of the tangibleness but also the continuity of a perceptual field—that constituted one of the major innovations of seventeenth-century painting; and especially in the work of Vermeer and Chardin, the seeming obliviousness of one or more figures to everything but the objects of their absorption contributes to an overall impression of self-sufficiency and repleteness that functions as a decisive hallmark of the "real."[2]

Hogarth belongs in this tradition, too, even though none of his works perhaps qualifies as absorptive in Fried's most rigorous sense (figs. 35 and 41). Critics since Greuze's own lifetime have recognized Hogarth as a major influence in the formation of his art and, although the moral dimension and the aspect of serial composition are usually stressed, Hogarth's realism and his dramatic yet unhistrionic presentation, in which figures address one another rather than the spectator, all form part of the prehistory of Greuze's manner.[3] Hogarth evinces both that preoccupation with the everyday—with the particulars of ordinary existence —and also that concern with cause and effect as principles governing the representation of action, character, and motive that identify realism.[4]

· I ·

Wright of Derby (1734–97), a slightly younger contemporary of Greuze who worked primarily in the midlands of England, seems to me eighteenth-century Britain's most absorptive painter. His realism, according to Robert Rosenblum, catches with "photographic truth, a flash-bulb record of the incontrovertible facts of modern life."[5] His prison subjects of the 1770s and 1780s epitomize the aesthetic of isolation in its absorptive dimension and graphically record the shift in the self-evidence of the means of representation that I have noted earlier in comparing Dance's New Newgate and Bentham's Panopticon. I am aware of no written account of Wright's views on prisons, but his circle of patrons and friends intersects provocatively with the membership of those dissenting academies and scientific societies in the middle and north of England that provided significant support to the reform movement associated with John Howard. William Hayley, a devoted admirer of Howard who composed an ode commemorating his prison visitations, was one of Wright's best friends. And so was Erasmus Darwin, who in 1783 moved to Derby, where he founded the Philosophical Society and, incidentally, wrote an elegy in Howard's honor. Josiah Wedgwood, a close friend and significant patron of Wright's, belonged to the Derby Society and to the precedent Lunar Society, which met at the house of Matthew Boulton, another friend, and which counted among its members James Watt and Joseph Priestley.[6]

Wright's painting *The Captive, from Sterne* (c. 1775–77) (fig. 58) refers to a famous passage in *A Sentimental Journey* (1768). Yorick, a hero of extreme *sensibilité*, having been visited by the *lieutenant de police*, is stricken with fear of imprisonment because he lacks the passport necessary to travel in France during hostilities with England. He begins lightheartedly by turning the Bastille into a place of unworldly contemplation and recuperation, but when a voice crying "I can't get out —I can't get out" interrupts these witty reflections, his mood alters dramatically. The cry is from a captive starling, which Yorick cannot free even by wrenching

58. Joseph Wright of Derby, *The Captive, from Sterne,* c. 1775–77. Wright's absorptive figure engages the moral sympathy yet, in recapitulation of Sterne's irony, is painted with an artful theatricality that holds the spectator at a distance.

at its cage with both hands. Later he places the trained bird on his coat of arms as a silent icon of liberty, ironically reflecting the truth that, even at large, its only words must always be "I can't get out." Liberty and confinement can be conceived only as dimensions of one another.[7]

Yorick rejects an affecting picture of the millions born to slavery, for though "I gave full scope to my imagination. . . . I could not bring it near me, and . . . the multitude of sad groups in it did but distract me." Instead, he conjures up a lone pathetic figure, clearly a picture of another man but also a phantom of the moral sentiment—the form Yorick would wish to take in the imagination of an impartial spectator (a role here played by Yorick himself).

> —I took a single captive, and having first shut him up in his dungeon, I then look'd through the twilight of his grated door to take his picture.

I beheld his body half wasted away with long expectation and confinement, and felt what kind of sickness of the heart it was which
arises from hope deferr'd. Upon looking nearer I saw him pale and
feverish: in thirty years the western breeze had not once fann'd his
blood—he had seen no sun, no moon in all that time—nor had the
voice of friend or kinsman breathed through his lattice—his children—
—But here my heart began to bleed—and I was forced to go on
with another part of the portrait.
He was sitting upon the ground upon a little straw, in the furthest
corner of his dungeon, which was alternately his chair and bed: a
little calender of small sticks were laid at the head notch'd all over
with the dismal days and nights he had pass'd there—he had one of
these little sticks in his hand, and with a rusty nail he was etching
another day of misery to add to the heap. As I darkened the little
light he had, he lifted up a hopeless eye towards the door, then cast
it down—shook his head, and went on with his work of affliction. I
heard his chains upon his legs, as he turn'd his body to lay his little
stick upon the bundle—He gave a deep sigh—I saw the iron enter
into his soul—I burst into tears—I could not sustain the picture of
confinement which my fancy had drawn.[8]

Until the end, when the captive shows a fleeting awareness of his audience, Yorick serves both as artist and as a spectator in the manner of
Diderot. The scene is visually framed and entirely pictorial until, with
clanking chains, it breaks into an intimate drama that acts out the paradox of absorptive spectatorship. Yorick imagines his own prospective
confinement as a painting of such immediacy that, upon the slightest
hint at any potential for direct address, it becomes too much to bear. It
is also too much for him to see since compassionate identification tran-
spires at the split second the object becomes something that cannot be
visualized: "I saw the iron enter into his soul."

Sterne introduces elements of parody that objectify Yorick's intense
emotionalism and throw the mechanism of conscience into high relief
as self-consciousness. The captive is a purposeful creation of Yorick, a
personification of the motives that lead him to Versailles in quest of the
passport which, by certifying his standing as a legal personage, will free
him to traverse the authoritative grid of the state. Sterne's final twist
emerges when Yorick, who declares that "there is not a more perplexing
affair in life to me, than to set about telling any one who I am," receives
a passport allowing him free passage as the king's jester. The outcome
of Yorick's prison fantasy is the opposite of incarceration: his new passport grants total liberty because of a mistake about his identity. To be
wholly free, he must become a fictional personage from a past era, the
court jester who, long dead even in *Hamlet,* lives through imagination

alone. Sterne's ironic distance in "The Captive" and its framing episodes confirms the existence, historically, of juridical self-consciousness much as, in *Tristram Shandy*, his sustained parody of narrative linearity, temporal order, causal consistency, and explicatory detail confirms that such devices of realism then conventionally defined the novel.

Wright of Derby makes *The Captive* into a powerful claustrophobic image, "a new type of prison picture in which," as Lorenz Eitner writes, "the whole emphasis falls on the pathos of man-inflicted suffering, witnessed at close range. [The figure affects us] with something of the stillness and solemnity of an *Ecce Homo*."[9] Wright's sculptural arches imply a massive entombment, but in order to create an impression of immediate proximity, he manipulates the space into a visual field subjectively much smaller than a ground-plot of the architecture would reveal. A bright slanting light falls from the single barred window at the upper left, etching the solitary captive into his shallow cell and provoking an immediacy that the figure's profound self-absorption at once contradicts and incites. We are drawn to speculate about the mind of the absorbed figure; indeed, Sterne's text requests that the picture be about such an act of imagination: an attempted entry by a spectator into the sensibility of another. Nonetheless, the artfulness of Wright's presentation—its quality as a set piece, which is so ironically loaded in Sterne—is necessarily part of a sophisticated experience of the image. Wright's baroque holdovers (the theatrical lighting, his captive's Italianate torso and exotic headdress, and of course the specified emblematic chain) may be taken as visual counterparts to Sterne's innuendo. In these respects, the picture's means of representation provoke a self-conscious experience of it. Crushing rustications, for instance, were standard to imaginary prison architecture, but their programmatic use here recalls the actuality of Dance's *architecture parlante* in New Newgate (see, e.g., figs. 8, 9, and 55). The image terrifies, it impresses, it moves, it provokes thought and moral sympathy; but in some measure it also asks to be seen in a theatrical mode. Both Wright and Sterne seem to me engaged in the very problematic that Fried explores in French painting of the period.

Wright's *The Prisoner* (1787–90) (fig. 59), painted at least a decade later than *The Captive* as part of a closely related group of prison pictures, reveals a freer, more purely visual approach and, by a variety of devices including a massive pier in the left foreground and some scoring on the floor that cuts perpendicularly against the imagined path of entry to the picture, marks off space into much more distinct gradients.[10] By setting the prisoner at a great distance and flooding him with intense light from the back of a darkened space, Wright creates a visual metaphor of sheer isolation. The image calls up Adam Smith's query: "What is it which

59. Joseph Wright of Derby, *The Prisoner*, c. 1787–90. Wright's late
images of captives place spectator, prisoner, and light source in a
panoptic relationship.

prompts the generous, upon all occasions, and the mean upon many, to
sacrifice their own interests to the greater interests of others? . . . It is
reason, principle, conscience, the inhabitant of the breast, the man within,
the great judge and arbiter of our conduct. . . . It is from him only that
we learn the real littleness of ourselves . . . and the natural misrepre-
sentations of self-love can be corrected only by the eye of this impartial
spectator."[11] One wants to enter into the absorption of Wright's prisoner,
and his simple anonymity seems to encourage this act of projection. The
spectator, like a prisoner, experiences a blocked urban view, implied only
by the tiniest of steeples. But this picture carries much further than *The*

Captive the split between the light source and the figure as alternate focuses of attention. The almost dazzling window, in one aspect, draws the eye forward; but it also, and much more powerfully I think, impels the spectator backward. The flood of light leaves the viewer hovering at the edge of the pictorial space, suspended between an objective view and absorptive spectatordom. The panoramic perceptual field coheres around the light illuminating the prisoner much more naturalistically—much less theatrically—than in *The Captive*. *The Prisoner* creates a sense of transparency that includes but goes beyond even the substantially absorptive effects of *The Captive*. *The Captive* is experienced as a picture, *The Prisoner* as a mysterious kind of reality: it engages in a realism the illusion of which substitutes magically for reality itself.

The solitary prisoners in Wright's late paintings appear against floods of light that outline their silhouettes. However tiny the figures, their every gesture is clear. These images have a panoptic resonance that distinguishes them from earlier prison pictures. As Foucault writes, not with Wright's paintings but with Bentham's Panopticon in view: "By the effect of backlighting, one can observe from the [central inspection] tower, standing out precisely against the light, the small captive shadows in the cells of the periphery. They are like so many cages, so many small theatres, in which each actor is alone, perfectly individualized and constantly visible. The panoptic mechanism arranges spatial unities that make it possible to see constantly and to recognize immediately" (fig. 54).[12] Furthermore, whereas *The Captive* follows Sterne in registering time emblematically by a calendar stick in the prisoner's hand, *The Prisoner* renders the idea of a sentence in time partly through the metaphor of architectural mass and partly through the measurement of space into gradations of light. If we imagine entering *The Prisoner*, we must do so obliquely from the far right, traversing a path marked off vertically by massive piers and horizontally by scorings on a pavement littered with fragments of plaster. Among these grid markers, near the window, the prisoner himself occupies a place. Wright inscribes this rendering of measured time into spatial order entirely within an envelope of light that radiates in minute gradations from an opening that glimpses the prospect of ordinary life—the denouement of a penitentiary sentence as contrasted to the dungeon's dark, limitless, unstructured incarceration or as opposed to the void beneath the hanged man at the instant of execution.[13]

· II ·

For centuries the London hangings at Tyburn were communal spectacles. The cart transporting the condemned from Newgate formed the focal point of a public procession that passed by Saint Sepulchre's, where he received a nosegay while the death knell pealed from the church tower, to Saint Giles, where he drank a cup of beer before moving out the Tyburn-Oxford road toward the gallows near the present-day Marble Arch (fig. 16; coordinates F/l, F/g, and F/e). What with the vast growth in metropolitan population and with the de facto observation of executions as public holidays, eighteenth-century Tyburn took on a tumultuous carnival aspect that, in view of the universally accepted justification of public executions as deterrents to crime, gave serious observers pause. Execution day was often called "Tyburn Fair" and, at least to its critics, comprehended every imaginable form of public disorder and private vice. The privileged few sat in expensive stands erected by concessioners, while the general public struggled like groundlings at a revel to catch sight of the ostentatious dress and braggadocio manner displayed by highwaymen and other hero criminals on the gallows. Hogarth's panoramic *Idle 'Prentice Executed at Tyburn* (fig. 44) details both the carnivalesque and theatrical aspects of execution day. At Tyburn, even more strikingly than in the old prisons, official power intertwined with license. So much so that, by mid-century, Tyburn became the scene of battles between the reigning authorities, who, as E. P. Thompson argues, maintained power in large measure through demonstrative public spectacles like executions, and popular interests that viewed governmental intervention as a usurpation of traditional rights.[14]

Henry Fielding specifically condemned the bloody theatricality of Tyburn as analogous to the excesses of earlier English drama and argued for a solemn, even private, manner of execution that, like off-stage murders in classical drama (or that of Duncan in Garrick's *Macbeth*) would increase the terror of death. The old poets followed the ancient priests, who "well knew the use of hiding from the eyes of the vulgar what they intended should inspire them with the greatest awe and dread. The mind of man is so much more capable of magnifying than his eye, that I question whether every object is not lessened by being looked upon."[15] Finally, in 1783, the sheriffs of London were able to prevail against Tyburn with arguments strikingly similar to Fielding's. They, too, emphasized the effect of Tyburn Fair on the "minds of the spectators" and noted that "their sentiments are inclined more to ridicule than pity." The sheriffs stopped short of advocating private execution, but they did urge ceremonial solemnity, recommending that a bell toll throughout, that the crowd be held at a distance, that the scaffold be "hung with black," and that no one be "permitted to ascend it than the necessary officers of justice, the clergyman, and the criminal."[16]

On 3 December 1783, the first convicts were hanged before Dance's New Newgate (fig. 60). Although a number of other places in London

60. Thomas Rowlandson, *An Execution outside Newgate Prison,* after 1790.
Imagery recalling Hogarth's "Idle 'Prentice Executed" assists Rowlandson
in displaying the odd conjunction between Tyburn's carnivalesque
disorder and Dance's austere New Newgate.

besides Tyburn had long been used for certain executions and would
have been obvious candidates, the new location may have seemed foreor-
dained since capital felons were lodged at Newgate. But Dance's architectural aesthetic also had created the physical circumstances that enabled the move to take place. During the quarter-century following
Dance's design, the penitentiary would emerge with astonishing rapidity,
but alterations in English criminal law—the "Bloody Code" that required
public executions as part of its theatrical apparatus—occurred belatedly
and at wide intervals. The aesthetic of isolation as observed in the management of public executions worked at a different pace and with different material facts than did the design of penitentiaries. But, viewed
over approximately a century's duration, the outcomes were similar since
the last public executions took place in England just when the few old-
style jails that remained were being demolished or remodeled. Dance's
Newgate shared, paradoxically, in both the emergent absorption of the
penitentiary and the residual theatricality of the Bloody Code; the build-

ing was a contradiction, an old-fashioned version of the new and a quint-essential distillation of the old. As such it presented the only possible choice once the executions were moved in from Tyburn.

Dance's design strikes the balance between reserved monumentality and gripping terror recommended in the 1750s by Jacques-François Blondel, who lay stress on the pictorial aspect of architecture generally and of prisons especially. The felons' prison, says Blondel, ought to "declare to spectators outside the confused lives of those detained inside, along with the force required for those in charge to hold them confined." While urging upon architects the "grave, orderly, plain and heroic" character of true monumentality, he reserved to prisons and scenic decoration alone the "gigantesque" devices of *architecture terrible* with its "mammoth heaviness" and its "repulsive" style "composed of ridiculously heavy, weighty masses."[17] This style, now considered part of the phenomenon known as *architecture parlante,* stressed the capacity of architecture to foster emotion in its spectators much as narrative paintings did.[18] No doubt techniques of communication differ vastly between canvas and stone, but *architecture parlante* appeared in tandem with Diderot's absorptive aesthetic in painting and dramaturgy, and Blondel's approach through his doctrine of architectural *caractère* reinforces the impression left by surviving designs that horrific prison exteriors ventured far beyond the classical emblematic tradition into the realm of realistic representation.[19] Dance's installation of real chains and shackles over the doorways of Newgate indicates a full comprehension of his purpose (fig. 61; see also figs. 55 and 56).

Dance knew Piranesi in Rome, and his admiration of the etchings is often cited as a formative influence on the exterior of Newgate even though no specific borrowings have been adduced (fig. 8).[20] The inspiration from Piranesi actually lies less in details such as festoons of chains than in the building's scenographic impact. Dance's visual considerations in fact went far beyond even the derivation of his facade's sculptural form from the overscaled classicism of Palladio and Giulio Romano.[21] The eighteenth-century engraver who relocated New Newgate in a piazza inspired by Piranesi's *Views of Rome* grasped something essential about the effect the architect worked to produce in his comprehensive redesign of his London site (fig. 62). Because the prospect available to anyone traveling in through Holborn onto the street that used to pass under the old City gate was exaggerated by a downhill slope (fig. 9), Dance could secure his main effect by situating the building so that the spectators' primary view resembled those plunging perspectives of massively rusticated piles so typical of Piranesi's prints (fig. 63). Early sketches clearly reveal his intentions. In one, the new ground plan is drawn over

61. George Dance, Jr.,
New Newgate, London,
designed 1768.
"Debtor's Door"
surmounted by a
drapery of real
fetters.

VUE PERSPECTIVE DE LA PRISON DE NEWGATE À LONDRES.

62. Ferdinand Bourjet, *Vue Perspective de la Prison de Newgate à Londres,*
c. 1790. A fanciful setting derived from Piranesi frames the structure as
originally built with a pedimented central pavilion. A violent crowd
spilling into the square may be meant to recall the Gordon Riots of June
1780, during which the prison was burned.

dark shapes that indicate the placement of the Old Newgate buildings straddling the road through the City walls (fig. 64). This plan, dating from 1768, shows the new prison located on Great Old Bailey, opposite a pie-shaped block of buildings that separated it from Little Old Bailey. During the course of construction, this block was eliminated to form the square shown in Malton's engraving (fig. 65). It is hard to believe that Dance seriously contemplated any other outcome, since his building would have had little impact situated on a narrow street and he would have been forced to design for a corner view. Dance, managing the site of his prison as brilliantly as the light and shade of its masonry, placed in the most engrossing possible perspective one of the earliest architectural representations of imprisonment as a stimulus to public reflection. By exploiting topography and engaging in a deliberate act of pictorial urban planning, Dance fabricated a scenic framework awaiting only its actors. He created a metropolitan space in which executions could be staged so as to become part of an absorptive tableau.

Just four years before Dance began his designs, Beccaria had argued in *On Crimes and Punishments* that imprisonment, because of its duration, was a more terrifying penalty than the brief spectacle of death by execution:

> And precisely this is the advantage of penal servitude, that it inspires terror in the spectator more than in the sufferer, for the former considers the entire sum of unhappy moments, while the latter is distracted from the thought of future misery by that of the present moment. All evils are magnified in the imagination, and the sufferer finds compensations and consolations unknown and incredible to spectators who substitute their own sensibility for the callous spirit of a miserable wretch.[22]

It would have been all but impossible for Dance to escape some knowledge of Beccaria's work with its stress on the sensory impact of confinement and the dilation of its effects in the beholder's imagination. This is one of many reasons to count New Newgate as perhaps the earliest realization of the penitentiary idea even though its interior plan would shortly be condemned by Howard as hopelessly old-fashioned.[23] The massive construction that so tangibly represented the terrors of imprisonment to passing beholders rendered New Newgate incapable of effecting the new technology of punishment that would soon overtake prison architecture. Like Greuze in Fried's account of absorption in French painting during the 1760s, Dance was forced to resort to extraordinary measures in order to make the classical mode of representation function. Finally, even the somewhat exaggerated scenic manner that Blondel considered necessary to prison architecture would not suf-

1. Ingresso della chiesa del Foro, occupata sopra dalla Chiesa, 2. del Monastero delle Religiose 3. veduta del Foro. 5. Pilastri della stessa Chiesa di maniera gotica aperta nel detto recinto. dell'Annunziata. 2. Uno degli Archi principali, che davano l'ingresso nel Foro date sotto l'Arco de'Pantani. 6. Case fabbricate ne'tempi bassi, si prettamente del moderno Monastero 3. Archi interiori, che formavano due con l'ingresso al Foro. 4. Terra della perduta Nicera aperta nell'antico 7. veduta s'entra al Foro de' PP. di S. Quirico.   Veduta degli avanzi del Foro di Nerva   Cav. Piranesi Architetto F.

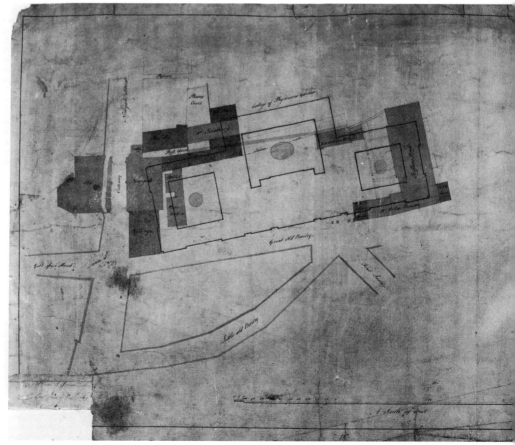

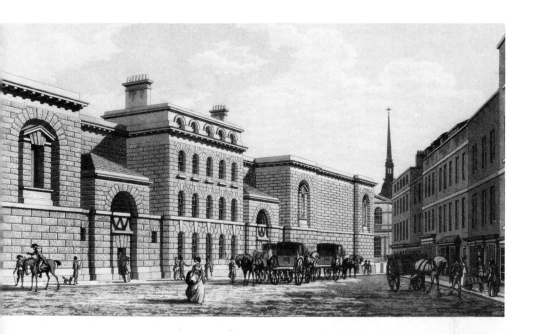

NEWGATE.

63. Above left: Giovanni Battista Piranesi, *Veduta degli Avanzi del Foro di Nerva.* Dance may have had in mind an exaggerated urban perspective like this when he designed the long, rusticated facade of New Newgate as one side of a newly cleared, wedge-shaped square.

64. Left: George Dance, Jr., Ground-Plan of New Newgate drawn over map of existing streets and buildings, c. 1768. Dance created a small piazza by removing the wedge of buildings that separated Great Old Bailey and Little Old Bailey. The downhill slope of Great Old Bailey assisted the illusion of a plunging perspective.

65. Above: Thomas Malton, *Newgate*, 1792. A full view of the square in ordinary use.

fice. No amount of manipulation of classical forms would yield an architecture sufficient to the penitentiary; new, technologically motivated structures had to be devised from the inside out.

By the same token, the extravagant theatricality of public executions could fit but awkwardly into the absorptive pictorialism of Dance's square. Tyburn, like the Globe Theatre of another age, had been outside the City. Its audience, like Shakespeare's, had accommodated tragedy and comedy comfortably together as alternate views of the same reality and had responded demonstratively to public spectacles that fused procession, pageantry, and oratory into theater. Largely without scenery, such theater was a rhetorical event that explicitly incorporated its audience. The new imagery was moving in quite different, absorptive ways. In front of New Newgate, the old Tyburn spectacle was delimited into illusionistic drama by the visual imagery of its new setting, and any view of a hanged criminal had to include the consideration of state authority present in this backdrop.

Dr. Johnson deplored the proposed move to Newgate as a "new way" of hanging and preferred executions under the "old method" precisely because they drew crowds: "If they do not draw spectators they don't answer their purpose." Johnson both saw the move as a radical change and, in discussing it as if it involved the removal of spectators from the scene of execution, intuited the eventual outcome. Boswell compliantly echoed Johnson's objections on this occasion, but the next June when he witnessed "the shocking sight of fifteen men executed before Newgate," he came away with impressions of a gravity that would surely have gratified the sheriffs who fostered the move:

> I was sure that human life was not machinery, that is to say, a chain of fatality planned and directed by the Supreme Being, as it had in it so much wickedness and misery. . . . Were it machinery it would be better than it is in these respects, though less noble, as not being a system of moral government. [Dr. Johnson] agreed with me now, as he always did, upon the great question of the liberty of the human will.[24]

Boswell, a connoisseur of executions, certainly seems to have experienced the Newgate hangings as different. For him, they fused visual response directly into a moral discourse that emphasized cause and effect. The new imagery was dramatically exclusive in quite specific ways. Divorced from their civic pageantry and from their potential for comedy or grotesquery, executions were forced into an absorptive pattern. To be present at but held at a distance from an intensely self-regarding spectacle seems to have provoked a profound moral self-consciousness. Certainly

Boswell's reflective engagement with the hangings he witnessed at Newgate contrasts sharply with the sheer terror he had experienced twenty-one years earlier following the execution at Tyburn of the glamorous highwayman Paul Lewis. Then he "was most terribly shocked" and thrown into such a deep melancholy that, three nights later, "I was still so haunted with frightful imaginations that I durst not lie by myself." At Tyburn he experienced ungoverned terror; at Newgate the quite different emotion that Lessing describes as tragic fear.[25]

At Newgate the introduction of the efficient mechanical "drop" reinforced the effect of Dance's horrific scene by shortening the heretofore drawn-out spectacle of execution and condensing its visual impact (fig. 66). The crowds really were more controllable and the imagery more emotionally focused. But the crowds remained too unruly for official taste and, as they grew with the vastness of metropolitan London, the impression of a tableau at Newgate executions was later increased by the introduction of a high platform (fig. 67). This "false stage," as the *Newgate Calendar* called it, made for a sharply demarcated relation between beholder and criminal and heightened the pictorial effect by holding the public at a distance and forcing their gaze upward to include a panoramic view of Dance's facade.[26] The spectators now stood in isolated correspondence with a mute spectacle. At other prisons, where the buildings were lower and the visual angle less steep than in the confined square before London Newgate, executions were removed to the roof leads (fig. 68). The fusion of architectural symbolism with the drama of execution had reached its technical limit. The requirement of public execution was met, but the interplay between spectator and event could be governed by principles analogous to the ones disclosed in Diderot's response to absorptive tableaux. Thus removed, executions were represented as actions so determined by their own rigorous laws of causation and by their own internally maintained web of attention that they provoked absolute fascination and intense imaginative projection. But finally the contradictions were insupportable: the demonstrative theatricality that always had motivated public executions overwhelmed the very imagery that had worked since the move to Newgate in 1783 to contain and maintain them.

The practice of public executions continued, as Radzinowicz observes, "long after the justifications that might once have supported them had disappeared," and not until 1868 had "the spectacle once thought so essential and potent a deterrent . . . dwindled to little more than a notice and a certificate on the gate of a prison."[27] Many factors combined to bring about their end: the overwhelming enormity of the crowds that massed for Victorian executions (fig. 69); profound revisions in criminal

The New Gallows in the Old Bailey.

66. *The New Gallows in the Old Bailey,* c. 1783. The new mechanical drop condensed the time required for multiple executions. Barriers and guards strictly separate spectators from the gallows, which can be entered only from Newgate's interior. A man in the foreground beholds the scene through an optical device.

VIEW OF AN EXECUTION BEFORE THE DEBTORS DOOR OF NEWGATE.

67. *View of an Execution before the Debtor's Door of Newgate,* 1809. Increasingly distant staging of executions heightened the scenographic tableau.

68. *Gaol for the County of Surrey,* 1800. Executions on the parapet of this scaled-down Newgate had to be viewed entirely within the pictorial context of the facade.

69. *Preparing for an Execution,* c. 1846. Victorian crowds thronged the scene of execution.

70. The drop inside New Newgate, photographed after 1868 and before demolition of the prison in 1902.

71. Execution shed inside New Newgate, photographed after 1868 and before demolition of the prison in 1902.

legislation, which by the 1860s had limited capital punishment to murder and to crimes against the crown; ever-increasing objections to the ancient assumption that the exhibition of capital punishment inspired an optimum of terror; a general sense that civilized punishment was not consonant with demonstrative spectacle.[28] The last public execution took place before Newgate on 26 May 1868.

A corresponding void opened in everyday life, for awful though the black hole beneath Newgate's private execution shed certainly was, its stark industrial structure discharged a mere technological function (fig. 70). The deterrent spectacle of executions henceforth would be staged solely in the transparent medium of conscience and the kindred genres of juridical imagination. When the hangings were moved out of public view into a brick and tin shed huddled at the corner of Newgate prison yard (fig. 71), the massive execution-day crowds, which Victorian reports numbered in the hundreds of thousands, were left to consult their own imaginations and, remarkably, to quest after realism in a parody of itself. Thereafter, on the execution days of celebrated murderers, the streets

72. The Chamber of Horrors, Madame Tussaud's Exhibition. The original gallows from Hertford Gaol, as shown in Madame Tussaud's during the 1960s.

around Madame Tussaud's Exhibition were thronged with crowds said to exceed thirty thousand. Mobs that once would have witnessed an actual execution crushed into the Baker Street rooms to catch a glimpse of the Chamber of Horrors, which, in Tussaud's Victorian practice, would have been freshly augmented that very day with a life-sized wax statue of the murderer just hanged—joined of course by an image of the current executioner, who would have deemed it an honor to cooperate with Tussaud's artists (fig. 72). In 1878 Tussaud's installed the gallows that had been in use at Hertford Gaol since 1824; a likeness of Marwood, the famous executioner, superintended, and Tussaud's often bought the murderer's actual clothes and memorabilia.[29] For a brief period in history, realism literally took the place of reality.

Notes

INTRODUCTION

Epigraphs: Freud's words come from the *Standard Edition of the Complete Psychological Works of Sigmund Freud* (London: Hogarth Press, 1953–74), 11: 38. The second quotation is from Geertz's *The Interpretation of Cultures* (New York: Basic Books, 1973), p. 451.

1. Burke's words come from *A Grammar of Motives* (Berkeley: University of California Press, 1969), p. xxii. Burke shows how language bridges the spheres of culture and social action, which, as Geertz suggests, are merely analytic categories: "One of the more useful ways—but far from the only one—of distinguishing between culture and social system is to see the former as an ordered system of meaning and of symbols, in terms of which social interaction takes place; and to see the latter as the pattern of social interaction itself. On the one level there is the framework of beliefs, expressive symbols, and values in terms of which individuals define their world, express their feelings, and make their judgments; on the other level there is the ongoing process of interactive behavior, whose persistent form we call social structure. Culture is the fabric of meaning in terms of which human beings interpret their experience and guide their action; social structure is the form that action takes, the actually existing network of social relations. Culture and social structure are then but different abstractions from the same phenomena" (*The Interpretation of Cultures*, pp. 144–45). On the history and significance of the word "culture," see the article in Raymond Williams, *Keywords* (New York: Oxford University Press, 1976), pp. 76–82. In the sentence that follows, I take the term "cognitive instrument" from Louis O. Mink, "Narrative Form as a Cognitive Instrument," in *The Writing of History: Literary Form and Historical Understanding*, ed. Robert H. Canary and Henry Kozicki (Madison: University of Wisconsin Press, 1978), pp. 129–49.

2. I define the novel as synonymous with narrative fiction (distinguished from nonfictional narrative on the one hand and from non-narrative fiction like drama and film on the other). I take the novel in general, and the realist novel in particular, to be defined by its unique technical capacity to represent consciousness in the form of unspoken thoughts, subjective responses, and sensations. This definition looks to Dorrit Cohn, *Transparent Minds: Narrative Modes for Pre-*

senting Consciousness in Fiction (Princeton: Princeton University Press, 1978), pp. 7–8. But unlike Käte Hamburger, whose book *The Logic of Literature*, 2d ed., trans. Marilynn J. Rose (Bloomington: Indiana University Press, 1973), provides the framework of Cohn's discussion, I do not distinguish sharply between first-person and third-person narration. As Ann Banfield says, the essential difference between narration and ordinary discourse is not "the presence or absence of any first person" but rather the presence or absence of ordinary communication. Banfield argues that "narrative fiction is structured linguistically by the conjunction of two unspeakable sentences, the sentence of narration and the sentence representing consciousness. Their coming together is a structural principle and a historical phenomenon" (*Unspeakable Sentences: Narration and Representation in the Language of Fiction* [Boston: Routledge and Kegan Paul, 1982], pp. 180, 257). This historical phenomenon is what I here call the realist novel.

3. Emile Durkheim, *The Division of Labor in Society*, trans. George Simpson (New York: Free Press, 1964), p. 97. Dan Sperber observes more generally that the symbolic "is not a means of encoding information, but a means of organizing it" (*Rethinking Symbolism*, trans. Alice L. Morton, Cambridge Studies in Social Anthropology 11 [Cambridge: Cambridge University Press, 1975], p. 70). For a comparable view, elaborated in terms eclectic enough to embrace significant ideas of both Marx and Durkheim, see Pierre Bourdieu, *Outline of a Theory of Practice*, trans. Richard Nice, Cambridge Studies in Social Anthropology, 16 (Cambridge: Cambridge University Press, 1977).

4. Fredric Jameson, *The Political Unconscious: Narrative as a Socially Symbolic Act* (Ithaca: Cornell University Press, 1981), p. 48.

5. See Mikhail M. Bakhtin, *The Dialogic Imagination*, ed. and trans. Michael Holquist and Caryl Emerson (Austin: University of Texas Press, 1981), pp. 262–64 et passim. According to Bakhtin, this dialogic exchange is possible because of "the novel's special relationship with extraliterary genres, with the genres of everyday life and with ideological genres. . . . Since it is constructed in a zone of contact with the incomplete events of a particular present, the novel often crosses the boundary of what we strictly call fictional literature—making use first of a moral confession, then of a philosophical tract, then of manifestos that are openly political, then degenerating into the raw spirituality of a confession, a 'cry of the soul' that has not yet found its formal contours. These phenomena are precisely what characterize the novel as a developing genre. After all, the boundaries between fiction and nonfiction, between literature and nonliterature and so forth are not laid up in heaven. Every specific situation is historical. And the growth of literature is not merely development and change within the fixed boundaries of any given definition; the boundaries themselves are constantly changing" (p. 33).

6. Gregory Bateson, "Metalogue: What Is an Instinct?" in *Steps to an Ecology of Mind* (New York: Ballantine Books, 1972), pp. 38–39. Newton's attitude toward hypotheses changed over the course of his career. See Alexandre Koyré, *Newtonian Studies* (Chicago: University of Chicago Press, 1965; reprt., 1968), chaps. 1 and 2; and Wesley Trimpi, "The Ancient Hypothesis of Fiction: An Essay on the Origins of Literary Theory," *Traditio* 27 (1971): Appendixes B and C.

7. Horace Freeland Judson, "Annals of Science (DNA—Part II)," *New Yorker*, 4 Dec. 1978, pp. 98–103. See also Ian Hacking, *Representing and Intervening: Introductory Topics in the Philosophy of Natural Science* (Cambridge: Cambridge

University Press, 1983), especially pp. 142–44. I doubt that Stephen Toulman's wish can be realized for theorists and critics to learn "the general historiographical lesson of Darwinism" before building explanations of the manner in which social institutions and relationships change. Still, the model he proposes holds distinct attractions: "In the development of historical entities or populations, it is not the *current* structure and relationships within that population which require to be explained as 'functional,' but rather the *changes* taking place in them which require to be explained as 'adaptive.' . . . Only when we consider the manner in which the current institutions or customs are changing, can we ask the operative question, 'What does this novel feature of society or culture achieve?' " (*Human Understanding: The Collective Use and Evolution of Concepts* [Princeton: Princeton University Press, 1972], pp. 349–50). For a corollary view of "fact" in scientific development, see Ludwik Fleck, *Genesis and Development of a Scientific Fact*, trans. Fred Bradley and Thaddeus J. Trenn (Chicago: University of Chicago Press, 1979).

8. See note 13 below for citations to Althusser. From Althusser's point of view, expressive causality underlies even the first paradigm, but see Jameson, *The Political Unconscious*, pp. 40–41.

9. Ibid., p. 34.

10. Jürgen Habermas, *Strukturwandel der Öffentlichkeit* (Neuwied: Hermann Luchterhand, 1962).

11. Weber and Durkheim use their characteristic methods to compare and contrast this process of rationalization and compartmentalization in modern European societies with similar developments in other cultures. See, for example, the selections on power, religion, and social structure in *From Max Weber*, trans. and ed. H. H. Gerth and C. Wright Mills (New York: Oxford University Press, 1958), and Durkheim, *The Division of Labor in Society*. For propositions about the ways in which these practices could have arisen from capitalist market conditions without reference to Marxian teleology, see Thomas L. Haskell, "Capitalism and the Origins of the Humanitarian Sensibility," *American Historical Review* 90 (1985): 339–61 and 547–66.

12. David Hume, *Treatise of Human Nature*, 2d ed., ed. L. A. Selby-Bigge and P. H. Nidditch (Oxford: Clarendon Press, 1978), 1.4.6, pp. 251–63. Ian Watt, *The Rise of the Novel* (Berkeley: University of California Press, 1959), p. 21, quotes the passage as it relates to identity and consciousness in the novel.

13. Pierre Macherey, *A Theory of Literary Production*, trans. Geoffrey Wall (London: Routledge and Kegan Paul, 1978), pp. 59–60. My description of the relations of literature and art to social forms, as well as my argument that the penitentiary idea took available shape at different historical moments in the literary, reformist, and architectural spheres, has been influenced by discussions of aesthetics in particular, and the phenomenon of emergence in general, in recent Marxism. Besides Fredric Jameson's *The Political Unconscious*, see Louis Althusser and Etienne Balibar, *Reading Capital*, trans. Ben Brewster (London: Verso Editions, 1979), pp. 99–102; and, especially, "A Letter on Art in Reply to André Daspre," in *Lenin and Philosophy*, trans. Ben Brewster (New York: Monthly Review Press, 1971), pp. 221–27. On the derivation of literary theory from Althusser's thought see James H. Kavanagh, "Marxism's Althusser: Toward a Politics of Literary Theory," *Diacritics* 12 (1982): 25–45. Works by Terry Eagleton also have been valuable: *Criticism and Ideology* (London: Verso Editions, 1978), chap. 3, especially pp. 89 and 100–101; and *Marxism and Literary Criticism* (Berke-

ley: University of California Press, 1976), pp. 20–36. Perhaps the most balanced synthesis is found in Raymond Williams, *Marxism and Literature* (Oxford: Oxford University Press, 1977). I adopt Williams's idea of cultural "emergence" and his term "structure of feeling." The works of Raymond Williams and Fredric Jameson, in particular *The Political Unconscious,* have proved especially valuable.

I draw freely on Marxist writers such as Macherey, Althusser, Bakhtin, Williams, Eagleton, and Jameson because they present highly developed theoretical accounts of the interaction between literary form and social institutions. Since most of these writers are primarily literary critics, they also provide analytical tools for the study of literary discourse as it relates to social process. But I cannot accept the a priori aspects of some versions of Marxism that privilege the economic bases of production by granting them ultimate causal, or at least explanatory, force. I adopt, rather, a critical but appreciative stance akin to that of Anthony Giddens in *A Contemporary Critique of Historical Materialism* (Berkeley: University of California Press, 1981). Similarly, I reject the notion of "mentality" as some ultimate force outside of and prior to texts. Mentality is not an object, not a container to be filled with meaning; it does not exist outside its cultural production. The interesting question is not the content of any particular construct we choose to consider as a "mentality," but how it is formed and how it changes as it renews itself. "Mentality" is always already changed as it is acted out in cultural process. For a Marxist analysis of Giddens's position see Erik Olin Wright, "Giddens's Critique of Marxism," *New Left Review,* no. 138 (1983): 11–35.

14. Williams, *Marxism and Literature,* p. 126.

15. This is no place to enter the vast controversy over the term "ideology." But see Williams, *Marxism and Literature,* sec. 1, part 4, as well as the entry in his *Keywords*; Althusser, "Ideology and Ideological State Apparatuses," in *Lenin and Philosophy,* pp. 127–86; Eagleton, *Criticism and Ideology,* chap. 2, and "Ideology, Fiction, Narrative," *Social Text* 2 (1979): 62–80; and Rosalind Coward and John Ellis, *Language and Materialism: Developments in Semiology and the Theory of the Subject* (London: Routledge and Kegan Paul, 1977), pp. 77–78.

16. Mikhail M. Bakhtin and Valentin N. Voloshinov, *Marxism and the Philosophy of Language,* trans. Ladislav Matejka and I. R. Titunik (New York: Seminar Press, 1973), p. 15 (italics omitted). See also "Discourse in Life and Discourse in Art (Concerning Sociological Poetics)," in *Freudianism: A Marxist Critique,* trans. I. R. Titunik, ed. Neal H. Bruss (New York: Academic Press, 1976), Appendix 1, pp. 93–116. Because of Bakhtin's apparent attempt to put his theories of "dialogic" discourse into actual practice, these works were published under the name of Voloshinov, a close associate. They are taken to be largely, if not exclusively, by Bakhtin. See Katerina Clark and Michael Holquist, *Mikhail Bakhtin* (Cambridge: Harvard University Press, 1984), chap. 6. Williams cogently treats both Bakhtin/Voloshinov's position in Marxism and his anti-Formalist, anti-Saussurean theory of the sign (*Marxism and Literature,* pp. 35–42).

17. Bakhtin gives the following definition in *Marxism and the Philosophy of Language:* "Behavioral ideology is that atmosphere of unsystematized and un-fixed inner and outer speech which endows our every instance of behavior and action and our every 'conscious' state with meaning. . . . The established ideological systems of social ethics, science, art, and religion are crystallizations of behavioral ideology, and these crystallizations, in turn, exert a powerful influence back upon behavioral ideology, normally setting its tone. At the same time, however, these already formalized ideological products constantly maintain the

most vital organic contact with behavioral ideology and draw sustenance from it; otherwise, without that contact, they would be dead, just as any literary work or cognitive idea is dead without living, evaluative perception of it. . . . This is what constitutes the vitality of an ideological production" (p. 91).

The most precise contemporary formulation I know of the role of literature and art within a Bakhtinian conception of ideology is by David E. Wellbery: "As a specific cultural code, an ideology exists only insofar as it is materialized, and such materialization inevitably takes place in texts (significant constructs). . . . Indeed, it seems a reasonable hypothesis that literary texts often represent innovative and problematic codifications from which reduced codes are later abstracted in such a way that they can generate subsequent materializations. In any case, it is clear that the description of the structure of a literary text is a necessary component in the account of that text's ideology precisely because [semiotic] structure is the locus of ideological materialization" ("Narrative Theory and Textual Interpretation: Hofmannsthal's "Sommerreise" as Test Case," *Deutsche Vierteljahrsschrift für Literaturwissenschaft und Geistesgeschichte* 54 [1980]: 331). I am indebted to Professor Wellbery for the previous citations to Sperber and Bourdieu.

18. Bakhtin, *Marxism and the Philosophy of Language*, p. 86.

19. Bakhtin, *The Dialogic Imagination*, p. 15. Ian Watt's *The Rise of the Novel* describes the inception of this phase of the enormous literary phenomenon that, for Bakhtin, the novel encompasses. Their ideas provide the broad framework within which I treat the novel in this book.

As Michael Holquist says, " 'novel' is the name Bakhtin gives to whatever force is at work in a given literary system to reveal the limits, the artificial constraints of that system. Literary systems are comprised of canons, and 'novelization' is fundamentally anticanonical. It will . . . always . . . insist on the dialogue between what a given system will admit as literature and those texts that are otherwise excluded from such a definition of literature. What is more conventionally thought of as the novel is simply the most complex and distilled expression of this impulse" (*The Dialogic Imagination*, p. xxxi). In the end, however, I deny Bakhtin's rather romantic insistence that the novel transcends the hegemony of official culture. I stress, instead, the ways in which realism, and especially the convention of transparency, enables the novel to participate in the containment, control, and reformation of social life. Collaterally, I believe my treatment of realism turns out to be less formalist than Watt's and my view of the novel's instrumental role in cultural formation more activist.

Although it has been criticized, Watt's classic definition of the realist novel's literary phenomenology has not been supplanted, and I employ it as a point of departure: "Formal realism . . . is the narrative embodiment of a premise that Defoe and Richardson accepted very literally, but which is implicit in the novel form in general: the premise, or primary convention, that the novel is a full and authentic report of human experience, and is therefore under an obligation to satisfy its reader with such details of the story as the individuality of the actors concerned, the particulars of the times and places of their actions, details which are presented through a more largely referential use of language than is common in other literary forms" (p. 32). I also find David Lodge's position congenial to my enterprise despite the questions about textuality raised by his "working definition of realism in literature" as "the representation of experience in a manner which approximates closely to descriptions of similar experience in nonliterary texts of the same culture" (*The Modes of Modern Writing: Metaphor, Metonymy, and the Typology of Modern Literature* [Ithaca: Cornell University Press, 1977], p. 25; italics omitted).

20. For a critique of the privileged position narrative construction of the mind has continued to enjoy in the twentieth century, see Donald P. Spence, *Narrative Truth and Historical Truth* (New York: W. W. Norton, 1982).

CHAPTER ONE

Epigraph: I quote here Peter H. Nidditch's edition of Locke's *Essay* (Oxford: Clarendon Press, 1975), 2.27.17, 2.27.18, and 2.27.26. For notes on the "forensic" concept of the self in these passages, see Alexander Campbell Fraser's two-volume edition (New York: Dover Publications, 1959), 1: 458–59 and 467. See also Henry E. Allison, "Locke's Theory of Personal Identity: A Re-Examination," in *Locke on Human Understanding,* ed. I. C. Tipton (Oxford: Oxford University Press, 1977), pp. 105–22; J. D. Mabbott, *John Locke* (London: Macmillan, 1973), pp. 58–64; Richard I. Aaron, *John Locke,* 3d ed. (Oxford: Clarendon Press, 1971), pp. 148–53, passim; and Christopher Fox, "Locke and the Scriblerians: The Discussion of Identity in Early Eighteenth-Century England," *Eighteenth-Century Studies* 16 (1982): 1–25.

1. Arthur Heiserman, *The Novel before the Novel* (Chicago: University of Chicago Press, 1977), p. 221; and Mikhail M. Bakhtin, *The Dialogic Imagination,* ed. and trans. Michael Holquist and Caryl Emerson (Austin: University of Texas Press, 1981), p. 124.

2. For a trenchant summary of conditions in eighteenth-century prisons and of the system of law enforcement in which they participated, see Gerald Howson, *Thief-Taker General: The Rise and Fall of Jonathan Wild* (London: Hutchinson, 1970), chap. 3. For detailed accounts of eighteenth-century prisons, see John Howard, *The State of the Prisons* (Warrington: William Eyres, 1777); reprinted, ed. Martin Wright (Abingdon: Professional Books, 1977); the posthumous fourth edition, as well as the second edition of Howard's *Lazarettos in Europe,* is reprinted in *Prisons and Lazarettos,* ed. Ralph W. England, Jr., 2 vols. (Montclair, N.J.: Patterson Smith, 1973), which is the edition to which subsequent citations refer unless otherwise noted. Informative modern works include Sidney and Beatrice Webb, *English Prisons under Local Government,* ed. Leon Radzinowicz (Hamden, Conn.: Archon Books, 1963), pp. 18–37; Max Grünhut, *Penal Reform: A Comparative Study* (Oxford: Oxford University Press, 1948), pp. 11–63; Leon Radzinowicz, *A History of English Criminal Law and Its Administration from 1750,* vol. 1, *The Movement for Reform 1750–1833* (New York: Macmillan, 1948), pp. 165–493; R. S. E. Hinde, *The British Penal System, 1773–1950* (London: Duckworth, 1951), pp. 11–47; U. R. Q. Henriques, "The Rise and Decline of the Separate System of Prison Discipline," *Past and Present* 54 (1972): 61–93; Michel Foucault, *Surveiller et punir: Naissance de la prison* (Paris: Gallimard, 1975), trans. Alan Sheridan as *Discipline and Punish: The Birth of the Prison* (London: Allen Lane, 1977), especially parts 2 and 3; Michael Ignatieff, *A Just Measure of Pain: The Penitentiary in the Industrial Revolution, 1750–1850* (New York: Pantheon, 1978), pp. 15–113; Seán McConville, *A History of English Prison Administration* (London: Routledge and Kegan Paul, 1981), 1: 49–134; and Robin Evans, *The Fabrication of Virtue: English Prison Architecture, 1750–1840* (Cambridge: Cambridge University Press, 1982), pp. 1–235. See also J. M. Beattie, "The Pattern of Crime in England, 1660–1800," *Past and Present* 62 (1974): 47–95, and "Crime and the

Courts in Surrey, 1736–1753," in *Crime in England, 1550–1800*, ed. J. S. Cockburn, (Princeton: Princeton University Press, 1977), pp. 155–86; for further references, see L. A. Knafla, "Crime and Criminal Justice: A Critical Bibliography," in Cockburn, *Crime in England*, pp. 270–98. Beattie's extensive treatment of the subject appeared as this book was going to press. See *Crime and the Courts in England, 1660–1800* (Princeton: Princeton University Press, 1986). My manuscript already was finished when I learned of Michael Ignatieff's important essay criticizing his own book, along with Foucault's *Discipline and Punish* and David J. Rothman's *The Discovery of the Asylum* (Boston: Little, Brown, 1971). See Ignatieff, "State, Civil Society, and Total Institutions: A Critique of Recent Social Histories of Punishment," in *Crime and Justice: An Annual Review of Research*, ed. Michael Tonry and Norval Morris (Chicago: University of Chicago Press, 1981), 3: 153–92. Although Foucault's and Ignatieff's ideas have strongly influenced my thinking about penitentiaries, both my general consideration of the novel as a phenomenon relatively autonomous of the state and, more specifically, my analysis of Adam Smith's *The Theory of Moral Sentiments* reflect concerns of the kind Ignatieff expresses about the tendency in revisionist history to treat quite diverse mechanisms of social regulation and control as deriving from the authority and the formal apparatus of state power.

3. See Radzinowicz, *A History of English Criminal Law*, 1: 632–42, for a detailed summary of the statutes. On the actual use of the death penalty as affected by the complex history of "benefit of clergy," see John H. Langbein, "Shaping the Eighteenth-Century Criminal Trial: A View from the Ryder Sources," *University of Chicago Law Review* 50 (1983): 36–41. Langbein says that, by 1717, transportation had "replaced death as the sanction for grand larceny and other clergyable felonies committed by first offenders" (p. 39). Despite this "fundamental alteration," "the death penalty still had a robust future" because statute law proceeded to remove benefit of clergy from aggravated felonies such as breaking and entering at night (p. 40).

4. See W. J. Sheehan, "Finding Solace in Eighteenth-Century Newgate," in Cockburn, *Crime in England*, pp. 229–45; and Joanna Innes, "The King's Bench Prison in the Later Eighteenth Century: Law, Authority, and Order in a London Debtors' Prison," in *An Ungovernable People: The English and Their Law in the Seventeenth and Eighteenth Centuries*, ed. John Brewer and John Styles (New Brunswick, N.J.: Rutgers University Press, 1980), pp. 250–98.

5. *Horace Walpole's Correspondence*, vol. 20, *Correspondence with Sir Horace Mann*, ed. W. S. Lewis, Warren Hunting Smith, and George L. Lam (New Haven: Yale University Press, 1960), p. 199. For an account of Maclaine's career, including the Hyde Park robbery in which Walpole "narrowly escaped being killed by the accidental going off of the highwayman's pistol, which . . . took off the skin of his cheekbone," see pp. 168–69.

6. Frantz Funck-Brentano, *Prisons d'autrefois* (Paris: Flammarion, 1935), p. 6. On Sheppard, see Daniel Defoe, *A Narrative of All the Robberies, Escapes, &c. of John Sheppard* (London: John Applebee, 1724) and *The History of the Remarkable Life of John Sheppard* (London: John Applebee, 1724). Sheppard escaped from various prisons four different times. For a readable modern account, see Christopher Hibbert, *The Road to Tyburn: The Story of Jack Sheppard and the Eighteenth Century Underworld* (London: Longmans, Green and Co., 1957).

7. *The Spectator*, ed. Donald F. Bond, 5 vols. (Oxford: Clarendon Press, 1965), 1: 350, notes the Englishness of imprisonment for debt. Failure to repay debt

can be regarded as a special kind of crime against property. Howard reveals that while imprisonment for debt was allowed in most Continental countries, the creditors usually had to pay for the upkeep of the debtor and therefore rarely took action. See Appendix 3 in the first volume of Radzinowicz, *A History of English Criminal Law*, for the impressions of foreign visitors on criminal justice in England, including many on the English imprisonment of debtors. Evans graphs figures from Howard and other sources to show that between 1775, when more than half of all prisoners (4,084) were debtors (2,437), and 1843 there was a steady increase in the imprisonment of nondebtors relative to a declining population of debtors. As Evans says, the figures reflect "the rapid and consistent development of the prison as the major legal sanction for crimes and misdemeanours, together with the dwindling of the debtor population" (*The Fabrication of Virtue*, p. 421, fig. 217). In 1843, the total of all prisoners was 15,792, of whom 1,796 were debtors.

8. Webb and Webb, *English Prisons*, pp. 24, 65, 119–20. As late as 1836 inspectors found petty debtors mixed into felons' wards at Newgate.

9. Ibid., pp. 16–17. See also Grünhut, *Penal Reform*, p. 25.

10. For Oglethorpe's account, see *A Report from the Committee Appointed to Enquire into the State of the Gaols of this Kingdom: Relating to the Fleet Prison* (London: Robert Knaplock, Jacob Tonson, John Pemberton, and Richard Williamson, 1729). Reports containing like findings at the Marshalsea Prison and additional details on the Fleet were published under the same imprint later in 1729; the next year the committee found worse conditions at the King's Bench Prison (London: Richard Williamson, 1730). For details see Leslie F. Church, *Oglethorpe: A Study of Philanthropy in England and Georgia* (London: Epworth Press, 1932), pp. 9–24; and Amos A. Ettlinger, *James Edward Oglethorpe, Imperial Idealist* (Oxford: Clarendon Press, 1936), pp. 89–95. Hall's pamphlet is reprinted in Philip Pinkus, *Grub Street Stripped Bare* (Hamden, Conn.: Archon Books, 1968), pp. 288–350. See also Moses Pitt, *The Cry of the Oppressed: Being a True and Tragical Account of the Unparallel'd Sufferings of Multitudes of Poor Imprison'd Debtors* (London: M. Pitt, 1691).

11. See Anthony Babington, *The English Bastille: A History of Newgate Gaol and Prison* (London: MacDonald and Co., 1971), p. 96; Ignatieff, *A Just Measure of Pain*, pp. 39–40.

12. Webb and Webb, *English Prisons*, pp. 21, 27. No predicament underlines the commonality of the old prisons more sharply than that of prisoners under accusation of felony: in law they were innocent until convicted and were supposed to enjoy special privileges while awaiting trial; in practice they could endure many months of treatment indistinguishable from that of convicts before judges arrived to conduct the Assizes or Quarter Sessions. Reformers complained in unavailing litany on behalf of such prisoners, but the old jails continued to defy even rudimentary categorizations. On this point see the Webbs (pp. 24, 57, 61, 65, and especially 77–82). In J. Mordaunt Crook and M. H. Port, *The History of the King's Works* (London: Her Majesty's Stationery Office, 1973), 6: 354, appears a quotation from 1773 in which the marshal of the King's Bench says that cramped quarters forced him to intermix prisoners.

Since the subcategories tended to merge and dissolve in actual practice, I usually shall refer simply to "prisons" and to "prisoners." I take this approach because I aim to consider the large patterns of confinement across the century. Where classifications in the old prisons matter to my argument, I of course take them into account. A recent historian has been criticized for treating the felons and debtors in Newgate as one population. Certainly it is worthwhile to seek out differences in detail; but there is reason to doubt that the differences arose from enforcement of official categories. See Joanna Innes, "The King's Bench Prison in the Later Eighteenth Century: Law, Authority, and Order in a London Debtors' Prison," p. 382, commenting on pp. 233–34 of W. J. Sheehan, "Finding Solace in Eighteenth-Century Newgate," in Cockburn, *Crime in England*.

13. On the physical conditions at Newgate, see Harold D. Kalman, "Newgate Prison," *Architectural History: Journal of the Society of Architectural Historians of Great Britain* 12 (1969): 50–61; on the dilapidation of walls, their reconstruction, and the liability of jailers for escapes, see Crook and Port, *The History of the King's Works*, 6: 627–28.

14. Samuel Johnson, *The Rambler*, ed. W. J. Bate and Albrecht B. Strauss, 3 vols. (New Haven: Yale University Press, 1969), no. 114. On eighteenth-century theories of deterrence see Radzinowicz, *A History of English Criminal Law* 1: 231–396.

15. *Dei Delitti e delle Pene* was translated into French by the Abbé Morellet (1766) and was being translated into English by an anonymous writer only eighteen months after its first appearance. See Cesare Beccaria, *On Crimes and Punishments*, ed. and trans. Henry Paolucci (Indianapolis: Bobbs-Merrill, 1963), p. x. On Beccaria's life, work, ideas, and influence, see Radzinowicz, *A History of English Criminal Law*, 1: 277–300; Marcello Maestro, *Cesare Beccaria and the Origins of Penal Reform* (Philadelphia: Temple University Press, 1973); and Coleman Phillipson, *Three Criminal Law Reformers: Beccaria, Bentham, Romilly* (London: J. M. Dent, 1923), pp. 3–106.

16. See, e.g., figs. 55 and 56. Convenient anthologies of photographs appear in Nikolaus Pevsner, *A History of Building Types* (Princeton: Princeton University Press, 1976), chap. 10, and in Helen Roseneau, *Social Purpose in Architecture: Paris and London Compared, 1760–1800* (London: Studio Vista, 1970), chap. 4; see also Evans, *The Fabrication of Virtue*, figs. 63, 86, and 129–35. For a brief account of these eighteenth-century developments, see Bruno Foucart, "Architecture carcérale et architectes fonctionnalistes en France au XIXe siècle," *Revue de l'Art* 32 (1976): 44–45. Emil Kaufmann, *Architecture in the Age of Reason: Baroque and Post-Baroque in England, Italy, and France* (Cambridge: Harvard University Press, 1955), p. 130, describes *architecture parlante* as "narrative architecture." The term, though not specifically Jacques-François Blondel's, crystallizes ideas set forth in lectures he began in the 1750s; they were published as his *Cours d'architecture*, 6 vols. (Paris: Desaint, 1771–77). See *Architecture in the Age of Reason*, pp. 102, 150, 154, 251 n.78 and passim; and Kaufmann's *Three Revolutionary Architects: Boullée, Ledoux, and Lequeu*, in *Transactions of the American Philosophical Society*, n.s. 42, pt. 3 (Philadelphia: American Philosophical Society, 1952), pp. 447, 514, 517, 520, 535.

17. Howard, *Prisons and Lazarettos*, 1:41,12; 2:226. On Howard's sense of personal guilt and on the intertwined strands of spiritualism and rationalism among English Nonconformists of the later eighteenth century, see Ignatieff, *A Just Measure of Pain*, pp. 47–52. Henriques traces into the nineteenth century the tensions between the rationalist and spiritualist elements in the prison reform movement but states that in the early stages there "was a wide area of agreement" ("Prison Discipline," p. 64). It seems to me artificial to draw extremely sharp distinctions between the two approaches since they so often intertwine and since

their proposals are founded upon the same mechanistic psychology. The reformers all assumed, even when they omitted to state it as a first principle, a psychology of impression and association, a materialistic connection between the actions of the body and the movement of the mind traceable first to Hartley and ultimately to Locke. On this psychology rested much of the reformers' public appeal because it explained mental phenomena in physical terms and encouraged the inference that they might therefore be brought under human control. See Henriques (p. 91) and Ignatieff (pp. 60, 66–67).

18. *Public General Acts*, 19 Geo. 3, c. 74 (1779). Published in *The Statutes at Large, anno decimo nono Georgii III Regis*, ed. Danby Pickering (Cambridge: Charles Bathurst, 1778–79), vol. 32, pt. 2, pp. 417–45. The quotation begins section 5 of the act. The many other sections of interest include section 14 listing the general architectural specifications; section 33 on solitary confinement; and, especially, section 38 outlining the classifications into which prisoners were to be divided and the three distinct phases of reformative punishment through which the classes would progress during the fulfillment of their sentences (exact particulars were to be devised by committee). Extracts from the Penitentiary Act (or Hard Labour Bill) are printed in the appendix to Helen Roseneau, *Social Purpose in Architecture*. On the Penitentiary Act of 1779, as well as reformist legislation that came before and after it, see volume 1 of Radzinowicz, *A History of English Criminal Law*; Ignatieff, *A Just Measure of Pain*, pp. 93–96; Evans, *The Fabrication of Virtue*, pp. 119–20; and McConville, *English Prison Administration*, pp. 86–87, 105–11. As McConville (pp. 88–98) and Evans (pp. 131–34) notice, local reforms prior to the Penitentiary Act also were influential: for example, in Sussex, the duke of Richmond instigated the construction of Horsham Gaol following Howard's principles; it opened in 1779.

The 1779 act took necessity as its occasion because transportation of condemned felons had ceased upon the outbreak of the American war; tightly packed jails became still worse when trade declined in the 1780s and soldiers returning unemployed from the war turned to crime. The situation was urgent. Howard reported an increase of 84 percent in the prison population between 1776 and 1788. These conditions allowed the reformers to experiment with a wealth of new buildings, but the rush to build new jails was such that many counties followed traditional or outdated plans. The penitentiary idea remained no more than an ideal in numerous counties. On the situation after the war, see Beattie, "The Pattern of Crime in England, 1660–1800," and Evans, *The Fabrication of Virtue*, p. 131 and fig. 217; on the rush to build new prisons and penitentiaries see Evans, chap. 4, and Webb and Webb, *English Prisons*, pp. 50–52.

19. For the Gloucestershire Act of 1785, along with the general regulations and rules governing the jails and penitentiaries of that county, see J. R. S. Whiting, *Prison Reform in Gloucestershire, 1776–1820: A Study of the Work of Sir George Onesiphorus Paul, Bart.* (London and Chichester: Phillimore and Co., 1975), Appendixes A and B. See also, on the Gloucestershire project, Ignatieff, *A Just Measure of Pain*, pp. 98–109; Evans, *The Fabrication of Virtue*, pp. 139–42; and McConville, *English Prison Administration*, pp. 98–104.

20. Cited by Evans, *The Fabrication of Virtue*, p. 132. On William Blackburn, see ibid., chap. 4; also H. M. Colvin, *A Biographical Dictionary of British Architects, 1600–1840* (London: John Murray, 1978), pp. 113–14.

The theory and practice of solitary confinement during the early phase of reform is a subject in itself. Henriques argues that the spiritualist reformers gravitated to schemes involving solitary confinement while the rationalists tended to put forth those involving supervised labor. This is a plausible framework in which to place the developments that culminated with the decision to construct the Model Prison at Pentonville (1842) using the separate system, but it understates the central role of theoretical speculation about solitary confinement in the emergence of the penitentiary idea during the eighteenth century. On the other hand, theoretical arguments in favor of reformative solitude came into question during the two decades following the Penitentiary Act as actual experience in the construction and management of real institutions revealed its enormous cost and often destructive psychological consequences. Bentham's original Panopticon appeared to solve the difficult problem of combining isolation and labor, but later he abandoned as uneconomical his early insistence upon solitary confinement. Howard's early enthusiasm for reformative solitude waned when he saw its destructive potential:

> It should . . . be considered by those who are ready to commit, for a *long* term, petty offenders to *absolute* solitude, that such a state is more than human nature can bear, without the hazard to distraction or despair. . . . The beneficial effects on the mind of such a punishment, are speedy, proceeding from the horror of a vicious person left entirely to his own reflection. This may wear off by long continuance, and a sullen insensibility may succeed. (*Prisons and Lazarettos*, 2: 169)

Only in the nineteenth century did the absolute separation of inmates become national policy. Even so, numbers of the earliest reformed penitentiaries provided for absolute separation, and solitary confinement had many strong adherents, including Sir George Onesiphorus Paul and various county magistrates like those of Berkshire, whom Howard reprimanded in the passage quoted above. I stress solitary confinement in this book because of its importance to thought about reformative punishment during the eighteenth century and because it remains central to the penitentiary idea, even in the present day, despite countless variants in the physical institutions designed to put it into practice as a social system.

21. A few early instances include Geffray Mynshul, *Essays and Characters of a Prison and Prisoners* (London: Mathew Walbacke, 1618); John Taylor, *The Praise and Virtue of a Jayle and Jaylers* (London, 1623); and John Frith, *Vox Piscis: or, the Book-Fish* (London, 1627). Mynshul says, for example, "Being once arriued at [the prison], all are not onely staid, but the inchantments are so strong, that it transformeth all that come thither. First, the greatest courages are here wracked, the fairest reuenues doe here come aground; it maketh a wise man to lose his wits, a foole to know himselfe, it turnes a rich man into a begger, and leaues a poore man desperate" (p. 2). Mynshul was in prison with Thomas Dekker, on whose *Villanies Discovered by Lanthornes and Candlelight* he often depends. See Mary L. Hunt, "Geffray Mynshul and Thomas Dekker," *Journal of English and Germanic Philology* 11 (1912): 231–43.

22. I lay stress here on Turner's initial essay, "Betwixt and Between: The Liminal Period in *Rites de Passage*," *Proceedings of the American Ethnological Society* (1964): 4–20; substantially reprinted in *The Forest of Symbols* (Ithaca: Cornell University Press, 1967) and in William A. Lessa and Evon Z. Vogt, eds., *Reader in Comparative Religion: An Anthropological Approach*, 3d ed. (New York: Harper and Row, 1972), pp. 338–47. The quotation appears on page 341 of this last edition; parenthetical references in my text are also to this printing of "Betwixt

and Between" unless noted. Turner based his definitions on Arnold van Gennep, *Les Rites de Passage* (Paris: E. Nourry, 1909), trans. Monika B. Vizedom and Gabrielle L. Caffee (London: Routledge and Kegan Paul, 1960). Subsequently, Turner developed his ideas in a variety of contexts, but for sake of precision and clarity I wish to adhere for the most part to his original definitions. The later works include *The Ritual Process: Structure and Anti-Structure* (Chicago: Aldine Publishing Co., 1969), especially chaps. 3 and 5; *Dramas, Fields, and Metaphors: Symbolic Action in Human Society* (Ithaca: Cornell University Press, 1974), especially chap. 6; "Variations on a Theme of Liminality," in *Secular Ritual*, ed. Sally F. Moore and Barbara G. Myerhoff (Assen: Van Gorcum, 1977); and "Process, System, and Symbol: A New Anthropological Synthesis," *Daedalus* 106, no. 3 (1977): 61–80; see also his "Comments and Conclusions," in *The Reversible World: Symbolic Inversion in Art and Society*, ed. Barbara A. Babcock (Ithaca: Cornell University Press, 1978), pp. 276–96. For an account of Turner's work as intermediary between social science and literary studies, see Clifford Geertz, "Blurred Genres: The Refiguration of Social Thought," *American Scholar* 49 (Spring 1980): 165–79, especially 172–73. See also Richard F. Hardin, "Ritual in Recent Criticism: The Elusive Sense of Community," *PMLA* 98 (1983): 846–62.

23. Alexander Smith, *A Complete History of the Lives and Robberies of the Most Notorious Highwaymen*, ed. Arthur L. Hayward (London: George Routledge and Sons, 1933), p. 108, reprinting the enlarged fifth edition (1719); Smith first published his work in 1714. See also *Memoirs of the Right Villainous John Hall* (1708); T. H., *A Glimpse of Hell; or, A Short Description of the Common Side of Newgate* (1704); and *The History of the Press Yard* (1717). Maximillian E. Novak discusses these and other works of criminal narrative in chap. 6 of *Realism, Myth, and History in Defoe's Fictions* (Lincoln: University of Nebraska Press, 1983), where he quotes part of this passage from Smith on page 127.

24. The first two quotations in this paragraph are from Turner, *Dramas, Fields, and Metaphors*, pp. 256 and 15, respectively.

25. W. Paget, *The Humours of the Fleet* (London, 1749). For a full account of the frontispiece (fig. 1), see Frederic George Stephens, *Catalogue of Prints and Drawings in the British Museum: Political and Personal Satires*, vol. 3, pt. 1 (London: Chiswick Press for the Trustees of the British Museum, 1877), no. 3049.

26. E. P. Thompson, "Eighteenth-Century English Society: Class Struggle without Class?" *Social History* 3 (1978): 154. See pp. 134–37 on the term "paternalistic" and its limitations. For Thompson's further exposition of these ideas, see also "Patrician Society, Plebeian Culture," *Journal of Social History* 7 (1974): 382–405; "The Moral Economy of the English Crowd in the Eighteenth Century," *Past and Present* 50 (1971): 76–136; and "Eighteenth-Century Crime, Popular Movements and Social Control," *Bulletin of the Society for the Study of Labour History* 25 (1972): 9–11. Related articles appear in Douglas Hay et al., *Albion's Fatal Tree: Crime and Society in Eighteenth-Century England* (New York: Pantheon, 1975); the legal historian John H. Langbein attacks this book in "*Albion's* Fatal Flaws," *Past and Present* 98 (1983): 96–120. For criticism of Thompson's work based on studies by John Brewer and others, see Lawrence Stone, "Plebes and Patricians," *New York Review of Books*, 29 May 1980, pp. 45–46 (reviewing *An Ungovernable People*); a substantial reply, stressing the "competing notions of order" at work in English society of the period, appears in a later review of Brewer by Susan Staves, *Eighteenth-Century Studies* 17 (1983): 102–7. J. M. Beattie's recent book *Crime and the Courts in England, 1660–1800* presents considerable

evidence that bears on the dispute. His broad conclusions harmonize with Thompson's, but see also Alan Macfarlane's review of Beattie (*London Review of Books*, 24 July 1986, pp. 8–9). In general, critiques of Thompson's thesis wrongly identify his use of the term "hegemony" with simple ideas of "class," not noticing his indebtedness to Gramsci's subtle definition. Various "classes" within a hegemonic social structure can serve its purposes and share its ideological dispositions; the point of cultural hegemony is that it works to displace class interest by substituting mystified ideological formulations for the objective recognition of "class" needs. See Ronald Paulson, *Popular and Polite Art in the Age of Hogarth and Fielding* (Notre Dame: University of Notre Dame Press, 1979), for an astute, wide-ranging use of Thompson's framework as a point of departure for the study of works of literature and art.

27. Ignatieff, *A Just Measure of Pain*, p. 38.

28. Howard, *Prisons and Lazarettos*, 1: 244. Howard says that sponging houses and bailiffs kept hold on those who had money (ibid., p. 5). Adventures in sponging houses were as common in the life of the eighteenth century as in its literature. Dr. Johnson, though already famous for the *Dictionary*, would have spent the night of 16 March 1756 in such a house had his friend Samuel Richardson not replied promptly to his request for five pounds, eighteen shillings. This was not a terribly large sum, but debtors might be jailed for much less. See James L. Clifford, *Dictionary Johnson: Samuel Johnson's Middle Years* (New York: McGraw-Hill, 1979), pp. 162–63, and *Boswell's Life of Johnson*, ed. G. B. Hill, revised and enlarged by L. F. Powell, 6 vols. (Oxford: Clarendon Press, 1934–64), 1: 303–4.

29. See, for example, Robert Darnton (*The Literary Underground of the Old Regime* [Cambridge: Harvard University Press, 1982], pp. 159–65) for rites of passage among Continental printers. As Darnton notes in "A Journeyman's Life under the Old Regime," *Princeton Alumni Weekly* 82, no. 1 (September 1981): 13–14, Benjamin Franklin, having refused the second of successive garnishes in the London shop where he apprenticed, suffered from practical jokes. All, says water-drinking Franklin, were "ascrib'd to the Chapel Ghost, which they said ever haunted those not regularly admitted." He eventually paid up, but then converted most of the shop to a healthy diet of porridge rather than the beer his garnish or *Bienvenu* had been meant to finance. The "chapel" was both the printing shop and the body of journeymen, just as Paget's mates in the Fleet formed its "college." Franklin's full account appears in his *Autobiography*, ed. Leonard W. Labaree et al. (New Haven: Yale University Press, 1964), pp. 100–101. On the revision of old customs governed by tradition in American ideology, where literary representation radically altered paternalistic social forms, see Jay Fliegelman, *Prodigals and Pilgrims: The American Revolution against Patriarchal Authority, 1750–1800* (Cambridge: Cambridge University Press, 1982), especially pp. 106–13 on Franklin.

30. Jürgen Habermas, *Strukturwandel der Öffentlichkeit* (Neuwied: Hermann Luchterhand, 1962), pp. 45, 64, 73. The Fleet from at least 1733, and the King's Bench, from at least 1754, both contained coffee houses formally recognized as such. See Bryant Lillywhite, *London Coffee Houses* (London: George Allen and Unwin, 1963), pp. 208–9, 313–14.

31. Howard, *Prisons and Lazarettos*, 1: 36.

32. The Webbs cite the dukes of Richmond and Devonshire as exceptions among leaders working for prison reform in the counties (*English Prisons*, pp.

54, 63n.). G. O. Paul had risen from a family in trade; Richmond and Devonshire, though exceptions, were both active in manufacturing and real estate development. See Ignatieff, *A Just Measure of Pain*, chaps. 3 and 4; Ralph W. England, Jr., discusses Howard's social status in Howard, *Prisons and Lazarettos*, 1: ix–xi.

33. Lawrence Stone argues that the chief weakness of Thompson's thesis is that "it completely ignores the central change of the period, mainly the remarkable, and probably unique, rise in numbers, wealth, leisure, and education of 'the middling sort' " (*New York Review of Books*, 29 May 1980, p. 45).

34. On the Wesleyan ministry in Bristol Newgate before and after its reform, see *The Journal of John Wesley*, ed. Nehemiah Curnock (London: Epworth Press, 1938), 2: 184–88; 4: 416–17, 427–28. See also Peter J. Collingwood, "The Prison Visitation in the Methodist Revival," *London Quarterly and Holborn Review* 24 (1955): 285–92, and McConville, *English Prison Administration*, pp. 78–80.

35. The quotations are from Thompson's "Eighteenth-Century Society: Class Struggle without Class?" p. 145. Thompson describes the assizes and Tyburn, but not the prisons, as part of the mystery of the law; he sees riot, to the degree it is a method of bargaining, as a means of social accommodation.

36. The speech is reprinted as an appendix in Frank Fowell and Frank Palmer, *Censorship in England* (London: Frank Palmer, 1913), pp. 357–68; see pp. 359–60 for the passage quoted. Steven Mullaney called my attention to this speech.

37. See E. P. Thompson, "Patrician Society, Plebeian Culture," p. 391, on the decline of the Church in this role. See also "Eighteenth-Century English Society: Class Struggle without Class?" pp. 156–57, which refers in turn to Thompson's review of Keith Thomas, *Religion and the Decline of Magic* in *Midland History* 1 (1972): 41–55, and to Thomas's response in *Journal of Interdisciplinary History* 6 (1975): 91–109.

38. Evans, *The Fabrication of Virtue*, p. 142.

39. See Ignatieff, *A Just Measure of Pain*, p. 106, for Wisdom's story. As Ignatieff says, "Solitary confinement was designed to wrest the governance of prisons out of the hands of the inmate subculture. It restored the state's control over the criminals' conscience" (p. 102). As G. O. Paul and others discovered, control of the prisons' subcultural area was expensive and, practically, much of the struggle between the two conceptions of social order focused on the costliness of reform. The proponents had to persuade local authorities—that is, other property owners like themselves—to assume financial and administrative responsibility for operating penitentiaries at state expense rather than following the old custom of contracting the jails out to private keepers whose motive was to improve profits from fees paid by inmates, not to alter anyone's soul. For a discussion of the difficulty of financing the new penitentiaries, and especially the refusal of Parliament to impose requirements, see Webb and Webb, *English Prisons*, p. 41. Given the obstacles, it is surprising that change occurred as rapidly as it did.

The high cost of penitentiaries, combined with controversy about their methods and with the dampening effect the French Revolution had on reform, meant that as late as 1812 James Neild, repeating Howard's survey, reported that just over half of the prisons he visited had been rebuilt or reformed. Evans (p. 236) and Ignatieff (p. 96) both consider the Howardian reforms to have been effective despite Neild's figure. Chiefly this is because of the marked trend to consolidate prisoners into comparatively few large institutions organized as penitentiaries. On the slow penetration of change to prisons outside county jurisdiction, nine-tenths of which remained in 1812 much as they had been in Howard's day, see

English Prisons, chap. 6, especially p. 64; the Webbs (pp. 60–62) quote a frightful account of an unreformed country prison in 1806. For charts showing the trend to consolidation see Evans, *The Fabrication of Virtue,* p. 238.

Not until the abolition of the Fleet in 1842 and the remodeling of Newgate in 1858–61 had change been fully consolidated. On the Fleet, see Crook and Port, *The History of the King's Works,* 6: 628–29; even after the abolition of the Fleet, the King's Bench continued on the old pattern with the Fleet and Marshalsea absorbed into it. The court that ordered the rebuilding of the King's Bench Prison in the 1780s, after the Gordon Riots, still insisted on special rooms for the socially better prisoners and the new prison followed the traditional plan (ibid., 6: 355). Henriques, "Prison Discipline," reports old practices in Newgate as late as 1880. The King's Bench ceased to be a debtors' prison in 1862 and was finally demolished in 1880. Henry Mayhew and John Binny give a full account of Newgate in *The Criminal Prisons of London and Scenes of Prison Life* (London: Charles Griffin and Co., 1862; reprt., Frank Cass and Co., 1968), pp. 588–611. They date certain minor reforms in diet and clothing from 1815, but cite a letter of 1817 (p. 593) from the Hon. Mr. Bennett, M.P., condemning the continuation of old practices. George Cruickshank caricatured the continued freedoms of Newgate in a print of 1818, reproduced as plate 176 in Evans, *The Fabrication of Virtue.*

40. William Paley, *Principles of Moral and Political Philosophy* (London: 1785), pp. 543–44.

41. Cited by McConville, *English Prison Administration,* p. 108.

42. On time measurement as a cultural phenomenon, see E. P. Thompson, "Time, Work-Discipline, and Industrial Capitalism," *Past and Present* 38 (1967): 56–97; and Niklas Luhmann, *The Differentiation of Society,* trans. Stephen Holmes and Charles Larmore (New York: Columbia University Press, 1982), pp. 239, 248.

43. Roland Barthes, "Introduction to the Structural Analysis of Narratives," in *Image-Music-Text,* ed. Stephen Heath (New York: Hill and Wang, 1977), pp. 83–84, 115–16. See also Louis O. Mink, "Narrative Form as a Cognitive Instrument," in *The Writing of History: Literary Form and Historical Understanding,* ed. Robert H. Canary and Henry Kozicki (Madison: University of Wisconsin Press, 1978), pp. 129–49, and "The Autonomy of Historical Understanding," in *Philosophical Analysis and History,* ed. William H. Dray (New York: Harper and Row, 1966), pp. 160–92; Julia Kristeva, *Desire in Language: A Semiotic Approach to Literature and Art,* ed. Leon S. Roudiez, trans. Thomas Gora et al. (New York: Columbia University Press, 1980), chap. 7, especially p. 174; Hayden White, "The Value of Narrativity in the Representation of Reality," in *On Narrative,* ed. W. J. T. Mitchell (Chicago: University of Chicago Press, 1981), pp. 1–23.

44. This change was adumbrated in the technical development of early modern Continental law as traced by John H. Langbein in *Torture and the Law of Proof* (Chicago: University of Chicago Press, 1977). Under Roman-canon law, a criminal could be declared guilty and sentenced to death or mutilation only on the basis of "full proof," which had to be founded upon reliable testimony by two eyewitnesses or upon confession—thus the use of torture. Historically, the use of torture declined with the emergence of technical devices in law that validated the kind of fine-grained, judicial inquiry (narrative construction) necessary to justify punishment based on circumstantial evidence. Such evidence could sustain only "half proof," and since no accumulation of half proofs constituted full proof,

it could not support condemnation but only time sentences in transient penal institutions. In countries with Mediterranean ports, the galleys served conveniently; while in the Low Countries workhouses that originally had been devised for vagrants, beggars, and misdemeanants allowed for punishments measured through time. The famous Amsterdam Rasphuis (opened 1596), for example, inspired a variety of projects during the reformist phase of the Enlightenment—most especially the Maison de Force, a great fortified house of correction opened at Ghent in 1772.

I join Robin Evans in laying stress on the vital difference between houses of correction and penitentiaries. The houses of correction were demonstrative, emblematic, and theatrical; their impact was corporal, though not final like execution or aggravated like torture. Their aim was *production* of goods through labor. Penitentiaries were psychological, sequential, and introspective; their aim was *reformation* of character through the controlled alteration of material circumstance over time. For this reason, as Evans argues, houses of correction could and did inhabit every variety of building from former royal palaces (London Bridewell) or convents (Amsterdam Rasphuis) to disused chapels or churches (Reading Bridewell), whereas the penitentiary idea brought into being an entirely new architectural type. See *The Fabrication of Virtue*, especially pp. 12–13 and 47–75. See also Webb and Webb, *English Prisons*, pp. 1–17; Thorsten Sellin, *Pioneering in Penology: the Amsterdam Houses of Correction in the Sixteeenth and Seventeenth Centuries* (Philadelphia: University of Pennsylvania Press, 1944); Grünhut, *Penal Reform*, pp. 11–22; and McConville, *English Prison Administration*, pp. 22–48.

On the Continent the technical judicial practices described by Langbein had obviated torture well before its much publicized official abandonment during the Enlightenment; these practices appear to have predicated modern, narratively structured conceptions of crime and punishment within a narrow legal sphere. But paradoxically it is in England—where the bridewells and workhouses, after their establishment during the sixteenth century, quickly subsided into the liminal pattern of the old prisons, and where, because of common law and the jury system, comparatively few formal strictures governed the judicial process itself—that one finds the first concerted institution of penitentiaries along modern lines. It was the English who, during the 1780s, constructed the model penitentiaries that later were re-exported from America to Europe during the penal reforms that swept the Continent throughout the first half of the nineteenth century. The introduction of lawyers (proffering contingent narratives of a case), as well as the subsequent imposition of rules of evidence in English courts, occurred after the period ordinarily associated with the rise of the novel and after an extended phase of narrative court accounts such as the Old Bailey Sessions Records, the Ordinary's accounts, the *Selected Trials*, and the *Newgate Calendar*. See Langbein, "The Criminal Trial before the Lawyers," *University of Chicago Law Review* 45 (1978): 263–316, and "Shaping the Eighteenth-Century Criminal Trial." Gerald Howson, in the bibliography to *Thief-Taker General*, provides a convenient summary of trial reports, Sessions Papers, and Sessions Records.

45. See, for example, the famous opening to Bentham's *Principles of Morals and Legislation*, as well as statements throughout his works. By far the most significant study of the major features of Bentham's philosophical thought is Ross Harrison's *Bentham* (London: Routledge and Kegan Paul, 1983); on the theory of fictions see chapters 2–4.

46. See *Bentham's Theory of Fictions*, ed. C. K. Ogden (London: Kegan Paul, Trench, Trubner and Co., 1932), pp. 17–18. Quotation is from *A Fragment on Ontology* in *The Works of Jeremy Bentham*, ed. John Bowring, 11 vols. (Edinburgh: William Tait, 1838–43), 8: 199. Subsequent citations refer to this edition as *Works*.

47. Ibid., p. 152, quoted from the abstract published by George Bentham in 1827. Bentham discusses these ideas more fully, and more technically, in a long note to the section "Nomenclature and Classification" in the appendix to the *Chrestomathia (Works,* 8: 126–27); see also the quotation from the same appendix (ibid., p. 174) that appears below as the epigraph to my chapter 7, where Bentham is more substantially considered.

48. See Lennard J. Davis, *Factual Fictions: The Origins of the English Novel* (New York: Columbia University Press, 1983).

49. The difference must exist, on Hume's general account, because the ideas in manifest fictions rely on imagination rather than on distinct impressions, which are physically closer to reality. For Hume on belief, see *A Treatise of Human Nature*, ed. L. A. Selby-Bigge, 2d ed. rev. by P. H. Nidditch (Oxford: Oxford University Press, 1978), 1.3.7–8 (pp. 94–106), plus Appendix (pp. 623–30); on poetic fictions, ibid., 1.3.9. (pp. 106–17), plus Appendix (pp. 630–39). See also John Passmore, *Hume's Intentions*, 3d ed. (London: Duckworth, 1980), pp. 99–104; and John J. Richetti, *Philosophical Writing: Locke, Berkeley, Hume* (Cambridge: Harvard University Press, 1983), pp. 208–11.

50. Hume, *Treatise*, 1.3.6 (pp. 261–62). Ian Watt quotes the last sentence in *The Rise of the Novel* (Berkeley: University of California Press, 1959), p. 21.

51. Hume, *Treatise*, 3.1.1 (p. 469); quoted by Halévy (see note 53 below). Ronald Paulson discusses this passage in *Satire and the Novel in the Eighteenth Century* (New Haven: Yale University Press, 1967), p. 6. See also Ian Ross, "Philosophy and Fiction: The Challenge of David Hume," pp. 60–71, in *Hume and the Enlightenment*, ed. William B. Todd (Edinburgh: Edinburgh University Press, 1974).

52. *Treatise*, 1.4.6 (p. 255).

53. The thirty-two *"circumstances influencing sensibility"* and, therefore, "the effect of *any* exciting cause" are

1. Health. 2. Strength. 3. Hardiness. 4. Bodily imperfection. 5. Quantity and quality of knowledge. 6. Strength of intellectual powers. 7. Firmness of mind. 8. Steadiness of mind. 9. Bent of inclination. 10. Moral sensibility. 11. Moral biases. 12. Religious sensibility. 13. Religious biases. 14. Sympathetic sensibility. 15. Sympathetic biases. 16. Antipathetic sensibility. 17. Antipathetic biases. 18. Insanity. 19. Habitual occupations. 20. Pecuniary circumstances. 21. Connexions in the way of sympathy. 22. Connexions in the way of antipathy. 23. Radical frame of body. 24. Radical frame of mind. 25. Sex. 26. Age. 27. Rank. 28. Education. 29. Climate. 30. Lineage. 31. Government. 32. Religious profession. (Bentham, *An Introduction to the Principles of Morals and Legislation, Works*, 1: 22. The modern edition edited by J. H. Burns and H. L. A. Hart [London: University of London, Athlone Press, 1970] contains an extensive topical index.)

Principles of Morals and Legislation was undertaken in the 1770s as part of a plan for a huge work. Mary P. Mack says that "Bentham wrote thousands of practice pages between 1769 and 1781. Some of them were incorporated in *The Principles of Morals*, printed in 1780, which was itself only a small fragment of his monumental plan to analyse the entire structure of law" (*Jeremy Bentham: An Odyssey of Ideas, 1748–1792* [London: Heinemann, 1962], p. 130). Radzinowicz considers these works under the rubric of the "subjective" or "individualistic" philosophy of punishment, by which he means punishment that endeavors "to assess the mental element in crime by investigating the mental processes of an accused person" (*A History of English Criminal Law,* 1: 374). Bentham's stress on solitary confinement in *A View of the Hard Labour Bill* (1778) follows from this approach to punishment, which implies a separate, individually controlled regime for each convict: "When I had read Mr. Howard's book on Prisons, one fruit of it was, a wish still more earnest than what I had been led to entertain from theory, to see some general plan of punishment adopted, in which solitary confinement might be combined with labour" (*Works,* 4: 3). For a variety of reasons, including observation of the actual effects of prolonged solitary confinement once the new penitentiaries began to be built during the 1780s, Bentham later changed his mind about the importance of isolation. Belief in the salutary effects of solitary confinement is characteristic of reformist discourse in the 1770s.

On Bentham see, besides Mack, Radzinowicz, *A History of English Criminal Law,* vol. 1, chap. 11, and Elie Halévy, *The Growth of Philosophic Radicalism,* trans. Mary Morris, ed. John Plamenatz (London: Faber and Faber, 1972), "The Youth of Bentham (1776–1789)," pp. 3–150. Halévy gives a lucid account of Bentham's relationship to earlier ideas, of his place in utilitarian thought (which Halévy calls "philosophic radicalism"), and of his theory of punishment. Evans offers the most detailed study of Bentham's complex, continuously evolving project for a penitentiary called the Panopticon (*The Fabrication of Virtue,* chap. 5). The Panopticon scheme, which dates from 1787, will be considered further in my last chapter.

54. Bentham, *Works,* 1: 34.

55. Ibid., pp. 164–68.

56. See Henriques, "Prison Discipline," pp. 63–64.

57. On the doctrine of exemplary punishment as the basis of deterrence, see Halévy, *The Growth of Philosophic Radicalism,* p. 67; McConville, *Prison Administration,* pp. 113–15; and Radzinowicz, *A History of English Criminal Law,* 1: 386–89.

58. Halévy, *The Growth of Philosophic Radicalism,* pp. 82–83, citing Bowring's edition of Bentham's *Works,* 4: 37–172.

59. These ideas are developed further in chapter 7 below. On paraphrasis and the theory of fictions, see Harrison, *Bentham,* pp. 53–74.

60. Gottfried Wilhelm Leibnitz, "Drôle de Pensée, touchant une nouvelle sorte de representation" (September 1675), ed. Yvon Belaval, *La Nouvelle Revue Française* 70 (1958): 753–68. Jacques Attali, *Noise: The Political Economy of Music,* trans. Brian Massumi (Minneapolis: University of Minnesota Press, 1985), p. 7, cites and translates the passage quoted.

CHAPTER TWO

Epigraph: I quote from G. D. H. Cole's two-volume edition of Defoe's *Tour* (London: Peter Davies, 1927), 1: 355. Gerald Howson says that in the early eighteenth century, metropolitan London had about 150 prisons of various types and sizes, plus 115 bailiffs' "Spunging Houses," and "an unrecorded number of private prisons belonging to thief-takers" (*Thief-Taker General: The Rise and Fall of Jonathan Wild* [London: Hutchinson, 1970], p. 28).

1. [James Arbuckle,] *Hibernicus's Letters,* no. 9, 29 May 1725. Cited in G. A. Starr, ed., *Moll Flanders* (London: Oxford University Press, 1971), p. xvii. Defoe's apparent belief that sensational criminal biographies provided useful negative

examples may have been disingenuous, but as Michael Shinagel says of Defoe's tracts on crime and criminals written during the 1720s when he was in Applebee's employ as a criminal reporter: "In all these works he addressed himself to the problems attending the sharp rise in the crime rate during this time and the very practices glorified by the criminal biographies of the 1720's. Defoe, in short, wrote as a social reformer anxious to discover ways of curtailing the crime rate and alerting the citizens of London on how to protect themselves and their property" (*Daniel Defoe and Middle-Class Gentility* [Cambridge: Harvard University Press, 1968], p. 170). J. Paul Hunter says that " 'reform' became a popular watchword at the beginning of the eighteenth century, and popular 'societies' for the suppression of vice sprang up everywhere. A 1700 pamphlet says that thirty-nine of these societies were operating in and about London and Westminster, with ten others in Dublin. . . . According to many acute contemporary observers, so much emphasis was everywhere placed upon 'manners' and conduct that Christianity itself was in danger of being reduced to a mere ethical system" (*The Reluctant Pilgrim* [Baltimore: Johns Hopkins University Press, 1966], pp. 24–25). On the criminal narrative as a literary form, see Maximillian E. Novak, *Realism, Myth, and History in Defoe's Fiction* (Lincoln: University of Nebraska Press, 1983), chap. 6.

2. Daniel Defoe, *Moll Flanders*, ed. G. A. Starr (London: Oxford University Press, 1971), pp. 273–74. Further citations refer to this edition.

3. Victor Turner, "Betwixt and Between: The Liminal Period in *Rites de Passage*," *Proceedings of the American Ethnological Society* (1964): 340; see chapter 1, note 22 for citation of reprints.

4. See G. A. Starr, *Defoe and Spiritual Autobiography* (Princeton: Princeton University Press, 1965), chap. 4; and *Defoe and Casuistry* (Princeton: Princeton University Press, 1971), pp. 159–64. On Defoe's representation of Moll's private, individualist consciousness through her self-control during the Newgate episode, see John J. Richetti, *Defoe's Narratives* (Oxford: Clarendon Press, 1975), pp. 133–40. Moll's equation of thought with being, of consciousness with self, surely echoes Descartes. Of course spiritual and secular values are closely interwoven here, as elsewhere, in Defoe. In *God's Plot and Man's Stories: Studies in the Fictional Imagination from Milton to Fielding* (Chicago: University of Chicago Press, 1985), which appeared when this book was in final preparation, Leopold Damrosch, Jr.'s analysis of the relationship between seventeenth-century Puritan narrative and the novel from Defoe to Fielding shows the considerable extent to which tensions between religious and secular values defined the early English novel. Maximillian Novak reveals the presence of such a tension during the later seventeenth century, when he finds in certain moralistic criminal narratives "a new kind of fictional metaphysic at work. Instead of the continual reminder of God's presence and impending revenge, the author speculates on cause and effect as if the world were not entirely under God's control. . . . It is clear that just as courts of law came to focus more and more on facts and evidence, so fiction came to function in a world of secondary causes and events" (*Realism, Myth, and History in Defoe's Fiction*, p. 125).

5. On irony in *Moll Flanders*, see especially Ian Watt, "The Recent Critical Fortunes of *Moll Flanders*," *Eighteenth Century Studies* 1 (1967): 109–26, and Novak, *Realism, Myth, and History in Defoe's Fiction*, chap. 4.

6. Works that have substantially revised previous estimates of Defoe by placing him in context with the thought of his period include Maximillian E. Novak,

Economics and the Fiction of Daniel Defoe (Berkeley: University of California Press, 1962) and *Defoe and the Nature of Man* (Oxford: Oxford University Press, 1963); Starr, *Defoe and Spiritual Autobiography* and *Defoe and Casuistry;* and Hunter, *The Reluctant Pilgrim.*

7. On shifts of theoretical content within stable terminologies during the Renaissance, see Phillip Damon, "History and Idea in Renaissance Criticism," in *Literary Criticism and Historical Understanding,* ed. Phillip Damon (New York: Columbia University Press, 1967).

8. The kind of writing we normally call allegorical never quite ran the equation backwards. This was precisely the Puritan objection to icons, fictions, etc., that they were vain and false imitations, not the real thing—that they were self-referential idols, not God-given signs of divine creation. See Hunter, *The Reluctant Pilgrim,* chap. 5, especially pp. 119–22; and Damrosch, *God's Plot and Man's Stories.*

9. Daniel Defoe, *Serious Reflections During the Life and Surprising Adventures of Robinson Crusoe,* ed. George A. Aitken (London: J. M. Dent, 1895), p. ix.

10. See Homer O. Brown, "The Displaced Self in the Novels of Daniel Defoe," *English Literary History* 38 (1971): 562–90; and Terry J. Castle, " 'Amy, Who Knew My Disease': A Psychosexual Pattern in Defoe's *Roxana,*" *English Literary History* 46 (1979): 81–96.

11. See Ian Watt, *The Rise of the Novel* (Berkeley: University of California Press, 1959), pp. 31, 102; and Novak, "Defoe's Theory of Fiction," *Studies in Philology* 61 (1964): 650–68, especially 661–62. See my chapters 1 and 7 for fuller discussion of the interrelation of empiricist philosophy, the novel, and the penitentiary.

12. Daniel Defoe, *Complete English Tradesman,* Letter 5, "Of Diligence and Application in Business" (London: Charles Rivington, 1726). Reprinted in *Robinson Crusoe and Other Writings,* ed. James Sutherland (New York: New York University Press, 1977), pp. 380–88. Quotation from p. 388.

13. Daniel Defoe, *Robinson Crusoe,* ed. J. Donald Crowley (London: Oxford University Press, 1972), p. 40. Further references are to this edition.

14. See Douglas Hay, "Property, Authority, and the Criminal Law," in *Albion's Fatal Tree: Crime and Society in Eighteenth-Century England,* ed. Douglas Hay et al. (New York: Pantheon, 1975), pp. 17–63.

15. On "polyglossia" as a form of contradiction and as the essence of the novel—that is, its ability to contain contradictory voices—see Mikhail Bakhtin, "From the Prehistory of Novelistic Discourse" and "Discourse in the Novel," in *The Dialogic Imagination,* ed. and trans. Michael Holquist and Caryl Emerson (Austin: University of Texas Press, 1981), especially pp. 50–60 and 277–84.

16. Here I treat the *The Surprising Adventures of Robinson Crusoe* as an autonomous work. As Maximillian Novak has shown, in an analysis that unifies the original *Surprising Adventures* with its sequel, *The Farther Adventures,* the second installment traces the evolution of Crusoe's colony from anarchy in a state of nature to a state of government under law. See "Crusoe the King and the Political Evolution of His Island," *Studies in English Literature* 2 (1962): 337–50. Since, in *Farther Adventures,* the Spanish captain defends Crusoe's ownership of the island and maintains allegiance to him in the face of anarchic claims by the mutineers, Crusoe's attempt to project his authority into the future succeeds in some measure. As Novak points out, Crusoe views himself as a paternalistic monarch despite his absolutist behavior in the *Surprising Adventures,* and even though what

actually happens on the island in *Farther Adventures* diverges significantly from his intentions. I would argue, along the lines advanced here, that Defoe shows Crusoe building a utopian city which becomes governmentally feasible only after the evolution that occurs in *Farther Reflections*. Crusoe's physical map of the island is as modern, novelistic, and urban as the point of view of his narrative; but isolation forces Crusoe and the others to retrace the origin and development of society.

17. Lewis Mumford, "University City," in *City Invincible*, ed. Carl H. Kraeling and Robert M. Adams (Chicago: University of Chicago Press, 1960), p. 7. Cited by Anthony Giddens, *A Contemporary Critique of Historical Materialism* (Berkeley: University of California Press, 1981), p. 96.

18. See especially Watt, *The Rise of the Novel*, pp. 45–46 and 177–82. My treatment of the relationship between narrative and cities, in general, and between the realist novel and the urban metropolis, in particular, is at once more literal, more encompassing, and less dependent upon the concept of class than Watt's. The newest and perhaps most probing examination of Watt's formulations was published by Michael McKeon after my text was complete. See "Generic Transformation and Social Change: Rethinking the Rise of the Novel," *Cultural Critique* 1 (1985): 159–81. A recent essay by Daniel R. Schwarz, "The Importance of Ian Watt's *The Rise of the Novel*," *Journal of Narrative Technique* 13 (1983): 59–73, notices the chief points made by earlier critics of the book. Watt's own "Serious Reflections on *The Rise of the Novel*," *Novel* 1 (1968): 205–18, discusses the work's genesis, its initial reception, and his views on its strengths and weaknesses.

19. Giddens, *A Contemporary Critique*, p. 96.

20. Ibid., p. 146.

21. See Robin Evans, *The Fabrication of Virtue: English Prison Architecture, 1750–1840* (Cambridge: Cambridge University Press, 1982), pp. 12–13, for a detailed list of the sites of English prisons.

22. Giddens, *A Contemporary Critique*, p. 95; Giddens cites Ruth Whitehouse, *The First Cities* (Oxford: Phaidon, 1977), p. 66, and Jack Goody, *The Domestication of the Savage Mind* (Cambridge: Cambridge University Press, 1977), chap. 5; see also Mason Hammond, *The City in the Ancient World* (Cambridge: Harvard University Press, 1972), pp. 36–37. Although I argue that affinities exist between the form cities take and the significance they assign to prison, I associate myself with Giddens in his criticism of Foucault for collapsing modern urban institutions as diverse as the factory, the clinic, and the penitentiary together under the rubric "sequestration." My argument runs parallel to Foucault's, but I stress that the selectivity of representational forms such as the realist novel and the penitentiary accounts at once for their clarity and for their power. By their nature they possess a formal closure, a totality, that metropolitan society imagines but, with the possible exception of large-scale authoritarian regimes of the twentieth century, has not achieved (see Giddens, pp. 169–74).

23. Bakhtin, *The Dialogic Imagination*, p. 3. Walter Benjamin makes some similar points in "The Storyteller: Reflections on the Works of Nikolai Leskov," in *Illuminations*, ed. Hannah Arendt, trans. Harry Zohn (New York: Schocken Books, 1969), pp. 83–109, especially p. 87.

24. The *New York Times* of 9 July 1977 (pp. 19–20) reports an analysis by Denise Schmandt-Besserat that links trade tokens from numerous Middle Eastern sites to the earliest known pictographic writing at Uruk in Iraq.

25. Throughout this paragraph and the next I employ Giddens's terms.

26. Elias Canetti, *Crowds and Power*, trans. Carol Stewart (New York: Viking Press, 1962), pp. 207–11. Canetti freely elaborates this idea. He says, for example, that the mouth, guarded by sharp teeth, is "the prototype of all prisons." The primitive prison ingests prey like the dragon, which symbolizes it. The modern penitentiary is the "puritanical" opposite: "The smoothness of teeth has conquered the world; the walls of cells are all smooth and even the window opening is small. For the prisoner, freedom is the space beyond the clenched teeth, and these are now represented by the bare walls of his cell" (p. 209). Terry Castle first called my attention to this passage in Canetti.

27. Lewis Mumford, *The City in History* (New York: Harcourt, Brace and World, 1961), p. 46. In this paragraph, and elsewhere, I assimilate Bakhtin's ideas about the novel's antiauthoritarian embrace of diversity (its "heteroglossia") into an account that runs opposite his main argument. Here I am concerned with the extent to which narrative order itself modifies the novelistic freedom as Bakhtin considers it; later, in chapter 7, I suggest that transparent representation in the realist novel encompasses, contains, and reshapes apparent heterodoxy.

28. The number remains indefinite, in part according to what one counts. John Robert Moore says: "At least seven times he was confined in Newgate, the Queen's Bench Prison, some debtors' prison, or the house of a Queen's messenger—once for a continuous period of four months" (*Daniel Defoe: Citizen of the Modern World* [Chicago: University of Chicago Press, 1958], p. 47). Pat Rogers has since found records showing Defoe in the Fleet prison (or its "rules") in 1692 and 1702. See "Defoe in the Fleet Prison," *Review of English Studies*, n.s. 22 (1971): 451–55; and also J. A. Downie, "Defoe in the Fleet Prison," *Notes and Queries*, n.s. 22 (1975): 343–45.

CHAPTER THREE

Epigraph: John Locke, *An Essay Concerning Human Understanding*, ed. Peter H. Nidditch (Oxford: Clarendon Press, 1975), 2.28.5.

1. Anthony Giddens, *A Contemporary Critique of Historical Materialism* (Berkeley: University of California Press, 1981), chap. 4; and Mason Hammond, *The City in the Ancient World* (Cambridge: Harvard University Press, 1972), pp. 43–46.

2. See Max Grünhut, *Penal Reform: A Comparative Study* (Oxford: Clarendon Press, 1948), pp. 11–14. Thus Justinian reaffirmed in A.D. 533 the principle articulated under Caracalla (A.D. 211–217) that "prison ought to be used for detention only, but not for punishment"; and the medieval code of Ferrara, like that of many Italian states, decreed that "prison has been 'invented' for custody, not for punishment." Quotations cited from Grünhut. In England imprisonment was used chiefly for debt and in the Star Chamber, and, as on the Continent, became increasingly common during the seventeenth century.

3. Consolidated building had extended well outside the city walls when Wenceslaus Hollar's *A Map or Ground-plot of the Citty of London . . . after the Fire of 1666* was published (see fig. 14). Hollar's map refers specifically to the "Suburbes," which reach out much farther than on earlier maps. See Philippa Glanville, *London in Maps* (London: Connoisseur, 1972), pp. 92–94 on Hollar and passim for earlier maps. Glanville stresses the concern about the extramural growth of London during this period: "The Stuarts recognised the problems created by an outer belt beyond the City's control, and the Council offered in 1633 'whether

they woulde accept of parte of the suburbs into their jurisdiction and liberty for better government,' but the City rejected the offer and it was not repeated" (p. 86).

Ian Watt says of Defoe's attitude toward London, by way of contrast with Richardson's suspicious negativity:

> Yet although the picture has its selfish and sordid aspects, it has one very significant difference from that presented by the modern city. Defoe's London is still a community, a community composed by now of an almost infinite variety of parts, but at least of parts which still recognise their kinship; it is large, but somehow remains local, and Defoe and his characters are part of it, understanding and understood.
>
> There are probably many reasons for Defoe's buoyant and secure tone. He had some memory of the days before the Great Fire, and the London he had grown up in was still an entity, much of it enclosed by the City Wall. But the major reason is surely that although Defoe had since seen enormous changes, he himself had participated in them actively and enthusiastically; he lived in the hurly-burly where the foundations of the new way of life were being laid: and he was at one with it. (*The Rise of the Novel* [Berkeley: University of California Press, 1959], p. 181)

Although I lay more stress than does Watt on Defoe's registration of London's metropolitan traits, my case depends upon the situation he so aptly describes. Defoe lives at a turning point; and his way of writing narrative works to preserve the minute particulars of the old life while reshaping them according to new predicates.

4. On gridiron development, see Lewis Mumford, *The City in History* (New York: Harcourt, Brace and World, 1961), pp. 421–23; he quotes North on p. 418.

5. Newcourt's plan is described in Glanville, *London in Maps*, p. 95. For discussion of plans by Wren, Evelyn, and others, see Michael Hanson, *Two Thousand Years of London* (London: Country Life, 1967), pp. 94–99. See also Thomas F. Reddaway, *The Rebuilding of London after the Great Fire* (London: Jonathan Cape, 1940).

Despite the occasion offered by the Great Fire, London traversed the seventeenth century with few marks of baroque city planning. Not even after the Great Fire did London adopt the axial symmetry that typified Continental urban renovations of the period. According to Mumford, the palatial forms, uniform street elevations, and repetitious patterning of these plans enforced the dominance of absolutist courts by repeating the ancient urban "implosion" in self-conscious, formally abstracted terms (*The City in History,* p. 367). The rebuilding of Saint Paul's and the City churches in Wren's vernacular adaptation of the baroque typifies the selective approach taken by a London that for the most part remained casual toward monumental architecture. The aristocratic attempt to perpetuate the illusion that the whole of urban life was identical to that of the court had its counterpart in a variety of English public buildings, ironically including Robert Hooke's palatial Bedlam Hospital (1675) (fig. 46); but purely from the point of view of urban planning, London bypassed the elaborations of the authoritarian baroque in favor of a direct move to the prototypical grid. The reasons for this situation had to do in some measure with insular politics; in the 1660s the imperious symbolism of ceremonial avenues cutting across the City surely would have gone against the grain of many Londoners. But the long-term significance of London's westward development is not so very different from that of systematic baroque planning, for both broke with the existing city forms in favor of ordered parcels arranged in reduplicating units, and both proposed idealized representations of the law, order, and uniformity necessary to mercantile trade. See Mumford (chaps. 12–14).

6. Daniel Defoe, *A Tour . . . of Great Britain*, 2 vols. (London: Peter Davies, 1927), 1: 325.

7. Mumford, *The City in History*, pp. 365–66 and 437–38. See also E. P. Thompson, "Time, Work-Discipline, and Industrial Capitalism," *Past and Present* 38 (1967): 56–97; and Niklas Luhmann, *The Differentiation of Society*, trans. Stephen Holmes and Charles Larmore (New York: Columbia University Press, 1982), pp. 239 and 248. Mumford's substitutional model, though suggestive in this context, oversimplifies: vicarious experience may indeed be diminished in emotional intensity and perceptual vividness but is also a symptom of the metropolitan organization and deployment of information, which allows both to individuals and to entities a vastly enlarged scope of comprehension and an unprecedented capacity to calculate plans and predict behavior. The emergence of organized philanthropy is a case study in the large-scaled effectuality of commodified, vicarious experience in modern society. On this, see Thomas Haskell, "Capitalism and the Origins of the Humanitarian Sensibility," *American Historical Review* 90 (1985): 339–61 and 547–66.

8. G. A. Starr, *Defoe and Casuistry* (Princeton University Press, 1971), especially chap. 1. Starr begins his book with the *OED*'s crisp definition, which continues: "Often (and perhaps originally) applied to a quibbling and evasive way of dealing with difficult cases of duty." Casuistry is, strictly, a device for dealing with the conflict of laws or rules in specific cases. Starr broadens the idea of casuistry (convincingly in my view) to include narration of the cases themselves.

9. Mikhail Bakhtin, *The Dialogic Imagination*, ed. and trans. Michael Holquist and Caryl Emerson (Austin: University of Texas Press, 1981), p. 15.

10. Maximillian E. Novak, "Crime and Punishment in Defoe's *Roxana*," *Journal of English and Germanic Philology* 65 (1966): 445. This essay appears in another form as chapter 5 of *Realism, Myth, and History in Defoe's Fiction* (Lincoln: University of Nebraska Press, 1983).

11. Watt, *The Rise of the Novel*, p. 32. As Watt says, "the novel in general, as much in Joyce as in Zola, employs the literary means [of] formal realism." The force of transparency as a primary convention is shown by the lengths to which novelists must go in order to call attention to their medium. The self-referential novel from *Tristram Shandy* to the present day defines itself in opposition to, and therefore depends upon, the convention of realism and the transparency it implies. These values implied by formal realism are borne by novelistic conventions in themselves, with no necessary reference to the specific subject matter.

12. "Only with the bureaucratization of the state and of law in general can one see a definite possibility of separating sharply and conceptually an 'objective' legal order from the 'subjective rights' of the individual which it guarantees. . . . This conceptual separation presupposes the conceptual separation of the 'state,' as an abstract bearer of sovereign prerogatives and the creator of 'legal norms,' from all personal 'authorizations' of individuals. These conceptual forms are necessarily remote from the nature of pre-bureaucratic, and especially from patrimonial and feudal, structures of authority. This conceptual separation of private and public was first conceived and realized in urban communities" (from "Bureaucracy," pp. 196–244, in *From Max Weber*, trans. and ed. H. H. Gerth and C. Wright Mills [New York: Oxford University Press, 1958], p. 239). This section translates part 3, chap. 6, pp. 650–78, of Weber's *Wirtschaft und Gesellschaft*.

13. Erving Goffman, "On the Characteristics of Total Institutions," in *Asylums: Essays on the Social Situation of Mental Patients and Other Inmates* (Garden City, N.Y.: Anchor Books, 1961), pp. 1–124; reprinted from *The Prison*, ed. Donald R. Cressey (New York: Holt, Rinehart and Winston, 1961).

14. Roland Barthes, "Dominici, or the Triumph of Literature," in *Mythologies*, trans. Annette Lavers (New York: Hill and Wang, 1972), p. 45. Earlier in this essay, Barthes says, "It is in the name of a 'universal' psychology that old Dominici has been condemned: descending from the charming empyrean of bourgeois novels and essentialist psychology, Literature has just condemned a man to the guillotine" (p. 43). See too *The Pleasure of the Text*, trans. Richard Miller (New York: Hill and Wang, 1975), p. 3: "How much penal evidence is based on a psychology of consistency!" See also D. A. Miller, "The Novel and the Police," *Glyph* 8 (1981): 127–47, as well as my chapter 7 below. On "internal distantiation," see Louis Althusser, "A Letter on Art in Reply to André Daspre," in *Lenin and Philosophy*, trans. Ben Brewster (New York: Monthly Review Press, 1971), pp. 221–27, especially p. 222.

15. For a listing of references, see Manuel Schonhorn, "Defoe's *Journal of the Plague Year*: Topography and Intention," *Review of English Studies*, n.s. 19 (1968): 399–402; and *A Journal of the Plague Year*, ed. Louis Landa (London: Oxford University Press, 1969), pp. 291–98. Citations appearing parenthetically in the text refer to this edition. The only mention of actual prisons occurs on p. 92, where H.F. lists several among the rebuilding projects undertaken after the Great Fire.

16. Maximillian E. Novak, citing Fielding's assertion in *Tom Jones* that the true novelist must above all have "a good Heart, and be capable of feeling," argues that "no narrator in realistic prose fiction before H.F. reveals this type of general sympathy for the human condition. . . . Like Fielding's humane historian, H.F. resists all temptation to blame and scold. . . . He set a pattern for fictional narrators that has been central to the development of the novel" ("Defoe and the Disordered City," *PMLA* 92 [1977]: 249–50). While I accept Novak's general characterization of H.F.'s empathetic quality and agree that the *Journal* defines this type of narrator, my stress lies on the formulation of authority latent in the methods of realistic fiction. From the point of view maintained in the following pages, the humane qualities Novak describes in H.F., as well as in later narrators, are themselves part of a representational alliance of self with authority that is characteristic of the realist novel. In these works effective magistrates and judges, like persuasive narrators, must be men of good heart. Similarly, this kind of speaker pervades reformist tracts and, in descriptions of the ideal keeper or warden, becomes central to the penitentiary idea.

17. On the (fictional) time of composition, see Schonhorn, "Defoe's *Journal*," p. 388.

18. Even in H.F.'s neighborhood beyond Aldgate on the far east, where growth was slower than on the west and north, development had extended to some depth beyond the walls and was spreading well down the river banks.

19. Schonhorn, "Defoe's *Journal*," p. 389.

20. See Barthes, *The Pleasure of the Text*, pp. 56–57: "Of course, it very often happens that representation takes desire itself as an object of imitation; but then, such desire never leaves the frame, the picture; it circulates among the characters; if it has a recipient, that recipient remains interior to the fiction (consequently, we can say that any semiotics that keeps desire within the configuration of those

upon whom it acts, however new it may be, is a semiotics of representation). That is what representation is: when nothing emerges, when nothing leaps out of the frame: of the picture, the book, the screen." Barthes's actual word, translated as "those upon whom it acts," is *actants,* a technical term in the structuralist analysis of narrative morphology. *Actants* are narrative roles usually lodged in single characters, but sometimes spread across several characters or vested in things: villain, hero, guide, quest object, and so forth. For the original see *Le Plaisir du texte* (Paris: Seuil, 1973), p. 90.

21. See Landa edition, pp. ix–x; and John Robert Moore, *Daniel Defoe,* p. 320.

22. See the last section of the previous chapter for full discussion of these ideas as they pertain to *Robinson Crusoe.*

23. W. B. Carnochan, *Confinement and Flight* (Berkeley: University of California Press, 1977), p. 75. I allude especially to Max Byrd, *London Transformed: Images of the City in the Eighteenth Century* (New Haven: Yale University Press, 1978), pp. 30–43; and to W. Austin Flanders, "Defoe's *Journal of the Plague Year* and the Modern Urban Experience," *Centennial Review* 16 (1972): 328–48, reprinted in *Daniel Defoe: A Collection of Critical Essays,* ed. Max Byrd (Englewood Cliffs, N.J.: Prentice-Hall, 1976), pp. 150–69. See also Jack Lindsay, *The Monster City: Defoe's London, 1688–1730* (New York: St. Martin's Press, 1978).

24. This density of texture extends outside the *Journal*'s formal boundaries in the sense that the work is one of several writings by Defoe which appear, simultaneously, to have increased public acceptance of the Quarantine Act and to have "reinforced the opposition to Walpole's proposals" (see Landa edition, p. x).

25. See ibid., p. 267n, for an account of the debate. On the expressive function of punishment, see Joel Feinberg, *Doing and Deserving: Essays in the Theory of Responsibility* (Princeton: Princeton University Press, 1970), pp. 95–118.

26. See *Journal,* pp. 73–75. Since, even under H.F.'s proposal, the master's only other choice would be the hated alternative of shutting up the house containing himself and his entire family along with the infected servant, avowals against force seem disingenuous. The assumption that disease, like crime, originates among the poor underlies the very legislation that Defoe transcribes into the *Journal.* The section on beggars closely resembles a number of criminal statutes. On Defoe's own, more sympathetic, attitude toward the poor, see Novak, "Defoe and the Disordered City."

27. See *Journal,* p. 182. In another passage, H.F. claims that greater ills would have resulted from carrying the sick to the pesthouses than would have followed from leaving them shut up at home (pp. 181–82). But here he refers to dangerous proposals that would have relied on the two grossly inadequate existing pest houses while abandoning the shutting up of houses.

28. See Maximillian E. Novak, *Defoe and the Nature of Man* (Oxford: Oxford University Press, 1963), pp. 14–21, passim, on Hobbes and pp. 157–58 on Locke. Novak cites *An Essay Concerning Human Understanding,* 3.11.24–25.

29. This passage suggests a more negative attitude toward the poor than Novak argues for in "Defoe and the Disordered City," but a sympathetic stance does not rule out accepting necessary solutions. Defoe's understanding of the social conditions that drove women to prostitution did not prevent his advocacy of shutting up their houses because they shelter robbers. See *An Effectual Scheme for the Immediate Preventing of Street Robberies* (1731).

CHAPTER FOUR

Epigraph: Again I quote Nidditch's edition of Locke's *Essay* (Oxford: Clarendon Press, 1975), 2.21.19.

1. Samuel Johnson's phrase from *Lives of the English Poets* is one of the many eighteenth-century testimonials to Gay's originality quoted by William Eben Schultz in *Gay's Beggar's Opera: Its Content, History and Influence* (New Haven: Yale University Press, 1923), p. 130.

2. Ian Donaldson, *The World Upside-Down: Comedy from Jonson to Fielding* (Oxford: Clarendon Press, 1970), p. 165. Donaldson (p. 196) credits the term "total irony" to C. S. Lewis, "A Note on Jane Austen," *Essays in Criticism* 4 (1954): 370.

3. See Schultz, *Gay's Beggar's Opera*, p. 237.

4. The suggestion that the progresses are like books appears in William Hogarth, *The Analysis of Beauty, With the Rejected Passages from the Manuscript Drafts and Autobiographical Notes*, ed. Joseph Burke (Oxford: Clarendon Press, 1955), p. 229. See Robert E. Moore for the idea that "with *A Harlot's Progress* modern fiction had arrived. The two arts had become one" (*Hogarth's Literary Relationships* [Minneapolis: University of Minnesota Press, 1948], p. 118). Ronald Paulson says that Hogarth "followed the practice of Daniel Defoe, who had invented a 'true' narrative of the career of a harlot, Moll Flanders, only a few years before (1722). Like Defoe, he supported the 'truth' of his biography by introducing actual streets, monuments, buildings, and people" (*Hogarth's Graphic Works*, 2 vols. [New Haven: Yale University Press, 1970], 1: 39). In *Hogarth: His Life, Art, and Times*, 2 vols. (New Haven: Yale University Press and Paul Mellon Centre for Studies in British Art, 1971), 1: 469–70, Paulson discusses Fielding's description of Hogarth as a "Comic History-Painter" in the preface to *Joseph Andrews* (1742). Paulson, noting that "Hogarth never seems to have used the term 'comic history painting' himself," goes on to show the painter's awareness that he had introduced a new genre.

5. *The Complete Works of Henry Fielding, Esq.*, 16 vols., ed. William E. Henley (London: Heinemann, 1903), 15: 331.

6. Mikhail Bakhtin, *The Dialogic Imagination*, ed. and trans. Michael Holquist and Caryl Emerson (Austin: University of Texas Press, 1981), pp. 6–7. Bakhtin goes on to speak of the novelization of the standard literary genres as part of a broader cultural process, the consequences of which emerged "with special force and clarity beginning in the second half of the eighteenth century" (p. 5):

> It is of course impossible to explain the phenomenon of novelization purely by reference to the direct and unmediated influence of the novel itself. Even where such influence can be precisely established and demonstrated, it is intimately interwoven with those direct changes in reality itself that also determine the novel and that condition its dominance in a given era. . . . The novel has become the leading hero in the drama of literary development in our time precisely because it best of all reflects the tendencies of a new world still in the making. (p. 7)

Bakhtin's actual theory of a dialogic relationship between the novel and the world it inhabits reaches well beyond the simple notion of reflection implied by this passage.

I take Bakhtin's idea of novelization as my point of departure and significantly rely on it. I find, however, that Bakhtin underestimates the extent to which, in the realist novel, causally sequenced plot structures, explanatory materials, and consciousness-centered narration contain and control the fundamentally parodic, multiple vocalization (the "heteroglossia") that for him defines the genre. Bakhtin's slight attention to plot and to narrative structure is consistent with the incompleteness of his theory. Thus, as my argument develops, I progressively reshape the term "novelization" to include the ideas of causal sequentiality and narratorial direction. In the previous chapter, I began to explore these aspects of realist fiction. Chapter 7 considers the authority latent in "transparent" third-person narration.

7. Schultz, *Gay's Beggar's Opera,* p. 173; see chapter 16, "Sources, Written and Unwritten." See especially the section "Satiric Realism" in Ronald Paulson, *Satire and the Novel in Eighteenth-Century England* (New Haven: Yale University Press, 1967), pp. 11–23. Even a recent editor who insists that Gay turned the low characters into "personae in a well-wrought play" and "endowed them with the speech of shopkeepers and businessmen," says: "The dramatization is realistic, however, to the extent that the action portrays the antagonism and injustice existing within the criminal class" (Edgar V. Roberts, ed., *The Beggar's Opera* [Lincoln: University of Nebraska Press, 1969], p. xix). Wild and Sheppard were assumed to be the prototypes for Peachum and Macheath.

8. Emmett L. Avery, ed., *The London Stage, 1660–1800* (Carbondale: Southern Illinois University Press, 1960), p. cx. See John Thurmond, *Harlequin Sheppard: A Night Scene in Grotesque Characters* (London: J. Roberts, 1724); Gay's lyrics appear on pp. 16–17. Both Rich's skill as an actor and his interest as a producer lay chiefly in pantomime and other forms of spectacle, though in order to remain competitive his theaters offered much the same fare as others. See Paul Sawyer, "John Rich's Contribution to the Eighteenth-Century London Stage," in *The Eighteenth-Century English Stage,* ed. Kenneth Richards and Peter Thomson (London: Methuen, 1972), pp. 85–104. On realistic scenery in Restoration and earlier eighteenth-century theaters, see Shirley Strum Kenny, "Theatre, Related Arts, and the Profit Motive: An Overview," in *British Theatre and the Other Arts,* ed. Shirley Strum Kenny (Washington: Folger Library, 1983), pp. 15–38, especially pp. 18–19; see also pp. 29–36 on the close relationship between the novel and drama in the eighteenth century.

9. Paulson says that *A Just View* appears to be a "portrait" of the Drury Lane stage (*Hogarth,* 1: 522 n. 10; see also 1: 138–39). For a detailed account of *A Just View,* see *Hogarth's Graphic Works,* 1: 109–11.

10. Paulson, *Hogarth,* 1: 180–88 and plates 61–62; and Marvin A. Carlson, "A Fresh Look at Hogarth's *Beggar's Opera,*" *Educational Theatre Journal* 27 (1975): 31–39. The prison setting in Hogarth's later versions of the picture is of the general type, derived ultimately from Bibiena (fig. 22), that appears as the frontispiece (fig. 26) to Gay's earlier tragedy *The Captives* (London, 1724) and again in Hogarth's drawing room "conversation" piece showing children acting the prison scene from Dryden's *The Indian Emperor* (1732) (fig. 25). See below for further discussion.

11. For a nineteenth-century print of the house before demolition, see Gerald Howson, *Thief-Taker General: The Rise and Fall of Jonathan Wild* (London: Hutchinson, 1970), plate 4; see also pp. 74 and 119.

12. See *The Works of Thomas Purney,* ed. H. O. White (Oxford: Basil Blackwell, 1933), and H. O. White, "Thomas Purney: A Forgotten Poet and Critic of the

Eighteenth Century," *Essays and Studies* 15 (1929): 67–97. Purney employed a deputy beginning in 1724, when he had to retire "into the Country to reestablish his Health."

13. On the Tuscan order, see, for example, William Chambers, *A Treatise on Civil Architecture* (London, 1759), p. 16. For the statues on Old Newgate see Anthony Babington, *The English Bastille* (London: MacDonald, 1971), p. 58. Babington and Paulson (*Hogarth,* 1: 137) agree in listing Security instead of Severity. The statues are listed in the caption to item 35.41 in the Museum of London. They were later installed on Dance's New Newgate.

14. See also Defoe's *A Narrative of All the Robberies, Escapes, &c., of John Sheppard* (London: John Applebee, 1724).

15. Preface to *The What D'Ye Call It,* in John Gay, *Dramatic Works,* 2 vols., ed. John Fuller (Oxford: Clarendon Press, 1983), 1: 174.

16. *The Letters of John Gay,* ed. C. F. Burgess (Oxford: Clarendon Press, 1966), p. 19. See Donaldson, *The World Upside-Down,* pp. 160–61, for a fuller discussion of this passage.

17. For a valuable compilation of sources and analogues, see J. V. Guerinot and Rodney D. Jilg, *The Beggar's Opera* (Hamden, Conn.: Archon, 1976).

18. See Schultz, *Gay's Beggar's Opera,* chaps. 8 and 9, for the stage history.

19. Information used in this paragraph is drawn from works cited above, as well as from Bertrand H. Bronson, "The Beggar's Opera," in *Facets of the Enlightenment* (Berkeley: University of California Press, 1968), pp. 60–90; H. T. Dickinson, *Walpole and the Whig Supremacy* (London: English Universities Press, 1973); William H. Irving, *John Gay: Favorite of the Wits* (Durham, N.C.: Duke University Press, 1940); Isaac Kramnick, *Bolingbroke and His Circle: The Politics of Nostalgia in the Age of Walpole* (Cambridge: Harvard University Press, 1968); Peter E. Lewis, *John Gay: The Beggar's Opera* (London: Edward Arnold, 1976); Yvonne Noble, ed., *Twentieth Century Interpretations of The Beggar's Opera* (Englewood Cliffs, N.J.: Prentice-Hall, 1975); John B. Owen, *The Eighteenth Century, 1714–1815* (New York: Norton, 1976); Patricia M. Spacks, *John Gay* (New York: Twayne, 1965).

20. On the Hobbesian equation, see Donaldson, *The World Upside-Down,* pp. 174–79. In a print of 1728, *"The Beggar's Opera* Burlesqued," the characters literally become animals in an outdoor performance where scenery and the actual topography of London merge. See Paulson, *Hogarth's Graphic Works,* 1: 297–99 and plate 320; Paulson and others have found the print too much in the "delicate" manner of Gravelot to give it to Hogarth without reservation.

21. Henry K. Miller, ed., *Miscellanies by Henry Fielding, Esq.* (Middletown: Wesleyan University Press, 1972), 1: 10.

22. Douglas Hay, "Property, Authority, and the Criminal Law," in *Albion's Fatal Tree: Crime and Society in Eighteenth-Century England,* ed. Douglas Hay et al. (New York: Pantheon, 1975), pp. 48–49.

23. This passage from Hawkins appears on pp. 253–54 of the convenient anthology provided by Schultz in chapter 21, "The Morality Question," of *Gay's Beggar's Opera.* See also the extracts in chapter 5, "The Morality Problem," of Guerinot and Jilg, *The Beggar's Opera.*

24. Swift's defense appeared in *The Intelligencer,* no. 3 (1729), and in *Mist's Weekly Journal,* 6 July 1728. Guerinot and Jilg, *The Beggar's Opera,* pp. 142–53, reprint the former; Schultz, *Gay's Beggar's Opera,* pp. 228–29, extracts from the latter. The quoted material comes from Schultz (p. 229).

25. Ibid., p. 75, citing *Biographia Dramatica*, ed. David E. Baker, Isaac Reed, and Stephen Jones, 3 vols. (London, 1812). See also Spacks, *John Gay*, pp. 124–25.

26. Gay's sequel, *Polly* (1729), plausibly showed Macheath transported to the West Indies in consequence of his reprieve. This outcome would have been likely in 1728, but it defies the original ending's spirit of unconditional operatic justice. As John Fuller observes, this invocation of conventional justice implies the dissolution and destruction of Macheath that follows. See John Gay, *Dramatic Works*, 1: 52–53.

27. At least in retrospect, the irony subsumes even the prison hulks since they were an expedient adopted by embarrassed authorities to replace transportation of convicted felons to America after the outbreak of the Revolution in 1776. These alterations occurred in the year Howard published *The State of the Prisons* and two years before the Penitentiary Act of 1779. On the Dodd case, see Gerald Howson, *The Macaroni Parson: A Life of the Unfortunate Dr. Dodd* (London: Hutchinson, 1973), especially chapter 25 and, for the petition itself, Appendix, pp. 248–51; the list of signatures was thirty-seven-and-a-half yards in length.

28. See Paulson, *Hogarth*, 1: 301–5. The parallels between these two theatrical pictures by Hogarth visually confirm that for Gay's audience the scene of Macheath torn between Polly and Lucy in Newgate (3.11) recalled prison episodes like Dryden's where, imprisoned and bound, Cortez confronts Almeria and Cydaria (*The Indian Emperor; or, The Conquest of Mexico*, 4.4) or the variant in act 4 of Gay's own tragedy *The Captives* (1724) where Cylene (the Captive) and Astarbe quarrel in the prison from which Sophemes has escaped in disguise under the veil of the captive who was to have executed him but who, like Fidelio after her, turns out to be his wife (fig. 26).

29. Donaldson, *The World Upside-Down*, p. 162.

30. Guildhall assumes the date of "An Exact Representation" to be 1724 though no date appears on the print. Parr's print appears to have been done specifically for *Select Trials at the Sessions-House in the Old-Bailey*, 4 vols. (London: J. Applebee, 1742). The Sheppard prints rely in some measure on the tradition of popular engravings produced in this format during the seventeenth century on the Continent. These included single plates containing a number of small scenes illustrating the careers of whores, rakes, and drunkards. Although Hogarth was influenced by these popular prints, as Paulson shows, the simple monumentality of his early cycles refers more to the great tradition of history painting. See *Hogarth*, 1: 269; also, Hilda Kurz, "Italian Models of Hogarth's Picture Stories," *Journal of the Warburg and Courtauld Institutes* 15 (1952): 136–68; and Frederick Antal, *Hogarth and His Place in European Art* (London: Routledge and Kegan Paul, 1962), pp. 97–98. In *Hogarth's Graphic Works*, 1: 39–40, Paulson discusses the relationship of Hogarth's progresses to earlier forms, "as old as the moral tracts or prints that contrast 'Before' and 'After,' " and to "the religious progress piece [that] traced the journey of the soul through the temptations of this life to its home with God." He says that "Hogarth consciously, though sometimes ironically, draws upon such works as Bunyan's *Pilgrim's Progress* and *The Life and Death of Mr. Badman*." The tradition of illustrating *Pilgrim's Progress* began very soon after its publication. Advertisements for sets of woodcuts (a cheap, popular form of illustration) are bound into many early editions, and "cuts" in ever increasing numbers ornament successive imprints. The first *Pilgrim's Progress* to include engraved illustrations (the more expensive form also used by Hogarth for his series) appeared in 1728, the work of John Sturt (1658–1730). On later

serializations of the Sheppard story and related popular narratives on the stage and in prints see Martin Meisel, *Realizations: Narrative, Pictorial, and Theatrical Arts in Nineteenth-Century England* (Princeton: Princeton University Press, 1983), chap. 13. Although Meisel does not refer to Bakhtin, his book traces the novelization of the theater and of painting that began in the eighteenth century.

31. A brief account appears in John Kerslake, *Early Georgian Portraits*, 2 vols. (London: Her Majesty's Stationery Office, 1977), 1: 331:

> Extortion in the Fleet debtors' prison had already become notorious during the wardenship, 1713–1728, of John Huggins. In 1728 his successor, Thomas Bambridge, caused the death of Robert Castell, a minor architect and friend of the prominent humanitarian MP James Oglethorpe, by exposing him to smallpox. In January 1729, Bambridge made the mistake of antagonizing a baronet Sir William Rich, who stabbed him in the course of a quarrel. A legal enquiry ensued.
>
> Meanwhile on 25 February on a motion from Oglethorpe, it was ordered in the House of Commons "That a Committee be appointed, to enquire into the State of the Gaols of this Kingdom, and report same, with their opinion thereupon, to the House: And it is referred to Mr. Oglethorpe . . . Colonel Onslow; And they are to meet this Afternoon, at Five of the Clock, in the Speaker's Chamber; and have Power to adjourn from Time to Time, and from Place to Place, as they shall find convenient; and to send for Persons, Papers and Records." Ninety-six names are subscribed. The Committee first went to the Fleet on 27 February 1729, when Rich was brought before them. Bambridge was questioned on 8 March and the irons worn by the prisoners, the "Articles of Complaint," were exhibited. The House heard the Committee's report on 20 March and passed a resolution ordering the prosecution of Huggins and Bambridge, and preventing Huggins from further wardenships. A supplementary report was submitted on 14 May 1729, but the committee was then at work on the Marshalsea which it subsequently investigated along with the Kings Bench prison. Reports were published on all three prisons, 1729–30.

For details see Leslie F. Church, *Oglethorpe: A Study of Philanthropy in England and Georgia* (London: Epworth Press, 1932), pp. 9–24; Amos A. Ettinger, *James Edward Oglethorpe, Imperial Idealist* (Oxford: Clarendon Press, 1936), pp. 89–95; and Paulson, *Hogarth*, 1: 196–202. For the committee's own very moving account, see *A Report from the Committee Appointed to Enquire into the State of the Gaols of this Kingdom: Relating to the Fleet Prison* (1729). Reports on the Marshalsea Prison and the King's Bench Prison appeared in 1729 and 1730 (see chap. 1, note 10 above). Hereafter, the first is cited as *A Report* and the others by the name of the prison.

32. I quote the 1730 version, ll. 340–70. For the complex textual history of the passage, see James Thomson, *The Seasons*, ed. James Sambrook (Oxford: Clarendon Press, 1981), especially pp. 220–21. For a full account, see Alan D. McKillop, "Thomson and the Jail Committee," *Studies in Philology* 47 (1950): 62–71. McKillop (p. 64) notes that Thomson's revisions in 1744 change the tone to that of exhortation in face of the, by then, slight impact of the Oglethorpe Committee. Note, in particular, the change to the imperative in the later version:

O great Design! if executed well,
With patient Care, and Wisdom-temper'd Zeal.
Ye Sons of Mercy! yet resume the Search;
Drag forth the legal Monsters into Light,
Wrench from their Hands Oppression's iron Rod,
And bid the Cruel feel the Pains they give.

(ll. 376–81)

33. *A Report . . . Relating to the Fleet Prison*, pp. 9–10. The appendix following page 40 of the *Report* contains thirty-three affidavits from prisoners relating further instances.

34. Later Thomson fully realized this line's Shakespearean quality by changing "robe" to "weed." See the Sambrook edition, p. 220, l. 369.

35. In some measure Thomson follows the *Report* (pp. 10–11, 13) in this association, which is made in indirect quotations from prisoners.

36. Preface to *Winter* (1726); Sambrook edition, p. 303.

37. Paulson, *Hogarth*, 1: 39. For details on the painting of the Oglethorpe Committee, see Kerslake, *Early Georgian Portraits*, 1: 330–38, and Paulson, *Hogarth*, 1: 196–202.

38. Ronald Paulson, *The Art of Hogarth* (London: Phaidon, 1975), p. 14; see also Paulson's *Emblem and Expression: Meaning in English Art of the Eighteenth Century* (Cambridge: Harvard University Press, 1975), pp. 45–46. Paulson, specifically linking the painter's early prison experience to the Oglethorpe picture, says that "the emphasis throughout his work is on prisons, real and metaphorical, on the relationship between the individual and institutions, on punishment hardly warranted by the crime, and on the image of the deluded and isolated individual. Even when he is not dealing with people who are in a prison of one sort or another he portrays rooms that are more like prison cells than boudoirs or parlors" (*Hogarth*, 1: 39).

39. Scholars agree that Hogarth must have been present at an actual meeting, but not about how he gained access. See especially Paulson, *Hogarth*, 1: 196–202, and Derek Jarrett, *The Ingenious Mr. Hogarth* (London: Michael Joseph, 1976), pp. 77–82.

40. On Castell see *A Report*, pp. 7–8; on Rich, *Marshalsea*, pp. 19–21; also Paulson, *Hogarth*, 1: 196–202.

41. Kerslake, *Early Georgian Portraits*, 1: 331, speculates that the torn notice may read "ALMANACK." On strong rooms and irons see *A Report*, pp. 11–13, passim.

42. The poem originally appeared on 15 May 1729; reprinted in Samuel Wesley, *Poems on Several Occasions* (London: Printed for the Author by E. Say, sold by S. Birt, 1736), pp. 173–91 (in D. F. Foxon, *English Verse, 1701–1750: A Catalogue of Separately Printed Poems*, 2 vols. [Cambridge: Cambridge University Press, 1975], W353). Wesley generalizes easily from the Fleet to other prisons, envisioning Newgate as Oglethorpe's next objective:

> Conscious of ill-us'd Pow'r, and publick Hate,
> Then other Tyrants fear'd approaching Fate;
> An universal Groan the Prisons gave,
> And Newgate trembled thro' her inmost Cave,
> Lest farther Searches farther Crimes reveal,
> Which Arts infernal labour to conceal;
> Lest Pity's Eye those Regions should explore,
> Where Beams of Mercy never reach'd before;
> Unwelcome Light on darkest Dungeons throw,
> And ev'ry latent Depth of Horror show. (p. 188)

See also Peter Fraser, *Iniquity Display'd; or, the Happy Deliverance* (London: Printed for the Author, 1729) (Foxon, F231). McKillop, "Thomson and the Jail Committee," pp. 64–65, lists the numerous pamphlets and poems occasioned by the committee.

43. From George Vertue, *Notebooks* (Oxford: Walpole Society, 1934–35), 3: 58; cited by Peter Jan De Voogd, *Henry Fielding and William Hogarth: The Correspondences of the Arts* (Amsterdam: Rodopi, 1981), p. 59.

44. Bishop Butler's "hospice" sermon of 1740 is the one possible exception, and it is usually cited as an isolated instance; see below, chapter 6.

45. Any interpretation of the progresses along the lines followed here is bound to be indebted at every turn to the work of Ronald Paulson. See, in addition to *Hogarth* and the detailed entries in *Hogarth's Graphic Works*, *The Art of Hogarth*, *Emblem and Expression*, and *Popular and Polite Art in the Age of Hogarth and Fielding* (Notre Dame: University of Notre Dame Press, 1979).

46. Prisoners had long complained of abuses of the fee system; the point is that the structure of feeling I am tracing enables this failing to become an issue like other manifestations of the randomness and the abdication of regulated authority in the old prisons. The long-term detention of debtors was "not a necessary consequence of the legal process, but a symptom of its (periodic) failure." See Joanna Innes, "The King's Bench Prison in the Later Eighteenth-Century: Law, Authority, and Order in a London Debtors' Prison," in *An Ungovernable People*, ed. John Brewer and John Styles (New Brunswick, N.J.: Rutgers University Press, 1980), p. 254.

47. *The Jew Decoy'd; or, the Progress of a Harlot* (London: W. Rayner, 1735), 2.6, p. 35.

48. Ibid., 2.5, p. 29.

49. Ibid., Air 12.

50. Paulson, *Emblem and Expression*, chap. 3.

51. Hogarth, *The Analysis of Beauty*, p. 42.

52. See Paulson, *Hogarth's Graphic Works*, 1: 142, and Moore, *Hogarth's Literary Relations*, pp. 29–31. Imitation of *The Rake's Progress* was equally rife. For instance, figure 48 below comes from a series after Hogarth. See Frederic George Stephens, *Catalogue of Prints and Drawings in the British Museum, Political and Personal Satires*, vol. 3, pt. 1 (London: Chiswick Press for the Trustees of the British Museum, 1877), no. 2186. The tradition of narrative commentary was well under way in the 1740s with Jean André Rouquet's *Lettres de Monsieur** à un de ses Amis à Paris, pour lui Expliquer des Estampes de Monsieur Hogarth* (London: R. Dodsley and M. Cooper, 1746) and continued with John Trusler's *Hogarth Moralized* (London: S. Hooper, 1768). By the later eighteenth century it was firmly established. See, besides the early standard commentaries on Hogarth by John Ireland, John Nichols, and George Steevens, *Lichtenberg's Commentaries on Hogarth's Engravings*, ed. and trans. Innes and Gustav Herdan (London: Cresset Press, 1966). Trusler, for example, was still being reprinted in the nineteenth century. One suspects that Hogarth's series were as much read in quasi-novelistic commentaries as inspected visually.

53. Paulson, *Hogarth*, 1: 238–59.

54. Bakhtin, *The Dialogic Imagination*, p. 7.

55. Paulson, *Hogarth*, 1: 240.

56. Ibid., pp. 181–95.

57. Hogarth's scenery in the two final pictures (Mr. and Mrs. Paul Mellon and Tate Gallery) refers to but does not fully adopt the Bibiena *scèna per angolo* that had been introduced into England earlier in the eighteenth century (fig. 22). The lofty palatial air, the double perspective, and the low vanishing points all recall the Bibienas even though Hogarth merely suggests the extreme asymmetry

that marked their style at its most distinctive. See Colin Visser, "Scenery and Technical Design," in *The London Theatre World, 1660–1800*, ed. Robert D. Hume (Carbondale: Southern Illinois University Press, 1980), pp. 66–118. As Visser indicates (p. 85), the *scèna per angolo* actually may have been invented by Juvarra rather than by Bibiena.

58. Kerslake, *Early Georgian Portraits*, 1: 332–33. In 1730–31, shortly after the Oglethorpe and *Beggar's Opera* pictures, Hogarth painted the serial pendants *Before* and *After* (Cambridge, Fitzwilliam Museum). In them, Paulson says, Hogarth "produces for the first time the sort of graphic narrative that came to be associated with his name" (*The Art of Hogarth*, plate 12 caption and p. 43); see also *Hogarth*, 1: 229–30. The commission for *Before* and *After* came from John Thomson, a member of Oglethorpe's Fleet committee.

59. Contemporary accounts and panegyrics viewed the Oglethorpe Committee's venture as a progress through hellish realms governed by petty tyrants to an essentially comic vindication of British liberty. From the perspective of my analysis, the two pictures imply a story where the realm of paradox that Gay centers in Old Newgate and identifies with government by patronage gives way to Oglethorpe's committee, a bureaucratic arm of a Parliament engaging in the interest-free inquiry that, according to Habermas, characterizes modern political discourse and state institutions.

60. *The Prisoners Opera* (London: At the Wells, 1730), p. 2.

61. Ibid., p. 12.

62. Paulson, *Hogarth's Graphic Works*, 1: 168. Samuel Wesley, in *The Prisons Open'd*, also had seen madness as the next step.

63. For a reproduction of a 1783 engraving, see Paulson, *The Art of Hogarth*, fig. 9; see also *Hogarth*, 1: 326–27 and 333.

64. Paulson, *Emblem and Expression*, chap. 5.

65. See chapters 5 and 6 below.

66. Both this symbolism and its increasingly problematic character are evident in a later eighteenth-century anecdote about Bedlam Hospital: "The design was taken from the Chateau de Tuilleries *at Versailles*. Louis XIV, it is said, was so much offended that his palace should be made a model for a hospital, that in revenge he ordered a plan of St. James's to be taken for offices of a very inferior nature" (Henry B. Wheatley, *London Past and Present: A Dictionary of Its History, Associations, and Traditions*, 3 vols. [London: John Murray, 1891], 1: 173). The story serves my point here despite Wheatley's justifiable skepticism about its accuracy concerning either Bedlam Hospital or Louis XIV.

67. *Stow's Survey of the Cities of London and Westminster*, ed. John Styrpe (London, 1720), p. 196. Paulson mentions the 1729 addition of bars at Bedlam Hospital in *Hogarth*, 1: 327.

CHAPTER FIVE

Epigraph: I quote from *The Complete Works of Henry Fielding, Esq.*, 16 vols., ed. William E. Henley (London: Heinemann, 1903), 13: 15 and 17. Unless noted otherwise, further references to writings by Fielding are to this edition. *An Enquiry* was first published by A. Millar (London, 1751).

1. On the novelization of culture that Bakhtin describes as having begun in the eighteenth century, see Mikhail M. Bakhtin, *The Dialogic Imagination*, ed. and trans. Michael Holquist and Caryl Emerson (Austin: University of Texas Press, 1981), pp. 5–7, and discussion in chapter 4 above, especially section 1.

2. On the distinction between cultural and social systems as analytic constructs, see Clifford Geertz, *The Interpretation of Cultures* (New York: Basic Books, 1973), pp. 144–45. Quoted above in my Introduction, note 1.

3. In devising the term "narrative resources," I extrapolate from Anthony Giddens, who argues in *A Contemporary Critique of Historical Materialism* (Berkeley: University of California Press, 1981) that both writing itself and prototypical chronicle lists were among the authoritative resources stored up in early cities.

4. The various chapters of Nikolaus Pevsner's *A History of Building Types* (Princeton: Princeton University Press, 1976) conveniently sketch the history of basic civic institutions. Public banks and exchanges, as opposed to the private banks of the Middle Ages and earlier Renaissance, began in the late Renaissance and became established in the seventeenth century. They anticipate later metropolitan developments on the European continent. The establishment of the Bank of England in 1694 inaugurated public banking in London well after the enormous growth that followed the Great Fire. See Pevsner's chapter 12, especially pp. 199–200.

5. See above, chapter 1, on Thompson's ideas.

6. Pat Rogers, *Henry Fielding: A Biography* (London: Paul Elek, 1979), pp. 165, 175–76, and 196.

7. Fielding, *Works*, 14: 174. My account of Covent Garden draws primarily on Robert Thorne, *Covent Garden Market: Its History and Restoration* (London: Architectural Press, 1980), pp. 2–11, and M. Dorothy George, *London Life in the Eighteenth Century* (London: Kegan Paul, Trench, Trubner, 1925), pp. 83–84; see also Michael Hanson, *Two Thousand Years of London* (London: Country Life, 1967), pp. 77–78. The term "liberties" continued to be applied to areas that until the seventeenth century had been sanctuaries from civil authorities because the lands had belonged to the Church prior to the Reformation; in Fielding's day, only the Mint continued as a sanctuary of this kind. For a convenient account of the "liberties," see Gerald Howson, *Thief-Taker General: The Rise and Fall of Jonathan Wild* (London: Hutchinson, 1970), pp. 22–24.

8. Leon Radzinowicz, *A History of English Criminal Law and Its Administration from 1750*, vol. 3, *Cross-Currents in the Movement for the Reform of the Police* (New York: Macmillan, 1957), pp. 1–7.

9. For fuller discussion of law enforcement in Fielding's day, and for detailed citations, see chapter 6.

10. These tracts, considered on Bakhtin's terms, record alterations in behavioral ideology occurring through dialogic exchange between literary discourse and social action. See *The Dialogic Imagination*, pp. 5–7, 33, and 262–64, passim, as well as works cited in my Introduction, notes 13–17.

There can be no doubt that Fielding worked to influence parliamentary thinking, and legal historians have generally maintained that he had some success in gaining legislative points. See Leon Radzinowicz, *A History of English Criminal Law and Its Administration from 1750*, vol. 1, *The Movement for Reform, 1750–1833* (New York: Macmillan, 1948), pp. 401–3. For dissenting views, see Malvin R. Zirker, Jr., *Fielding's Social Pamphlets* (Berkeley: University of California Press, 1966), pp. 39–42; and Hugh Amory, "Henry Fielding and the Criminal Legislation of 1751–2," *Philological Quarterly* 50 (1971): 175–92. John H. Langbein, "Shaping the Eighteenth-Century Criminal Trial: A View from the Ryder Sources," *University of Chicago Law Review* 50 (1983): 65–66, summarizes the Commons committee report of 17 January 1752 (around which most of the controversy has swirled), and remarks that he sees "a closer correspondence between Fielding's views and the proposal in the Commons report than does Amory." Martin C. Battestin says in his introduction to *Amelia* (Middletown: Wesleyan University Press, 1984) that "there can be no doubt that [Fielding] was the most articulate and authoritative writer who addressed these grave issues, and that his advice was sought at the highest levels of government—by the Lord Chancellor, by the Secretary of State, by the Prime Minister" (p. xxxv). Battestin's summation is sufficient to my argument, which is concerned with the relation of Fielding's social pamphlets to changes in practice and to reformist consciousness in the public sphere, not with the precise effect of his views in one Parliament. Unfortunately, Battestin's edition became available too late for me to take full advantage of its rich annotation and commentary.

11. Ronald Paulson, *Satire and the Novel in the Eighteenth Century* (New Haven: Yale University Press, 1967), p. 106. See J. Paul Hunter, *Occasional Form: Henry Fielding and the Chains of Circumstance* (Baltimore: Johns Hopkins University Press, 1975), pp. 212–14, for an account of the symmetries between Fielding and Richardson. Richardson has hovered in my thoughts all through the composition of this book: the most extreme instance of a problem with no satisfactory solution. How could I ever treat enough novels when my argument required the presence of a rather complicated conceptual framework, of considerable historical material, and of enough textual explication to allow readers to explore the ideas in my company? As the book grew longer, it became clear that Defoe and Fielding would have to be the test cases and that chapters about Richardson, Smollett, Goldsmith, Sterne, Godwin, and others would have to be sacrificed. The additional pair of chapters necessary to a proper analysis of Richardson alone would have stretched the book unconscionably. Here, and at a few other points, the reader will find the briefest indications of the way my treatment of these various writers might have gone. Some of my ideas on Goldsmith are worked out in a forthcoming essay, "Prison Reform and the Sentence of Narration in *The Vicar of Wakefield*."

12. Although an early dating is congenial to the discussion of *Jonathan Wild* that follows, my argument does not hinge upon any specific theory about its date of composition. Like Ian Donaldson (*The World Upside-Down* [Oxford: Clarendon Press, 1970], chap. 8), I write as if the work was substantially conceived before *Shamela* or *Joseph Andrews*, forming a bridge along with *The Champion* between Fielding's careers as a playwright and novelist. As Pat Rogers says, however, "no one knows quite when the book came to be written." It is certain only that essays in *The Champion* for 4 and 24 March 1740 refer to Wild. *The Champion* for 4 October 1740 mentions the author's suppression of a work against Walpole, and "the likeliest candidate seems to be *Jonathan Wild*, first published in 1743 but—as many suppose—drafted some time earlier" (Rogers, *Fielding*, pp. 136 and 104–5). Alan D. McKillop observes of *Jonathan Wild* that "the evident intention to satirize Walpole and the sustained burlesque suggest the tone of the late 1730's"(*The Early Masters of English Fiction* [Lawrence: University of Kansas Press, 1956], p. 117). Claude J. Rawson accepts Dudden's theory that the mock-heroic sections that satirize Walpole by attacking Wild as a "great" man were drafted about 1740 along with Mrs. Heartfree's travels; he thinks the balance of the Heartfree materials probably date from 1742 and the assemblage of the work from 1742/43 (*Henry Fielding and the Augustan Ideal under Stress* [London: Routledge and Kegan Paul, 1972], pp. 165–66 and 256–57). See F. Homes Dudden, *Henry Fielding: His Life, Works, and Times*, 2 vols. (Oxford:

Clarendon Press, 1952), 1: 482–83. J. Paul Hunter, citing "lingering uncertainties about its process of composition" and "the probability that its 1743 form . . . represents more than one stage of Fielding's thinking," still inclines toward an early dating: "*Jonathan Wild* may well be Fielding's first step toward prose fiction. Its focuses are narrower than either *Shamela* or *Joseph Andrews*, and my guess is that Fielding wrote a draft of it before the occasion of *Shamela* came up" (*Occasional Form*, p. 235). See also William R. Irwin, *The Making of Jonathan Wild* (New York: Columbia University Press, 1941), pp. 36–37.

13. Paulson, *Satire and the Novel*, p. 96. See also B. M. Jones, *Henry Fielding: Novelist and Magistrate* (London: George Allen and Unwin, 1933), pp. 76–78.

14. Rogers, *Fielding*, p. 124.

15. Bakhtin, *The Dialogic Imagination*, pp. 13–15 and 20–22. On Fielding and Lucian, see Henry K. Miller, *Essays on Fielding's Miscellanies* (Princeton: Princeton University Press, 1961), chap. 6.

16. On Fielding's adaptation of the mock heroic to prose fiction, see Rawson, *Henry Fielding and the Augustan Ideal under Stress*, especially chaps. 5 and 6, and J. Paul Hunter, *Occasional Form*, especially pp. 130 and 139.

17. The treatise now survives only in scattered fragments. See William B. Coley, "Henry Fielding's 'Lost' Law Book," *Modern Language Notes* 76 (1961): 408–13, and Hugh Amory, "A Preliminary Census of Fielding's Legal Manuscripts," *Papers of the Bibliographical Society of America* 62 (1968): 587–601.

18. For a discussion of the mock trial in Fielding's earlier works see Ronald Paulson, *Satire and the Novel*, pp. 95–96. On the place of this issue of the *True Patriot* in Fielding's life, see Rogers, *Fielding*, pp. 141–47, and Wilbur L. Cross, *The History of Henry Fielding*, 3 vols. (New Haven: Yale University Press, 1918), 2: 1–44.

19. Battestin, *Amelia*, pp. xl–xliv.

20. Ibid., pp. xv and 539. *A Journal of the Plague Year* comes to mind as a possible exception, but it differs because Defoe's fictional chronology consists only in the consciousness of H.F. as it unfolds within the framework provided by historical documents like plague bills and by a selective mapping of London of that day. One can track, and usually time, the steps of Fielding's characters in *Amelia* through a "London" in which every place named in fact existed. *A Journal of the Plague Year* is much more impressionistic despite its attempt at precise reconstruction. On the other hand, as Battestin shows, Fielding does not consistently coordinate his plot with references to specific historical details even though the novel is set in London during a few months of 1733 when, for the most part, he must have been in residence there (if Fielding were Joyce, his oratorio would not be on the wrong day of the week). But Fielding's numerous small anachronisms, and his few enormous ones, should not obscure the remarkable correlation of time and place that distinguish *Amelia* as a landmark in the history of the novel.

21. Robin Evans, *The Fabrication of Virtue: English Prison Architecture, 1750–1840* (Cambridge: Cambridge University Press, 1982), pp. 53–56.

22. Fielding, *Works*, 13: 169. The second section of Fielding's *Proposal* sets forth the rules in fifty-nine numbered paragraphs (ibid., pp. 145–68). Evans notes that because of the centrality of labor to Fielding's plan it "had no real heirs within the mainstream of penal reform" (*The Fabrication of Virtue*, p. 56). Labor also figured in Bentham's much later Panopticon scheme; but it is true that apart from the striking fact of the County House's enormous metropolitan

size, Fielding's innovations are submerged in a proposal, not for the first penitentiary, but for one of the last houses of correction. However, in a manner akin to that of John Howard and the other eighteenth-century advocates of the penitentiary who cited Fielding as a pioneer, I am noting that he opened the penitentiary idea to consideration. Fielding's writings are among the circumstances of its emergence. Certainly, as Zirker has shown in *Fielding's Social Pamphlets,* Fielding's thought finds root in received wisdom and he draws particulars from a variety of previous tracts. But Evans allows us to understand that however commonplace many aspects of Fielding's plan may have been in proposals for houses of correction, they take on different significance when magnified in size and tailored into a materially articulate architecture. On Fielding as a pioneer in the consideration of "a new intermediate penalty suitable for minor felonies," see Michael Ignatieff, *A Just Measure of Pain: The Penitentiary in the Industrial Revolution, 1750–1850* (New York: Pantheon, 1978), pp. 45–47, passim. For a summary of Evans's distinction between houses of correction and penitentiaries, see above, note 44 to chapter 1.

23. Fielding, *Works,* 13: 183–86.

24. Evans advances this argument in *The Fabrication of Virtue,* p. 66, citing D. P. Walker, *The Decline of Hell: Seventeenth-Century Discussions of Eternal Torment* (London: Routledge and Kegan Paul, 1964); see especially pp. 8–11, 40–42, and 59–70.

25. Fielding, *Jonathan Wild, Works,* 2: 10 and 188 (originally all in capitals). Henley's edition is based on Fielding's revised version of 1754, which omitted two digressive chapters and blunted the satire against Walpole, altering the emphasis to a more general attack on politicians and great men as types. Further citations to *Jonathan Wild* appear in the text. Although Fielding may be read as guiding us to view Mrs. Heartfree's statement as inadequate, even simple-minded, his irony is too feeble and diffuse to alter the validation of her view by the outcome of the plot; a happy ending may be ironically colored, but it is still happy. Fielding probably did not mean to imply that the virtuous are always rewarded on earth. For a full treatment of the complex relationship between Fielding's apparent intentions in *Jonathan Wild* and those in the preface to the *Miscellanies,* and, in turn, of how these relate to questions about his purely technical powers of execution in the earlier novels, see Rawson, *Henry Fielding and the Augustan Ideal under Stress,* chap. 7.

The literary history of Wild's story included a version by Defoe, *The True and Genuine Account of the Life and Actions of the Late Jonathan Wild* (London: J. Applebee, 1725), where, in contrast to his earlier first-person treatment of Sheppard in a manner rather like that of *Moll Flanders,* Defoe continually intrudes and interprets in a heavily moralistic vein. Although they are not narratives, the two satiric articles equating Wild and Walpole that appeared in *Mist's Weekly Journal* on 12 and 19 June 1725, are more akin in their ironic tone to Fielding. They once were mistakenly attributed to Fielding, and there has been speculation that they might be by Defoe even though he broke with Mist in 1724. See Irwin, *The Making of Jonathan Wild,* p. 24 and passim, for Fielding's awareness of these and other works about Wild; for a convenient reprint of the Mist articles, see Guerinot and Jilg, *The Beggar's Opera,* pp. 71–74.

26. Donaldson, *The World Upside-Down,* p. 202–3.

27. *Miscellanies by Henry Fielding, Esq.,* ed. Henry K. Miller (Middletown: Wesleyan University Press, 1972), 1: 10; further references are to this edition and

are hereafter cited parenthetically in the text. See above p. 100 for full quotation of the paragraph. See, besides Donaldson, John Preston, "The Ironic Mode: A Comparison of *Jonathan Wild* and *The Beggar's Opera*," *Essays in Criticism* 16 (1966): 268–80.

28. John Gay, *Dramatic Works*, 2 vols., ed. John Fuller (Oxford: Clarendon Press, 1983), 2: 64 (3.16).

29. On Fielding's views concerning human nature and ethics, see Martin C. Battestin, *The Moral Basis of Fielding's Art: A Study of Joseph Andrews* (Middletown: Wesleyan University Press, 1959), especially chap. 5; Irwin, *The Making of Jonathan Wild*, chap. 2; Morris Golden, *Fielding's Moral Psychology* (Amherst: University of Massachusetts Press, 1966), chaps. 2 and 5; and Miller, *Essays on Fielding's Miscellanies*, pp. 189–228. Bernard Harrison, *Fielding's Tom Jones: The Novelist as Moral Philosopher* (London: Chatto and Windus for Sussex University Press, 1975), chaps. 4 and 6, offers an overall account of Fielding's place in the moral thought of his period.

30. David Hume, *A Treatise of Human Nature*, ed. L. A. Selby-Bigge, 2d ed. rev. P. H. Nidditch (Oxford: Clarendon Press, 1978), 3.1, pp. 468–69. I quote the balance of this paragraph in the final section of chapter 1. Slightly later in the same book Hume says: "I am sensible, that, generally speaking, the representations of [selfishness] have been carried much too far; and that the descriptions, which certain philosophers delight so much to form of mankind in this particular, are as wide of nature as any accounts of monsters, which we meet with in fables and romances. So far from thinking, that men have no affection for any thing beyond themselves, I am of opinion, that tho' it be rare to meet with one, who loves any single person better than himself; yet 'tis as rare to meet with one, in whom all the kind affections, taken together, do not over-balance all the selfish" (pp. 486–87). Miller, in his edition of Fielding's *Miscellanies* (p. 10), cites classical precedents for the idea of the "Judge in every Man's Breast" but does not mention Hume. Given, as Leo Braudy says, that Fielding "knew much of Hume's work," his name seldom appears in studies of the novelist and more rarely still has the relationship between Hume and Fielding been the subject of sustained inquiry. The chief exception, besides Braudy's *Narrative Form in History and Fiction: Hume, Fielding, and Gibbon* (Princeton: Princeton University Press, 1970), is Martin C. Battestin's fine essay, "The Problem of *Amelia:* Hume, Barrow, and the Conversion of Captain Booth," *English Literary History* 41 (1974): 613–48. Battestin traces the awkwardness of *Amelia* to "an intellectual drama unfolding in the novel—a drama residing in Fielding's anxious response to a new and particularly disturbing species of philosophical scepticism whose cogency, in part, he seems to have felt" (p. 616). See also George R. Swann, *Philosophical Parallelisms in Six English Novelists: The Conception of Good, Evil, and Human Nature* (Philadelphia: University of Pennsylvania, 1929), chap. 4; Paulson, *Satire and the Novel*, pp. 5–6 and 153–56; Bernard Harrison, *Fielding's Tom Jones*, chap. 6; Miller, *Essays on Fielding's Miscellanies*, pp. 225–26; and Sabine Nathan, "Humes Auffassung von Moral und Fieldings *Amelia*," *Zeitschrift für Anglistik und Amerikanistik* 28 (1980): 219–25.

31. Hume, *Treatise*, 3.2, p. 496 (italicized in the original).

32. For discussion of Adam Smith, *The Theory of Moral Sentiments*, see chapter 7.

33. On the term "liberal state," see Anthony Giddens, *A Contemporary Critique*, p. 228.

34. Ibid., p. 94 (italicized in the original).

35. See, for example, the opening pages of Fielding's *Proposal for Making an Effectual Provision for the Poor, Works,* 13: 135–37. The stress on the labor force in Fielding's economics may be broadly characterized as "mercantilist." See Zirker, *Fielding's Social Pamphlets,* chap. 6.

36. Margaret Doody, Introduction to *Pamela, or Virtue Rewarded,* ed. Peter Sabor (New York: Penguin Books, 1980), p. 9.

37. Radzinowicz, *A History of English Criminal Law,* 1: 682–84.

38. Ibid., 1: 724; and Howson, *Thief-Taker General,* chap. 11. On the equivocal opinions of Wild among the educated public, see Howson (pp. 124–28). Howson (p. 8) says that the fullest biography of Wild is still the account in *Select Trials at the Sessions House in the Old Bailey,* 2 vols. (London: J. Wilford, 1734–35). Fielding owned a copy of one of the several four-volume editions published in 1742 in London by L. Gilliver and J. Applebee, and also in Dublin. For a reproduction of the sale catalog of Fielding's library, see the appendix to Ethel M. Thornbury, *Henry Fielding's Theory of the Comic Prose Epic* (Madison: University of Wisconsin Studies in Language and Literature, 1931), pp. 168–89; the *Select Trials* are no. 552.

39. Defoe, *Jure Divino* (London, 1706), book 2, p. 4. Cited by Maximillian E. Novak, *Defoe and the Nature of Man* (Oxford: Oxford University Press, 1963), p. 17.

40. Fielding's gloss informs us that the cant term for "thief" is "prig" (p. 14). On the allegory in this chapter of *Jonathan Wild,* see Cross, *The History of Henry Fielding,* 1: 421–22, and Dudden, *Henry Fielding,* 1: 462–63. On the historical Roger Johnson, see Howson, *Thief-Taker General,* p. 290. Cross says, "The only modern philosopher that Fielding cared much for was Locke" (3: 79). Richard I. Aaron gives a convenient account of the historical position of Locke's views on government in *Two Treatises of Government* (see *John Locke,* 3d ed. [Oxford: Clarendon Press, 1971], pp. 270–86). Fielding owned an edition of Locke's *Works* and one of the *Treatises;* see the appendix to Thornbury, *Henry Fielding's Theory of the Comic Prose Epic,* nos. 456 and 239.

CHAPTER SIX

Epigraph: Joseph Butler, *A Sermon* (London: J. and P. Knapton, 1740), pp. 20–21. Quoted by Seán McConville, *A History of English Prison Administration,* vol. 1 (London: Routledge and Kegan Paul, 1981), p. 97. John Howard approvingly cites both Butler and Fielding, though he dates Butler's sermon ten years too late. See John Howard, *Prisons and Lazarettos,* 2 vols., ed. Ralph W. England, Jr. (Montclair, N.J.: Patterson Smith, 1973), 1: 22, 40, and 42.

1. In the countryside, where cases of felony were few, justices of the peace served in effect as volunteers from the landed elite. But the traditional system could not manage heavy metropolitan case loads and had to be supplemented in counties around London by the appointment of additional magistrates. These were called "trading justices" because the gentry felt they lowered the office to the level of a trade by supporting themselves on fees and, further, because of the imputation that their judgments might be bought. Though of gentle background, Fielding supported himself on his offices as justice for Middlesex and Westminster; legitimate fees were skimpy, however, and he in fact collected a secret salary from Bedford. Both Henry and John Fielding campaigned through-

out their lives for justices to be paid a living wage. John H. Langbein gives accounts of eighteenth-century practice in "The Criminal Trial before the Lawyers," *University of Chicago Law Review* 45 (1978): 280–81, and in "Shaping the Eighteenth-Century Criminal Trial: A View from the Ryder Sources," *University of Chicago Law Review* 50 (1983): 55–83. On special arrangements concerning metropolitan magistrates, see the latter article, pp. 57–60; and on "sitting aldermen," pp. 76–81. On the Marian statutes, see Langbein, *Prosecuting Crime in the Renaissance* (Cambridge: Harvard University Press, 1974), pp. 1–6. See also Norma Landau, *The Justices of the Peace, 1679–1760* (Berkeley: University of California Press, 1984); and J. M. Beattie, *Crime and the Courts in England, 1660–1800* (Princeton: Princeton University Press, 1986).

2. *The Complete Works of Henry Fielding, Esq.,* 16 vols., ed. William E. Henley (London: Heinemann, 1903), 6: 16. Unless noted otherwise, further references to writings by Fielding are to this edition. Further references to *Amelia* appear parenthetically in the text.

3. Leon Radzinowicz gives a full account of the police in the eighteenth century, including the role of the Fieldings, in *A History of English Criminal Law and Its Administration from 1750,* vol. 3, *Cross-Currents in the Movement for the Reform of the Police* (New York: Macmillan, 1957), pp. 1–62. See also T. A. Critchley, *A History of the Police in England and Wales, 900–1966* (London: Constable, 1967), pp. 18–35; J. J. Tobias, *Crime and Police in England, 1700–1900* (New York: St. Martin's Press, 1979), pp. 1–56; Patrick Pringle, *Hue and Cry: The Birth of the British Police* (London: Museum Press, 1955); Gilbert Armitage, *The History of the Bow Street Runners, 1729–1829* (London: Wishart, 1932); B. M. Jones, *Henry Fielding: Novelist and Magistrate* (London: George Allen and Unwin, 1933); R. Leslie-Melville, *The Life and Work of Sir John Fielding* (London: Lincoln Williams, 1934); and Anthony Babington, *A House in Bow Street: Crime and the Magistracy, London 1740–1881* (London: Macdonald, 1969). Gerald Howson gives an excellent brief account of law enforcement in metropolitan London of the earlier eighteenth century in chapter 3 of *Thief-Taker General: The Rise and Fall of Jonathan Wild* (London: Hutchinson, 1970).

4. This paragraph is based primarily upon Langbein, "The Criminal Trial before the Lawyers," pp. 272–300.

5. John Fielding, *Extracts from Such of the Penal Laws as Particularly Relate to the Peace and Good Order of this Metropolis* (London, 1761), p. 4. Quoted by Langbein, "Shaping the Eighteenth-Century Criminal Trial," p. 75.

6. Quoted by Radzinowicz, *A History of English Criminal Law,* 3: 43–44. Radzinowicz also cites *The Public Advertiser* for 17 December 1754 and 15 January 1755; Langbein, "Shaping the Eighteenth-Century Criminal Trial," pp. 67–69, quotes a substantially identical text from 7 February 1755.

7. Quoted by Radzinowicz, *A History of English Criminal Law,* 3: 43.

8. On Fielding's system as a method of coordinating information, see Langbein, "Shaping the Eighteenth-Century Criminal Trial," p. 64, and, for an extended treatment of the use of crown witnesses, pp. 84–114.

9. Quoted by Radzinowicz, *A History of English Criminal Law,* 3: 43, 46. Both Fieldings emphasized the value of knowing the ins and outs of London's streets; Sir John attached an essay, "Some Proper Cautions," to *A Brief Description of the Cities of London and Westminster* (London, 1776), which contained an alphabetical list of streets and squares. See Radzinowicz (3: 42).

10. On the time-scheme of *Amelia,* see Martin Battestin's edition of *Amelia* (Middletown: Wesleyan University Press, 1984), Appendix 1, pp. 535–39. Battestin treats both the novel's precision of chronology and its exactness of reference to London's geography. But even the revised version, which eliminates the most glaring anachronisms, mislocates some events historically. Fielding seems to have attempted, and largely to have achieved, internal consistency of time and both internal and external coordination with the geography of London. He appears either not to have concerned himself with minutiae or to have made substantial errors in the somewhat different matter of historical detail.

11. Gerald Howson writes a brief history of thief-taking in chap. 4 of *Thief-Taker General;* he lists the chief London gangs of Wild's lifetime in Appendix 3.

12. Wild used newspaper advertisements and reports with a subtlety unexcelled by modern media consultants. See ibid., pp. 66–68 and 116–20.

13. Ibid., p. 86.

14. Ibid., p. 5.

15. Ibid., pp. 257–58. Howson's tabulation in Appendix 2 raises the count to 101.

16. Ibid., pp. 7 and 283.

17. Radzinowicz, *A History of English Criminal Law,* 3: 56–57.

18. For summary accounts of Wild's methods, including the points stressed here, see Howson, *Thief-Taker General,* pp. 73, 75, and 115–16. Howson gives much detail on the Lost Property Office in chap. 9.

19. Ibid., p. 240.

20. Howson reprints the warrant in full (ibid., pp. 238–40).

21. See chap. 5, n. 38. Howson gives a bibliography of the *Select Trials* (*Thief-Taker General,* pp. 317–27).

22. Langbein,"Shaping the Eighteenth-Century Criminal Trial," p. 130.

23. Langbein, "The Criminal Trial before the Lawyers," pp. 306–14. Langbein is responsible for pushing this date back to the 1730s through his research in the Old Bailey Sessions Papers. For a characterization of these publications, see ibid., pp. 267–72, and Howson, *Thief-Taker General,* p. 325.

24. Langbein, "Shaping the Eighteenth-Century Criminal Trial," p. 124.

25. The following two paragraphs draw substantially upon Langbein, especially the section "First Stirrings of Adversary Procedure," in ibid., pp. 123–34.

26. This is about one-third of the case load. Activity by other magistrates is traceable in 9 other fully reported cases, and 10 are given slight notice both by Ryder and the reporters. See Langbein ibid., pp. 69–75. The Bow Street system actually had a far wider impact than these figures imply. Langbein, notes (p. 75), for example, that pawnbrokers, who were key figures in the Fielding scheme, figured in 30 of the 171 Ryder cases—a vastly disproportional figure considering both that a large number of thieves were apprehended by hue and cry before making it to a broker and that many crimes did not involve marketable goods.

27. Ibid., p. 129.

28. Mikhail M. Bakhtin, *The Dialogic Imagination,* ed. and trans. Michael Holquist and Caryl Emerson (Austin: University of Texas Press, 1981), pp. 50 and 277–84, passim. For discussion of my differences with Bakhtin, specifically on the extent to which the realist novel authoritatively contains and shapes the "polyglossia" of social discourse as a whole, see chapter 7.

29. Langbein, "The Criminal Trial before the Lawyers," p. 306.

30. Ibid., p. 315.

31. From the lecture "Science as a Vocation," in *From Max Weber: Essays in Sociology*, trans. and ed. H. H. Gerth and C. Wright Mills (New York: Oxford University Press, 1946; reprinted 1981), pp. 144–45. Ian Watt says that "formal realism is . . . like the rules of evidence, only a convention; and there is no reason why the report on human life which is presented by it should be in fact any truer than those presented through the very different conventions of other literary genres" (*The Rise of the Novel* [Berkeley: University of California Press, 1959], p. 32). For a discussion of Fielding's reforms in a broadly Weberian frame of reference, see Horst Breuer, "Zur Geschichte der Justizreform in England: Der Beitrag Henry Fieldings," *Deutsche Vierteljahrsschrift für Literatur Wissenschaft und Geistesgeschichte* 53 (1979): 378–93.

32. Bakhtin defines "heteroglossia" as central to the novel: "These distinctive links and interrelationships between utterances and languages, this movement of the theme through different languages and speech types, its dispersion into the rivulets and droplets of social heteroglossia, its dialogization—this is the basic distinguishing feature of the stylistics of the novel." For full exposition of the term, see *The Dialogic Imagination*, pp. 263–73; I quote p. 263.

33. *The Letters of Gustave Flaubert*, 2 vols., ed. and trans. Francis Steegmuller (Cambridge: Harvard University Press, 1980), 1: 230. James Joyce introduces similar ideas into a discussion of literary aesthetics in chap. 5 of *A Portrait of the Artist as a Young Man* (New York: Viking, 1956), pp. 214–15.

34. Dorrit Cohn, *Transparent Minds: Narrative Modes for Presenting Consciousness in Fiction* (Princeton: Princeton University Press, 1978), p. 100. Cohn says that "most writers on the novel have taken the transparency of fictional minds for granted. . . . [But] narrative fiction is the only literary genre, as well as the only kind of narrative, in which the unspoken thoughts, feelings, perceptions of a person other than the speaker can be portrayed" (p. 7). Cohn follows Käte Hamburger, *The Logic of Literature*, trans. Marilynn J. Rose (Bloomington: University of Indiana Press, 1973), in arguing that "the representation (mimesis) of consciousness [is] the subject that distinguishes narrative fiction from non-fictional narrative to the one side, from non-narrative fiction to the other (i.e., from drama and film, the other genres populated by invented persons)" (pp. 7–8). Cohn's term "narrated monologue" includes and somewhat redefines "free indirect discourse," indicating "its position astride narration and quotation" (p. 14); see pp. 13–17, in which she demonstrates that the concept has been little known in English criticism, where the technique it identifies is often confused with others under the term "interior monologue." For discussion of the long history of the term in Continental scholarship, see Cohn (pp. 290–91) and Roy Pascal, *The Dual Voice* (Manchester: Manchester University Press, 1977), pp. 2–32. Cohn does not cite Bakhtin and Voloshinov's treatment of the technique and its ideological significance in the final chapter of *Marxism and the Philosophy of Language*, trans. Ladislav Matejka and I. R. Titunik (New York: Seminar Press, 1973). Cohn's full discussion of free indirect discourse occurs in chapter 3, where, quoting *Emma*, she cites Austen as "one of the first writers to use the narrated monologue frequently and extensively":

> How could she have been so deceived! He protested that he had never thought seriously of Harriet—never! . . . The picture! How eager he had been about the picture! And the charade! And a hundred other circumstances; how clearly they had seemed to point at Harriet! To be sure, the charade, with its "ready wit"—but then, the "soft eyes"—in fact it suited neither; it was a jumble without taste or truth. Who could have seen through such thick-headed nonsense? (p. 113)

The most complete modern study of the grammar and syntax that define free indirect discourse is by Ann Banfield, *Unspeakable Sentences: Narration and Representation in the Language of Fiction* (Boston: Routledge and Kegan Paul, 1982). My consideration of transparency and free indirect discourse in chapter 7 takes her views and those of Bakhtin/Voloshinov into account. After this book was finished, I encountered two provocative treatments of the *style indirect libre*. See Elizabeth Ermarth, *Realism and Consensus in the English Novel* (Princeton: Princeton University Press, 1983), part 1, chap. 3; and Dominick LaCapra, *Madame Bovary on Trial* (Ithaca: Cornell University Press, 1982), chap. 6. LaCapra debates Cohn and others who have considered the subject.

35. Fielding, *Works*, 5: 185. See also the passage following the quoted monologue in the chapter "Containing a Conversation which Mr. Jones had with Himself": "And now having taken a resolution to leave the country, he began to debate with himself whither he should go. . . . All his acquaintance were the acquaintance of Mr. Allworthy; and he had no reason to expect any countenance from them" (3: 337). As Cohn (following Watt) points out, in *Tom Jones* Fielding usually avoids direct entry to the minds of characters. Nonetheless, she presents him as one of the earliest authors to introduce the techniques she called "psycho-narration" and "quoted monologue" (*Transparent Minds*, pp. 22–23, 58, 89, and 112–13).

36. Leo Braudy, *Narrative Form in History and Fiction: Hume, Fielding, and Gibbon* (Princeton: Princeton University Press, 1970), p. 92; the previous treatments of Fielding's judging narrator in *Amelia* to which I am most indebted are by Braudy (pp. 180–212) and by Ronald Paulson, *Satire and the Novel in the Eighteenth Century* (New Haven: Yale University Press, 1967), pp. 141–50.

37. The requirement for "natural" resolution set forth at the beginning of book 1 of *Tom Jones* exactly parallels that specified in book 4, chaps. 4 and 6, of *Jonathan Wild*.

38. Braudy, *Narrative Form in History and Fiction*, pp. 181–82.

39. Quoted by Cohn, *Transparent Minds*, p. 8.

40. On *Amelia*'s publication and reception see the Battestin edition, pp. xliv–lxi.

41. Fielding, *Works*, 6: 14. On "trading justices" see note 1 above.

42. Claude Rawson, *Henry Fielding and the Augustan Ideal under Stress* (London: Routledge and Kegan Paul, 1972), p. 73. Rawson argues that "the Newgate vignettes of *Amelia* must be distinguished from those brief moral set-pieces of similar shape which Fielding had produced from time to time in the past (for example, in the Lucianic judgment-pieces in the *Champion* and the *Journey from This World to the Next*)" (p. 74), and, especially, that the portrait of Blear-eyed Moll "strikes a new note in Fielding, and perhaps in eighteenth-century literature" (p. 81).

43. Braudy, *Narrative Form in History and Fiction*, p. 210.

44. Fielding, *Works*, 5: 20.

45. Fielding, *Covent Garden Journal*, 4 January 1752, in *Works*, 14: 77; and Radzinowicz, *A History of English Criminal Law*, 3: 12.

46. Malvin R. Zirker, Jr., *Fielding's Social Pamphlets* (Berkeley: University of California Press, 1966). Of course I do not concur with Zirker's portrait of Fielding as a reactionary, though he is correct that the traditional account romanticizes him as a liberal. Useful as Zirker's study is, the terms on which he conducts his analysis are unable to cope with the complex web of changing

practice and thought Fielding's later career presents. For a summary of criticisms of Zirker's view, see H. George Hahn, *Henry Fielding: An Annotated Bibliography* (Metuchen, N.J.: Scarecrow Press, 1979), pp. 193–94.

47. For an inventory that reveals the astonishing pervasiveness of prisons and metaphoric imprisonment in *Amelia*, see Peter V. LePage, "The Prison and the Dark Beauty of 'Amelia,' " *Criticism* 9 (1967): 338–43, and 348, on which I rely here. On the Verge of the Court, see John C. Stephens, Jr., "The Verge of the Court and Arrest for Debt in Fielding's *Amelia*," *Modern Language Notes* 63 (1948): 104–9, and the note on p. 476 of Tobias Smollett, *Roderick Random*, ed. Paul-Gabriel Boucé (Oxford: Oxford University Press, 1979).

48. J. Paul Hunter, *Occasional Form: Henry Fielding and the Chains of Circumstance* (Baltimore: Johns Hopkins University Press, 1975), p. 205.

49. See LePage, "The Prison and the Dark Beauty of 'Amelia,' " pp. 348–53, for an account of the elaborate causal structures that connect large and small elements of the plot in *Amelia*.

50. Terry Castle, *Masquerade and Civilization: The Carnivalesque in Eighteenth-Century English Culture and Fiction* (Stanford: Stanford University Press, 1986), p. 232.

51. Martin Battestin, "The Problem of *Amelia*: Hume, Barrow, and the Conversion of Captain Booth," *English Literary History* 41 (1974): 635.

52. For a detailed account of Fielding's struggle with these opposite tendencies, see Henry K. Miller, *Essays on Fielding's Miscellanies* (Princeton: Princeton University Press, 1961), pp. 205–28. For a closely argued essay that runs counter to the view accepted here, see Tulvia Bloch, "*Amelia* and Booth's Doctrine of the Passions," *Studies in English Literature* 13 (1973): 461–73. See also Frederick G. Ribble, "The Constitution of the Mind and the Concept of Emotion in Fielding's *Amelia*," *Philological Quarterly* 56 (1977): 104–22.

53. Montesquieu is seldom mentioned in studies of Fielding, who praised an imitation of the *Lettres persanes* written by his friend George Lyttelton (*Letters from a Persian in England,* 1735) in his preface to Sarah Fielding's *Familiar Letters on David Simple* (1747). See Wilbur L. Cross, *The History of Henry Fielding*, 3 vols. (New Haven: Yale University Press, 1918), 2: 48, and Miller, *Essays on Fielding's Miscellanies*, p. 88. The preface is reprinted in Ioan Williams, ed., *The Criticism of Henry Fielding* (New York: Barnes and Noble, 1970), pp. 131–36. I am unaware of direct evidence that Fielding read the *Esprit des Lois* (1748), but the work was quickly noticed in England. Thomas Gray, Thomas Wharton, Horace Walpole, and Lord Chesterfield all had read it by 1750 (the latter three times). In July and October of 1749, prior to the appearance of Thomas Nugent's translation the next year, the *Monthly Review* devoted substantial space to the *Esprit des Lois*, parts of which it translated. Fielding's publisher had connections with the *Monthly Review*, where John Cleland's favorable essay on *Amelia* appeared in December of 1751. Although it is difficult to disentangle Bolingbroke's influence from Montesquieu's, the emphasis on the corruption of manners as the cause of the decline of government and civil liberty in Fielding's *Enquiry Into the Causes of the Late Increase of Robbers* (1751) parallels that in the *Esprit des Lois*. Given his interests, Fielding could hardly have escaped some knowledge of the work. See F. T. H. Fletcher, *Montesquieu and English Politics (1750–1800)* (London: Edward Arnold, 1939), pp. 21–27; Fletcher specifically discusses Fielding on pp. 157 and 189. Another reformist commonplace appears in the discussion of justice that Dr. Harrison has with a young clergyman and his father. When the doctor

quotes scripture to recommend benevolence, the young man cries, "There must be an end of all law and justice, for I do not see how any man can prosecute his enemy in a court of justice." The doctor replies: "Indeed, as an enemy merely, and from a spirit of revenge, he cannot, and he ought not to prosecute him; but as an offender against the laws of his country he may, and it is his duty so to do. Is there any spirit of revenge in the magistrates or officers of justice when they punish criminals? Why do such, ordinarily I mean, concern themselves in inflicting punishments, but because it is their duty? and why may not a private man deliver an offender into the hands of justice, from the same laudable motive?" (Fielding, *Works*, 7: 164–65).

54. Hume, *Enquiries Concerning Human Understanding and Concerning the Principles of Morals*, ed. L. A. Selby-Bigge, rev. P. H. Nidditch (Oxford: Clarendon Press, 1975), pp. 5–6. Miller, *Essays on Fielding's Miscellanies*, pp. 225–27.

55. Miller cites the praise Fielding's narrator bestows on Amelia because daily education of her children "had, in their tender minds, so strongly annexed the ideas of fear and shame to every idea of evil of which they were susceptible, that it must require great pains and length of habit to separate them" (6: 191); he also mentions the argument in Fielding's *Enquiry* that the main purpose of executions is "to unite the ideas of death and shame" (*Works*, 13: 123). Hume's *Enquiry* of 1748 is listed as number 539 in the catalog of Fielding's library reprinted in Ethel M. Thornbury, *Henry Fielding's Theory of the Comic Prose Epic* (Madison: University of Wisconsin Studies in Language and Literature, 1931), pp. 168–89. On "the beginning of the Utilitarian century," see Elie Halévy, *The Growth of Philosophic Radicalism*, trans. Mary Morris (London: Faber and Faber, 1972), pp. 5–11.

56. For a brief description, see Langbein, "Shaping the Eighteenth-Century Criminal Trial," p. 66.

57. Radzinowicz, *A History of English Criminal Law*, 3: 43–55.

58. Ibid., pp. 50–51. The quotation comes from a circular letter of 1772; official approval came in 1773.

59. Bakhtin, *The Dialogic Imagination*, p. 33. Bakhtin continues: "The novel often crosses the boundary of what we strictly call fictional literature—making use first of a moral confession, then of a philosophical tract, then of manifestos that are openly political."

60. See Battestin edition of *Amelia*, pp. lix–lx and pp. 535–39; and Cross, *The History of Henry Fielding*, 2: 337–38, 352, and 356. On the Universal Register Office, see R. Leslie-Melville, *The Life and Work of Sir John Fielding*, pp. 9–26.

61. Braudy, *Narrative Form in History and Fiction*, p. 199.

62. Sheldon Sacks, *Fiction and the Shape of Belief: A Study of Henry Fielding* (Berkeley: University of California Press, 1964), chap. 3; I quote p. 110.

63. "Disappearing exemplar," J. Paul Hunter's alternative to Sacks's term, is particularly suitable in this context. See *Occasional Form*, p. 208.

64. Thomas Hobbes, *Leviathan*, ed. Herbert W. Schneider (New York: Bobbs-Merrill, 1958), p. 23.

65. Ibid., part 1, chap. 16, pp. 132–33 (Hobbes's emphasis, except for first sentence, which the original put entirely in italics).

66. Ibid., p. 134.

67. See note 53 above for the complete quotation.

68. Fielding, *Works*, 13: 190–91. See chapter 5, section 1, for an account of the place of Fielding's proposals in the history of the penitentiary.

69. On the progress of *Amelia*'s composition, see Battestin edition, pp. xl–xliv.

70. Fielding, *Works*, 13: 186–87.

71. The words from William A. Guy, "Address on John Howard," *Journal of the Statistical Society* 38 (1875): 438, are quoted by Seán McConville, *English Prison Administration*, 1: 56.

72. See the epigraph to this chapter and chapter 5, part 1, quoting *Works*, 13: 183–85. Butler might be called the bishop of the conditional. The majority of his proposals, observations, and arguments, especially in the famous *Analogy of Religion Natural and Revealed*, chapter 2 of which is entitled "Government of God by Rewards and Punishments, and Particularly the Latter," are couched in the conditional, subjunctive, optative, or interrogative mood. The tone of reformist discourse from the 1750s onward strikes a more aggressive note.

73. Fielding, *Works*, 13: 183.

74. *The Works of Jeremy Bentham*, 11 vols., ed. John Bowring (Edinburgh: William Tait, 1838–43), 4: 47.

CHAPTER SEVEN

Epigraphs: I quote the appendix to the *Chrestomathia* as printed in *The Works of Jeremy Bentham*, 11 vols., ed. John Bowring (Edinburgh: William Tait, 1838–43), 8: 174. Unless noted otherwise, further references to writings by Bentham are to this edition.

In the selection from Smith's *Theory of Moral Sentiments*, I quote the edition by D. D. Raphael and A. L. Macfie (Oxford: Clarendon Press, 1976), pp. 84–85. Further references are to this edition.

1. I do not dwell here on the aspect of sublimity in the aesthetic of isolation, partly because the subject is of great enough interest and importance that full treatment of it would be very lengthy, and partly because a framework within which to understand it has been fully discussed by Thomas Weiskel and the commentators on his book, *The Romantic Sublime: Studies in the Structure and Psychology of Transcendence* (Baltimore: Johns Hopkins University Press, 1976). Weiskel says:

> The power of anything is ultimately "its ability to hurt" [Burke]. The fear of injury points genetically and synecdochically to castration anxiety. We know that the castration fear of the young boy is not realistic; nevertheless it operates subjectively as a real fear. A fantasy of aggression or resistance toward a superior power is played out in the imagination, and the boy sees at once that he would lose. . . . The fantasized character of castration anxiety seems related to the mediated conditionality of the sublime moment: on the one hand, the "ability to hurt" must be objective and obvious; on the other hand, it must not be actually directed against oneself, or the fantasy dissolves into genuine panic and the objective defense of flight. . . . This makes possible a positive resolution of the anxiety in the delight of the third phase, which is psychologically an identification with the superior power. . . . The boy must have introjected or internalized an image of the superior power in order to picture to himself the consequences of aggression, and in the reactive defense this introjected image is reinforced as the affects line up on its side. The identification which thus establishes the superego retains an essential ambiguity. The boy neutralizes the possibility of danger by incorporating or swallowing it: it is now within and can't hurt him from without. But he must also renounce the aggression and turn himself into—be swallowed by—the image, now an ideal, with which he is identifying. . . . The sublime moment recapitulates and thereby reestablishes the oedipus complex, whose positive resolution is the basis of culture itself. (pp. 93–94)

This central passage from the pivotal chapter of Weiskel's book is discussed by Neil Hertz in *The End of the Line: Essays on Psychoanalysis and the Sublime* (New York: Columbia University Press, 1985), pp. 49–53, and by Michael Fried in "Realism, Writing, and Disfiguration in Thomas Eakins's *Gross Clinic*, with a Postscript on Stephen Crane's Upturned Faces," *Representations* 9 (1985): 73–76. My quotation follows Fried's apt abridgment. For critiques of Weiskel, see Hertz (chap. 3) and Steven Knapp, *Personification and the Sublime: Milton to Coleridge* (Cambridge: Harvard University Press, 1985), chap. 3, especially pp. 76–77 and 80. Weiskel does not mention Adam Smith, but the internalization of authority through which he accounts psychoanalytically for the pleasurable dynamic effects of the sublime resembles that personified in Smith's "impartial spectator." For a comparison of Smith's impartial spectator with the Freudian superego see R. F. Brissenden, "Authority, Guilt, and Anxiety in *The Theory of Moral Sentiments*," *Texas Studies in Literature and Language*, 11 (1969), 945–62. Of course there are major differences, the chief of which is that Smith has no idea of the unconscious mind and the complexes lodged in it.

2. On Pentonville see Michael Ignatieff, *A Just Measure of Pain: The Penitentiary in the Industrial Revolution, 1750–1850* (New York: Pantheon, 1978), chap. 1; and Robin Evans, *The Fabrication of Virtue: English Prison Architecture, 1750–1840* (Cambridge: Cambridge University Press, 1982), chap. 8.

3. Bentham, *Works*, 4: 78–79. Bentham's original proposal had mentioned a chapel only in passing, and then conditionally (4: 43). Later, even upon elaboration in the *Postscript*, he said that the chapel was not "a characteristic part of the design." He seems to have considered the chapel itself as residual and certainly to have associated it with the "*stage effect*" that marked the old forms of punishment. The doubtful standing of theatricalism at the time is evident from Bentham's defensive tone and from the anxiety with which he works to dissociate his spectacle from the frivolous aspects of theater. In *Principles of Penal Law*, he again suggests that masks be used when prisoners are in public view and that they be "made more or less tragical, in proportion to the enormity of the crimes of those who wear them. The air of mystery which such a contrivance will throw over the scene, will contribute in great degree to fix the attention, by the curiosity it will excite, and the terror it will inspire" (*Works*, 1: 431).

4. Evans says that the history of reformed prison design "is the history of the removal of power from those who worked and lived within to those who ruled the prison from outside" (*The Fabrication of Virtue*, p. 46). Chapter 1 above treats the point in somewhat more detail. On the removal of governance from prisoners during the course of reform, see Ignatieff, *A Just Measure of Pain*, p. 102, passim.

5. See Ann Banfield, *Unspeakable Sentences: Narration and Representation in the Language of Fiction* (Boston: Routledge and Kegan Paul, 1982), pp. 225–26. Michael Fried describes the consolidation of analogous, "absorptive," techniques in French painting from the mid-eighteenth century onward, a period during which he finds that the nature of pictorial representation itself became problematic (*Absorption and Theatricality: Painting and the Beholder in the Age of Diderot* [Berkeley: University of California Press, 1980]). See below, chapter 8, on the relationship between "absorption" and realism.

The approach to realism developed in this chapter, and elsewhere in this book, differs significantly from that of Georg Lukács. He considers realism as a phenomenon specific to the nineteenth century, and he links it to a particular idea of history in the period following the French Revolution. I view realism as a broader historical phenomenon than Lukács and ground it more specifically in technical devices. See Georg Lukács, *The Historical Novel*, trans. Hannah and Stanley Mitchell (London: Merlin, 1965), and *Studies in European Realism*, trans. Edith Bone (New York: Grosset and Dunlap, 1964).

6. Bentham's nomination of the "two sovereign masters" opens *An Introduction to the Principles of Morals and Legislation* (*Works*, 1: 1). For fuller treatment of "paraphrasis" see below, section 3. Robin Evans argues, in describing Bentham's aspiration to a Panopticon of "universal transparency," that he "tacitly redefined" architecture: "In the Panopticon the principle of utility was to have been translated directly into architecture without the intervention of academic rules of composition. While it is ironic that the act of designing was finally divorced from visualization in a project so fundamentally concerned with the eye, the significant thing was the change in focus: the eye of the beholder and of the designer no longer rested on the building (as it did for example in Ledoux's famous contemporary engraving of the theatre at Besançon reflected on a retina) but on the human figures within it" (*The Fabrication of Virtue*, pp. 222–24). The Ledoux engraving is reproduced below as figure 57.

7. Numerous works cited in chapter 1 trace the history of the penitentiary in terms of specific buildings, plans, schemes, and projects. Only a few actual institutions have approached full realization of the penitentiary idea. Perhaps because they are among those to have done so, places like Pentonville, the Eastern Penitentiary near Philadelphia, Sing Sing, La Santé, Strangeways, and later Alcatraz have assumed a popular fascination. The spell of Alcatraz remains alive even though many thousands each year now visit it as a national park.

8. The standard history by Leon Radzinowicz is characteristic. See *A History of English Criminal Law and Its Administration from 1750*, vol. 1, *The Movement for Reform, 1750–1833* (New York: Macmillan, 1948).

9. Samuel Johnson, *The Idler and the Adventurer*, ed. W. J. Bate et al. (New Haven: Yale University Press, 1963), p. 120 (no. 38, Saturday, 6 January 1759). Howard quotes Johnson loosely.

10. *Citizen of the World* was written 1760–61. On the composition of these works by Goldsmith, see Arthur Friedman, ed., *Collected Works of Oliver Goldsmith*, 5 vols. (Oxford: Clarendon Press, 1966), 2: ix–xiv; 4: 3–4. Friedman places the composition of *The Vicar of Wakefield* in 1761–62. In the appendix to *The Notable Man: The Life and Times of Oliver Goldsmith* (London: Hamish Hamilton, 1977), pp. 363–70, John Ginger convincingly argues that Goldsmith was still at work on the novel at least as late as 1763. On excerpts from the novel in periodicals, see Morris Golden, "Goldsmith, *The Vicar of Wakefield*, and the Periodicals," *Journal of English and Germanic Philology* 76 (1977): 525–36.

11. Evans points out the neologism (*OED*, A.3) in *The Fabrication of Virtue*, p. 119. Public awareness of reformed penitentiaries was fostered from the very beginning by architectural competitions. The earliest of these, staged by the official supervisors of the act, attracted sixty-three entries including surviving designs by John Soane and Thomas Baldwin. One of the two winners was William Blackburn, whose plan for the male penitentiary is now lost (see ibid., pp. 121–31).

I refer here to a wide variety of regimes, both those proposed and those put into practice, but not to Bentham's scheme for the Panopticon. Public access was included at every stage of Bentham's proposal on the ground that it would provide incentives to keep the jailers honest (the idea was based on Bentham's theory of motives, not on observation of how public access in fact affected the old prisons). This feature, along with Bentham's adamant insistence upon contract management rather than government operation of the penitentiary, runs counter to the penitentiary idea as I describe it and as it developed in historical fact. Bentham's Panopticon is a remarkably trenchant, but still incomplete, fulfillment of the idea. One of several reasons the other reformers had for excluding the public was, of course, that isolation and visitation are mutually contradictory. Only Bentham's idiosyncratic architecture could allow for both. Indeed, in the Panopticon, visitation actually reinforced Bentham's principle of inspection by multiplying the unseen but hypothetical inspectors to infinity. For examples of penitentiary rules that excluded visitors (apart from official reviewers), see Jonas Hanway, *Solitude in Imprisonment* (London: J. Bew, 1776), pp. 111–24; J. R. S. Whiting, *Prison Reform in Gloucestershire, 1776–1820* (London and Chichester: Phillimore and Co., 1975), Appendix B, especially p. 208; and Seán McConville, *A History of English Prison Administration* (London: Routledge and Kegan Paul, 1981), 1: 91.

12. On Bentham and Blackburn as technical innovators, see Evans, *The Fabrication of Virtue*, pp. 126–31, 170–74, 195–235, passim.

13. See David Lyons, *In the Interest of the Governed: A Study in Bentham's Philosophy of Utility and Law* (Oxford: Clarendon Press, 1973), especially pp. 62–64. On Bentham's sensationalist background, see Evans, *The Fabrication of Virtue*, pp. 214–15. Bentham himself thought the concept of conscience a fiction; he wished to describe the "real" entity of process in relation to which he considered the idea of conscience to stand as a useful if unjustified fiction. On Bentham's omission of "conscience" from his "simple springs of action," see Leslie Stephen, *The English Utilitarians*, 3 vols. (London: Duckworth, 1900; reprt., New York: Augustus M. Kelley, 1968), 1: 251–54.

14. Evans, *The Fabrication of Virtue*, pp. 202–9.

15. Jonas Hanway, *Solitude in Imprisonment*, pp. 98–99 and 102; further citations appear parenthetically in the text. Ignatieff says in *A Just Measure of Pain*, p. 54, that this work contains "the first mention of the idea of using solitary on offenders under sentence." On Hanway see R. Everett Jayne, *Jonas Hanway: Philanthropist, Politician, and Author, 1712–1786* (London: Epworth Press, 1929); and John H. Hutchins, *Jonas Hanway, 1712–1786* (London: Society for Promoting Christian Knowledge, 1940). Hanway was connected with Sir John Fielding, especially in his work on the Magdalen Hospital beginning in the 1750s.

16. Mikhail Bakhtin and V. N. Voloshinov, *Marxism and the Philosophy of Language*, trans. Ladislav Matejka and I. R. Titunik (New York: Seminar Press, 1973), p. 146.

17. Rosalind Coward and John Ellis, *Language and Materialism: Developments in Semiology and the Theory of the Subject* (London: Routledge and Kegan Paul, 1977), compressed from pp. 46–47 and 49; the quotation within this passage is from Jacques Derrida, *Positions* (Paris: Minuit, 1972), pp. 32–33. Terence Hawkes has noted that "a central tenet of structuralism and semiotics is . . . that even in cases where the aim of the work is utter realism . . . this 'transparency' of writing, this 'innocence' of literature, remains an illusion" (*Structuralism and Semiotics* [Berkeley: University of California Press, 1977], p. 143). Barthes broached these ideas first in *Writing Degree Zero*, trans. Annette Lavers and Colin Smith (London: Cape, 1967; first published 1953); they are developed more technically in his "Introduction to the Structural Analysis of Narratives," in *Image-Music-Text*, ed.

and trans. Stephen Heath (New York: Hill and Wang, 1977; first published 1966); and they are presented in terms of an exhaustive analysis of Balzac's *Sarrasine* in *S/Z,* trans. Richard Miller (New York: Hill and Wang, 1974; first published 1970). For a contemporary philosophical account of "transparency theory," see A. C. Danto, *The Transfiguration of the Commonplace* (Cambridge: Harvard University Press, 1981), pp. 156–64.

18. Bakhtin and Voloshinov, *Marxism and the Philosophy of Language,* p. 147; Bakhtin and Voloshinov devote part 3, chap. 4, to the term and its history. See my chapter 6 above for the definition of "free indirect discourse" and for a discussion of it in relation to Fielding; my colleague William M. Todd III informs me that "impersonal direct discourse" is a more literal translation than "quasi-direct discourse" for Bakhtin's Russian equivalent of "free indirect discourse" (*Nesobstvenno-priamaia rech'*). In *The Dialogic Imagination,* p. 260, Bakhtin denounces the "widespread point of view that sees novelistic discourse as . . . an artistically neutral means of communication"; see also pp. 307–8.

19. The first part of this summation relies on Dorrit Cohn, *Transparent Minds: Narrative Modes for Presenting Consciousness in Fiction* (Princeton: Princeton University Press, 1978), pp. 7–8.

20. Compressed from Bakhtin and Voloshinov, *Marxism and the Philosophy of Language,* pp. 143 and 152–53.

21. See Margaret A. Doody, "George Eliot and the Eighteenth-Century Novel," *Nineteenth-Century Fiction* 35 (1980): 260–91, especially pp. 283–91. I located this important article, which contains the first account of the development of free indirect discourse in later eighteenth-century English fiction, too late to make complete use of it. Doody raises fascinating points about the connection of the technique with the quest of female writers for a distinct voice. Our emphases diverge to some extent when she argues that the "technique turns upon a discrepancy between a character's thoughts and authorial respeaking of them. The effect depends upon the reader's noticing a gap" (p. 288). I have found instances of the technique not only in Burney but in Inchbald, Radcliffe, and Wollstonecraft.

22. As Philippe Sollers writes, "The novel is this society's mode of communication. . . . Our identity depends on the novel, what others think of us, what we think of ourselves, the way in which our life is imperceptibly moulded into a whole. How do others see us if not as a character from a novel?" *Logiques* (Paris: Seuil, 1968), p. 228. Quoted by Jonathan Culler, *Structuralist Poetics* (Ithaca: Cornell University Press, 1975), p. 189. The translation is Culler's except for the opening, which is my own. Coward and Ellis (*Language and Materialism,* pp. 35–36) quote Stephen Heath's statement of similar ideas from the point of view of structuralist Marxism: " 'Reality' . . . needs to be understood not as an absolute and immutable given but as a production within which representation will depend on (and, dialectically, contribute to) what the French Marxist philosopher Louis Althusser has described as 'practical ideology,' a complex formation of *montages* of notions, representations, images and modes of action, gestures, attitudes, the whole ensemble functioning as practical norms which govern the concrete stance of men in relation to the objects and problems of their social and individual existence; in short, the lived relation of men to their world. In this sense, the 'realistic' is not substantial but formal (a process of significant 'fictions'), and, in connection with the novel, it may be described in the notion of the *vraisemblable* of a particular society, the generally received picture of what may be regarded as 'realistic'. . . . Evidently, this *vraisemblable* is

not recognized as such, but rather as, precisely, 'Reality'; its function is the naturalisation of that reality articulated by a society as *the* 'Reality' and its success is the degree to which it remains unknown as a form" (*The Nouveau Roman* [London: Elek, 1972], p. 20).

23. Banfield, *Unspeakable Sentences*, pp. 254 and 227. "Represented speech and thought" is Banfield's equivalent of "free indirect discourse," *style indirect libre, erlebte Rede,* etc. Her position, based in Chomskian linguistics, varies from Bakhtin's in other respects since he views written language as a record of utterance (the "inwardly impelled word") whereas she argues that represented speech and thought have no basis in spoken language and asserts that written narration releases "language from its subjection to communication" (p. 227). See also Banfield's earlier article, "Where Epistemology, Style, and Grammar Meet Literary History: The Development of Represented Speech and Thought," *New Literary History* 9 (1978): 415–54. Leo Spitzer argues that written narration, especially that employing *erlebte Rede,* expresses causal connections in an entirely different, much more strict, way than spoken language. See "Pseudoobjektive Motivierung bei Charles-Louis Philippe," *Zeitschrift für französische Sprache und Literatur* 46 (1923): 359–85; reprinted in *Stilstudien* (Munich, 1928), 2: 166–207; I have had access to a translation forthcoming in a volume of Spitzer's work to be published by the Stanford University Press. See also "Zur Entstehung der sogennanten 'erlebten Rede,'" *Germanisch-romanische Monatsschrift* 16 (1928). Herbert Lindenberger points out that Bakhtin's treatment of Dickens in *The Dialogic Imagination,* pp. 305–8, develops Spitzer's term "pseudo-objective motivation."

24. Bakhtin and Voloshinov, *Marxism and the Philosophy of Language,* p. 123. Todorov notes that Bakhtin views the evolution of the novel as "dominated by the perpetual, infinitely changing conflict between a tendency toward unification and a contrary tendency that maintains diversity," but that "the conflict between the two tendencies is ultimately won by the impulse toward diversity" (Tzvetan Todorov, *Mikhail Bakhtin: The Dialogic Principle,* trans. Wlad Godzich [Minneapolis: University of Minnesota Press, 1984], p. x).

25. My revision of Bakhtin's discussion of authority in the novel adopts many of his techniques and his theory of ideology as communicational practice while sharply modifying his concept of novelization to include substantial emphasis on the enactment of narrative forms in cultural and social systems. Bakhtin's treatment of the novel lays comparatively little stress on the issue of narrative structure. My own dialogue with Bakhtin picks up other strands in his thought. One strand illuminates the reflections here on character and conscience as historical productions of a juridical nature:

> Witness and judge. As soon as consciousness appears in the world ... being in its (unattainable) whole becomes altogether other because, on the stage of earthly being, for the first time, a new and decisive character in the event makes his entrance: the witness and the judge. And the sun, which retains its physical identity, becomes other, through the act of consciousness that the witness and judge have of it. It has ceased just being ... because it is reflected in the consciousness of another. (Quoted and translated in Todorov, *Mikhail Bakhtin,* p. 97, from p. 341 of "Iz zapisej 1970–71 godov," which appears in Bakhtin's *Estetika slovesnogo tvorchestva,* ed. S. G. Bocharov [Moscow: "Iskusstuo," 1979]).

The other connects him with Weber's account of the diffraction of authority and the specialization of knowledge in state-governed cultures:

The victory of extreme forms of the picturesque style in reported speech is not . . . to be explained in terms either of psychological factors or the artist's own individual stylistic purposes, but is explainable in terms of the general, far-reaching subjectivization of the ideological word-utterance. . . . This stage in the vicissitudes of the word in present-day bourgeois Europe . . . can be characterized as the stage of transformation of the word into a thing, the stage of depression in the thematic value of the word. (*Marxism and the Philosophy of Language*, pp. 158–59; italics omitted)

Todorov's translation of this passage (quite different in many respects) renders the last phrase as "can be defined as the *reification of discourse*, as the deterioration of the semantic dimension of discourse" (*Mikhail Bakhtin*, pp. 101–2).

26. Ross Harrison, *Bentham* (London: Routledge and Kegan Paul, 1983), p. 59. This paragraph summarizes my understanding of Bentham's position in the phase of his career that precedes or includes most of his work on the Panopticon. Later, Bentham's epistemological thought developed in much more subtle directions on the point of the direct accessibility of perceptible reality independent of the constituents of language. As Harrison shows, Bentham then argues that the "distinction between real and fictitious entities is made inside language" and that "we work from language to reality" (p. 82). In Bentham's own words: "The division of entities into real and fictitious, is more properly the division of names into *names* of real and *names* of fictitious entities"; and "a fictitious entity is an entity to which, though by the grammatical form of discourse employed in speaking of it, existence be ascribed, yet in truth and reality existence is not meant to be ascribed" (*Works*, 8: 198n and 197). On the role of Bentham and his disciples in shaping opinion during the period prior to the legal reforms of the 1830s, see Harrison, *Bentham*, chap. 1. My treatment here of Bentham's epistemology depends upon Harrison's.

27. Ibid., p. 67.

28. The quotations are from ibid., pp. 64 and 65. This paragraph refers especially to pp. 66–67.

29. Ibid., p. 66 (quoting Russell). On the disputed question of the standing of discursive statements in fictional narrative, see Barbara Herrnstein Smith, *On the Margins of Discourse: The Relation of Literature to Language* (Chicago: University of Chicago Press, 1979), and Mary L. Pratt, *Towards a Speech Act Theory of Literary Discourse* (Bloomington: Indiana University Press, 1977).

30. The idea that "a narrative is a long sentence just as every constative sentence is in a way the rough outline of a short narrative," is developed by Roland Barthes in his "Introduction to the Structural Analysis of Narratives," in *Image-Music-Text*, especially pp. 82–85. One of Julia Kristeva's remarks takes on a useful specificity in context with Bentham's ideas on exposition: "In the narrative, the speaking subject constitutes itself as the subject of a family, clan, or state group; it has been shown that the syntactically normative sentence develops within the context of prosaic and, later, historic narration. The simultaneous appearance of *narrative* genre and *sentence* limits the signifying process to an attitude of request and communication" (*Desire in Language: A Semiotic Approach to Literature and Art*, ed. Leon S. Roudiez, trans. Thomas Gora, Alice Jardine, L. S. Roudiez [New York: Columbia University Press, 1980], p. 174).

31. The quotations from Bentham appear, respectively, in *Works*, 9: 57, and 8: 197. Harrison discusses them in *Bentham*, pp. 79 and 83. Also see Harrison (p. 86) on the difference between "real entities," which are subject to "physical analysis," and "qualities," which are subject to "logical analysis."

32. Ibid., p. 25; see also p. 79.

33. On Bentham's technological innovations and the evolution of the Panopticon plan, see Evans, *The Fabrication of Virtue*, chap. 5.

34. Bentham, *Works*, 9: 105. Bentham's "Plan of an Industry House" includes rubrics like "universal transparency" and "simultaneous inspectability" (ibid., 8: 375).

35. Ibid., 9: 104. The *Panopticon* of 1791 included a plan showing the wall (BM Press No. 1651/999).

36. John Howard, *The State of the Prisons*, 4th ed. (1792), p. 12. Reprinted as volume 1 of *Prisons and Lazarettos*, 2 vols. (Montclair, N.J.: Patterson Smith, 1973). On the personal and religious dimensions of Howard's expressions of guilt, see Ignatieff, *A Just Measure of Pain*, pp. 47–52.

37. Harrison, *Bentham*, p. 122. Bentham was studying *The Wealth of Nations* during the 1780s, when he published with the *Defense of Usury* (1787) an open letter to Smith in which he declared, "I owed you everything" (Harrison, p. 121). The identification of social and individual interest is perhaps the central mystification of utilitarianism, an identification that requires, in turn, some mechanism like Smith's "impartial spectator." As John Rawls points out in *A Theory of Justice* (Cambridge: Harvard University Press, 1971), pp. 26–27, "The most natural way, then, of arriving at utilitarianism . . . is to adopt for society as a whole the principle of rational choice for one man. Once this is recognized, the place of the impartial spectator and the emphasis on sympathy in the history of utilitarian thought is readily understood. For it is by the conception of the impartial spectator and the use of sympathetic identification in guiding our imagination that the principle for one man is applied to society. It is this spectator who is conceived as carrying out the required organization of the desires of all persons into one coherent system of desire; it is by this construction that many persons are fused into one."

38. R. F. Brissenden argues in *Virtue in Distress: Studies in the Novel of Sentiment from Richardson to Sade* (London: Macmillan, 1974), p. 37, that Smith's book was "paradigmatic" in Thomas S. Kuhn's sense of works "that some particular scientific community acknowledges for a time as supplying the foundation for its further practice." See Kuhn, *The Structure of Scientific Revolutions*, 2d ed. (*International Encyclopedia of Unified Science*, vols. 1 and 2) (Chicago: University of Chicago Press, 1970), p. 10.

39. Smith, *Moral Sentiments*, p. 9; further references in this section appear parenthetically in the text. The relevance of *The Theory of Moral Sentiments* to this study became apparent to me upon reading Jonas Barish, *The Antitheatrical Prejudice* (Berkeley: University of California Press, 1981), especially pp. 243–55. I have also relied upon A. L. Macfie, *The Individual in Society: Papers on Adam Smith* (London: George Allen and Unwin, 1967); D. D. Raphael, "The Impartial Spectator," in *Essays on Adam Smith*, ed. Andrew S. Skinner and Thomas Wilson (Oxford: Clarendon Press, 1975), pp. 83–99; R. F. Brissenden, "Authority, Guilt, and Anxiety in *The Theory of Moral Sentiments*," and *Virtue in Distress*, especially chap. 2; and David Marshall, "Adam Smith and the Theatricality of Moral Sentiments," *Critical Inquiry* 10 (1984): 592–613 (Marshall gives a remarkably subtle exposition of Smith's main thesis).

40. The contrast between shame and guilt as cultural orientations and modes of social control is compactly developed by Alvin W. Gouldner in *Enter Plato: Classical Greece and the Origins of Social Theory* (New York: Basic Books, 1965), pp. 81–87.

41. On the "generalized other" see Mead's *Mind, Self, and Society*, ed. Charles W. Morris (Chicago: University of Chicago Press, 1934), part 3. David Wellbery first called my attention to the work of Gouldner and Mead; my phrasing here relies in part on his comments about Mead. The phrase from Johnson's *Idler* no. 38 (6 January 1759) is quoted in context in section one of this chapter.

42. Smith, *Moral Sentiments*, p. 80, cites the arguments of Henry Home, Lord Kames, to the effect that justice is uniquely different from, and more significant than, the other social virtues. Smith goes on to insist that without justice (the social manifestation of the mechanism of the impartial spectator) civilization would collapse: "Justice . . . is the main pillar that upholds the whole edifice. If it is removed, the great, the immense fabric of human society . . . must in a moment crumble into atoms" (p. 86). Although Smith argues that the passion of resentment on the part of individuals works to the desirable ends of punishment, his theory of justice is not fundamentally retributive; justice, though comprehending the passions, achieves its end in social utility, which in the case of punishment means correction and deterrence. Smith's approach is generally consonant with that of virtually all theorists after Montesquieu. See Radzinowicz, *A History of English Criminal Law*, 1: 337.

43. Quoted by Michael Ignatieff, *A Just Measure of Pain*, p. 74. Ignatieff trenchantly sums up dialogue within the penitentiary movement around the time of Smith's death in 1790: "By cords of love, Brewster meant the reformative and utilitarian justifications of punishment that would persuade the offender to accept his sufferings and face his own guilt. It is important to see these new theories of punishment as arguments directed at the prisoner. Reformative theory presented punishment to offenders as being 'in their best interests' while utilitarian theory cast it as an impartial act of social necessity. In rejecting retributive theory, the reformers sought, in effect, to take the anger out of punishment. As it was legitimized to the prisoner, punishment was no longer to be, in Bentham's words, 'an act of wrath or vengeance,' but an act of calculation, disciplined by considerations of the social good and the offenders' needs" (pp. 74–75).

44. Bentham, *Letter to Lord Pelham* (1802), quoted by Ignatieff, *A Just Measure of Pain*, p. 66.

45. Bentham, *Works*, 1.1: 22; for discussion see chapter 1 above.

46. For further discussion of this passage, see Raphael, "The Impartial Spectator," pp. 93–94.

47. David Marshall, "Adam Smith and the Theatricality of Moral Sentiments," p. 597. I borrow the term *dédoublement* from Marshall's discussion.

48. See ibid., p. 598, and the passage quoted above from *Moral Sentiments*, p. 113. In his drafts of this passage, Smith wrote "the pannel," which is a Scots term for "the accused."

49. See also Marshall's discussion, ibid., pp. 599–600.

50. Barish, *The Antitheatrical Prejudice*, p. 244, and Marshall, "Adam Smith and the Theatricality of Moral Sentiments," p. 604.

51. Banfield, *Unspeakable Sentences*, pp. 16–17.

CHAPTER EIGHT

Epigraphs: I quote first from the Durand edition of Helvétius's work (Paris, 1758), p. 11 (author's translation). The previous paragraph of *De l'Esprit* is concerned to show how the poet or orator directs an audience to an instantaneous idea of justice by presenting, to the senses, three imaginary tableaux that juxtapose a harsh but valid judgment of execution, a scene of misguided mercy, and one showing the murderous rampage of an ungoverned criminal.

The second quotation is from Victor Lange's edition of Lessing's *Dramaturgy*, trans. Helen Zimmern (New York: Dover, 1962), no. 74, p. 178.

The third quotation is from the David McCracken edition of *Caleb Williams* (London: Oxford University Press, 1970), p. 326. Godwin bitterly opposed all prisons, especially the use of solitary confinement in the new penitentiaries. In *Political Justice* (1793) he specifically attacked Howard. See Michael Ignatieff, *A Just Measure of Pain* (New York: Pantheon, 1978), pp. 117–18 and 128–29; and Peter H. Marshall, *William Godwin* (New Haven: Yale University Press, 1984), pp. 108, 150–51, and 264. At the end of *Realism, Myth, and History in Defoe's Fiction* (Lincoln: University of Nebraska Press, 1983), pp. 140–41, Maximillian E. Novak places *Caleb Williams* in the tradition of the eighteenth-century Newgate novel.

1. See Michael Fried, *Absorption and Theatricality: Painting and the Beholder in the Age of Diderot* (Berkeley: University of California Press, 1980). The complexity, precision, and thoroughness of Fried's argument defy summary. My condensation of his analysis and my application of some of its terms to materials outside the half-century of French painting to which he confines his book inevitably, but I hope not willfully, alter his emphasis. David Marshall was the first to have published writings that link Fried's ideas to Adam Smith's; see "Adam Smith and the Theatricality of Moral Sentiments," *Critical Inquiry* 10 (1984): 592–613.

Several classic mid-eighteenth-century texts attack theatricality, as opposed either to life itself or to persuasively illusionistic drama. Fried's book gives considerable attention to writings on the theater by Diderot and includes an appendix on Rousseau. Diderot's most significant works on the theater are *Entretiens sur le Fils naturel* (1757), *Discours sur la poésie dramatique* (1758), and *Paradoxe sur le comédien* (begun 1769). On them see also Arthur M. Wilson, *Diderot* (New York: Oxford University Press, 1972), pp. 268–71, 326–31, 620–28. Rousseau's main effort is his *Lettre à M. d'Alembert sur les spectacles* (1758). On this see Lester G. Crocker, *Jean-Jacques Rousseau*, 2 vols. (New York: Macmillan, 1973), 2: 5–21; and Jonas Barish, *The Antitheatrical Prejudice* (Berkeley: University of California Press, 1981), chap. 9. Lessing's central ideas were first formulated in 1757 in correspondence with Mendelssohn, and later worked out at length in essays known as the *Hamburgische Dramaturgie* (1767–69). See J. G. Robertson, *Lessing's Dramatic Theory* (Cambridge: Cambridge University Press, 1939), and, especially on Lessing's ideas about pity (compassionate identification), David E. Wellbery, *Lessing's Laöcoon: Semiotics and Aesthetics in the Age of Reason* (Cambridge: Cambridge University Press, 1984), pp. 165–66.

2. Michael Fried, "Realism, Writing, and Disfiguration in Thomas Eakins's *Gross Clinic*," *Representations* 9 (1985): p. 59. Fried here expands upon ideas also treated in *Absorption and Theatricality*, pp. 43 and 194.

3. Fried, while confining his attention to France alone, grants the possibility that the developments he traces there in painting after mid-century may have been influenced by precursors in foreign countries and that they may resemble events elsewhere. He notes that some earlier scholars have given British art a measure of priority; he does not mention Hogarth. See *Absorption and Theatricality*, p. 2 and p. 180 n. 4. Frederick Antal, in *Hogarth and His Place in European Art* (London: Routledge and Kegan Paul, 1962), pp. 197–202, finds that Hogarth was a major influence on both Greuze and David. Antal argues that Hogarth's

"realism and directness of expression" were significant to the new French history painting and that his works "distinctly foreshadow the new French classicism from a formal viewpoint" (p. 200). He singles out Joseph-Marie Vien's "famous religious composition heralding the new style," *St. Denis Preaching* (1767, St. Roch, Paris), and *Marchande d'Amour* (1763, Fontainebleau), pictures that for Fried (and Diderot) sum up the absorptive style. Antal also discovers the influence of Hogarth's *Analysis of Beauty* in Diderot's *Salons* and asserts that "when Diderot advised Greuze to imitate the pantomimes in his paintings, he was fundamentally reiterating Hogarth's views" (p. 199). See also Anita Brookner, *Greuze* (Greenwich, Conn.: New York Graphic Society, 1972), pp. 47–48, 88, 136–37 and passim. Works of Hogarth that partake of the absorptive mode seem to me to include *Sarah Malcolm* (1733), *Moses Brought to Pharaoh's Daughter* (1746), *Paul before Felix* (1748), *Garrick and His Wife* (1757), *The Cockpit* (1759), as well as some of the "conversation pieces" and several plates in the "progresses."

4. On the relation of the "everyday" to absorption, see Fried, *Absorption and Theatricality*, p. 61; on the major role of cause and effect in Diderot's aesthetic, see pp. 85–87.

5. Robert Rosenblum, *Romantic Art in Britain: Paintings and Drawings 1760–1860* (Philadelphia: Philadelphia Museum of Art, 1968), p. 12. Rosenblum finds "what amounts, in such works, to a quiet pictorial revolution that will ultimately lead to the more programmatic realism of the 1840s and 1850s." Ellis Waterhouse parallels Wright with Greuze and argues that his pictures fit Diderot's criteria for *le genre sérieux* (*Painting in Britain 1530 to 1790*, 4th ed. [Harmondsworth: Penguin, 1978], p. 285).

6. On Wright's friends and associations, see Benedict Nicolson, *Joseph Wright of Derby: Painter of Light*, 2 vols. (London: Routledge and Kegan Paul, 1968), especially part 3, chaps. 5, 6, and 8. On Hayley as a patron, see Victor Chan, *Leader of My Angels: William Hayley and His Circle* (Edmonton Art Gallery, 1982). On Howard's relationship to intellectual and scientific circles, see Michael Ignatieff, *A Just Measure of Pain*, pp. 62–63 and passim. Ignatieff names Wedgwood and Boulton along with Jedediah Strutt, whom Wright painted, as among "the creators of the new factory discipline" (p. 215), and describes them as having devised such features of industrial labor as punch clocks, bells, rules, and fines. He also writes that, "in order to reduce turnover and stabilize the labor force in their early factories, they provided schools, chapels, and homes for their workers in model villages" (p. 62). These phenomena correlate closely with the legislative institution of the penitentiary.

7. Lorenz Eitner argues persuasively that the imagery of confinement during the period deals centrally with this truth. See "Cages, Prisons, and Captives in Eighteenth-Century Art," in *Images of Romanticism: Verbal and Visual Affinities*, ed. Karl Kroeber and William Walling (New Haven: Yale University Press, 1978), pp. 13–38.

8. Laurence Sterne, *A Sentimental Journey Through France and Italy By Mr. Yorick with The Journal to Eliza and A Political Romance*, ed. Ian Jack (Oxford: Oxford University Press, 1984), p. 73; the quotations above come from pp. 71–72; in the next paragraph, from p. 85.

9. Eitner, "Cages, Prisons, and Captives," p. 34. Eitner actually refers to an earlier version of the painting (now known only in a copy) in which the iconographic allusion to the *Ecce Homo* is unmistakable.

10. On the dating of *The Captive* (Derby Museum and Art Gallery) and *The Prisoner* (Yale Center for British Art, Paul Mellon Collection), see Nicolson, *Joseph*

Wright of Derby, 1: 242 (where the title *Small Prison Scene* is used). Nicolson (2: plates 285 and 286) catalogs another late prison painting that, with a related drawing, shares several features of the Mellon picture; a photograph in the Witt Library records an extremely close variant of the Mellon painting that was sold at Christie's on 22 June 1979.

11. Smith, *The Theory of Moral Sentiments* (Oxford: Clarendon Press, 1976), p. 137.

12. Michel Foucault, *Discipline and Punish: The Birth of the Prison*, trans. Alan Sheridan (London: Allen Lane, 1977; first published 1975), p. 200. Foucault gives passing mention to Goya's images of madhouses and prisons from the 1790s but none to those of Wright or other painters. Eitner, "Cages, Prisons, and Captives," p. 34, discusses Goya's drawings of solitary captives. I think that Goya's strongly backlighted painting, *Interior of a Prison* (Bowes Museum, Barnard Castle), offers particularly interesting points of comparison with Wright. For a color reproduction, see Enriqueta Harris, *Goya* (London: Phaidon, 1969), plate 35.

13. Ronald Paulson argues that, even in landscapes, the cell-shaped, lighted hollow is one of Wright's basic visual metaphors. See *Emblem and Expression: Meaning in English Art of the Eighteenth-Century* (Cambridge: Harvard University Press, 1975), chap. 11, especially pp. 195–96.

14. On Thompson's position in general see above, chapter 1; for a detailed treatment of mid-century Tyburn inspired by Thompson's approach, see Peter Linebaugh, "The Tyburn Riot against Surgeons," in *Albion's Fatal Tree: Crime and Society in Eighteenth-Century England*, ed. Douglas Hay et al. (New York: Pantheon, 1975), pp. 65–117. On Tyburn in the eighteenth century, see Leon Radzinowicz, *A History of English Criminal Law and Its Administration from 1750*, 4 vols. (New York: Macmillan, 1948–68), 1: chap. 6, and Anthony Babington, *The English Bastille: A History of Newgate Gaol and Prison Conditions in Britain 1188–1902* (London: Macdonald, 1971), pp. 30–36.

15. *The Works of Henry Fielding*, ed. William E. Henley (London: Heinemann, 1903), 13: 123–24. Others before Fielding had doubted the deterrent effect of Tyburn executions. See, for instance, Bernard Mandeville, *An Enquiry into the Causes of the Frequent Executions at Tyburn* (London: J. Roberts, 1725).

16. See Radzinowicz, *A History of English Criminal Law*, 1: 201–2; Babington, *The English Bastille*, p. 145; and Ignatieff, *A Just Measure of Pain*, pp. 88–89.

17. Jacques-François Blondel, *Cours d'architecture*, 6 vols. (Paris: Desaint, 1771–77), 1: 377 and 426–27. Harold D. Kalman, "Newgate Prison," *Journal of the Society of Architectural Historians of Great Britain* 12 (1969): 55–56, points to these ideas and, noting that this passage occurs near the start of Blondel's lectures (which began in 1750), observes that Dance could have heard his theories early in 1765 on a visit to Paris. Another possibility is that Dance learned about Blondel during his stay in Rome, where the French Academy was a significant point of contact among Italian, French, and English artists of advanced views. See André Chastel et al., eds., *Piranèse et les Français, 1740–1790* (Rome: Edizioni dell'Elefante, 1976). Kalman cites Dora Wiebenson, " 'L'Architecture Terrible' and the 'Jardin Anglo-Chinois,' " *Journal of the Society of Architectural Historians* (U.S.A.) 27 (1968): 137, for her discussion of Blondel. A few phrases in my translation are based on Wiebenson's. On Blondel and prisons, see also Bruno Foucart, "Architecture carcérale et architectes fonctionnalistes en France au XIXᵉ siècle," *Revue de l'Art* 32 (1976): 44–55. Kalman also cites Edmund Burke's *Philosophical*

Enquiry into the Origin of Our Ideas of the Sublime and the Beautiful (1757) and notes that, years later, Dance said in his diary that it was "a very excellent work." On Burke's importance to architecture, see Eileen Harris, "Burke and Chambers on the Sublime and the Beautiful," *Essays in the History of Architecture Presented to Rudolf Wittkower,* ed. Douglas Fraser et al., 2 vols. (London: Phaidon, 1967), 1: 207–13. See, in addition, on the parallel between painting and architecture, Allan Braham, *The Architecture of the French Enlightenment* (Berkeley: University of California Press, 1980), pp. 16–17.

18. Emil Kaufmann, *Architecture in the Age of Reason: Baroque and Post-Baroque in England, Italy, and France* (Cambridge: Harvard University Press, 1955), p. 130, says that *architecture parlante* is "narrative architecture." On the concept and its origins, see *Architecture in the Age of Reason,* pp. 102, 150, 154 and passim; and Kaufmann's *Three Revolutionary Architects: Boullée, Ledoux, and Lequeu,* in *Transactions of the American Philosophical Society,* n.s. 42, pt. 3 (Philadelphia: American Philosophical Society, 1952), pp. 447, 514, 517, 520, and 535.

19. The idea that this architectural *caractère* consists in and reveals essential traits, on the analogy with human character, is clearly intended. Blondel says, for example, that "every building needs a character which determines its general nature and declares what the structure is." He goes on to stress that external attributes like sculptural decoration are not sufficient to determine character (*Cours d'architecture,* 2: 229, author's translation).

20. Dorothy Stroud, *George Dance, Architect, 1741–1825* (London: Faber and Faber, 1971), chap. 3; Harold D. Kalman, "Newgate Prison," p. 55; John Summerson, *Architecture in Britain, 1530–1830,* 5th ed. (Harmondsworth: Penguin, 1969), p. 274. Dance was in Rome for just over five years beginning in May of 1759. The suggestion that he may have been inspired by Piranesi's *Carceri,* though perhaps unprovable, is entirely plausible since the revised states of the etchings appeared, during Dance's stay, in 1760–61. John Wilton-Ely says that "it was Piranesi's *Carceri* that taught Dance's generation the expressive potential of design based on the highly original handling of Classical forms amplified by exaggeration in scale and texture" (*The Mind and Art of Giovanni Battista Piranesi* [London: Thames and Hudson, 1978], p. 90).

21. Palladio's Palazzo Thiene at Vicenza, Romano's own house, and his Palazzo del Tè at Mantua are often cited. For these and other analogues see Stroud, *George Dance,* pp. 98–99 and fig. 29a; and Kalman, "Newgate Prison," pp. 54–55.

22. I quote from Henry Paolucci's translation, *On Crimes and Punishments* (Indianapolis: Bobbs-Merrill, 1963), pp. 48–49; Beccaria's sensationalist emphasis is clear when he says, for example, that "the multitude adopt no fixed principles of conduct and will not be released from the sway of that universal principle of dissolution which is seen to operate both in the physical and moral universe, except for motives that directly strike the senses" (p. 12).

23. John Howard, *Prisons and Lazarettos,* 2 vols. (Montclair, N.J.: Patterson Smith, 1973) 1: 213–15.

24. *Boswell's Life of Johnson,* ed. R. W. Chapman (London: Oxford University Press, 1953), pp. 1211–12 and 1318–19.

25. *Boswell's London Journal, 1762–1763,* ed. Frederick A. Pottle (New York: McGraw-Hill, 1950), pp. 252–54. This episode also illustrates the reflexivity of tragedy and comedy in the Tyburn experience: Boswell's friend Dempster "prescribed to me to cut two or three brisk capers round the room, which I did, and

found attended with most agreeable effects" (p. 253). Boswell's terror at this hanging is understandable, at least in part, as the other side of his own comic but intense identification with Macheath. When Boswell saw Lewis at Newgate the previous day, he seemed "just a Macheath. He was dressed in a white coat and blue silk vest and silver, with his hair neatly queued and a silver-laced hat, smartly cocked" (p. 251). Just two weeks after the Lewis execution, for example, Boswell found "two very pretty little girls" in Covent Garden: "I toyed with them and drank about and sung *Youth's the Season* and thought myself Captain Macheath; and then solaced my existence with them, one after the other, according to their seniority" (pp. 262–64). The editor observes that "in one way or another the figure of Macheath dominates this entire journal" (p. 252). See also, e.g., *Boswell in Search of a Wife, 1766–1769*, eds. Frank Brady and Frederick A. Pottle (New York: McGraw-Hill, 1956), p. 81. See also Boswell's May 1783 *Hypochondriack* column, "On Executions," in which he declares himself to have been "convulsed with pity and terror" after witnessing his first execution but asserts that his "sensibility abated" thereafter by degrees and that he now views them in "a philosophical manner" (*Boswell's Column*, ed. Margery Bailey [London: William Kimber, 1951], pp. 343–48).

Lessing's distinction is central to his view of pathetic identification, an effect rendered impossible by theatrical pomp. See Victor Lange, ed., *Hamburg Dramaturgy*, no. 59, p. 164; no. 74, pp. 175–78; no. 75, pp. 178–82; and no. 80, p. 198. See also Robertson, *Lessing's Dramatic Theory*, pp. 352–65; and Wellbery, *Lessing's Laöcoon*, pp. 165–66.

26. *The Newgate Calendar*, 5 vols. (London: J. and J. Condee; Liverpool: Nuttal, Fisher, and Dixon, c. 1810), p. x.

27. Radzinowicz, *A History of English Criminal Law*, 4: 352–53; chap. 8 of this volume treats the legal developments and public controversies leading up to the abolition of public execution.

28. For a concise illustration of aversion to the old theatricalism, see Radzinowicz's account of the successful outcry against the tradition of offering tickets to the condemned sermon, which took place in the Newgate chapel the Sunday before execution, as well as against allowing journalists at the prisoner's confession and final preparation (ibid., pp. 347–49). Estimates of the attendance at Victorian executions sometimes run into the hundreds of thousands. On the other hand, in the "notorious" case of Mr. and Mrs. George Manning, hanged together in 1849 for the murder of her lover, Radzinowicz says thirty thousand people attended but "more than two and a half million copies of broadsheets . . . describing the last moments . . . were sold at the time" (ibid., p. 349).

29. Ibid., p. 349. In 1903 Tussaud's acquired the Old Toll Bell and other relics following the demolition of Dance's Newgate the previous year. I first became aware that frustrated execution-day crowds turned their attention to Madame Tussaud's Exhibition upon reading Peter Lovesey's novel, *Waxwork* (Harmondsworth: Penguin Books, 1980). This paragraph refers in part to Mr. Lovesey's research, forwarded to me in correspondence. Tussaud's current catalog gives information on the phenomenon, as well as on artifacts acquired. A catalog from the 1890s, now in the Huntington Library (HEH 223613), describes a large and up-to-date Chamber of Horrors full of murderers from the 1880s. The executioners Marwood and Berry both are present. The preface that introduces the Chamber of Horrors picks up the traditional idea that it is "natural" to attend to "whatever is unusual and enormous in crime, equally as it is [to be] excited

by exceptional genius, heroism, and virtue." But it also sounds surprisingly close to John Howard's forward-looking arguments when it states that the "capacity for the worst of crimes" can lurk "beneath the outward appearance of eminent respectability" (*Madame Tussaud and Sons' Exhibition Catalogue* [London, 189?], p. 43). An 1882 catalog, also in the Huntington (HEH 235400), quotes the *Daily Telegraph* for 20 March 1868: "He is a shallow critic who wonders at the public interest in great crimes, and finds fault with it." See also John Theodore Tussaud, *The Romance of Madame Tussaud's* (London: Odhams, 1920), pp. 249–67; and Peter Aykroyd, *Evil London* (London: Wolfe, 1973), pp. 177–80. Unfortunately, Tussaud's archive was destroyed by fire in 1925. I discovered the existence of Pauline F. Chapman's *Madame Tussaud's Chamber of Horrors: Two Hundred Years of Crime* (London: Constable, 1984) too late to locate or consult it. I am indebted to Tussaud's archivist, Undine Concannon, for locating press cuttings and releases which show that, as late as 1948, the nine-fold murderer John George Haigh bequeathed to the exhibition his green hopsack suit, green socks, and red tie with green squares. His figure was on view within an hour of the execution and over fifty thousand people thronged the exhibition to see it.

Index

Abbati, Pietro Giovanni, 93
Absorption: aesthetic of isolation and, 202, 233–38, 300n.5; defined, 231–32; executions in tableaux of, 243, 246–47
Acedia, 45
Actants, 278n.20
Action, modes of: language and thought as, 1; substitution of vicarious experience for direct, 65–66, 276n.7; reform as (for Fielding), 185
Aesthetic discipline, literature as (Foucault), xv
Aesthetic of isolation. *See* Isolation
Aesthetics: dimension of, in policy events, 231; recent Marxism and, 255–56n.13
Aesthetic works. *See* Art (works of)
Affidavits, 171, 182
Alcatraz, 301n.7
Alchemist, The (Jonson), 125
Aldermen, duties of, 167
Alibi (the), 174–75
Allegorical figures: in *Moll Flanders*, 45–48, 50; in *Robinson Crusoe,* 55; Puritan objections to, 272n.8
Allegory, Fielding on, 163
Allworthy, Squire (*Tom Jones*), 178–79, 191
Althusser, Louis, 5, 72, 303n.22
Amelia (Fielding), 28, 129, 139, 147, 163, 166, 169, 180–96, 289n.20

Amsterdam Rasphuis, 268n.44
Anachronisms: in *Amelia*, 189–90, 294n.10; threat to realist novel of, 195–96. *See also* Contradictions
Analysis of Beauty, The (Hogarth), 121
Anthropological terms, 26–29
Architecture (general), Renaissance ideals of city, 134. *See also* Cities (early modern)
Architecture parlante, 21, 216, 218, 236, 241, 261n.16, 311n.18
Architecture (prison): emergence of genre, 3; fanciful renderings of, 13; special construction of, 14, 15; reimagining penitentiary, 19–25; horrific faces of, 20–22, 216, 218, 219, 247; transparency of penitentiary, 23–25, 208–9, 215–17, 301n.6; inspection principle (surveillance) in new, 40, 203, 216, 217; plans for protopenitentiary (Fielding and Gibson), 147–50; penitentiary idea and, 185, 204–8, 210; aesthetic of isolation, public executions, and, 240–51; pictorial aspect of, 241; competitions for reformed penitentiary, 301–2n.11. *See also specific buildings*
Architecture terrible, 241
Aristotle, 161
Art (works of), in cultural context, xv, 1–9, 253n.1, 255–56n.13; relationships between social

315